BRITISH IMPERIALISM:
CRISIS AND DECONSTRUCTION 1914–1990

Also available

British Imperialism: Innovation and Expansion 1688–1914

P.J. CAIN and A.G. HOPKINS

British Imperialism: Crisis and Deconstruction 1914–1990

P.J. Cain and A.G. Hopkins

Longman
London and New York

Longman Group UK Limited,
Longman House, Burnt Mill,
Harlow, Essex, CM20 2JE, England
and Associated Companies throughout the world.

Published in the United States of America
by Longman Publishing, New York

First published 1993
Second impression 1993

ISBN 0 582 20966 8 CSD
ISBN 0 582 20965 X PPR

British Library Cataloguing-in-Publication Data

A catalogue record for this book is
available from the British Library

Library of Congress Cataloguing in Publication Data

Cain, P. J., 1941–
    British imperialism : crisis and deconstruction, 1914–1990 / P.J.
Cain and A.G. Hopkins.
        p.   cm.
    Includes bibliographical references and index.
    ISBN 0–582–20966–8. – ISBN 0–582–20965–X (pbk.)
    1. Great Britain – Colonies – History – 20th century. I. Hopkins,
A. G. (Antony G.) II. Title
JV1018.C35   1993
325′.341′0904 – dc20   92–21715
                                                            CIP

Set by 9 in Bembo
Produced by Longman Singapore Publishers (Pte) Ltd
Printed in Singapore

Contents

List of Tables

List of Maps

Preface

The origins, scope and argument of this study are set out in detail in P. J. Cain and A. G. Hopkins, *British Imperialism: Innovation and Expansion, 1688–1914*. Chapter one of this companion book provides a summary of our interpretation of the period after 1914. We have also acknowledged specific debts to enlisted scholars at appropriate points throughout the text. It remains for us to express here our appreciation of those who have done so much, in different ways, to keep the whole enterprise afloat. We should like to record our gratitude to the Social Science Research Council for Personal Research Grants in 1980–81 and 1983, to colleagues in the University of Birmingham and the Graduate Institute of International Studies for their advice and tolerance of our various impositions, to our students, whose exposure to several versions of our interpretation helped to educate their teachers, and to libraries and librarians, especially in the University of Birmingham and the University of California, Los Angeles, for their resourcefulness in supplying the wide range of materials needed for this study. Special thanks are also due to Sue Kennedy and Diane Martin for unwavering secretarial support. Finally, and most important of all, we must pay tribute to our families, who have borne the deprivations imposed by slow-moving authors with unwavering fortitude and whose limitless support has finally been rewarded by an event that is as surprising as it has been long-promised: this time, the book really is finished.

P.J.C.
University of Birmingham
A.G.H.
The Graduate Institute of International Studies, Geneva
May 1992

Note on Sources

Since our text makes judgements that rest upon a wide range of detailed research, we have placed our notes at the foot of the page so that our sources can be easily recognised and traced. We hope that this arrangement will give prominence, and hence acknowledgement, to the many scholars whose work has made our own study possible, and that it will be helpful to readers who wish to pursue particular topics or lines of enquiry of their own. In the text and notes the two books which comprise this study are referred to, for the sake of simplicity, as Volume I and Volume II. Books and articles are cited in full on first mention in each chapter, are referred to subsequently by short titles, and should therefore be readily identifiable. The place of publication of books is London unless another location is given. Presenting our citations in this way removes the need to produce a separate bibliography; had we added a consolidated list of references we would also have required a third volume – a prospect that neither the authors nor even their accommodating publishers could have faced.

Acknowledgements

The publishers would like to thank the following for permission to reproduce copyright material: Cambridge University Press for table 3.2 from *National Income, Expenditure and Output of the United Kingdom, 1856–1965*, C.H. Feinstein (1972), and table 6.3 from *Abstract of British Historical Statistics*, B.R. Mitchell and P. Deane (1962); Oxford University Press for table 3.6 from *British Economic Growth 1856–1973*, R.C.O. Matthews, C.H. Feinstein and J.C. Odling-Smee (1983); the Editor of the *Australian Economic Papers* for table 6.2 from 'The Australian Balance of Payments on Current Account, 1901 to 1964–5', I.W. McLean (Vol. 7., 1968); Croom Helm for table 8.4 from *Men of Property: The Very Wealthy in Great Britain Since the Industrial Revolution*, W.D. Rubinstein (1981)

Abbreviations

African Aff.	African Affairs
African Econ. Hist.	African Economic History
African Stud. Rev.	African Studies Review
Austral. Econ. Hist. Rev.	Australian Economic History Review
Brit. Jour. Internat. Stud.	British Journal of International Studies
Brit. Jour. Pol. Sci.	British Journal of Political Science
Bus. Hist.	Business History
Bus. Hist. Rev.	Business History Review
Canadian Jour. Hist.	Canadian Journal of History
Comp. Stud. in Soc. and Hist.	Comparative Studies in Society and History
Dip. Hist.	Diplomatic History
Econ. Hist. Rev.	Economic History Review
Econ. Jour.	Economic Journal
Eng. Hist. Rev.	English Historical Review
Hisp. Am. Hist. Rev.	Hispanic American Historical Review
Hist. Jour.	Historical Journal
Hist. Stud.	Historical Studies
Indian Econ. and Soc. Hist. Rev.	Indian Economic and Social History Review
Int. Jour. African Hist. Stud.	International Journal of African Historical Studies
Jour. African Hist.	Journal of African History
Jour. Asian Stud.	Journal of Asian Studies
Jour. Comm. and Comp. Pol.	Journal of Commonwealth and Comparative Politics
Jour. Contemp. Hist.	Journal of Contemporary History

Jour. Econ. Hist.	*Journal of Economic History*
Jour. Eur. Econ. Hist.	*Journal of European Economic History*
Jour. Imp. and Comm. Hist.	*Journal of Imperial and Commonwealth History*
Jour. Latin Am. Stud.	*Journal of Latin American Studies*
Jour. South-East Asian Stud.	*Journal of South-East Asian Studies*
Jour. Southern African Stud.	*Journal of Southern African Studies*
Mod. Asian Stud.	*Modern Asian Studies*
Pac. Aff.	*Pacific Affairs*
Pacific Hist. Rev.	*Pacific Historical Review*
PP	*Parliamentary Papers*
Rev. Internat. Stud.	*Review of International Studies*
Soc. and Econ. Stud.	*Socical and Economic Studies*
South Afr. Hist. Jour.	*South African Historical Journal*
Trans. Royal Hist. Soc.	*Transactions of the Royal Historical Society*

PART ONE
Introduction

CHAPTER ONE

The Imperialist Dynamic: From World War I to Decolonisation

Britain's position in the world, as we have described it, was much stronger in 1914 than is customarily thought.[1] This claim does not arise from counting heads or estimating acres within the British empire, sizeable though they were at the point when war broke out. It depends, rather, upon a reassessment of the basis of Britain's global influence in the pre-war era. Although Britain's manufactured exports were running into increasing difficulties in overseas markets, as is well known and widely emphasised, Britain's financial presence continued to grow and it remained strong, indeed pre-eminent, right down to 1914. Moreover, the financial presence, in the various forms we have discussed, dominated policy towards the management of the formal empire, and also gave Britain substantial interests and considerable influence outside it. Far from being in decline in the late nineteenth century, Britain's 'invisible empire' was expanding at precisely that point. To a degree that has often been underestimated, mounting international rivalries and growing nationalist resistance from this time onwards were symptoms less of the erosion of Britain's 'hegemonic' status than of the continuing extension of her global influence. On our interpretation, then, Britain remained a dynamic power, and the anxieties, alarms and difficulties which beset the

---

1. Readers should note that a full statement of the argument, concepts and methodology deployed in this study can be found in Volume I, Chapter 1. In all other respects this volume is self-contained and can be read independently of its predecessor.

builders of the second Rome, though real enough, need to be placed in the context of their strikingly successful record in upholding British interests throughout the world.

After 1914, the gentlemanly order was compelled to operate in a more hostile global environment. The war disrupted the international economy, enabled the United States to emerge as a competitor on a global scale and seriously damaged Britain's ability to act as banker to the world. Thereafter, the slow and incomplete recovery of international trade hampered Britain's efforts to return to 'normality' and checked her influence overseas. Exports and foreign investment dwindled during the war, and failed in the 1920s to recover the levels attained in 1913. The gold standard, the evocative symbol of Britain's power, had to be suspended in 1913 and was abandoned in 1919. Returning to gold in 1925 involved an immense effort which probably accelerated Britain's relative economic decline. The onset of the world slump in 1929 ensured that the 1930s were, in most respects, an even gloomier period. Export values fell to new levels and foreign investment was reduced to a trickle. In 1931 Britain was forced to abandon the gold standard again; in the following year she replaced free trade with a preferential commercial system centred on the formal empire.

It would be easy to infer from this catalogue of economic set-backs and disappointed expectations that the gentlemanly elite and its interests steadily lost ground during the inter-war years and that Britain was in irreversible decline as an imperial power. Indeed, this is the conclusion that is conventionally reached. Standard interpretations of the period after 1914 emphasise Britain's economic weakness, her faltering will-power and her diminishing ability to maintain political control inside the empire and influence beyond it. These judgements are not to be thrown aside, but there are grounds for thinking that they are not as robust as their frequent repetition might suggest. One temptation, easily entered into, is of reading the present into the past, so that contemporary preoccupations with Britain's loss of status as a great power encourage the search for ever more distant intimations of decline. The danger here is that, in seeking to verify the favoured hypothesis, other evidence regarding the continuing vigour of Britain's presence in the world may be minimised or overlooked, and with it alternative approaches to understanding both her present predicament and the end of empire. A further hazard, which historians are inclined to hit head-on, though frequently without seeming to notice the impact, consists of discussing decline without defining the concept or specifying how it is to be measured. One consequence of this procedure is that connections between, for example, economic performance and political strength are often assumed rather than demonstrated.

Our stress on the enduring vitality of British imperialism begins by emphasising the fact that the complex of services and consumer industries which sustained wealth in the south-east of England continued to flourish after World War I, thus providing the means of perpetuating gentlemanly values, status and power. The City of London retained its independence and its central position in British economic life throughout the inter-war period, despite the fall in income from overseas investment and the rise of large-scale manufacturing in Britain. The City was not absorbed into a monopoly-capitalist structure dominated by manufacturing in the way that banks had become linked to large-scale industry in Germany and the United States; its priorities continued to imprint themselves on economic policy and on the empire, as they had done before the war. It is true, of course, that the City could no longer mobilise funds with the ease that had made it the world's largest creditor before 1914, and in the 1930s foreign investment fell to very low levels. But even this limitation does not provide straightforward evidence that Britain's power was on the wane. Power, considered as a measure of the ability to influence others, is relative as well as absolute, and potential as well as real. The resources at Britain's disposal were less plentiful after 1914 than before, but relatively she still remained a long way ahead of her European rivals, while the United States, which could have deployed forms of economic and military might far in excess of Britain's, was only just beginning to emerge as a world power. Moreover, and partly for this reason, Britain's position in relation to her various satellites and dependencies also remained strong, either because they lacked alternative sources of external support or because, during a period of considerable difficulty for primary producers, they relied heavily on the British market or on finance and services provided by the City to gain access to other markets.

From this perspective, it becomes easier to see why policy-makers did not accept that Britain's future lay behind her after 1914. The strenuous efforts made in the 1920s to return to pre-war 'normality', both at home and abroad, represented a rational choice on the part of Britain's gentlemanly elite rather than a rearguard action against the tide of history. Britain had, after all, won the war, not lost it; although the conflict had raised the standing of the United States, it had also greatly reduced that of Germany and France. The war had dented Britain's resources, too, but it had stiffened her resolve to win the peace and given her the chance of doing so. The struggle to restore the gold standard, for example, demonstrates Britain's determination to repel the challenge of the United States and to reassert financial authority on the periphery as well as traditional orthodoxy at home. As our case studies show, Britain did not relax her grip on matters of vital interest within the empire, and she had considerable success in retaining or regaining her informal influence outside it. In seeking to reconstruct the pre-war international system after 1918, the gentlemanly order also rose to a higher challenge: the need to reinvigorate liberal capitalism both to frustrate predictions of its imminent demise and to ward off the new dangers presented by Bolshevism and, later on, fascism. After 1918, as after 1815, Britain's hard-headed policies were infused with an element of crusading zeal which rallied the gentlemanly elite and gave it a mission to accomplish.

Although Britain suffered in the world slump that began in 1929, she was far less affected than her rivals, including the United States, whose global economic influence shrank rapidly. Indeed, it is important to remember that Britain was the only truly world power of consequence in the 1930s. The decade saw a resurgence of her imperialist ambitions, as she pieced together the Sterling Area, which emerged as the most important international economic bloc, and encroached on positions that the United States had begun to occupy in Canada, South America and China. The overriding purpose of British policy, within the empire and beyond it, was to restore or enhance her financial influence. This priority gave direction and momentum to important decisions on international policy, from the Ottawa agreements to appeasement; it shaped Britain's other dealings with the Dominions and the colonies; and it dominated her aims in South America and China. In pursuing these goals, Britain showed a degree of energy and agility that is hard to reconcile with the view that, by the close of the 1930s, she had become an elderly and arthritic power. She held on resolutely to her central overseas interests against the claims of Germany and Japan, as imperialist rivalries gathered pace from the mid-1930s; and she showed both determination in pursuing her debtors and flexibility in adjusting to developments on the periphery by investing in joint-ventures and by working with nationalists instead of against them.

What halted this promising strategy was not renewed American expansionism, which was only just reappearing at the close of the 1930s, but the coming of another world war. From the perspective of the present study, World War II itself was the culmination of international rivalries which accelerated under the pressures generated by the world slump. Failure to accommodate or control the 'have-not' powers of Germany and Japan finally made war inevitable and reduced Britain to financial dependence on the United States. Antici-pations of this fate in London had done much to inspire efforts to keep the peace, to restrain defence costs, and thus to uphold the value of sterling and the prospects of a British-led recovery in international trade. After 1939, with these plans in ruin, Britain's gentlemanly capitalists became players, albeit important ones, in an orchestra conducted jointly in Washington and New York.

Nevertheless, the outbreak of World War II did not mark the end of Britain's long history of imperial expansion. Britain's war aims included regaining and regrouping the empire, and in this she was remarkably successful – given the desperate situation in 1940 and the fact that her main ally and chief paymaster was a former colony with an anti-colonial bias. As the principal component of the Sterling Area, the empire also made a vital contribution to Britain's post-war reconstruction plans in the decade after 1945. The acts of decolonisa-tion which gathered pace from the late 1950s were neither fortuitous events nor the inevitable culmination of a long process of decay. In the end, as is well known, nationalist aspirations could not be contained at a price that was worth paying, or perhaps at any price. But by that time, too, as is less well appreciated, the empire had served its purpose. It did not simply fall apart but was taken apart by the proprietors as well as by its prospective new owners. However, even as the debris of deconstruction went overboard, the gentlemen of the City had already changed course and were heading towards new horizons, where global opportunities – above the nation state and beyond the empire – beckoned.

PART TWO
The Gentlemanly Order

CHAPTER TWO

'The Power of Constant Renewal': Services, Finance and the Gentlemanly Elite, 1914–39[1]

MANUFACTURING, SERVICES AND THE SOUTH-EAST

The need to create a mass army and the disruption caused by the suppression of international trade led to a fall in total output in Britain after 1914. Pre-war levels of output were not recovered until the mid–1920s. Thereafter, despite the crisis of 1929–33, the economy grew at an average rate of over 2 per cent per annum until the late 1930s, a rate in excess of that achieved between 1870 and 1913.[2] Productivity rose sharply in wartime, too, partly to compensate for losses of manpower to the defence forces, and in the 1920s and 1930s increased at rates comparable with those of late Victorian Britain.[3] Another marked feature of the post-war economy was the rapid growth of manufacturing which, at over 3 per cent per year, was much higher than pre-war: by contrast, service growth was slower than before 1914. Manufacturing's share of output increased from around 30 per cent in 1913 to 35 per cent in 1937, while the share of services fell. Manufacturing productivity also rose at a much higher rate than previously, whereas productivity in services may well have declined.[4]

The output of industries dependent on export sales sometimes fell between the wars but this was more than compensated by the growth

1. The phrase is taken from François Bédarida, *A Social History of England, 1850–75* (1979), p. 303.
2. R.C.O. Matthews, C.H. Feinstein and J.C. Odling-Smee, *British Economic Growth, 1856–1973* (Oxford, 1982), Table 2.1, p. 22.
3. Ibid. Table 7.3, p. 210.
4. Ibid. Table 8.3, pp. 228–9, and Table 8.1, pp. 222–3.

of manufactures based on domestic demand.[5] This rapid growth has led some historians to argue that, despite the difficulties produced by an ailing export sector, the inter-war period was one of far-reaching economic transformation led by new, technologically dynamic industries.[6] But the 'new industries', such as chemicals and motor vehicles, accounted for only one-fifth of manufacturing output in 1937. Also, much of the improved productivity performance in the 1930s was a result of the 'rationalisation' of older industries, like textiles, where employment fell faster than output.[7] Investment in manufacturing between the wars remained low: around 70 per cent of net investment between 1920 and 1938 was in housing.[8] This low level of industrial investment was a reflection of reduced profits compared with the period before 1914 and the uncertainty generated by severe cyclical fluctuations, as well as the capital-saving nature of some important innovations.[9] Despite mergers, rationalisation and the increasing significance of 'big business' in Britain, technological backwardness and managerial inefficiency remained features of much of British industry, including some of the more rapidly growing sectors, which needed protection in the 1930s to preserve their domestic market and could not compete abroad outside the confines of empire.[10] Although the United States' economy suffered greatly in the 1930s, the productivity gap in manufacturing between Britain and the USA was wider in 1939 than in 1914. Measured against her European neighbours, Britain held her own between the wars in terms of productivity, but no more than that.[11]

5. Ibid. Table 9.10, p. 281.
6. See Derek H. Aldcroft and Harry W. Richardson, *The British Economy, 1870–1939* (1969), pp. 190–288; H.W. Richardson, *Economic Recovery in Britain, 1932–39* (1967); D.H. Aldcroft, 'Economic Growth in the Inter-War Years: a Reassessment', *Econ. Hist. Rev.*, 2nd ser. XX (1967), reprinted in Derek H. Aldcroft and Peter Fearon, eds. *Economic Growth in 20th-Century Britain* (1969).
7. Nick Crafts, 'The Assessment: British Economic Growth in the Long Run', *Oxford Review of Economic Policy*, 4 (1988), p. vi; Neil K. Buxton, 'The Role of the "New" Industries in Britain during the 1930s: a Reinterpretation', *Bus. Hist. Rev.*, XLIX (1975); J.A. Dowie, 'Growth in the Inter-war Period: some More Arithmetic', *Econ. Hist. Rev.*, 2nd ser. XXI (1968).
8. C.H. Feinstein, *Domestic Capital Formation in the United Kingdom, 1920–38* (Cambridge, 1965), Table 3.40, p. 49.
9. Matthews, Feinstein and Odling-Smee, *British Economic Growth*, Table 6.1, p. 164, and pp. 383–6.
10. B.W.E. Alford, 'New Industries for Old? British Industry between the Wars', in Roderick Floud and Donald N. McCloskey, eds. *An Economic History of Britain, II : 1860 to the 1970s* (1981); Crafts, 'The Assessment', pp. vi-viii.
11. Stephen Broadberry, 'The Impact of the World Wars on the Long Run Performance of the British Economy', *Oxford Review of Economic Policy*, 4 (1988), Table 2, p. 27. Charles Feinstein, 'Economic Growth Since 1870: Britain's Performance

The rapid development of manufacturing in the inter-war period did not mean, either, that there was any change in the patterns of regional dominance which had established themselves before 1914. The south-east's share of manufacturing output rose from about one-fifth just after the war to over one-quarter thirty years later; this was the chief reason why the region's share of total employment also increased in the same period.[12] Of all new firms formed in industry, transport and services, 50 per cent took place in the south-east between the two wars, attracted by the well-established high levels of per capita income in the region;[13] in many ways the development of the south-east followed the same pattern as pre-1914, when high incomes generated in services increased the demand for locally produced consumer manufactures. The south-east had a higher concentration of new industries, a higher rate of employment growth and a lower rate of unemployment than any other region.[14] It also attracted the bulk of the direct industrial investment from overseas, mainly the United States, which flowed into Britain in this period.[15] The boom in private housing, which was so important in sustaining growth in Britain after 1918, was much more marked in the south-east than elsewhere, and was a direct result of the high concentration of income-taxpayers there.[16] Manufacturing had become a more

---

in International Perspective', ibid. Table 3, p. 10. For a detailed study of British industry see N.K. Buxton and D.H. Aldcroft, *British Industry Between the Wars: Instability and Economic Development, 1919–1939* (1979).

12. Christopher M. Law, *British Regional Development Since World War One* (1980), Table 22, p. 110. The south-east's share of total employment rose from 28 per cent to over 31 per cent between 1911 and 1951. Figures from C.H. Lee, *British Regional Employment Statistics* (1979).

13. James S. Foreman-Peck, 'Seedcorn or Chaff? New Firm Formation and the Performance of the Inter-War Economy', *Econ. Hist. Rev.*, 2nd ser. XXXVIII (1985), Table 4, p. 412, p. 415 and Table 5, p. 416. See also C.H. Lee, *The British Economy since 1700: A Macroeconomic Survey* (Cambridge 1986), pp. 213–14, 230–1.

14. Law, *British Regional Development*, Table 12, p. 74; Sidney Pollard, *The Development of the British Economy, 1914–1980* (1983), Table 2.9, p. 78. On regional unemployment see M.E.F. Jones, 'The Economic History of the Regional Problem in Britain, 1920–1938', *Journal of Historical Geography*, 10 (1984). Contrary to the usual assumptions of historians, it has recently been suggested that unemployment was higher in the older industrial regions than in the south of England before 1914 as well as after. This conclusion would be consistent with the idea, presented in this book, of a dynamic south-eastern economy both before and after 1914. See Humphrey R. Southall, 'The Origins of the Depressed Areas: Unemployment, Growth and Regional Economic Structures in Britain before 1914', *Econ. Hist. Rev.*, 2nd ser. XLI (1988).

15. Foreman-Peck, 'Seedcorn or Chaff?', p. 416; Law, *Regional Development*, pp. 175–7.

16. See J.L. Marshall, 'The Pattern of Housebuilding in the Inter-War Period in England and Wales', *Scottish Journal of Political Economy*, 15 (1968), Table 1, p. 185; and

important element within the economy than before 1914 but its development reinforced the influence of the south-east corner of Britain. Shifts in the location of industry fused the centres of manufacturing and service sector power more closely together; London's dominance, as registered by the locations of the head offices of firms, increased.[17]

FINANCE AND INDUSTRY AFTER 1914

Before World War I there was, as we have seen, a divide between industrial capitalism and the major financial institutions, whose concentration in London became more marked over time. The bulk of industry remained self-financing up to 1914 or relied on local stock exchanges; even had they wished to do so, the majority of manufacturing firms would have been too small to benefit from the services offered by leading City issuing houses. On their side, the merchant bankers and the finance houses of the City were occupied with the business of government and public-utility finance either in Britain or overseas. The great clearing banks, reduced by amalgamation to the 'Big Five' in 1921, had, of necessity, a closer relationship with industry, but what they offered was short-term accommodation and overdraft facilities rather than long-term loans.

After 1914 the two spheres or 'fractions' of capital, as Marxists prefer to call them, came closer together. In one important respect this was an accidental process. In the great restocking boom of 1919–20, cotton, coal, shipbuilding and other major exporting interests made large additions to their capital in anticipation of rapid growth in overseas markets once 'normality' had been restored. The clearing banks often shared their customers' febrile optimism and offered accommodation on an unprecedented scale. When the new markets anticipated in 1920 proved non-existent, much of the new capital was wasted and, as profits collapsed, the banks were left

---

Mark Swenarton and Sandra Taylor, 'The Scale and Nature of the Growth of Owner-Occupation in Britain Between the Wars', *Econ. Hist. Rev.*, 2nd ser. XXXVIII (1985). A good example of linkage between services and industry is that between the growth of the professions, the suburbs and the motor car. See Bédarida, *Social History of England*, pp. 205–7.

17. David J. Jeremy, 'Anatomy of the British Business Elite', Table 9, p. 19.

with overdrafts which could be called in only at the risk of bank-ruptcy.[18]

At the end of the decade and in the 1930s, when the ailments of the export industries had proved to be chronic and heavy regional unemployment was a fixture, more positive efforts were made to marry finance with industry. Led by Norman, as Governor, the Bank of England launched a series of initiatives designed to bring City and provincial industry together. The Bank was acutely aware of the increasing criticism of financial policy in the 1920s. Norman, in particular, was convinced that the failure of the financial sector to show some interest in reviving older industries would give the green light to politicians, particularly Labour politicians, to interfere – with disastrous effects on the market system which the Bank supervised.[19] He also recognised, frankly enough, that in an age when opportunities for overseas investment were shrinking, City institutions needed to look more to the domestic market for business. As Norman put it in 1930:

> I believe that the finance which for 100 years has been directed by them abroad can be directed by them into British industry, that a marriage can take place between the industry of the North and the finance of the South.[20]

The Bank often urged the clearing banks to use their new financial position with major industries to impose mergers or more efficient management upon them. It also launched, in 1929, the Bankers Industrial Development Corporation, which brought City and industry together in an endeavour to promote 'rationalisation', especially in the steel industry;[21] it played a leading role in National Shipbuilders Security, which was designed to reduce capacity in shipbuilding and lower costs;[22] and in the late 1930s it took part, with the Treasury, in the Special Areas Reconstruction Association, a body composed of

18. Jeffrey H. Porter, 'The Commercial Banks and the Financial Problems of the English Cotton Industry', *Revue internationale d'histoire de la banque*, 9 (1974), pp. 1–10; Stephen Tolliday, *Business, Banking and Politics: The Case of British Steel, 1918–1939* (Cambridge, Mass., 1988), pp. 176–8.

19. Tolliday, *Business, Banking and Politics*, pp. 197–210; Carol E. Heim, 'Limits to Intervention: the Bank of England and Industrial Diversification in the Depressed Areas', *Econ. Hist. Rev.*, 2nd ser. XXXVII (1984), pp. 535, 543–4.

20. From Norman's evidence to the Sankey Commission 1930, quoted in Tolliday, *Business, Banking and Politics*, p. 183.

21. Ibid. Pt. II; Leslie Hannah, *The Rise of the Corporate Economy* (2nd edn, 1983), pp. 64–5. See also Stephen Tolliday, 'Steel and Rationalization Policies, 1918–50', in Bernard Elbaum and William Lazonick, *The Decline of the British Economy* (Oxford, 1986).

22. Tolliday, *Business, Banking and Politics*, pp. 238–9, 323–4.

City and industrial firms which invested capital in areas of high unemployment.[23]

One of the Bank's main aims was the creation of efficient big business. The war, by effecting a coordination of output in many industries, and the intensity of international competition in the 1920s, gave a significant boost to the creation of oligopoly in Britain. The share of the leading 100 companies in British output rose from 15 per cent in 1907 to around 26 per cent in the later 1920s, though levels of concentration appear to have fallen slightly in the 1930s.[24] Many mergers in the 1920s were carried through with the aid of Stock Exchange finance[25] and, as the large corporations became more typical members of the British industrial landscape, there began to emerge a new class of managerial capitalists – Mond of ICI is a good example – who had a more central role in British economic (and political) life than hitherto.

Furthermore, domestic issues of capital on the Stock Exchange were a more dominant part of the capital market after 1919 and domestic industrial and commercial issues were the most prominent element. Domestic issues as a whole were over twice the value of overseas issues between the wars, whereas on average only two-fifths of all issues were raised for domestic concerns between 1865 and 1914 and, in the last few years before the war, only three-tenths (Table 2.1).[26] Some specialist firms arose to deal with domestic industrial finance,[27] but even the traditional merchant bankers responded to some degree to changing times. Although Barings remained primarily an overseas issuing house, they acted as advisers to Armstrongs, the armaments firm, and underwrote flotations for underground railways, breweries and even tyre firms.[28] Kleinworts were more adventurous and promoted issues for cotton firms and shipbuilders, while

23. Heim, 'Limits of Intervention', passim. For earlier overviews of Bank of England involvement see R.S. Sayers, *The Bank of England*, Vol. I (Cambridge, 1970), pp. 314–30; and Sir Henry Clay, *Lord Norman* (1957), Ch. VIII.

24. Hannah, *Rise of the Corporate Economy*, pp. 91–2, 180. For slightly different figures see Lewis Johnmann, 'The Largest Manufacturing Companies of 1935', *Bus. Hist.*, XXIV (1986), p. 229.

25. Hannah, *Rise of the Corporate Economy*, pp. 55–7.

26. Lance E. Davis and Robert A. Huttenback, *Mammon and the Pursuit of Empire: The Political Economy of British Imperialism* (Cambridge, 1986), pp. 40–1; R.C. Michie, 'The Stock Exchange and the British Economy, 1870–1939', in J.J. Van-Helten and Y. Cassis, eds. *Capitalism in a Mature Economy: Financial Institutions, Capital Export and British Industry, 1870–1939* (1989), p. 98.

27. W.A. Thomas, *The Finance of British Industry, 1918–76* (1978), p. 49.

28. Philip Zeigler, *The Sixth Great Power Barings, 1792–1929* (1988), pp. 342–5.

Table 2.1 New capital issues, 1919–38 (quinquennial averages, £m.)

	Public	Industry and commerce	Total Domestic	Domestic %	Overseas	%
1919–23	37.1	119.0	156.1	61.1	99.3	38.9
1924–28	55.1	96.4	151.5	55.2	123.3	44.8
1929–33	41.3	60.4	101.7	61.7	63.2	38.3
1934–38	47.5	90.7	138.2	82.3	29.7	17.7

Source: T. Balogh, *Studies in Financial Organizations* (Cambridge, 1947), Table XLVIa, pp. 249–50; W.A. Thomas, *The Finance of British Industry* (London, 1978), Table 2.1, p. 27.

Morgan Grenfell could probably claim a greater involvement in industrial issues than any other firm between the wars.[29]

By 1939, the large corporation was well established in Britain, and finance and industry had intermingled to a novel degree; but whether the outcome could be described as 'finance capitalism', in Hilferding's sense of the term, is doubtful. Even in 1939 the large firms which had merged with the help of the London Stock Exchange still made little use of it for new capital, which was mainly raised internally,[30] and smaller firms still found London too expensive a place to find finance.[31] Nor did the closer involvement of the clearing banks in financing industry lead to fundamental changes in the relationship between them. Encouraged by the Bank of England, the banks most closely involved with cotton textiles did use their influence, via the Lancashire Cotton Corporation, to push through a policy of scrapping excess capacity owned by the firms beholden to them, on pain of having overdrafts withdrawn.[32] This action, however, was unusual: the clearers normally had little influence on industrial policy and wanted less. Norman's hope that they might use their position to force industry into efficiency did not materialise.[33] The clearers did

29. Stephanie Diaper, 'Merchant Banking in the Inter-War Period: the Case of Kleinwort, Sons and Co.', *Bus. Hist.*, XXVIII (1986), pp. 57–60; Kathleen Burk, *Morgan Grenfell, 1838–1988: The Biography of a Merchant Bank* (1989), pp. 91–8, 157–66.
30. Hannah, *Rise of the Corporate Economy*, pp. 62, 66.
31. This is the famous 'Macmillan Gap'. See Thomas, *The Finance of British Industry*, pp. 116–21.
32. Porter, 'The Commercial Banks and the Financial Problems of the English Cotton Industry', pp. 11–16; Hannah, *Rise of the Corporate Economy*, p. 65; Tolliday, *Business, Banking and Politics*, pp. 197–9.
33. Tolliday, *Business, Banking and Politics*, esp. Ch. 9.

not evolve into industrial banks and they were still dependent for their income on investment outlets dominated by the City of London and its money market. As such, they remained rather uneasily placed between provincial industry and the dominant financial sector in London centred on the Bank of England. Their status and their influence remained limited. Industry was given representation on the Bank of England's directorate in 1928; but the clearers had to wait until 1934 before one of their number was invited to join.[34]

Even successful industrial mergers often turned out to be no more than the bringing together of disparate elements which resisted fundamental change in managerial structures and methods.[35] As for the clearers, when profits rose in the 1930s, their advances to industry actually fell quite sharply.[36] This disengagement from industry can be interpreted either as a determination by the banks to free themselves to pursue their primary goal of maintaining a high degree of liquidity or as a conscious repudiation of long-term involvement with bank capital by industry.[37] Either way, the result was that the two sides of capitalism were not indissolubly committed to each other.

Like the clearers, the merchant banks often found that their experiences in industrial finance were unhappy ones: Kleinworts, for example, burned their fingers badly on occasions.[38] Stock Exchange investors were also wary of industry. The number of industrial companies quoted on the Exchange rose from 569 in 1907 to 1,712 in 1939 and their combined market value was five times greater in 1939 than before World War I.[39] But, partly because of the massive increase in public debt as a result of the war, industrial securities still made up

34. For a rather more positive view of relations with industry see Duncan M. Ross, 'The Clearing Banks and Industry – a New Perspective on the Inter-War Years', in Van-Helten and Cassis, *Capitalism in a Mature Economy*.

35. Michael H. Best and Jane Humphries, 'The City and Industrial Decline', in Elbaum and Lazonick, *The Decline of the British Economy*, p. 231.

36. Tolliday, *Business, Banking and Politics*, p. 184. Best and Humphries, 'The City and Industrial Decline', p. 230.

37. One chairman of a major clearing bank declared in 1930 that a commitment to an industrial policy by the banks would be wrong because 'it would militate against the liquidity of the banks and that would in turn militate against our large foreign earnings and that in turn would militate against our balancing our imports and exports'. Quoted in Ross, 'The Clearing Banks and Industry', p. 54. For a strong argument that banks did not offer long-term funding mainly because there was little demand from industry, see Thomas, *The Finance of British Industry*, pp. 74–5.

38. Diaper, 'Merchant Banking in the Inter-War Period', pp. 60–1; idem, 'The Sperling Combine and the Shipbuilding Industry: Merchant Banking and Industrial Finance in the 1920s', in Van-Helten and Cassis, *Capitalism in a Mature Economy*.

39. Hannah, *Rise of the Corporate Economy*, p. 61.

only 10 per cent of the value of all quoted securities in the 1930s, as opposed to 8 per cent in 1913.[40] Although industrial issues were slowly increasing in importance, low returns on capital and the insecurities surrounding industrial profits were still powerful deterrents which inhibited outsiders from making long-term investments in manufacturing. The raising of new industrial finance on the Stock Exchange was also inhibited after 1914 by the growth of the national debt, which diverted income to rentiers whose inclination was to look for safer domestic investment outlets than industry could offer.[41]

It is important, too, not to magnify the novelty of the Bank of England's own initiatives in this field. It was resolutely opposed to providing much new money for industry;[42] it saw its role mainly as facilitating contacts with financiers and promoting self-help. Some of its schemes were, in fact, little more than gestures designed to divert criticism from financial policy in general and to keep the state at bay. Like the National Government itself, which encouraged industries to raise profits by concocting price and output schemes in the 1930s, the aim was to make industry help itself while preserving the orthodoxies of balanced budgets, low government spending and a strong pound, all of which found support in industrial circles.[43]

What little direct help the Bank of England or the Treasury did give often went to older industries because the underlying assumption of policy remained one of attempting to revive exports and the international economy.[44] London remained cosmopolitan in outlook. The Macmillan Committee's verdict of 1930, that 'in some respects the City is more highly organized to provide capital to foreign countries than to British industry',[45] was still correct at the end of the period. It is also possible that the chief result of Bank of England and

---

40. W.J. Reader, *A House in the City: A Study of the City and of the Stock Exchange Based on the Records of Foster and Braithwaite, 1825–1975* (1979), pp. 141–6. Investment trusts also took a greater interest in domestic industrial investment after 1919, but the amounts of capital involved were not large. See Youssef Cassis, 'The Emergence of a New Financial Institution: Investment Trusts in Britain, 1870–1939', in Van-Helten and Cassis, *Capitalism in a Mature Economy*.

41. As we have already seen, the investment of capital in domestic manufacturing was not high between the wars, despite high levels of output. For the effects of the national debt, see Michie, 'The Stock Exchange and the British Economy', pp. 105, 109.

42. Hannah, *Rise of the Corporate Economy*, p. 65.

43. For a profound study of these relationships see Tolliday, *Business, Banking and Finance*, Chs. 12–14.

44. Heim, 'Limits of Intervention', pp. 544–5.

45. *Report of the Committee on Finance and Industry*, Cmd 3897 (1931), para. 397. The merchant bankers were 'reproached for being better informed on conditions in Latin America than in Lancashire or Scotland'. Thomas, *The Finance of British Industry*, p. 48.

government involvement in industry was to create a more conscious and vocal set of vested interests, dependent on cartelisation and protection, whose power was often used to forestall change rather than to encourage it.[46] Thus, the emergence of the large corporation in British industry did promote the growth of a more coherent, politically aware, industrial interest which had more influence than in the past and was closer to centres of power in London, where the head offices of these major companies were based. But the incorporation of industrial capital did not lead to any fundamental shifts in the structure of relations between the principal segments of capital in Britain and, as a consequence, it had little influence upon the distribution of power or any new, determining effect upon economic policy.

WEALTH AND POWER BETWEEN THE WARS

Recent studies of the distribution of wealth in Britain all show a remarkable continuity between the inter-war period and preceding times. In the first place, landed wealth continued to decline in relative importance. In all fortunes of £0.5m. or above declared at death, the share of landed wealth was two-fifths in 1880–99 but fell to a mere 15 per cent by 1920–39 (Table 2.2). The rising importance of other sectors, land taxes and death duties, and the low level of agricultural prices and profits after wartime state support was removed, all contributed to this decline. Land sales were very high in the immediate post-war years. About one-quarter of all land changed hands, the main movement being from landlords to farmers who exchanged tenancy for ownership. Most major landed estates survived, although with a diminished acreage, and the proceeds of sales were invested in other forms of economic activity, mainly financial, integrating the landed elite more firmly into the structures of a gentlemanly capitalism which contained them rather than being dominated by them.[47]

Secondly, despite the rapid growth of manufacturing output after 1914 and the tendency towards industrial concentration, the relative

46. Tolliday, *Business, Banking and Finance*, pp. 330, 335–7.
47. On the fortunes of landed wealth after 1914 see F.M.L. Thompson, *English Landed Society in the Nineteenth Century* (1963), Ch. XII; John Scott, *The Upper Classes: Property and Privilege in Britain* (1983), pp. 133–4; John Stevenson, *British Society, 1914–45* (1984), esp. pp. 333–5; Perkin, *The Rise of Professional Society: England since 1880* (1989), pp. 251–5. See also Marion Beard, *English Landed Society in the 20th Century* (1989).

importance of manufacturers among top wealth-holders did not change much. The number of deceased half-millionaires who owed their fortunes either to manufacturing or to the food, drink and tobacco industries was always around one-half of all non-landed fortunes and, between the wars, the share of the purely manufacturing wealthy declined slightly (Table 2.2). A fall in the importance of wealth made in cottons and woollens was to be expected; but newer industries did not generate outstanding new concentrations of wealth.

Table 2.2 Non-landed fortunes at death, 1880–1969 (£0.5m. or more)

	1880–99	%	1900–19	%	1920–39	%	1940–69	%
Manufacturing and mining	82	36.7	124	34.2	153	30.4	164	32.1
Food, drink and tobacco	36	16.1	48	13.2	97	19.3	86	16.8
Finance	47	21.1	79	21.9	90	17.9	211	41.3
Commerce	47	21.1	101	27.9	138	27.4		
Other	11	4.9	10	2.8	24	4.8	50	9.8
Total	223		362		502		511	
(Land)	(174)		(140)		(91)		(n/a)	

Source: derived from W.D. Rubinstein, *Men of Property: The Very Wealthy in Great Britain Since the Industrial Revolution* (London, 1981), Tables 3.3, 3.4 and 8.3

Note: Rubinstein's figures do not include the value of the land of those whose property was subject to legal settlements forbidding sale and in which any particular owner had only a life interest. The compilation of the groups is as follows: *Manufacturing and mining* comprising columns 1–11 of the original tables: *Food, drink and tobacco*, columns 12–15; *Finance*, columns 16–18, 22 and 23; *Commerce*, columns 19–21, 24 and 25; and *Others*, columns 26–32.

The engineering and chemical industries together produced 26 half-millionaire fortunes or above in 1880–98 and only 32 between 1920–39. Although the food, drink and tobacco sector was buoyant, this was partly due to the importance of traditional industries such as brewing and distilling, which produced 43 out of the 96 half-millionaire fortunes in this sector between the wars.[48]

Thirdly, as before 1914, commerce and finance provided about two-fifths of all large estates. Not surprisingly, merchant banking's dependence on the international economy caused a decline in its

48. W.D. Rubinstein, *Men of Property: The Very Wealthy in Great Britain Since the Industrial Revolution* (1981), Tables 3.3 and 3.4.

relative importance,[49] but banking in general, stockbroking, insurance and, most of all, shipowning more than compensated for this. Estates above £0.5m. in value derived from shipbuilding increased from 10 in 1880–99 to 24 in 1900–19, and then rose dramatically to 56 in 1920–39.[50]

Nor were there any notable changes in the geographical distribution of large fortunes (Table 2.3). London's share was stable at just under two-fifths: the City's share fell slightly but still amounted to well over one-fifth of the total in 1920–39. Given the increasing concentration of big business, both financial and industrial, between the wars and the growth of manufacturing in the south-east, it is surprising that London's share of great wealth did not increase. On the other hand, the major industrial areas did not improve their position *vis-à-vis* the metropolis, and because the south-east was the most dynamic centre of industrial development, the Midlands increased its share of top wealth only marginally (Table 2.3).

Table 2.3 Geographical origins of non-landed fortunes, 1900–39 (£0.5m. or more)

	1900–19	*%*	*1920–39*	*%*
City	82	22.7	106	21.1
Other London	47	13.0	67	13.4
Lancashire	24		36	
Yorkshire	25		38	
North-east	26		31	
Midlands	25		38	
Northern Ireland	3		6	
South Wales	7		6	
Total, industrial	110	30.5	155	30.9
Clydeside[a]	28⎫	15.8	40⎫	15.9
Merseyside[a]	29⎭		40⎭	
Others	66		94	
Grand total	362		502	

Source: Rubinstein, *Men of Property*, Tables 3.11 and 3.12.

Note: [a] Merseyside and Clydeside have been listed separately from the industrial areas because of the predominance there of commercial fortunes.

49. S. Diaper, 'Merchant Banking in the Inter-War Period', pp. 69–70.
50. See Rubinstein, *Men of Property*, pp. 62–6. Why there should have been such a dramatic increase in top wealth in shipowning when world shipping was in the doldrums is not obvious, but it may have been related to high levels of concentration in the industry.

It can, of course, be argued that the estates of those dying in the period 1920–39 are a very inadequate index of wealth concentration between the wars since so many of those who left fortunes between the wars had made their mark on the pre-1914 economy, while many who made their fortunes between 1914 and 1939 died long after. However, what information there is on wealth at death in the period 1940–69 shows a very similar distribution, both by sector and by region (Tables 2.3 and 2.4). This evidence confirms that, despite the shift from overseas to domestic sources of income and wealth after 1914 and the rise of new industry, there were no sweeping changes in the nature of wealth-holding in Britain in the inter-war period. The south-east remained the most rapidly developing region; the service–consumer industry complex formed its central activities; the City of London remained the main source of its economic strength; and its wealth provided the economic basis for the social and political power of the gentlemanly service class, which was one of the south-east's outstanding products.

Table 2.4 Geographical origins of non-landed fortunes, 1940–69 (£0.5m. or more)

	1940–69	%
City[a]	95	18.1
Other London[a]	85	16.1
Greater Manchester	17 ⎫	
West Yorkshire	24 ⎬	13.6
Greater Birmingham	31 ⎭	
Clydeside[b]	28 ⎫	10.4
Merseyside[b]	27 ⎭	
Total[c]	526	

Source: Rubinstein, *Men of Property*, Table 8.4.

Notes: [a] The number of large fortunes declared after 1940 is severely affected by taxation and estate-duty avoidance: the wealthy of the City were more adept at hiding their wealth than others. See Rubinstein, *Men of Property*, pp. 235–6.
[b] Merseyside and Clydeside have been listed separately from the industrial areas because of a predominance there of commercial fortunes.
[c] The total figure includes a number of fortunes made in Britain by foreigners.

There was an 'establishment' in Britain between the wars and, as before 1914, its material foundation was the service wealth which funded the activities of the 'service class' – the higher civil servants, lawyers and other professionals, clergy and military men. The establishment had a strong association with aristocracy, though the latter's direct power was fading, with Eton and Harrow, with Oxford and Cambridge; and its members filled many of the jobs at the 'commanding heights' of society.[51] But it was not a caste. As Bédarida has noted, what

> gave the top class the power of constant renewal and adaptation to change was its capacity to absorb and assimilate. It welcomed outsiders and, by investing them with its own aura, perpetuated itself. It knew how to inculcate its own norms and values on those it took under its wing.[52]

Indeed, the powerful and the influential in society were the top echelons of a complex structure of service employment, revolving around London and the Home Counties, which reached even farther down into the world of white-collar employment than before 1914. Upward mobility was a significant feature of this economy: bishops, higher civil servants, university figures and other leading professionals were often recruited from the lower reaches of the middle class, who had little capital and no connections, and whose careers mainly depended on success at public school and Oxbridge.[53] Power was meritocratic in origin rather than purely hereditary but, as before 1914, there was little recruitment from outside the service sector itself. Of Wykehamists born in the 1880s (who would have been at the height of their careers in the 1920s and 1930s) only 15 per cent had fathers in business or engineering and only one-fifth took up careers in these areas, most of them outside manufacturing.[54] The career paths of the products of other prestigious public schools were very similar: of boys entering Rugby and Harrow in 1880 only one-quarter and one-sixth respectively chose business careers, and the importance of business did not increase with time.[55] The concen-

51. Scott, *The Upper Classes*, Ch. 7.
52. Bédarida, *A Social History of England*, p. 303.
53. W.D. Rubinstein, 'Education and the Social Origins of British Elites, 1880–1970', *Past and Present*, 112 (1986). Rubinstein points out (p. 203) that a significant number of recruits to elite positions did not come from public school backgrounds; but many of these came from traditional grammar schools which were strongly imbued with public school values.
54. Thomas J.H. Bishop and Rupert Wilkinson, *Winchester and the Public School Elite: A Statistical Analysis* (1967), Table 5, p. 106, and Table 10, p. 67. The occupations of 30 per cent of fathers of entrants born in 1880–9 could not be traced. The term 'Wykehamist' refers to someone educated at Winchester, whose founder was William of Wykeham (1323–1404).
55. Thomas William Bamford, *The Rise of the Public Schools: A Study of Boys' Public Boarding Schools in England and Wales from 1837 to the Present Day* (1967), Table 12, p. 210.

tration of both public school and Oxbridge recruits and the families of 'top people' in government and the professions around London and the south-east was also obvious since this was where the bulk of the service-sector middle class was found.[56] Bound together by a common background in service-sector capitalism and by a similar education, the establishment was the product of a system which preferred the security offered by bureaucratic or professional employment to the hazards of business.[57] Gentlemen continued to give 'service' rather than to make profits, and this ideal of service formed a bond of union across the whole professional class – from permanent officials in the Foreign Office to underpaid London clerks.[58]

The colonial service remained a strong branch of this particular culture up to World War II and indeed beyond. Between 1919 and 1948 recruitment was in the hands of one man, Sir Ralph Furse, assisted by two close and long-serving colleagues.[59] Furse came from an old and well-connected gentry family and was educated at Eton (where the future Lord Salisbury was his 'fag') and Oxford before entering the Colonial Office in 1910. His family links to Church and state (his grandfather had been Archdeacon of Westminster) were extended by his marriage to Sir Henry Newbolt's daughter, who was related to the Montagus. Furse's method of recruitment favoured selection by interview from a pool of candidates created very largely by his own actively cultivated contacts at Oxford and Cambridge, and his experience as an undergraduate gave him 'a keen eye for the merits of that admirable class of person whom university examiners consider worthy only of third-class honours'.[60] His life in London and his travels throughout the empire provide an insight into the continuing vitality of the gentlemanly diaspora: no matter where he went, Furse was certain to run into other men of influence who were known to him through family connections, Eton or Balliol. Furse's dedication and integrity were accompanied by a sense of purpose that was as unswerving as it was uncritical. His belief in England's mission

56. Rubinstein, 'Education and the Social Origins of British Elites', pp. 199–200.

57. W.D. Rubinstein, 'Social Class, Social Attitudes and British Business Life', *Oxford Review of Economic Policy*, 4 (1988).

58. See also Perkin, *The Rise of Professional Society*, pp. 258–66.

59. Sir Ralph Furse, *Aucuparius: Recollections of a Recruiting Officer* (1962). India, Ceylon and Hong Kong recruited by a separate system; so too did Malaya until the 1930s, when it came within Furse's remit. One of Furse's assistants was his brother-in-law, Francis Newbolt; the other was Greville Irby, who left in 1942 when he inherited the title and estates of his uncle, Lord Boston. Robert Heussler, *Yesterday's Rulers: The Making of the British Colonial Service* (New York, 1963) provides a fascinating commentary on Furse's career.

60. Furse, *Aucuparius*, p. 9.

was inspired by an Elizabethan spirit of adventure and directed by rules of conduct that were drawn from the disciplines of military life and team games, especially cricket. As soon as war broke out in 1939, Furse began to make plans for the recruiting drive that would be needed after it had been won.

The impressions evoked by Furse's autobiography have been confirmed by recent research.[61] An analysis of 200 colonial governors between 1900 and 1960 shows that they came predominantly from the south-east of England and had close family connections with the service sector. Virtually all of them were educated at public schools and over half had been to Oxford or Cambridge. Variations from this pattern occurred but were inconsiderable. As in the case of many other professional groups, the future governors emerged from a wide range of public schools and only a small minority (14 per cent) had been educated at the top nine 'Clarendon' schools. They also tended to come from the less affluent, non-industrial middle class. As one of their number wrote in retirement, they were

> mostly the younger sons of the professional middle class, and had been given a Sound Old-fashioned Liberal Education in the humanities at preparatory and public schools ending with an arts degree at one of the older universities.[62]

Insofar as they had any direct contact with business, it was likely to be with firms in the City;[63] and this was also true of other sections of the service elite.[64] Of all business centres, the City remained the one most thoroughly in touch with the world of gentlemanly employment. The proportion of merchant bankers and the chairmen of other leading banking firms going to Eton, or the other top public schools which educated so many of the political elite, was very high. The family connections between financiers remained much stronger than they were in other businesses;[65] despite the problems of some houses

61. I.F. Nicolson and Colin A. Hughes, 'A Provenance of Pro-Consuls: British Colonial Governors, 1900–1960', *Jour. Imp. and Comm. Hist.*, 4 (1974–5), Table VI, p. 97; See also A.H.M. Kirk-Greene, 'On Governorship and Governors in British Africa', in L.H. Gann and Peter Duignan, eds. *African Proconsuls: European Governors in Africa* (1978), pp. 196–9.

62. K. Bradley, *Once a District Officer* (1966), pp. 3–4, quoted in Nicolson and Hughes, 'A Provenance of Pro-Consuls', p. 104. For an example of the 'benign colonialism' which this training produced, see the autobiography of a former governor of Honduras and Fiji, Sir R. Garvey, *Gentleman Pauper* (1984).

63. Nicolson and Hughes, 'A Provenance of Pro-Consuls', p. 90.

64. Robert W. Boyce, *British Capitalism at the Crossroads, 1919–1932: A Study in Politics, Economics and International Relations* (Cambridge, 1987), p. 31.

65. Philip Stanworth and Antony Giddens, 'An Economic Elite: a Demographic Profile of Company Chairmen', in Philip Stanworth and Anthony Giddens, eds. *Elites and Power in British Society* (1973), pp. 92–3.

which were very dependent on overseas income, the levels of wealth attainable in the City were still much higher than in most of the manufacturing sector.

Some of the older houses felt the need to draw on outside talent after 1919 in order to increase their performance, but the gentlemanly quality of life in the City remained undisturbed.[66] In assessing London's virtues in the mid-1930s, Truptil thought that the concentration of a multitude of different commercial and financial activities in one small space was an important aid to efficiency because it allowed for 'economy of time and staff' and 'a multiplicity of contact between all the various people who have to work together'.[67] But, besides that, he emphasised that the City was characterised by 'closer personal relationships in which direct family ties were an important element but not outstandingly so, for to have been at the same college at Oxford or Cambridge frequently forms a far closer bond between two men then the fact that they may be cousins'. It was for this reason, Truptil believed, that the sense of community in London was much stronger than in Paris and made it possible, for example, for the Bank of England and the Treasury to operate embargoes on overseas loans without legal sanctions. 'Team spirit' and 'a sporting sense of discipline' could ensure a certain amount of self-regulation, solidarity and mutual self-help in the face of crisis.[68] The personal element in City business was one of the factors which gave financiers an affinity with the professionals and bureaucrats who ran the rest of the service sector and distanced them to some degree from the world of industry.[69]

The status of industry, though improving, still lagged somewhat behind that of the professions and the City. The broad swathe of industrialists whose firms were small, together with the growing managerial element in manufacturing, came from backgrounds that differed markedly from those of the leading members of the service sector. Jeremy's study of the 270 businessmen (mainly industrialists and industrial managers) who figure in the first volume of the *Dictionary of Business Biography* shows that only one-fifth of those born between 1870 and 1899 (and who would have been most active

---

66. Ziegler, *The Sixth Great Power*, pp. 336–7. The new partners in Morgans were very much of the gentlemanly capitalist type: Burk, *Morgan Grenfell*, pp. 99–100, 159–60.
67. R.J. Truptil, *British Banks and the London Money Market* (1936), pp. 172–5.
68. Though the embargo did encourage British investors to take their capital to the New York market instead. Burk, *Morgan Grenfell*, pp. 88–9.
69. Truptil, *British Banks and the London Money Market*, pp. 196–7.

between the wars and immediately after that) went to public school, though the public school component for later birth cohorts was significantly higher. Only one-ninth of the group had been educated at one of the ancient universities and half had fathers who were craftsmen, clerks, tradesmen or were similarly occupied.[70]

Nonetheless, industrialists' links with centres of power certainly strengthened after 1914. As big business increased in significance, the connections between finance and industry became closer. The leaders of large manufacturing companies enjoyed an educational background similar to that of non-traditional members of the elite,[71] the chief difference being that, like top City men, these leading industrialists often came from rather wealthier backgrounds than did recruits to the professions.[72] On the whole, however, industrialists still lacked entry into the circles of influence to which the City had long been admitted.

There is no doubt that, as a result of the war and its effects, there emerged a new breed of industrialists who moved between manufacturing business on one side and finance and politics on the other to a degree unheard of before 1914. On the whole, though, it would seem that those who became more prominent at the centre of affairs were frequently absorbed by gentlemanly culture without making any major impact upon it. One excellent example of this was the eagerness with which industrialists accepted the honours system. After 1914, they played a much fuller part in this remnant of the 'gentlemanly meaning system of the nineteenth century', dignifying their calling by accepting status rewards in return for their 'services' to the community. In doing so, they joined the traditional gentlemanly elite in playing down the importance of the profit motive, notwithstanding the fact that, in Lloyd George's time at least, honours had to be bought rather than won.[73]

Among the bigger corporations, where integration had gone furthest, there is some evidence that the influence of gentlemanly values on industrial life was becoming strong enough to affect policy and attitudes. In many important boardrooms there was 'a vague but persistent belief that some things were indeed more important than profits', a view which may well have hindered innovation and adaptation to the times.[74] By contrast, the 'practical men', who still

---

70. Jeremy, 'Anatomy of the British Business Elite', pp. 3–13.
71. Stanworth and Giddens, 'An Economic Elite', pp. 93–7.
72. Rubinstein, 'Education and the Social Origins of British Elites', pp. 180–2.
73. Scott, *The Upper Classes*, Ch. 6, esp. pp. 157, 160.
74. D.C. Coleman, 'Gentlemen and Players', *Econ. Hist. Rev.*, 2nd ser. XXVI (1973). The quotation is from p. 114.

dominated the small firm or held important managerial or technical positions in the larger firms, were too close to the machinery of industry to possess high status and often lacked the broad vision which, at its best, a traditional liberal education could bring: a great many of those involved in industry thus remained 'provincial' not just in geographical terms but also in a cultural sense.

On the political front, the most noticeable feature from our perspective was the extent to which all kinds of propertied interests, gentlemanly or otherwise, herded together within the Conservative Party, as Labour replaced the Liberals and as working men began to enter Parliament in strength for the first time. The movement of provincial propertied interests from Liberalism to Conservatism, already evident before 1914, was registered strongly at the election of 1918, when nearly half of all new recruits to the Conservative-dominated coalition government were businessmen. Landed representation in Parliament fell sharply, never recovering its former levels, and the ranks of public school men and Oxbridge graduates were thinned.[75] Overall, the party became more of a coalition of propertied interests than it had been before 1914: the 181 Conservatives identified as directors of companies in 1939 held a vast range of appointments in which finance, transport, distribution and manufacturing were all well represented;[76] and the changes which took place in party composition were enough to provoke alarm among traditionalists.[77] Nonetheless, business interests, whether provincial or otherwise, were hardly dominant after 1918. Aristocrats remained heavily over-represented in Cabinets and, in 1937, 19 out of 21 Cabinet members were public-school men, a high proportion of them old Etonians.[78] In 1939 three-fifths of all Conservative MPs were from public school backgrounds; the same percentage had connections with the land, the professions or other service occupations. Of the remaining two-fifths, a commercial background was still far more common than an industrial one. It remained the case, too, that the safest seats went to those who came from traditionally privileged backgrounds.[79]

The Conservative Party – which was in power for most of the

75. John M. McEwan, 'The Coupon Election of 1918 and Unionist Members of Parliament', *Journal of Modern History*, 34 (1962), pp. 297–304.

76. Simon Haxey, *Tory M.P.* (1939), p. 37.

77. McEwan, 'The Coupon Election of 1918', p. 306.

78. Stevenson, *British Society, 1914–45*, pp. 349–50; Bédarida, *A Social History of England*, p. 237.

79. John Ramsden, *The Age of Balfour and Baldwin, 1902–1940* (1978), pp. 360–1.

period, though sometimes under the guise of 'Coalition' or 'National' governments – needed a deeper well of support than that provided by a congerie of nation-wide propertied interests. As before 1914, the main source of Conservative strength was the south-east, where the middle-class population was extensive and trade unionism less influential. With one or two traditional exceptions, Conservatism was much weaker in areas where heavy industry was concentrated.[80] As Labour captured the industrial working-class vote and post-war industrial disputes became more bitter, manufacturing interests, big and little, were driven into Conservatism. In doing so, they became part of a movement whose heartland was the service-consumer industry complex of the south-east of England,[81] and they were contained within a traditional power structure whose cultural authority rested upon gentility and whose fulcrum of economic power was the City of London. 'The City counted on the party to provide the climate of political stability essential for its role as the world's financial capital; the party in turn relied on the City for financial advice and support'.[82] The intimacy between the two was such that the City could effectively veto 'unsuitable' candidates for the post of Chancellor of the Exchequer, as it had done before 1914.[83]

80. J.P.P. Dunbabin, 'British Elections in the Nineteenth and Twentieth Centuries: a Regional Approach', *Eng. Hist. Rev.* XCV (1980), Table 3, p. 37.

81. On this south-eastern hegemony see the suggestive comments in W.J.M. Mackenzie, *Politics and Social Science* (1967), pp. 351–2.

82. The quotation is from Boyce, who also claims that the movement of industrialists into the party 'did more to turn industrialists into Conservatives than Conservatives into the party of industry': *British Capitalism at the Crossroads*, p. 21.

83. The City objected to the appointment of Sir Robert Horne as Chancellor in 1923 because of his association with groups which were sceptical about restoring the gold standard. Ibid. pp. 21, 72–3.

CHAPTER THREE

Industry, the City and the Decline of the International Economy, 1914–39

World War I devastated international trade, and recovery was slow and incomplete in the 1920s. Britain's invisible trade was as badly affected by this, by the succeeding great depression of 1929–33 and by the protectionism which characterised the 1930s, as was the export trade in manufactures. The problems of the latter were compounded by further competitive failures in markets which had been particularly important to Britain before 1914. Invisible exports were also threatened by increased competition, and New York proved to be an effective rival source of long-term international investment in the 1920s. In the 1930s, however, when neither London nor New York could lend abroad, the City of London remained the headquarters of the largest commercial and financial bloc in the world, the Sterling Area, and its development was restrained as much by lack of opportunity as by competition.

The tribulations of industrial exports after World War I are one of the best documented episodes in the history of inter-war Britain. Declining competitiveness, evident well before 1914, would have brought severe problems for Britain's traditional exporters eventually; but the shock of war, and of the depression which began in the late 1920s and ran across the globe like a virulent disease, accelerated the process of decline by closing down markets and encouraging import substitution. Exports of goods never regained their pre-war levels, in terms of volumes, before 1939. After a decade spent assuming that pre-1914 conditions could somehow be restored, it was generally accepted in the 1930s that the staple industries of provincial Britain would recapture no former international glories. Despite the rapid growth of manufacturing output, the 'new industries' were not competitive enough to do well outside the Sterling Area.

What is less well appreciated is the severity of the decline in income from 'invisible' exports, which were equally devastated by war and its aftermath: measured against the standards of 1913, the City of London was performing less well in the 1920s than were the much-maligned exporters of industrial goods. In the 1930s, just as industry became dependent on protection and imperial markets, so the City had to abandon cosmopolitanism and settle for dominance within a sterling bloc centred on the empire. In this sense, the overseas interests of industry and finance converged markedly after 1914 and especially in the 1930s.

COMMODITY TRADE

The value of exports was much higher after the war than before, averaging £718m. between 1925 and 1929 as against £455m. for 1909–13. But prices had risen sharply during the war and fell only slowly after it; an index of the volume of exports (1913 = 100) shows them running at 91 in 1909–13 against 80.5 by 1925–9 and 86.3 in 1929, the height of the post-war boom.[1] In 1914–18 some markets were lost because they were cut off, encouraging import substitution and allowing less harassed rivals, notably the United States and Japan, to take advantage of Britain's difficulties. The demands of the

1. Volumes are arrived at by using the figures in B.R. Mitchell and Phyllis Deane's *Abstract of British Historical Statistics* (Cambridge, 1962), p. 284, and applying C.H. Feinstein's price indices, which can be found in *Statistical Tables of National Income, Expenditure and Output for the U.K., 1855–1965* (Cambridge, 1972), Table 64. The figures include trade with Eire from 1923 onwards. The most comprehensive study of British foreign trade in this period is still Alfred E. Kahn, *Britain and the World Economy* (1946). There are a number of obvious discrepancies here and in other chapters between some of the trade and payments statistics quoted. The figures for the invisible items in the balance of payments and for the balance of payments surpluses and deficits are from Feinstein, *Statistical Tables*. Like the Bank of England's figures (*Quarterly Bulletin*, 12 (1972), pp. 345ff), they do not tally with the data presented in the *Statistical Abstracts* and in Mitchell and Deane. On the other hand, neither Feinstein's nor the Bank's figures allow for a geographical breakdown of the trade statistics. Since this is vital to our purpose, we have used the older statistics where necessary. It is comforting to note, however, that the trends shown in both the older figures and the newer estimates are very similar. Nonetheless, it is only by using Feinstein's figures that it is possible to conclude as readily as we do that the balance of trade gap in the 1920s was less than is usually assumed, that the performance of invisibles in the 1920s was worse than is usually assumed, and that invisibles did better in the 1930s than the conventional wisdom usually allows. The only real problem arises from the first of these judgements concerning the trade gap. There are simply no figures for invisibles to compare with those of Feinstein, and all serious work in this area must begin from his starting points.

domestic economy in total war also reduced the volume of goods available for export. But, despite the rapid rise to prominence of the United States during the war, Britain's share of world trade may have actually been higher in the early 1920s compared with 1913; this reflected the economic dislocation of Britain's European rivals.[2] In the boom of 1924–9, however, Britain's share fell sharply. Lewis puts Britain's share of the world's manufactured exports at about 26 per cent in 1913, falling to 21 per cent by 1929; Germany's share was also lower in 1929 (19 per cent) than in 1913 (23 per cent), while the USA's share had gone up from 11 per cent to 18 per cent.[3] Britain's relative decline had been clear since the late nineteenth century and, in the 1920s, it continued for broadly similar reasons: the inability of the old staples to fend off competition and the failure to replace them adequately. The most obvious decline was in cotton textiles, Britain's leading commodity export, which accounted for £127m. or 25 per cent of exports in 1913, and maintained its share in 1924. But between 1924 and 1929 exports fell from £199.2m. to £135.4m., or 18.6 per cent of the total.[4]

During the 1920s most efforts in Britain, the United States and elsewhere were devoted to trying to make the pre-1913 world economy work again. After 1929, the system, so carefully patched up over the previous decade, suddenly fell apart. The world depression, centred on the collapse of the economies of the United States and of many leading primary producers, led to a severe contraction of world trade and to financial panic; protectionism and the bloc system took the place of the cosmopolitan world economy which still existed in 1929.

The value of exports fell in the depression and averaged £451m. in 1934–8, slightly less than the average for 1909–13. Volumes fell even further – from 80.5 in 1925–9 (1913 = 100) to 63.2 in 1934–8 and to 69.4 in the best year of the decade, 1937. But the slump was universal, and Britain's share of world trade actually rose a little in the early 1930s following the stimulus of devaluation in 1931 and, at 19.1 per

2. Gerd Hardach, *The First World War, 1914–18* (1977), p. 148 and Table 18. This gives Britain's share of world trade in 1913 as 15.3 per cent compared with 16.3 per cent in 1924. World trade was, of course, lower in 1924 than in 1913.

3. W. Arthur Lewis, 'International Competition in Manufactures', *American Economic Review: Papers and Proceedings*, XLVII (1957), p. 579. For different figures, which nonetheless indicate similar trends, see: Alfred Maizels, *Industrial Growth and World Trade* (1963), p. 189; and H. Tysynski, 'World Trade in Manufactured Commodities, 1899–1950', *Manchester School*, 19 (1951), p. 286.

4. Figures from Mitchell and Deane, *Abstract*, pp. 305–6.

cent in 1937, was only fractionally lower than in 1929.[5] The shift away from the nineteenth-century staple exports also continued in the 1930s. Cotton textiles' share of domestic exports fell to 13 per cent in 1937; on the other hand, 'new' industries – machinery, chemicals, electrical goods, vehicles and aircraft – accounted for 12 per cent in 1924, 16.5 per cent in 1929 and nearly 22 per cent in 1937.[6]

In contrast to exports, import volumes were higher after 1914 than before. They showed a 5 per cent rise over 1913 volumes in 1924, and were 16 per cent higher in 1929.[7] Part of this increase stemmed from the improvement in living standards which accompanied growth in Britain after 1919, and part was generated by increased demand for raw materials which could not be obtained at home (e.g. petroleum). But imports of manufactures also grew rapidly after 1924, when 'normality' was restored, moving from 21 per cent of gross imports in that year to 25 per cent in 1929 (Table 3.1). Net exports of articles wholly and mainly manufactured (exports and re-exports of British produce minus imports) did extremely badly in the mid- and late 1920s.

Table 3.1 Imports and net exports of articles wholly or mainly manufactured, 1924–37[a]

	Imports (£m.)	Share of gross imports (%)	Net exports[b] (£m.)
1924	298.8	20.8	354.4
1925	318.7	21.8	330.0
1926	314.0	23.3	251.2
1927	321.8	24.4	268.1
1928	317.0	24.4	288.6
1929	333.6	25.0	269.9
1930	306.8	27.1	157.9
1931	261.3	28.3	48.8
1932	157.4	20.8	130.7
1933	150.4	20.7	142.2
1934	170.9	21.9	144.3
1935	184.5	22.6	157.6
1936	212.7	23.2	143.9
1937	274.9	24.4	154.1

Source: *Statistical Abstract for the United Kingdom* for 1939 (HMSO).
Notes: [a] Figures are not strictly comparable with those for pre-1913.
  [b] Exports of British produce and re-exports minus gross imports.

5. Lewis, 'International Competition in Manufactures', and other sources as in n. 3.
6. Derived from Mitchell and Deane, *Abstract*, pp. 305–6.
7. Figures obtained as for n. 1.

Overall, net exports fell by about £85m. between 1924 and 1929. Practically the whole of that fall (£76m.) can be attributed to increased imports from foreign countries, although there was also a small fall in net exports to the empire.

Import volumes fell in the depression from 116 in 1929 (1913 = 100) to 1913 levels in 1932 but then rose rapidly to a new high of 121 in 1937.[8] Manufactured imports increased sharply in 1929–31, when exports were falling fast, and reached 28 per cent of total imports in 1931. The rise in manufactured imports, partly induced by anticipations of protectionist measures, which duly came in 1932,[9] meant that net exports fell catastrophically from £270m. in 1929 to £49m. in 1931, and a net export surplus on manufactures with foreign countries of £25m. was converted into an import surplus of £66m. in 1931. Net exports of manufactures to empire countries also fell, by over 50 per cent in two years, as their income from exports of primary produce exports shrank. Once protection had been imposed on foreign manufactures in 1932, the share of manufactures in imports fell to less than 21 per cent in 1933, but then rose steadily to reach nearly 25 per cent again in 1937 (Table 3.1). Net exports of manufactures to foreign countries were positive in 1933–6, but a small import surplus appeared again in 1937. Over the whole period, and despite protection in the 1930s and the surge in manufacturing output in Britain between the wars, Britain's position as a manufacturing trader continued to worsen. The ratio of exports and re-exports of manufactures to imported manufactures, which was 2.27:1 in 1913 and 2.18:1 in 1924, fell sharply to 1.56:1 in 1937. Britain's comparative advantage still lay in the labour-intensive older staple industries which were in decline as traded goods, and her 'new' industrial output was not competitive enough to provide adequate compensation.[10]

What eased Britain's position as a trading nation after 1914 was a very favourable shift in the terms of trade. Import prices rose less than export prices during the war and fell more quickly during the 1920s. Despite favourable price movements, exports and re-exports bought only 60 per cent of gross imports in 1914–18, but after 1918 exports recovered some ground, aided by a world restocking boom, the devaluation of sterling below its fixed wartime level of $4.76 (it reached

8. Figures obtained as for n. 1.

9. Forrest Capie, 'The Pressure for Tariff Protection in Britain, 1917–31', *Jour. Eur. Econ. Hist.*, 9 (1980).

10. N.F.R. Crafts and M. Thomas, 'Comparative Advantage in U.K. Manufacturing Trade, 1910–35', *Econ. Jour.*, 96 (1986); Alec Cairncross and Barry Eichengreen, *Sterling in Decline: The Devaluations of 1931, 1949 and 1967* (Oxford, 1983), pp. 32–3.

$3.40 in March 1920) and the disorganisation of European rivals. This trend, together with favourable terms of trade, sent the ratio of exports and re-exports to imports up to 85 per cent in 1919–23. The ratio then fell to 77 per cent between 1924 and 1928, when Britain revalued sterling on returning to the gold standard, when her European rivals were moving back to 'normality', and when competition in the old staple commodities was extremely fierce (Table 3.2). Although the buying power of exports in the 1920s was disappointing compared with the boom of 1911–13, it was on a par with experience in the 1890s (Table 3.2). In the 1930s, though, despite a further favourable shift in the terms of trade as import prices fell drastically from 1929 to 1933, exports and re-exports were only 69 per cent of the value of imports in 1929–33 and slightly less than that in 1934–8 (Table 3.2).

Table 3.2 Exports, re-exports and invisible surplus as percentage of gross imports, 1896–1948

	Net property income	Other services	All invisibles[a]	Exports and re-exports	All credits[b]
1896–1900	22.6	17.3	39.9	73.1	113.0
1901–05	22.4	13.5	35.9	73.0	108.9
1906–10	25.7	16.4	42.1	83.3	125.4
1911–13	27.6	16.2	43.8	87.7	131.5
1914–18	19.7	18.8	38.5	60.3	98.8
1919–23	15.1	13.6	28.7	85.2	113.9
1924–28	19.6	9.0	28.6	77.2	105.8
1929–33	21.9	8.6	30.5	69.0	99.5
1934–38	23.6	5.3	28.9	67.8	96.7
1939–43	14.4	−26.6	−12.2	40.9	28.7
1944–48	10.5	−21.2	−10.7	75.1	64.4

Source: C.H. Feinstein, *Statistical Tables of National Income, Expenditure and Output of the United Kingdom, 1856–1965* (Cambridge, 1972), Table 15.

Notes: [a] Net property income plus other services.
[b] All invisibles plus exports and re-exports.

One of the most noticeable features of the inter-war period was the increased importance of trade with the empire, and more especially with the white Dominions of Canada, Australia, New Zealand and South Africa (Table 3.3). In the 1930s, when world trade was collapsing, the British not only adopted protection for their manufactures but also created a preferential system centred on the empire, particularly the white colonies. Nonetheless, although the Ottawa agreements did increase British trade with the Dominions, it

Table 3.3 Regional shares in British exports and imports, 1846–1938 (per cent)

Regional shares in exports of British produce

	1846–50	1871–75	1896–1900	1909–13	1925–29	1934–38
Developed countries	44.8	47.2	39.4	35.1	31.1	33.4
Newly settled countries	18.7	21.3	25.2	28.7	30.2	34.0
Underdeveloped countries	35.6	31.1	34.3	35.9	37.0	33.8
Dominions	8.7	12.0	16.7	17.5	20.6	25.9
India and Burma	9.4	8.9	11.8	11.9	11.6	8.0
Rest of British empire	9.2	5.9	5.6	5.6	5.0	7.4
British empire	27.3	26.8	34.1	35.0	37.2	41.3

Regional shares in net imports into Britain

	1846–50	1871–75	1896–1900	1909–13	1925–29	1934–38
Developed countries	n/a	48.1	61.8	49.9	46.2	38.2
Newly settled countries	n/a	17.7	17.7	24.9	28.0	34.5
Underdeveloped countries	n/a	34.1	20.1	24.7	25.3	26.4
Dominions	n/a	9.6	12.6	14.3	16.9	24.3
India and Burma	n/a	9.9	6.2	7.3	6.1	6.5
Rest of British empire	n/a	5.3	3.9	5.3	9.9	11.4
British empire	n/a	24.8	22.7	26.9	32.9	41.2

Source: B.R. Mitchell and P. Deane, *Abstract of British Historical Statistics* (Cambridge, 1962); and *Statistical Abstracts for the United Kingdom* (HMSO).

Notes: Eire has been treated as UK internal trade in 1925–9 and 1934–8 in order to allow comparisons with earlier years. South Africa appears under 'Newly settled' and 'Dominions' throughout.

is clear that the 1930s preferential system merely formalised an interdependence which had been growing rapidly before 1914 and continued to expand in the 1920s. At the same time, however, as trade with the Dominions and with the more recently acquired parts of the underdeveloped empire was growing in relative significance, Britain's links with India slackened, especially in the 1930s. Moreover, the empire was only a part, albeit the largest part, of the Sterling Area which emerged in the 1930s and which included some of the smaller countries of Europe. The share of exports going to the area as a whole rose from just over one-half to three-fifths between 1929 and 1937, and European members contributed a significant part of the increase.

Table 3.4 British trade in manufactures, 1924 and 1937 (£m.)

	Imports		Exports and re-exports		Balance of trade[a]	
	1924	1937	1924	1937	1924	1937
Industrial countries[b]	−222.9	−139.2	+178.2	+76.6	−44.8	−62.6
European Sterling Area[c]	−15.1	−19.4	+31.5	+39.7	+16.4	+20.3
Rest of Europe	−10.3	−13.1	+29.5	+26.6	+19.2	+13.5
Other foreign	−16.9	−40.8	+117.1	+67.7	+100.2	+26.9
All foreign[d]	−265.2	−212.5	+356.2	+210.6	+91.0	−1.9
Dominions[e]	−12.3	−35.3	+132.9	+118.5	+120.6	+83.2
India	−11.8	−13.0	+86.8	+35.7	+75.0	+22.7
Other empire	−10.5	−14.1	+76.9	+64.4	+66.4	+50.3
All empire[f]	−34.6	−62.4	+296.6	+218.6	+262.0	+156.2
Total trade[g]	−299.8	−274.9	+652.8	+429.2	+353.0	+154.3

Source: *Annual Statement of Trade of the United Kingdom.*

Notes: [a] Difference between imports and exports/re-exports.
[b] Industrial countries comprise Germany, Belgium, The Netherlands, Luxembourg, France, Italy, Switzerland and the United States.
[c] European Sterling Area comprises Finland, Norway, Sweden, Denmark, Estonia, Latvia, Lithuania, Iceland and Portugal.
[d] Industrial countries plus European Sterling Area plus Rest of Europe plus Other foreign.
[e] Dominions include South Africa.
[f] Dominions plus India plus Other empire.
[g] All foreign plus All empire. These figures do not always tally with Table 3.1. Some rough estimates of the trade of small countries have had to be made because the tables in the *Statement* are not sufficiently specific.

In contrast, the erosion of Britain's position in industrial markets continued apace. Exports to four major Western Europe countries and the United States, which were 24 per cent of the total in 1913, fell to 21 per cent in 1929 and to 19.5 per cent in 1937, though the fall owed something to protectionism as well as a further decline in competitiveness.[11] In areas of traditional informal influence, trade performance between the wars was very poor. Latin America's share of British exports in the 1930s was lower than at any time since the 1870s. China, usually singled out as the area with the greatest potential for growth, proved even more disappointing: in 1934–8 China and Hong Kong together took 1.9 per cent of British exports as against 3.7 per cent in 1871–5.

A close look at the fate of trade in manufactures confirms the shrinkage of Britain's influence between the wars (Tables 3.4 and 3.5). What is remarkable is not the deficit on manufacturing trade with other industrial countries, which was worsening (a deficit on trade with the United States appeared after 1914), but the erosion of the British position in other areas, including some parts of the empire. Net exports to the European members of the Sterling Area kept up well, partly because Britain managed to sign some highly favourable treaties with them in the 1930s, as we shall see. But net exports to 'other foreign' countries fell very sharply between 1924 and 1937. This was due, to some degree, to the spread of industrialisation on the periphery and increased protectionism; but it also owed something to the decline of British competitiveness in areas of traditional informal influence such as Latin America, the Middle East and the Far East. More specifically, however, the erosion occurred across the 'semi-industrial' periphery identified earlier, which included countries within the empire. Net exports to India declined significantly following the demise of textile exports, and Britain developed a deficit with Canada on trade in manufactures in the 1930s. Trade with the Dominions as a whole was disappointing, especially in view of the preferential system brought in after 1932. Broadly speaking, it would be fair to say that Britain's exporters became increasingly dependent on Sterling Area countries after 1919, mainly because trade with them declined less dramatically than trade with other customers.

11. The four European countries are France, Germany, the Netherlands and Belgium. The percentages are computed from figures in Mitchell and Deane, *Abstract*.

Table 3.5 British trade in manufactures, 1924 and 1937: trade ratios (exports and re-exports ÷ imports)

	1924	1937
Industrial countries	0.80	0.55
European Sterling Area	2.09	2.05
Rest of Europe	2.86	2.03
Other foreign	6.93	1.54
All foreign	1.34	0.99
Dominions	10.81	3.36
India	7.36	2.75
Other empire	7.32	4.57
All empire	8.57	3.50
Total trade	2.18	1.56

Source: *Annual Statement of Trade of the United Kingdom.*
Note: In this table numerals less than 1 indicate a deficit on manufactured trade and above 1 indicate a surplus. Thus in 1924 Britain's exports to other industrial countries were only four-fifths the value of British imports from them. In the same year, exports to the Dominions were almost eleven times greater in value than imports from them. See also notes for Table 3.4.

THE CITY AND INVISIBLES

The decline of visible exports is a commonplace of inter-war history but the drastic slump in Britain's invisible income was of equal significance. In value terms, the invisible surplus was worth £317m. in 1913, £359m. in 1929 and £289m. in 1937.[12] In real terms, though, the decline in invisible income after 1913 was severe. Measured by pre-war prices, the purchasing power of invisible income was only three-fifths of the 1913 level in 1929 and 54 per cent of the pre-war level in 1937.[13] Invisible income had grown very rapidly before 1914, when the chief driving force was income from investments and property overseas. This income was badly affected by the war. Some investments were permanently lost, most notably those placed in Russia, which were repudiated by the Bolsheviks in 1917. Others had to be liquidated, especially those held in the United States, to pay for war supplies. British assets abroad were reduced by about £1bn.

12. Feinstein, *Statistical Tables*, Table 38.
13. These results are arrived at by deflating the current value figures by an index of the prices of consumer goods and services. See Feinstein, *Statistical Tables*, Tables 15 and 61.

(roughly one-quarter) during the war.[14] In addition, the British government incurred a dollar debt of about £750m.[15] American debts, permanent loss of assets, the disruption of the world economy and, after 1919, the devaluation of sterling (in which invisible payments to Britain were made) all reduced net income on overseas property in the early 1920s. The invisible surplus was equivalent to 44 per cent of the value of imports just before World War I but was worth only 29 per cent of imports in the 1920s (Table 3.2). The return to gold in 1925, and the resumption of foreign lending by Britain in the 1920s, pushed up property income relative to imports. The improvement continued in the early 1930s, mainly owing to the tremendous fall in import prices and to the fact that very few of Britain's debtors actually defaulted on their loans, although many of them paid reduced rates of interest.

Other forms of invisible income suffered even more severely. Shipping income fell in the 1920s as competition increased and freight rates collapsed; it contracted even more sharply in the 1930s as the world economy shrank.[16] Returns on the provision of short-term credit and other business services were also badly hit by the war and by depression (Table 3.2). The war shook confidence in credit, and many assets were frozen for the duration. In 1914 many London firms could not have met their obligations on bills accepted without help from the Bank of England and the Treasury.[17] Those firms, such as the merchant banker, Kleinworts, which had been heavily involved in extending credit to Germany and other enemy powers, were most seriously affected by the crisis.[18] New business also declined drastically as international trade shrank: former customers, cut off from London credit, had to make new arrangements, and American competition proved keen.[19] During the war, business centred more and more on the handling of growing amounts of government short-term debt although, on the foreign front, some of the more presti-

---

14. United Nations, *International Capital Movements in the Inter-War Period* (1949), pp. 4–5.
15. Hardach, *The First World War*, Table 18, p. 148.
16. Shipping returns fell from just under £30m. per year on average during 1921–9 to around £15.5m. per year in 1930–8. See Feinstein, *Statistical Tables*, Table 38.
17. Thomas Balogh, *Studies in Financial Organization* (Cambridge, 1947), p. 243; Henry Roseveare, *The Treasury: The Evolution of a British Institution* (1969), pp. 236–8. See also the lucid 'eyewitness' account given by J.M. Keynes, 'War and the Financial System', August 1914', in *Econ. Jour.*, XXIV (1914).
18. Suzanne Diaper, 'Merchant Banking in the Inter-war Period: the Case of Kleinwort, Sons and Co.', *Bus. Hist.*, XXVIII (1986), p. 64.
19. Balogh, *Studies in Financial Organization*, p. 179. For Barings' experience see Philip Ziegler, *The Sixth Great Power: Barings, 1762–1929* (1988), pp. 321–4.

gious houses, such as Barings, made a comfortable living by facilitating inter-allied financial arrangements.[20]

Once the war was over, continental business picked up quickly and, insofar as Britain became a centre for the operation of the gold exchange standard in the 1920s, this brought considerable funds into the London short market.[21] Nonetheless, most United States business was permanently lost;[22] confidence in London was never quite the same again. Merchant banks and discount houses involved in short-term credit adopted limited liability status in the 1920s – a clear sign of diminishing credibility.[23] Furthermore, a great deal of business during the decade was in the form of 'reimbursement credits' in which borrowers had their credit status guaranteed by their bankers before funds were made available in the City: the old system of doing business through contacts between City institutions, and their family and other personal contacts abroad, began to break down under the strain of war and the uncertainties that war left behind.[24] The absolute volume of bills in the London market in 1929 may have been similar to the pre-war figure,[25] because world trade volumes were higher in the late 1920s than before 1914 and because the loss of American business had been compensated by increased volume in Europe.[26] Returns, however, were sharply lower than before the war because the discount houses and acceptance houses in London had to face competition not only from New York (and later in the decade, Paris) but also from the domestic clearing banks, which invaded this field of operations in the 1920s.[27]

In the succeeding decade, the commercial bill market shrank rapidly and, despite the fact that the joint-stock banks withdrew from direct competition with the specialist houses, competition between the latter was so fierce that returns were driven down to very low levels. Again, those most involved in European business were the worst affected: German assets were first frozen, then rigidly con-

20. Ziegler, *The Sixth Great Power*, p. 328.

21. Balogh, *Studies in Financial Organization*, pp. 178, 247–8.

22. Diaper, 'Merchant Banking in the Inter-War Period', p. 64.

23. R.J. Truptil, *British Banks and the London Money Market* (1936), pp. 134–5.

24. Truptil, *British Banks*, p. 136; Diaper, 'Merchant Banking in the Inter-War Period', p. 66; Balogh, *Studies in Financial Organization*, p. 244.

25. Balogh (*Studies in Financial Organization*, p. 248) argues for this, but Gordon A. Fletcher claims that there was an absolute decline in the volume of bills. See his *The Discount Market in London: Principles, Operation and Change* (1976), pp. 39–40.

26. Ziegler, *The Sixth Great Power*, pp. 339–40. For the experience of some acceptance houses in the 1920s see Diaper, 'Merchant Banking in the Inter-War Period', p. 67; also Kathleen Burk, *Morgan Grenfell, 1838–1988: The Biography of a Merchant Bank* (Cambridge, 1989), pp. 85–6.

27. Balogh, *Studies in Financial Organization*, pp. 224–5; Diaper, 'Merchant Banking in the Inter-War Period', p. 66.

trolled later in the decade.[28] In all, net returns on 'financial and other services' were around £45m. in the 1920s, reached a low of £15m. in 1932 and had recovered only to £25m. by 1937.[29] Profits fell and survival for the bill specialists, such as the discount houses, depended on amalgamation, encouraged by the Bank of England, and opening new lines of business on the domestic front, especially in Treasury bills, government stock and even, after devaluation in 1931, currency speculation. For their part, the merchant bankers also turned to domestic industrial issues.[30]

The troubles of merchant bankers were shared by the British overseas banks, which faced greater local competition, often spiced with nationalist hostility, as well as a decline in international business. Many were bought out by British clearing banks which moved into international business for the first time between the wars and were encouraged in the 1930s by the Bank of England, which feared that some international banks would otherwise fail.[31] However, the removal of American competition, and very low interest rates in the 'cheap money' era after 1932, probably meant that London's comparative advantages in short-term credits increased in the 1930s.[32] The French financial expert, R.J. Truptil, writing in the mid–1930s, felt that, though New York and Paris had made up some ground on London in comparison with 1913, 'there can be little doubt that a return to stability in money matters will result in such a revival in the City that it will once more become the world centre for the financing of international trade'.[33] In practice, trade was so restricted in the 1930s that the City was forced to operate mainly within the confines of the empire and the Sterling Area.

The overall effect of the crisis in both visible and invisible trade after 1914 was that the large balance of payments surplus of the immediate pre-war period was much reduced in the 1920s and disappeared in the 1930s. The current account surplus of over £200m. was reduced by two-thirds in the late 1920s, and the deficit between 1934 and 1938 averaged about £25m. per annum.[34] The surplus was

28. Diaper 'Merchant Banking in the Inter War Period', pp. 67–9; Balogh, *Studies in Financial Organization*, pp. 263–5.

29. Feinstein, *Statistical Tables*, Table 38.

30. Fletcher, *The Discount Market in London*, pp. 35–41; Diaper, 'Merchant Banking in the Inter-War Period', pp. 57–61.

31. Geoffrey Jones, 'Competitive Advantages in British Multinational Banking since 1890', in idem, ed. *Banks as Multinationals* (1990), pp. 42–8.

32. Balogh, *Studies in Financial Organization*, pp. 178, 180.

33. Truptil, *British Banks and the London Money Market*, pp. 199–200.

34. Figures are from Feinstein, *Statistical Tables*, Table 15.

equivalent to nearly one-third of imports in 1911–13, fell to about 5 per cent in the mid–1920s and became negative in the 1930s, at which point Britain was having to reduce her assets overseas to cover payments on her imports (Table 3.2). In the 1920s the principal problem was invisible income, which fell more heavily than income from visible exports. In that decade, when Britain was attempting to lead the world back to pre-1913 'normality', commodity exports as a percentage of GDP actually rose compared with pre-war from an average of 17.7 between 1891 and 1913 to 18.2 in 1921–9; and the balance of trade deficit was lower on average in the second period than in the first. But the decline in the invisible surplus, from 11 per cent of GDP in the 20 years before the war to 7.3 per cent in the 1920s, reduced the overall balance of payments surplus from 5 per cent of GDP on average before 1913 to just over 2 per cent in 1921–9, a level lower than at any time since the early nineteenth century. In the 1930s during the world economic crisis, exports fell drastically as a proportion of GDP, but imports dropped almost as much and the balance of trade gap was only as great as that experienced in the period 1891–1913. Even so, when the deficit on commodity trade was added to a further fall in the contribution of invisibles to national income, the British found themselves disinvesting overseas at a rate equivalent to 1 per cent of GDP per year in the 1930s (Table 3.6).

Table 3.6 Balance of payments on current account, 1891–1964: ratios to GDP (average of annual percentages)

	Exports of goods	Imports of goods	Balance of trade[a]	Net property income	Net other services	All invisible income[b]	Balance of payments on current a/c (new overseas investment)[c]
1891–1913	17.7	−23.8	−6.1	6.8	4.3	11.1	5.0
1921–29	18.2	−23.3	−5.1	5.1	2.2	7.3	2.2
1930–38	10.9	−16.9	−6.0	4.2	0.9	5.1	−0.9
1952–64	16.6	−17.5	−0.9	1.3	0.2	1.5	0.6

Source: R.C.O. Matthews, C.H. Feinstein and J.C. Odling-Smee, *British Economic Growth, 1856–1973* (Oxford, 1983).

Notes: [a] Difference between exports and imports.
[b] Net property income plus net other services.
[c] Balance of trade plus all invisible income.

It was recognised quite early in official circles that Britain's lending capacity would be much reduced compared with the heady days immediately before the war.[35] Overseas loans in the 1920s were running at roughly £100m. per annum, much below the levels of 1900–14, especially remembering that the price level was much lower before the war than in the 1920s (Table 3.7). Besides this, domestic issues were of greater significance than overseas issues after 1919, as we shall see.

Table 3.7 New capital issues, empire and foreign, 1900–38 (average per year)

	Empire		Foreign		Total	
	£m.	%	£m.	%	£m.	%
1900–14	53.5	39.1	83.9	60.9	137.4	100
1919–23	65.4	66.4	27.9	33.6	93.3	100
1924–28	72.5	58.8	50.8	41.2	123.3	100
1929–33	44.0	69.6	19.2	30.4	63.2	100
1934–38	25.6	86.2	4.1	13.8	29.7	100
1919–38	51.9	67.1	25.5	32.9	77.4	100

Sources: Calculated from T. Balogh, *Studies in Financial Organization* (Cambridge, 1947), Table XLVIa, pp. 249–50; L. Davis and R. Huttenback, *Mammon and the Pursuit of Empire: The Political Economy of British Imperialism 1860–1912* (Cambridge, 1987), pp. 40–1 (intermediate estimate).

The Bank of England used a great deal of unofficial pressure at times to persuade City institutions not to lend abroad lest the flow should jeopardise Britain's attempts to get back to gold before 1925 or to stay on gold after that date.[36] Barings had to refuse an offer to take up a large loan for Argentina in 1925 because of Bank of England disapproval, and other merchant bankers also responded to similar calls for restraint.[37] Despite embargoes, some foreign issues were positively encouraged by the authorities in the 1920s as part of the European reconstruction schemes which British governments and officials felt were crucial to the recovery of the world economy. Loans to Austria and Hungary fell into this category.[38] Moreover, in the late 1920s, when embargoes were lifted, foreign issues did increase in importance. But embargoes apart, the British lost a great deal of their traditional foreign loan business in the 1920s because the London

35. J.M. Atkin, *British Overseas Investment, 1918–1931* (1977), p. 53.
36. Idem, 'Official Regulation of British Overseas Investment, 1914–31', *Econ. Hist. Rev.*, 2nd ser. XXIII (1970).
37. Ziegler, *The Sixth Great Power*, pp. 349–50. The Argentine business had originally been lost to the USA in the war (ibid. pp. 345–5). See also below, pp. 150, 155–6, 168.
38. Atkin, *British Overseas Investment*, pp. 93–7, 133–4.

rate on loans was often too high in comparison with that prevailing in New York, and much of the European business which did come London's way was of the 'second class' variety.[39] Trustee status (extended to underdeveloped parts of the empire in the late 1920s) ensured that the empire could still borrow in London at rates New York could not match;[40] embargoes on empire loans were rarely applied because 'empire development' was officially in vogue. As a result, empire issues came to predominate over foreign ones when Britain invested overseas (Table 3.7).

A further important change in the nature of foreign investment in the 1920s was the predominance of borrowing by public authorities compared with the position before the war. Public-authority borrowing accounted for about one-third of all foreign loans on average between 1865 and 1914 and just over one-half of imperial ones.[41] In the period 1918–31 the proportions rose to 47 per cent and 70 per cent respectively.[42] This change may reflect not only state reconstruction schemes after the war but also a diminution in confidence in private borrowers after the traumas of 1914–18.

Despite lending on a reduced scale compared with the Edwardian age, Britain was still probably the world's largest overseas investor in 1929,[43] but it seems likely that she overstretched herself as a long-term lender in the 1920s. Allowing for the purchase of about 10 per cent of issues by foreigners and also adjusting for loan repayments, it has been estimated that Britain sent £542m. of new money abroad between 1924 and 1930.[44] Although this foreign investment probably had a positive influence on Britain's exports, the accumulated balance of payments surplus for these years was roughly £70m. less.[45] Britain had to borrow short in Europe in order to lend long to the empire. Although the short-term liabilities which resulted from over-extended, long-term lending were only a small fraction of all the short money held in

39. Ibid. pp. 147–54.
40. Ibid. pp. 76–86. British investment by multinationals became most concentrated on the empire after 1914. Stephen J. Nicholas, 'British Multinational Investment before 1939', *Jour. Eur. Econ. Hist.*, 11 (1982).
41. Lance E. Davis and Robert A. Huttenback, *Mammon and the Pursuit of Empire: The Political Economy of British Imperialism, 1860–1914* (Cambridge, 1986), Table 2.2, pp. 44–5.
42. Atkin, *British Overseas Investment*, Table 14, p. 130.
43. United Nations, *International Capital Movements in the Inter-War Period* (New York, 1949), estimated total UK overseas assets in 1929 to be $16.86bn. as against $14.6bn. for the USA (p. 29).
44. Atkin, *British Overseas Investment*, p. 246. The figures probably underestimate the outflow since they do not cover some private direct overseas investment.
45. Feinstein, *Statistical Tables*, Table 37.

London in the 1920s, worries about over-commitment undoubtedly contributed to the crisis which took sterling off gold in 1931.[46]

Overseas lending diminished after 1929 and reached levels on a par with early-nineteenth-century experience in the 1930s (Table 3.7). Borrowing was almost entirely confined to empire countries by the mid–1930s and the trickle of money going to foreigners went largely to those within the Sterling Area. Capital export was on a very tight rein in the 1930s and lending to the empire and to foreign countries fell sharply although, despite embargoes, governments did not attempt to prevent British investors from subscribing to stocks issued in foreign capitals. In fact, repayments on existing loans exceeded new issues in every year between 1932 and 1938 by a huge margin.[47]

Once the gallant attempt to restore a cosmopolitan economy in the 1920s had failed, finance and industry were forced into an increased dependence upon the Sterling Area and upon the domestic market as the free-trading, expanding world economy which had existed before 1914 disappeared. And just as, before 1914, visible and invisible trade had interacted in a dynamic way so, in the less favourable post-war atmosphere, the weakness of the one sometimes increased the difficulties of the other. Thus the reduction in the volume of exports affected shipping income and returns on commercial business and insurance. The smaller balance of payments surplus which resulted from this fall meant less foreign investment and hence fewer exports of goods. Similarly, attempts to maintain high levels of foreign investment in the 1920s meant that high interest rates had to be imposed to attract the short money which would ease the strain imposed by lending long: this inhibited the growth of investment in industries which were important contributors to exports. Most important of all, the attempt to restore London's position by returning to the gold standard led to an overvaluation of the pound which harmed Britain's export industries and encouraged manufactured imports.[48]

46. For the role played by the collapse of invisible income in precipitating a balance of payments crisis in 1931 see Donald Moggeridge, 'The 1931 Financial Crisis – A New View', *The Banker*, CXX (1970); and Cairncross and Eichengreen, *Sterling in Decline*, pp. 56–7. Of equal significance in our view was the £230m. shrinkage in the net export of manufactures between 1929 and 1931.

47. Kahn, *Britain in the World Economy*, pp. 188–95: Cairncross and Eichengreen, *Sterling in Decline*, p. 96.

48. M.E.F. Jones, 'The Regional Impact of the Overvalued Pound in the 1920s', *Econ. Hist. Rev.*, 2nd ser. XXXVIII (1985). The assumption that the pound was overvalued in the late 1920s has recently been attacked by K.G.P. Matthews, 'Was Sterling Overvalued in 1925?', ibid. XXXIX (1986). We do not find his argument convincing.

The City suffered as badly as industry, and its area of effective control covered only the Sterling Area by the 1930s, but its long-term future was brighter. The concentration of commercial and financial power connected with overseas trade in London continued to grow between the wars, and London's dominance was shown by its increasing relative importance as a centre for import traffic and shipping.[49] Moreover, as already indicated, the City's problems over short-term credit instruments had more to do with the chaotic state of world trade than with lack of competitiveness; if Britain's own savings were much diminished and New York had the capital, London still had much to offer in terms of the 'expertise, the clients and the market' should the international economy revive.[50] In terms of both markets and policy, City and industry were more at one with each other in the 1930s than before; but if a protected Sterling Area was a necessity for uncompetitive industry it was more of a temporary refuge in hard times for the City.[51]

Moreover, given the continued influence of gentlemanly values upon government and administration, the main emphasis in international economic policy was on the problems of Britain's financial sector and how to overcome them. In the 1920s restoring London's position as the main international money market, fighting off the American financial challenge and encouraging the recovery of invisible income were the chief concerns. In the 1930s the most pressing matter was how the emerging sterling bloc could make payments on accumulated debt, when foreign trade had been devastated by depression and loans from Britain were few and small. This debt crisis posed a threat to the stability of the bloc and, as we shall see, the emergence of a new policy in the 1930s is understandable only in relation to it, and to the determination to win back the ground lost to the United States in the previous decade.

49. In 1913 the tonnage of shipping entered and cleared in London was 25 million tons; in Liverpool it was 23 million. By 1936 the figures were 42 million and 27 million respectively. The information is from the *Statistical Abstract of the United Kingdom*. The concentration of financial control of colonial trade in London between the wars is evident in Kathleen Stahl, *The Metropolitan Organization of British Colonial Trade* (1951), pp. 295–6.
50. Burk, *Morgan Grenfell*, p. 86.
51. It is worth noting here that, although invisible income declined in the 1930s, the ratio of invisible exports to invisible imports was 2.58:1 in 1929, fell to 2.2:1 in 1933 and then rose to 2.64:1 in 1937. The ratio was, however, much more favourable to Britain before 1914. See Feinstein, *Statistical Tables*, Tables 38–9.

CHAPTER FOUR

Upholding Gentlemanly Values: The American Challenge, 1914–31

INDUSTRY, THE STATE AND WAR, 1914–21

When war broke out in 1914, and for some months afterwards, the British government assumed that fighting Germany was compatible with (in the words of Churchill) 'business as usual'. Britain's small expeditionary force would supplement the much larger French army and we would supply them and our other Allies with financial and material aid in what, it was confidently expected, would be a short campaign similar to the Franco–German conflict of 1870. By the end of 1915 these assumptions had been overturned. A mass army now had to be organised and the nation had to accept the prospect of a long, exhausting war and the mobilisation of all available material resources in order to survive. Under the strain, the market economy failed to deliver the goods and it was soon recognised that the state had to extend its authority to a degree unimagined in peacetime. Central allocation of resources and price fixing began with munitions and were then extended further and further into the economy to ensure adequate war supplies and a proper division of output between military and civilian needs. By 1918 two-thirds of the economy and nine-tenths of imports were subject to direction by bodies authorised by government.[1]

One inevitable outcome of this development was a much greater involvement of governing elites in the mechanics of the industrial

1. For a useful summary of the evolution of the war economy see Sidney Pollard, *The Development of the British Economy, 1914–1980* (1983), pp. 14–47. See also G.C. Peden, *British Economic and Social Policy: Lloyd George to Margaret Thatcher* (1985), pp. 36–47; David French, 'The Rise and Fall of "Business As Usual"', in Kathleen Burk, ed. *War and the State* (1982); and an older, but still riveting, account in R.H. Tawney, 'The Abolition of Economic Controls, 1918–21', *Econ. Hist. Rev.*, 1st ser. XIII (1943).

production process, from which they had been so remote in 1914. Numerous ad hoc commissions and boards were set up in industry for the purpose of coordinating, and inevitably centralising, the production of hitherto scattered industries. These new bodies brought owners and managers, whose horizons had previously been irredeemably provincial, into intimate contact with each other and with authority in London.[2] One outcome of the war was an acceleration in the development of big business in Britain; another was the evolution of peak organisations to represent industrialists who were becoming conscious of themselves as an interest over against, not only labour, but also that traditional centre of economic power, London finance. The most important of these organisations, the Federation of British Industries (FBI), was established in 1916.[3]

The entry of provincial industry into the power structure after 1914 was made a great deal easier by the appearance in 1916 of Lloyd George's coalition government, which was free from the normal restraints of party allegiance.[4] By contrast, the influence of traditional finance and of the City in general was curbed by the war. The illiquidity crisis, involving the acceptance houses at the outbreak of war, was only resolved by government guarantees and was a grave blow to the City's self-confidence.[5] More important in its long-term effects was the rapid decline in the international service economy, and the permanent rupture of many of the delicate commercial and financial threads which had linked London with the world economy before 1914. The gold standard was virtually suspended at the outbreak of war and the control of the money supply slipped out of the grip of the Bank of England as government expenditure soared and the economy endured inflation at a rate unheard of since Napoleon's time. The Treasury strove mightily to contain expenditure but during the war the power of the main spending ministries, especially munitions, could not be controlled effectively.[6]

2. Scott Newton and Dilwyn Porter, *Modernization Frustrated: The Politics of Industrial Decline in Britain Since 1900* (1988), pp. 37–8.
3. John Turner, 'The Politics of "Organized Business" in the First World War', in John Turner, ed. *Businessmen and Politics: Studies of Business Activity in British Politics, 1900–1945* (1984); R.T.P. Davenport-Hines, *Dudley Docker: The Life and Times of a Trade Warrior* (Cambridge, 1984), Ch. 5.
4. Newton and Porter, *Modernization Frustrated*, p. 32.
5. Henry Roseveare, *The Treasury: The Evolution of a British Institution* (1969), pp. 238–40; Teresa Seaborne, 'The Summer of 1914', in Forrest Capie and Geoffrey Wood, *Financial Crises and the World Banking System* (1986); also J.M. Keynes, 'War and the Financial System, Aug. 1914', *Econ. Jour.*, XXIV (1914).
6. Roseveare, *The Treasury*, pp. 238ff; Kathleen Burk, 'The Treasury: the Impotence of Power', in Burk, *War and the State*.

By 1917 there was a considerable body of support for the view that the role of the state in the economy should be greatly enhanced even in peacetime. In certain areas, state control appeared to promise more efficient production than the market; there was also a strong lobby which argued that the powers used to create weapons in war ought to be turned to the production of social amenities, once peace was declared, to reward the nation for its fortitude.[7] Equally if not more important than the zeal of the reconstructionists in focusing attention on the state was the fear that outright victory against Germany might not be achieved.[8] Any compromise peace might be followed by an economic assault from Germany as she tried to refloat her economy by a massive export drive and a policy of 'dumping', thus undermining British industry and producing heavy unemployment. It was this fear which led the principal Allies to sign the Paris Agreements in 1916. Here, the Allies pledged themselves to measures designed to counteract post-war German dumping and agreed to deny her and Austria most-favoured-nation status after the war. Plans were drawn up for coordinated Allied production and a common post-war reconstruction policy was promised.

To achieve their ends, the Allies were prepared to use extensive government intervention in the economy and heavy protection, and to draw on the resources of their empires through preferential tariffs and other forms of discrimination.[9] Protection had a general appeal to propertied interests by 1916 since it held out the prospect of raising revenues to pay off escalating war debts without placing too high a burden on personal taxation.[10] But the Paris Agreements were most enthusiastically received by pre-war supporters of Chamberlain's programme.[11] Within government, the pressures making for an 'imperial' strategy and for a renewed emphasis on the centrality of

---

7. On reconstructionist ideas see Pollard, *The Development of the British Economy*, pp. 48–50; Peden, *British Economic and Social Policy*, pp. 47ff; Newton and Porter, *Modernization Frustrated*, pp. 45–54. There is also a highly detailed account in P.B. Johnson, *Land Fit For Heroes: The Planning of British Reconstruction, 1916–19* (Chicago, 1968).

8. Peter Cline, 'Winding Down the War Economy: British Plans for Peacetime Recovery, 1916–19', in Burk, *War and the State*, pp. 160–4.

9. Cline, 'Winding Down the War Economy', pp. 164–9; Robert E. Bunselmeyer, *The Cost of the War, 1914–18: British Economic War Aims and the Origin of Reparations* (Hamden, Conn., 1975), pp. 35ff. Details of the Paris Agreements can be found in Parliamentary Paper Cd 8271 for 1916 and in Albert O. Hirschman, *National Power and the Structure of Foreign Trade* (1945; 1980), App. B, pp. 163–5. See also V.H. Rothwell, *British War Aims and Peace Diplomacy* (Oxford, 1971), Ch. 8.

10. Bunselmeyer, *The Cost of the War*, pp. 13–17.

11. Ibid. pp. 24–32.

empire were enhanced by the presence of 'social imperialists', like Milner, in the war Cabinet after 1916. Social imperialists were ready to accept that Germany could not be completely defeated and were convinced that this did not matter fundamentally, provided that she was confined to Europe. To ensure her own independence Britain should, they believed, retire behind a heavily protected empire dominated by British industry. From this perspective, 'only the failure of "Britons" to make the empire strong and cohesive enough to ignore the balance of power in Europe had required war against German domination of the Continent'. What they now wanted was the freedom for the 'Southern British World . . . to go about its peaceful business without constant fear of German aggression'.[12] Germany would have to be relieved of her colonies and British naval predominance maintained: that apart, imperial self-sufficiency was the key to survival.

The rising power of the social-imperialist element in government in the latter part of the war was paralleled by an increased clamour from provincial businessmen, involved in engineering and other industries subject to severe pre-war German competition, who were strongly protectionist, empire-minded and often hostile to the City and to pre-war *laissez-faire*. They favoured a much enhanced role for the state after the war in order to repel German competition by tariffs and by creating new institutions to finance the export trade and to divert funds from overseas to home purposes. As one of their number expressed it, without protection Britain would soon be 'a national scrapheap'; he also voiced the usually unspoken resentments of many industrialists when he claimed that 'financiers' were 'a sort of nation apart, with the City of London for its metropolis, but possessing no territory and no sentiment'.[13]

Britain had already moved away from free trade in 1915, when the McKenna duties were placed on luxury goods for revenue purposes and to clear the shipping lanes for imported war supplies. By 1917 there was excited talk in 'imperial' circles about empire self-sufficiency in foodstuffs and about a strategy of planned emigration to the Dominions. At the Imperial Conference in 1917, an imperial emigration programme was proposed, and it was agreed that the Dominions

12. Paul Guinn, *British Strategy and Politics, 1914–18* (Oxford, 1965), pp. 193–4. For the strategic implications of the battle between the social imperialists and those – the Continentalists – who were more concerned with the need to defeat Germany, see Paul Kennedy, *The Realities Behind Diplomacy: Background Influences on British External Policy, 1865–1980* (1981), pp. 179–90.
13. Davenport-Hines, *Dudley Docker*, pp. 107–8 and Chs. 6 and 7.

should be allowed preferences on items that Britain felt needed protection.[14] A year later, the Balfour Committee on 'Commercial and Industrial Policy After the War' put its weight behind the Paris Agreements. Although it remained suspicious of a general tariff on efficiency grounds, the Committee advocated tariffs on a list of commodities assumed to be vital to national security and acknowledged the openings for imperial preference.[15] During the 1918 election campaign, Lloyd George's successful Coalitionists argued for imperial preference in principle. By this time, the dominant party within the Coalition, the Conservatives, were sure that imperial economic unity offered far greater benefits than the prospects of inter-Allied cooperation.[16]

Late in the war, therefore, a new economic policy was beginning to take shape based on close consultation between government, business and trade unions,[17] and offering industrial protection, closer union with the empire and far greater prospects of state intervention in the economy than would have been considered desirable before war broke out. But proposals that seemed to be moving to the centre of the political agenda in 1917–18 were no longer practical politics by 1921. By then, the economy had been almost entirely decontrolled; free trade was largely reaffirmed; restoring balanced budgets and the gold standard were again the chief aims of government; and the Treasury, the Bank of England and the City of London had reasserted their authority over economic policy. How did this come about?[18]

Four years of economic transformation were insufficient to eradicate the deep suspicion of government felt by many in business or to temper their eagerness to be rid of its influence as soon as the emergency was over.[19] What this reflected, in part, was a conflict between businessmen in older industries who were more inclined to accept traditional roles and ideologies, and those in the new industries who felt a need for drastic change. This split, together with that

14. Rothwell, *British War Aims*, p. 171; Ian M. Drummond, *Imperial Economic Policy, 1917–39: Studies in Expansion and Protection* (1974), pp. 25–6; see also idem, *British Economic Policy and the Empire, 1919–39* (1972), pp. 55–7, 143–50.

15. *Final Report of the Committee on Commercial and Industrial Policy After the War*, PP 1918 XIII (Cd 9035), Paras 317–52.

16. Bunselmeyer, *The Cost of the War*, pp. 47–51.

17. For this 'corporatist' strategy see Turner, 'The Politics of "Organized Business"', p. 2. There is detailed study in Keith Middlemass, *Politics in Industrial Society: The Experience of the British System Since 1911* (1974), Chs. 3–6.

18. The most comprehensive guide to the politics of the Coalition after the war is Kenneth O. Morgan, *Consensus or Disunity: The Lloyd George Coalition Government, 1918–22* (Oxford, 1979).

19. Newton and Porter, *Modernization Frustrated*, p. 39.

between the free traders, chiefly represented by cotton interests, and those on the receiving end of German competition, who favoured protection, seriously weakened the FBI, for example, and often made it impossible for it, or other industrial pressure groups, to speak with one voice, or even any voice at all, on matters of national import-ance.[20] Impatient with the apparent passivity of the FBI, some of the leading protectionist and imperially minded industrialists, such as Dudley Docker and Sir Alan Smith, tried to create organisations which could keep their ideas before the public; but they could not gather enough support on their own to be effective.[21] At the end of the war, British industry was still too small in scale, too fragmented and too bitterly competitive to allow any strategy to emerge which could match that offered by the City in terms of coherence and simplicity.[22] Even when industrialists did manage to offer a distinctive viewpoint, they found that the message failed to rise to the political heights because most channels of communication after 1918 were controlled by the traditional financial and commercial communities. Before the Cunliffe Committee in 1918, the FBI argued strongly that recreating the export economy should precede any attempt to reintro-duce the gold standard. The Committee ignored this completely in its report arguing, mainly from the first principles of conventional wisdom, that restoring the standard was a prerequisite of Britain's economic success and that industry concurred with this view.[23]

The entry of the United States into the war in 1917, followed by Germany's unexpectedly rapid collapse in the following year, also undermined the position of those who advocated a revolution in economic management. Germany's comprehensive defeat made an 'economic war after the war' unnecessary, undermined the 'seige economics' of the social imperialists and made liberal normality seem plausible again, reinforcing the opinion of those who viewed the

20. Davenport-Hines, *Dudley Docker*, pp. 117–19; Turner, 'The Politics of "Organ-ized Business"', pp. 38–45.

21. Davenport-Hines, *Dudley Docker*, Chs. 5–7; John Turner, 'The British Com-monwealth Union and the General Election of 1918', *Eng. Hist. Rev.*, XCIII (1978); Turner, 'The Politics of "Organized Business"', pp. 46–8; Terence Rodgers, 'Sir Alan Smith, the Industrial Group and the Politics of Unemployment, 1919–24', *Bus. Hist.*, XXXVIII (1986).

22. In *Modernization Frustrated*, Newton and Porter claim that one of the big weaknesses of the FBI was its failure to attract membership from consumer industries in the south of England (p. 56).

23. R.W.D. Boyce, 'Creating the Myth of Consensus: Public Opinion and Britain's Return to the Gold Standard in 1925', in P.L. Cottrell and D.E. Moggridge, eds. *Money and Power: Essays in Honour of L.S. Pressnell* (1988), p. 175; and idem, *British Capitalism at the Crossroads*, p. 31.

state's intrusion into economic life in wartime as being temporary and accidental.[24] Then in 1919 and 1920, many of those who had remained faithful to the idea that social and economic reconstruction was essential lost their credibility because the rapid inflation which accompanied the restocking boom gave the Treasury and the Bank their chance to reassert the need for discipline in government expenditure.[25] Inflation terrified the nation and drove it back to orthodoxy for, as Keynes wrote at the time, it meant that

> all permanent relations between debtors and creditors, which form the ultimate foundation of capitalism, become so utterly disordered as to be almost meaningless. Lenin was certainly right. There is no subtler, no surer means of overturning the existing bases of society than to debauch the currency.[26]

In this atmosphere, and with the Chancellor of the Exchequer in 1921 'prophesying ruin for the country if expenditure were not cut drastically',[27] those in power who were either imperialists or sympathetic to reconstruction schemes were panicked into assuming that the cure for the disease must be the traditional medicine administered by the usual gentlemanly doctors.[28]

Between 1918 and 1921 the policies proposed by radical industrialists and politicians were swept from the agenda. Immediately the war ended, despite formally accepting the message of the Cunliffe Committee, Lloyd George's coalition let the pound float down from its fixed wartime level of $4.76. Freed from the need to protect a fixed rate of exchange, the government could have gone whole-heartedly for a policy of social reform and imperial preference. Social reconstruction and an empire policy seemed to go naturally together for, as the Cabinet were informed early in 1919, 'if large sums of capital are locked up in slow maturing investments (e.g. housing) the trade of the country must be reduced and emigration on a large scale is necessary.'[29] In fact, as the incompatibility between these new policies and established financial rectitude became apparent, it was the dreams of imperial tariffs and state-led emigration schemes which were shattered first of all. Although the Conservative Party wavered briefly on the issue in 1923, the free-trade policy remained largely intact in

24. Cline, 'Winding Down the War Economy', pp. 171–7.
25. On the inflation and its effects see Susan Howson, 'The Origins of Dear Money, 1919–20', *Econ. Hist. Rev.*, 2nd ser. XXVII (1974); and on the boom, J. A. Dowie, '1919–20 is in Need of Attention', ibid. 2nd ser. XXVIII (1975).
26. *Collected Writings of J.M. Keynes*, IX (Cambridge, 1972), p. 57.
27. Burk, 'The Treasury', p. 101.
28. Newton and Porter, *Modernization Frustrated*, pp. 41–4.
29. Johnson, *Land Fit for Heroes*, pp. 364–76.

the 1920s: only a few commodities were protected, in 1921, for the purposes of national defence and a few minor concessions were made on imperial preference.

Plans for a massive resettlement of Britons on the white imperial frontier also failed to materialise. Discussion of state-supported emigration had first arisen in the context of a debate on resettling ex-servicemen after the war. In the enthusiastic atmosphere of 1918–19, Milner and Amery had translated this mundane issue into a grand strategy for peopling the empty spaces of empire and encouraging inter-imperial flows of both labour and capital. The main colonial enthusiasts were the Australians, then busy planning a significant extension of their agricultural frontier. The Treasury's reaction was cold: spending on emigration would drain British savings, reduce domestic investment, raise interest rates and make a return to gold more difficult. In the atmosphere of 1921–2 this might have been enough to torpedo the scheme completely had not rising unemployment meant that assisting emigrants might be no more expensive than paying out additional unemployment pay. So the Treasury agreed reluctantly to spend between £1.5m. and £3m. per year for the next fifteen years to place British migrants on colonial land, and the Empire Settlement Act of 1922 was born.[30] Plans for social reconstruction lingered longer but were soon washed away in the tide of fear produced by the inflation of early 1920.[31] The pound fell to $3.4 and industrial unrest, aggravated by falling real wages, sent the propertied interests scuttling behind the barricades provided by ancient financial verities.

Orthodoxy triumphed because the Bank of England's determination to control the money supply, the Treasury's interest in curbing government spending, and the City's urgent demand that the international service economy be restored as quickly as possible, offered a consistent and well-established set of priorities and policies with which to meet the frightening problems of 1919–21. They owed their weighty appeal not only to their simplicity and coherence, which the radical critics of orthodoxy simply could not emulate, but also to the fact that the City and the controlling financial institutions were the visible manifestations of a dominant gentlemanly capitalist culture which still had control over the 'commanding heights' of the economy and a prestige which producers – industrialists and trade unionists

30. Drummond, *Imperial Economic Policy, 1917–39*, Ch. 2. See also his *British Economic Policy and the Empire*, pp. 70ff.
31. The best account of the whole episode remains S.M.H. Armitage, *The Politics of the Decontrol of Industry: Britain and the United States* (1969), pp. 8–15.

alike – could not match. In the 1920s it was still possible for a City MP to claim 'that because of its national services, the City as a whole occupied a special position' in matters of political economy, and it was sincerely believed, as one historian has recently pointed out, that 'City parliamentarians were expected to preserve more independence from their political parties than most other M.P.s'.[32] The City still represented the nation: industry was seen as provincial and self-interested and this was inevitable as long as the latter remained fragmented and divided.

No complete 'return to 1913' was, of course, possible. The McKenna duties remained and several industries were given protection in 1921 because domestic production was thought to be vital in the event of another war. The Treasury, as we have seen, grudgingly supported a limited scheme of emigration to the empire; some measures of social reform in education, housing and social services survived the crisis of 1919–21. More important than this was the fact that industry and the trade unions were both more politically self-aware after 1919. Gentlemanly capitalists, in or out of government, now had to justify their policy preferences: the rules of the game had to be made explicit after the war and thus open to argument and contradiction. In pursuing financial discipline, too, it had to be accepted that budgets would balance only at much higher levels of expenditure in real terms than before the war, mainly because of the high level of the national debt and increased commitments to social services. If industrial peace after 1919 could be bought only at the price of a higher level of real wages than before 1914, a price also had to be paid for re-establishing financial peace: orthodoxy, at levels of taxation which did not provoke mutiny, was achievable only by ruthlessly cutting defence expenditure in the 1920s.

After the war, the problems of holding together a more fragile social and economic order pushed the British towards disarmament, towards appeasement of their former enemies and towards international economic liberalism, which offered the greater promise of peace.[33] This weakening of Britain's defence came at a time when her global dominance was also challenged by the United States, for whom the war proved to be an entry point into world power status. As we shall

32. Phillip Williamson, 'Financiers, the Gold Standard and British Politics, 1925–1931', in Turner, *Businessmen and Politics*, p. 110.

33. For some of the wider political and defence implications of changing economic structures see Paul Kennedy, 'Strategy versus Finance in Twentieth Century Britain', in idem, *Strategy and Diplomacy* (1983); and Wolf D. Gruner, 'The British Political, Social and Economic System and the Decision for Peace or War: Reflections on Anglo-German Relations, 1800–1939', *Brit. Jour. Internat. Stud.*, 6 (1980).

see, the rise of the United States proved more troublesome to Britain's gentlemanly capitalists than did the increased assertiveness of domestic industry.

THE IMPACT OF THE UNITED STATES

For the gentlemanly capitalist class, the mushroom growth of the United States' influence after 1914 presented a serious and abiding challenge. To defeat Germany, Britain had to enlist first the financial, and then the military, strength of the United States with the result that there was a permanent shift in the world balance of power. After 1914 Britain faced a fresh global challenge, a renewed threat of a 're-division of the world', though one more subtle and more difficult to resist than that offered by the Kaiser's empire. The years 1917–19 apart, the American impact was not overtly political because of her strong tradition of isolationism. The pressure came largely from the unparalleled economic dynamism of the republic spilling out dramatically into the world in the shape of trade and finance, and undermining the British position just as surely as Britain's own market power had once undermined the economic foundation of the international power of Portugal, The Netherlands, Spain and France. So, although there were tense moments of naval rivalry, the central battle was between economies, Treasuries, central banks and stock markets rather than between armies and navies. For British elites, the battle was also confused in that the Americans were difficult to identify clearly as an enemy. They appreciated the importance of the global struggle for informal economic influence set in train after 1914. But the strident anti-imperialist ideology suitable to an ex-colony, which they feared and resented, was often accompanied by the language of an economic internationalism which the gentlemanly capitalist class could instinctively appreciate as the foundation of their own power and influence. Similarly, their hostility to the brashness and assertiveness of the United States was muted by a strong feeling that the republic was, after all, part of 'Anglo-Saxondom', a genuinely liberal state, one more like a Dominion than a foreign country.[34]

34. The best recent overview of the relationship is D. Cameron Watt, *Succeeding John Bull: America in Britain's Place, 1900–1975* (Cambridge, 1984). Also helpful are David Reynolds, *The Creation of the Anglo-American Alliance, 1937–41: A Study in Competitive Co-operation* (1981), Ch. 1, which has many interesting general insights. A useful review article in this context is A.J. Thompson, 'From the Monroe Doctrine to the Marshall Plan', *Hist. Jour.*, 22 (1979).

Wartime dependence on the United States stemmed from her crucial position as a supplier of vital war materials and from Britain's role as financier of her own, and the Allies', international needs.[35] Many British investments in the United States were liquidated and gold reserves run down in order to pay for supplies; but, as early as 1915, the British had a dollar problem which required extensive borrowing on Wall Street, using Morgans as their principal agent.[36] In 1916 the American authorities, unused to foreign lending, became sufficiently alarmed at the extent of the borrowing to discourage investors. Had Britain been unable to continue borrowing then her plight, and the Allied cause, would have been desperate: it is difficult to see how Germany could have been defeated without a liberal supply of American aid.[37] The situation might have been eased had Britain let the exchange rate fall from its fixed wartime level of $4.76. For the Treasury, however, this not only threatened inflation but also meant a loss of prestige 'equivalent to the loss of a major battle'.[38] The Allied cause was saved in 1917 by the United States' entry into the war, which opened the way to public, as well as to a renewal of private, loans. By the end of the war, the time-honoured financial relationship between Britain and the United States had been turned upside down, and the British had borrowed a total of $3.7bn.[39] Britain was now a 'permanent debtor' thus 'making it impossible for London alone to continue as the principal effective financial centre of the world'.[40]

It may not be too cynical to suggest that one motive for American intervention on the Allied side was to safeguard her loans and her burgeoning export markets, which would have been imperilled by an Allied defeat or by a stalemate peace among increasingly protectionist powers:[41] the United States raised her share of world exports from 13.5

---

35. Kathleen Burk, *Britain, America and the Sinews of War, 1914–1918* (1985); idem, 'The Diplomacy of Finance: British Financial Missions to the United States, 1914–1918', *Hist. Jour.*, 22 (1979).

36. Kathleen Burk, 'A Merchant Bank at War: the House of Morgan 1914–18', in Cottrell and Moggridge, *Money and Power*.

37. Keynes recognised in 1917 that without America's support 'the whole financial fabric of the Alliance will collapse'. See Kathleen Burk, 'J.M. Keynes and the Exchange Rate Crisis of 1917', *Econ. Hist. Rev.*, 2nd ser. XXXII (1979), p. 411. See also J.M. Cooper, 'The Command of Gold Reversed: American Loans to Britain, 1915–17', *Pacific Historical Review*, 45 (1976), p. 230.

38. Burk, 'A Merchant Bank at War', p. 164.

39. Gerd Hardach, *The First World War, 1914–18* (1977), Table 18, p. 148.

40. Max Beloff, *Imperial Sunset: Britain's Liberal Empire, 1897–1921* (1969), p. 178.

41. Roberta A. Dayer, 'Strange Bedfellows: J.P. Morgan and Co., Whitehall and the Wilson Administration during World War I', *Bus. Hist.*, XVIII (1978), pp. 130, 142–3.

per cent in 1913 to over 25 per cent by 1920.[42] The administration, and many export-minded business and financial circles in the United States, were certainly alarmed by the implications of the Paris Agreements, and entry into the conflict gave them the opportunity to put their weight behind a liberal solution to the world's problems. The fear that the United States' expanding economic interests would be curbed by rampant militarism and imperialism lay behind Wilson's demand for a liberal peace which would bring a democratised Germany back into the world economy quickly and, by preserving freedom of trade, would encourage the flow of American capital into Europe and elsewhere.[43] With British policy still under the influence of social imperialist sentiment, Anglo–American relations were often imbued with a deep economic antagonism even while the common fight against Germany continued; at one point, late in 1918, the British went so far as to slow down the shipment of American troops to the battlefield in order to release British shipping to counter American trade competition. Fear of American competition also influenced Britain's decision to seize the German merchant fleet after the war was over.[44]

Fortunately for the Allies, the war ended quickly enough to prevent the United States from attaining the overwhelming authority which ever-increasing Allied indebtedness would have given her. Germany's decisive defeat marked the end of the Paris Agreements but, as they faded from view, they were replaced by bitter and unreasoning demands that Germany should pay huge, if not precisely specified, reparations to cover Allied war costs.[45] After the German defeat, the 1918 general election in Britain was dominated by ideas of economic revenge:[46] it has been claimed that, at the Versailles Peace Conference, the British were, if anything, more intransigent than the French on this issue,[47] as Lloyd George dreamed of financing social reform by taxing

---

42. Edward B. Parsons, 'Why the British Reduced the Flow of American Troops to Europe in August–October 1918', *Canadian Historical Review*, III (1977), p. 178.

43. Carl P. Parrini, *Heir to Empire: United States Economic Diplomacy, 1916–23* (Pittsburgh, Pa, 1969), esp. Ch. I; Michael J. Hogan, *Informal Entente: The Private Structure of Co-operation in Anglo-American Economic Diplomacy, 1918–1928* (Columbia, Miss., 1977), Ch. I.

44. Parsons, 'Why the British Reduced the Flow', passim.

45. For the evolution of thinking on reparations in Britain see Bunselmeyer, *The Cost of the War*, pp. 55–105.

46. Ibid. pp. 106–84; Seth P. Tillman, *Anglo-American Relations of the Paris Peace Conference of 1919* (Princeton, NJ, 1961), pp. 230–56. See also M.L. Dockrill and J.D. Goold, *Peace without Promise: Britain and the Peace Conferences, 1919–23* (1981), pp. 45–56.

47. Marc Trachtenberg, 'Reparations at the Paris Peace Conference', *Jour. Mod. Hist.*, 51 (1979).

the Germans 'till the pips squeak'.[48] The United States opposed reparations as being unworkable and as a sure recipe for continued antagonism between the Allies and Germany. But Wilson's ideas were ignored and the United States was also defeated on the colonial issue as Britain, encouraged by her Dominions, demanded a large share of the German empire as it was dismembered.[49] Nor could the Americans prevent the Allies from agreeing to discriminate against Germany in trade for five years after the war.[50]

British and American aspirations were still far apart in 1918. In Britain, reconstruction and empire unity remained part of the political agenda and the fear of American competition went with a fear of social disorder which a return to liberalism might bring. For the United States the chief economic worry at the end of the war was the possibility of a slump; this increased their determination to press for a liberal solution to European problems. Export markets had to be maintained and, since the domestic American market was protected by tariffs which no administration had the power to reduce, it was clear that American capital export would become a vital part of her expansion abroad. In an essentially free-market society the capital would have to be privately funded; these private funds would not flow into Europe until American investors were satisfied that peace there was well established and the liberal order permanently restored. Only then would the American economic invasion get under way and the English 'monopoly' of financial services be broken.[51]

From 1919 onwards, as we have seen, the 'industrial elite' who had strongly influenced the Coalition government in Britain and was responsible for its 'burst of economic nationalism' was in decline.[52] By 1921 the gentlemanly capitalists were in charge again, and their implicit internationalist assumptions once more guided British economic policy. This inevitably brought the United States and Britain closer together. Once convinced of the paramount need to restore a cosmo-

48. On the link between reconstruction policy and reparations see Bunselmeyer, *The Cost of the War*, pp. 137–40.
49. On the German colonial issue see W. Roger Louis, *Great Britain and Germany's Lost Colonies* (Oxford, 1967), pp. 2–9, 108–35. As Louis observes, despite Wilson, German and Turkish colonies were divided in a manner that was similar to the scramble of the late nineteenth century (p. 155). See also Tillman, *Anglo-American Relations*, pp. 85–100; Dockrill and Goold, *Peace without Promise*, pp. 64–8; and below, pp. 211–13.
50. Tillman, *Anglo-American Relations*.
51. Parrini, *Heir to Empire*, Chs. 4 and 5. See also Frank Costigliola, *Awkward Dominion: American Political, Economic and Cultural Relations with Europe, 1919–1933* (Ithaca, NY, 1985), pp. 33–6, 38.
52. Cameron Watt, *Succeeding John Bull*, pp. 47–8.

politan world order rather than to retreat into their empire, the British gave up their futile attempt to stamp out Bolshevism in Russia, an attempt encouraged by imperialists fearful for Indian security, and began to think about how to tempt Lenin back into the liberal fold under British auspices.[53] On reparations, they were now of Keynes's opinion that huge exactions would hold back German recovery and damage the world economy. Their position thus shifted towards the United States and away from France.[54]

The reassertion of control by the gentlemen in Britain by no means eliminated all sources of conflict with the United States. One potent source of difficulty was the issue of war debts. Britain's position was that if her debts to the United States were scaled down she could be equally generous to her allied debtors and the pressure to collect reparations would be reduced.[55] No American administration would admit any connection between war debt and reparations and all insisted on full repayment. The British fear was that, if they had to pay, 'the effect of such payment would be to enable the American government to reduce taxation and so place the American manufacturer in a favourable position as regards British competition'.[56] In insisting on British payment, the Americans certainly appreciated this; they could not see why the British, whose imperial wealth they regarded as being unlimited, could not respond by liquidating other foreign investments or cutting down the flow of new loans, incidentally giving New York a further edge over London in the financial war. Finally, at the Washington Conference in 1922, the British repudiated their naval alliance with Japan and agreed to parity with the United States in capital ships, partly to reduce defence expenditure but partly also to influence favourably the American position on war debt. But in 1923,

53. On this fascinating sea-change see Stephen White, *Britain and the Bolshevik Revolution: A Study in the Politics of Diplomacy, 1920–1924* (1979), pp. 3–26; M.V. Glenny, 'The Anglo-Soviet Trade Agreement, March 1921', *Jour. Contemp. Hist.*, 2 (1970). When faced with the demand to carry on the fight against Bolshevism, Lloyd George argued that this would precipitate economic collapse in Britain and bring 'bankruptcy and Bolshevism in these islands'. C.J. Lowe and M.J. Dockrill, The *Mirage of Power: British Foreign Policy, 1902–1922* (1973), II, p. 324.

54. Dockrill and Goold, *Peace without Promise*, pp. 75–6, 85–6. Lowe and Dockrill claim that Britain adopted a conciliatory attitude towards Germany and Russia after 1920 because she saw them as being important to the world economy, while Turkey, a far less weighty economic entity, continued to be treated harshly. *The Mirage of Power*, II, p. 374.

55. Roberta Allbert Dayer, *Finance and Empire: Sir Charles Addis, 1861–1945* (1988), pp. 114–15.

56. A British Cabinet minute quoted in Roberta A. Dayer, 'The British War Debts to the United States and the Anglo-Japanese Alliance, 1920–3', *Pacific Historical Review*, 45 (1976), p. 584.

Britain had to accept full repayment, at a fairly high rate of interest, and a scaling down of her own demands on her former allies and Germany.[57]

THE RETURN TO GOLD

Insistence on war debt repayment was one way of asserting New York's financial primacy;[58] a common belief in the need for a liberal world order stimulated rather than damped down the conflict between the two leading money markets. Britain's determination to restore the gold standard was a vital part of London's post-war rehabilitation. The United States supported the policy of restoration because it was seen as an essential step in recreating a fully functioning international system. But returning to the gold standard was acutely difficult. While the United States had huge stocks of gold, Britain's own holdings were small and the fear of the authorities was that, in order to achieve a balance of payments strong enough to give a restored gold standard credibility, such continuous and massive deflationary pressures would have to be applied that economic growth would be curtailed and the social order imperilled. This is why, at the Genoa Conference in 1922, the British authorities proposed that, in the wake of the war and post-war inflation, European currencies should be restabilised using either dollars or sterling as reserves rather than gold, as had been the case before 1914.[59]

Had this plan been universally accepted, Britain's problem as a

---

57. Apart from Dayer, the war debt issue is also treated in Hogan, *Informal Entente*, pp. 50–6 and Costigliola, *Awkward Dominion*, pp. 38–9, 81–6. Costigliola emphasises the fact that the British had to pay up in the end if they were to remain a great international financial centre (p. 106). For some strategic implications of the Washington Agreements see R.B. Holland, *Britain and the Commonwealth Alliance, 1918–39* (1981), pp. 11–15.

58. An excellent overview of the decade is given in Frank Costigliola, 'Anglo-American Financial Rivalry in the 1920s', *Jour. Econ. Hist.*, 37 (1977).

59. The Genoa Conference is now beginning to receive the attention it deserves from those interested in post-war British economic foreign policy. This account is based largely upon Parrini, *Heir to Empire*, Ch. 6; Hogan, *Informal Entente*, pp. 45–7; Stephen V.O. Clarke, 'The Reconstruction of the International Financial System: the Attempts of 1922 and 1933' (Princeton Studies in International Finance, No. 33, 1978); Costigliola, *Awkward Dominion*, pp. 107–8; Costigliola, 'Anglo-American Financial Rivalry', pp. 913–20. See also the recent study by Anne Orde, *British Policy and European Reconstruction after the First World War* (Cambridge, 1990), Chs. 5 and 6; and Carole Fink, *The Genoa Conference: European Diplomacy, 1921–1922*, (Chapel Hill, NC, 1984).

financial centre in the 1920s would have been eased considerably and it would have been much easier to manage the gold standard after 1925. The system would have economised on gold and concentrated much of it in London. Increased gold reserves would have allowed for easier money and lower interest rates in Britain and given a stimulus to economic growth. The 'gold exchange standard', as it was known, would also have led, interestingly enough, to a considerable extension of the use of sterling in Europe, where Britain's financial writ had not run before 1914. In pre-war days the franc and, to a lesser extent, the mark had been the dominant currencies of Europe. The power of both had been destroyed by the war and the British, building on their position as wartime Allied paymaster, were keen to compensate themselves in Europe for the loss of financial position they had suffered in, for example, parts of Latin America at the hands of the United States. Not surprisingly, the gold exchange standard was bitterly opposed by the French, but it also fell foul of the United States, who viewed it with deep suspicion as being likely to produce inflation and were wary of supporting any proposal which looked likely to promote the power of the pound. It seems ironic in retrospect that the gentlemanly capitalists who preached deflation to the British voter and supported the gold standard with almost religious fervour were actually hoping to establish a different gold standard from that which existed in 1914, and one which could legitimately be attacked as being unorthodox and dangerous.

The universal acceptance of a gold exchange standard would have solved another puzzle for the British: how to attract American capital to Europe without surrendering their position at the centre of the world economy. To create a prosperous, liberal world economy and restore London's glory, a sustained recovery was necessary in Europe. This was impossible without United States' capital, but if that capital came would Britain and Europe become a part of an American economic empire? Britain's answer to this conundrum was given in the context of the Genoa discussions on the future of the Soviet Union.[60] The British proposed to create a financial consortium, led by themselves, to invest massively in the Soviet Union. Bolshevism would be killed off by kindness, the Soviet Union would be reintegrated into the world economy, benefiting in particular the Germans, whose trade links with Tsarist Russia had been so important to her prosperity. In return for this capital, and for *de facto* recognition of their regime, the

---

60. As well as the sources referred to in n. 59, see White, *Britain and the Bolshevik Revolution*, Ch. 3.

Bolsheviks were to acknowledge, rather than repay, their debts and allow foreign entrepreneurs to operate freely in the Soviet Union. The proposals failed. Lenin would not accept loans at the price of subverting communism and the Soviet Union's creditors, especially the French, demanded repayment of old loans. The plan also failed because the United States' government believed, rightly, that the British were aiming at a settlement which would induce American private capital to flow to Europe through London channels (since shares in the proposed Consortium were to be issued in sterling), allowing Britain to extend her financial empire within Europe and turn the Soviet Union into a financial colony,[61] without having to raise much capital from her own diminished post-war stores. The objections of the United States alone would have been sufficient to kill off this scheme for, without her tacit approval, no private capital would flow into Europe, and the British themselves were in no position to provide it.

Genoa was only the beginning of Britain's pursuit of a new empire for sterling in Europe. Under the leadership of Montagu Norman, its long-serving and highly influential Governor, the Bank of England organised a syndicate to buy up the ailing Anglo-Austrian bank and to establish a separate Anglo-Czech bank on similar lines. The creation of the latter was soon followed by a £10m. reconstruction loan orchestrated by Barings with encouragement from the Bank of England. Then, using his influence over the Financial Committee of the League of Nations, Norman took the lead in persuading London financiers to acquire the largest share in loans designed to bring financial stability to two of the war's greatest casualties, Austria and Hungary, in 1923–4.[62] In this endeavour, the Bank drew some support from American banking circles, including the Federal Reserve.

Norman was also keen to encourage the establishment of central banks throughout Europe. Like their prototype, the Bank of England, they would be free of political control and would manage the new financial order on the basis of informal cooperation:[63] the central banks proposed for both Austria and Hungary were strictly enjoined to be independent of government and their statutes disallowed financial

---

61. Lowe and Dockrill, *The Mirage of Power*, II, p. 332.

62. R.S. Sayers, *The Bank of England, 1891–1944*, I (Cambridge 1976), pp. 163, 166–73; Hogan, *Informal Entente*, pp. 60–6; Orde, *British Policy and Reconstruction*, pp. 135–44, 266–74. See also Atkin, *British Overseas Investment*, pp. 93–7, and Kathleen Burk, *Morgan Grenfell, 1838–1988: The Biography of a Merchant Bank* (Cambridge, 1989), pp. 139–4. For a broad view of policy see W. Adam Brown, *The International Gold Standard Reinterpreted, 1914–1934*, I (New York, 1940), pp. 346–50.

63. Dayer, *Sir Charles Addis*, pp. 152–3; Clarke, 'The Reconstruction of the International Financial System', pp. 13–14.

entanglement with the state.[64] No doubt with their own history at the front of their minds, leading English bankers were convinced that 'if politicians would leave the financiers alone, they could solve the world's economic problems'; they would do so by relying 'on personal relationships rather than official structures, academic theory or statistics'.[65] Unfortunately, finance and politics could no longer be so easily separated. Outside some financial circles in the United States,[66] the impression remained strong that the British were using their power with the League to create a new Europe financed by New York but controlled in London.[67]

While spreading to Europe the gospel of sound money based on sterling reserves, the Bank of England was also encouraging the Dominions to think along the same lines. When the Imperial Conference of 1923 took place sterling was, of course, still floating and Dominion currencies, such as those of Australia and New Zealand, had actually begun to diverge in value from the British pound for the first time. At the Conference, the British urged the Dominions to accumulate sterling assets as London funds and assumed rather than argued that the latter would want to retain parity between their currencies and London. Ideally, it was claimed, the best way to do this would be to create central banks free of government control – South Africa had led the way in 1920[68] – which would cooperate with the monetary authorities in London in minimising fluctuations in exchange rates.[69] With Genoa in mind, the Bank of England was eager to train the colonial 'savages' in the niceties of financial management,[70] and was intent on setting up the same machinery to manage money in the Dominions as it was attempting to establish in Central Europe.

In 1923 there were twenty central banks holding sterling reserves

64. Sayers, *Bank of England*, I, pp. 160, 168.
65. Dayer, *Sir Charles Addis*, pp. 173–4. On the Bank's role, see also Alicia Teichova, 'Versailles and the Expansion of the Bank of England into Central Europe', in N. Horn and J. Kocka, eds. *Recht und Entwicklung in Grossunternehmen im 19.und frühen 20. Jahrhundert* (Göttingen, 1979).
66. Norman was encouraged in his ideas of informal cooperation between central banks through his friendly relationship with Benjamin Strong, Governor of the Federal Reserve Bank. But the 'Fed.' did not have the authority in the United States possessed by the Bank of England in Britain. See Sayers, *The Bank of England*, I, pp. 154–62, and Dayer, *Sir Charles Addis*, p. 140.
67. Costigliola, *Awkward Dominion*, pp. 113–4.
68. Sayers, *Bank of England*, I, pp. 302–3.
69. Lyndhurst Falkiner Giblin, *The Growth of a Central Bank: The Development of the Commonwealth Bank of Australia, 1924–45* (Melbourne, 1951), pp. 17–18.
70. The word was used by Otto Niemeyer, then of the Treasury, later of the Bank of England. Dayer, *Sir Charles Addis*, p. 165.

compared with only four in 1914.[71] But none of these countries was an important economic power, save for Germany, whose financial future was still to be decided, and France, which was ready to remove the indignity of dependence on sterling as soon as the franc could be restabilised. The test case for the Bank of England's ability to make Europe dependent upon London finance was the restabilisation of the German mark in 1924. The French invasion of the Ruhr in 1923 – intended to exact reparations from Germany – not only gave an upward twist to spiralling German inflation but also simultaneously led to a collapse in the value of the franc. With French power reduced, Britain and the United States were able in 1924 to impose the Dawes Plan, which cut Germany's reparations bill and fixed payments over a long period of time.[72] But Germany could not be brought back to the centre of European affairs without the restabilisation of the mark. To accomplish this, the British revived their Genoa proposals and pressed Germany to hold sterling and dollars as reserve assets. Much German capital had fled to London during the great inflation; if Germany had adopted a sterling reserve system this would have made London the financial heart of Europe. Reconstructing the German central bank, the Reichsbank, was a crucial element in the policy of stabilisation, and the Bank of England hoped for an institution independent of government with which it could cooperate informally in managing an international economy free of the corrupting influence of politicians.[73] Nonetheless, it was the United States which subscribed the major part of the stabilisation loan and which also insisted on Germany holding at least three-quarters of her reserves in gold.[74] Washington feared that if Germany was pulled into a Sterling Area then Britain would have neither the incentive nor the desire to return to gold at all.[75] In this they were probably wrong, but the manner of the German stabilisation effectively ended Britain's bid to colonise the continent financially in compensation for her losses elsewhere, and it also meant that the gentlemanly capitalists could not avoid the implications of a return to a full gold standard.

The Dawes Plan and financial reconstruction offered the stability

71. Sayers, *Bank of England*, I, pp. 202–3.

72. Stephen A. Shuker, *The End of French Predominance in Europe: The Financial Crisis of 1924 and the Adoption of the Dawes Plan* (Chapel Hill, NC, 1976), pp. 383–93; Alan Cassells, 'Repairing the *Entente Cordiale* and the New Diplomacy', *Hist. Jour.*, 23 (1980).

73. See Sayers, *Bank of England*, I, pp. 181–3, and Burk, *Morgan Grenfell*, pp. 141–3.

74. For good accounts of this episode see Hogan, *Informal Entente*, pp. 66–71; S.V.O. Clarke, *Central Bank Co-operation, 1924–31* (New York, 1967), pp. 58–67.

75. Costigliola, *Awkward Dominion*, p. 128.

that the private investor craved, promised rapid development in Germany and general European growth, and loosed a flood of American capital on Europe. If London were to play a central part in this process, a quick return to the gold standard was imperative.[76] German stabilisation on gold made a similar British move unavoidable because Britain could not hope to retain world financial leadership with a floating currency when her close rivals were adopting stable exchange rates.[77] It is apparent also that the Dominions, especially South Africa, were becoming restless with a floating currency by 1924, and there were vague threats about stabilising on the dollar. Whether the Dominions, as primary exporters, would have received any benefit from transferring their allegiance from free-market Britain to the heavily protectionist United States is doubtful. However, the restlessness of the white empire seems to have influenced Churchill, as Chancellor of the Exchequer, and helped to convince him that the time for a return to $4.86 had come.[78]

Churchill still had his doubts; he would have preferred to leave sterling at its 1924 level of roughly $4.40 because this was better for exports and, he hoped, for employment. He was worried 'at the spectacle of Britain possessing the finest credit in the world simultaneously with a million and a quarter unemployed', and would have liked to 'see Finance less proud and Industry more content'.[79] The response from the Bank of England and the Treasury gave clear expression to hitherto unspoken gentlemanly assumptions on the nature of economy and policy. London had to remain the financial capital of the world because, as a Treasury official put it in 1924,

> mercantile business tends to be transacted at the centres from which it is financed. The greatest factor in the material prosperity of this country is not

76. Boyce, *British Capitalism at the Crossroads*, pp. 57–60, emphasises this. Clarke argues that 'it is clear that Germany's imminent stabilization had put Norman under great pressure to commit himself to an early return', Clarke, *Central Bank Co-operation*, p. 66.

77. R.G. Hawtrey, then an economist at the Treasury, warned his colleagues in 1924 that 'the transition to a general gold standard may be a very short one, and London may be left isolated with a paper currency in a gold-using world. Should this occur, the danger to the position of London would be aggravated'. Quoted in Adrian Ham, *Treasury Rules: Recurrent Themes in British Economic Policy* (1981), p. 46.

78. Sources for this rather curious episode include L.S. Pressnell, '1925: the Burden of Sterling', *Econ. Hist. Rev.*, 2nd ser. XXXI (1978), pp. 71–3; Costigliola, 'Anglo-American Financial Rivalry', pp. 920–3; Costigliola, *Awkward Dominion*, pp. 128, 130–1; Dayer, *Sir Charles Addis*, pp. 170–1. See also Bruce Dalgaard, *South Africa's Impact on Britain's Return to Gold, 1925* (New York, 1981).

79. Quoted in D.E. Moggridge, *British Monetary Policy, 1924–31: The Norman Conquest of $4.86* (Cambridge, 1972), p. 76; also quoted in Costigliola, 'Anglo-American Financial Rivalry', p. 925.

manufacturing, important as that is, but *commerce*. The diversion of commerce to other centres is the severest loss to which we could be exposed.[80]

This was the voice, not of crude and conspiratorial 'City interests', but of a whole, hugely successful, service economy dominated by gentlemen, in which the City of London, for whom industrialism and provincialism were synonymous, played the crucial coordinating role. Already condemned as marginal, manufacturers struggled – vainly – to be noticed. While some industrialists did offer support for the gold standard as the bringer of stability, there were deep worries in the provinces about deflation and high interest rates,[81] but both Churchill *and* the officials who advised him were effectively insulated from this branch of opinion.[82]

For officialdom, a return to $4.86 was a necessary means of disciplining all those, capitalists and workers alike, who apparently wished to use state economic power for their own, obviously selfish, ends. The gold standard was as important to the nation as 'A Police Force or Tax Collector': in returning to it, the views of 'the merchant, the manufacturer workmen etc should be considered (but not consulted any more than about the design of battleships)'.[83] The gentlemen who controlled policy never hesitated in their belief, nurtured by the successes of the pre-war era, that they alone understood what the true economic interests of the nation were: behind their confidence in their

---

80. Quoted in Boyce, *British Capitalism at the Crossroads*, pp. 65–6. These sentiments chimed in with deep worries about the level of invisible income (ibid. p. 67).

81. Ibid. pp. 79–90, and idem, 'Creating the Myth of Consensus', pp. 178–9, 181–7, 189–91. Also R.E. Catterall, 'Attitudes to, and the Impact of, British Monetary Policy in the 1920s', *Revue internationale d'histoire de la banque*, 12 (1976); and Geoffrey Ingham, *Capitalism Divided? The City and Industry in British Social Development* (Cambridge, 1984), pp. 175–87. For an earlier view see L.J. Hume, 'The Gold Standard and Deflation: Issues and Attitudes in the Nineteen Twenties', *Economica*, new ser. XXX (1963), reprinted in Sidney Pollard, ed. *The Gold Standard and Employment Policies Between the Wars* (1970). See also R.S. Sayers, 'The Return to Gold, 1925', in L.S. Pressnell, ed. *Studies in the Industrial Revolution* (1960), and W. Adams Brown, *England and the New Gold Standard, 1919–26* (1929), Ch. 10. Both are reprinted in Pollard, *Gold Standard*.

82. 'The Chancellor finally decided in favour of a return to gold – partly as he himself said, because he knew that if he adopted this course Niemeyer [at the Treasury] would give him irrefutable arguments to support it, whereas if he refused to adopt it he would be faced with criticism from the City authorities against which he would not have any effective answer'. Frederick Leith Ross, *Money Talks* (1968), p. 92, quoted in Ham, *Treasury Rules*, p. 54. Leith Ross became Deputy Controller of Finance at the Treasury in 1925.

83. Norman, quoted in Moggridge, *British Monetary Policy*, pp. 270–1. See also the discussion of policy in ibid. pp. 64–70, and Hogan, *Informal Entente*, pp. 71–5.

own authority lay generations of gentlemanly financial success.[84] And, if they could not have the gold exchange standard of Genoa, then the rigours of the full gold standard had to be faced. Industry might be hurt immediately by revaluation and the high interest rates needed to attract investors into sterling, but the benefits of stability and of London's prosperity would also, it was assumed, eventually rub off on them. Meanwhile, the imperative matter was London's ability to meet the challenge of New York and to recapture the invisible income lost during the war. By restoring the pre-1914 exchange rate regime, Britain was honouring her obligations in full, proving that a gentleman's word was his bond,[85] and, it was hoped, restablishing that confidence in London which was such a vital element in restoring its fortunes.

Confidence was indeed the key issue. Arguments by Keynes, for example, that Britain should have stabilised at a rate about 10 per cent below the old rate could be countered with the claim that this might have triggered off competing devaluations in Europe and undermined the stability which was the prime aim of policy.[86] Given industry's fragmentation and inability to come forward with a clear alternative strategy, and the general lack of interest in 'managed money', it is difficult, in retrospect, to see what other policy could in practice have been adopted in 1925, especially when one considers that a more flexible gold standard system – such as that proposed at Genoa – had been ruled out by international hostility. The gentlemanly capitalists who ran British economic policy were certainly arrogant in assuming that they knew what was good for industry, but industry was too divided to speak for itself with authority; it had no effective counter to the argument that a return to internationalism on the old terms was the most practical way of restoring Britain's economic fortunes.

Unfortunately, trying to maintain the gold standard after 1925 proved to be a constant, unrewarding struggle. At first, the British monetary authorities still had high hopes of establishing a viable gold

84. For an interpretation of the return to gold as a restoration of authority by the Bank and the Treasury, see Jim Tomlinson, *Problems of British Economic Policy, 1870–1914* (1981), Ch. 6.

85. The City saw the return as 'a vindication of British financial integrity, and an assurance that British financial prestige and power would regain much that it had lost'. Brown, 'England and the New Gold Standard', in Pollard, *The Gold Standard*, p. 61.

86. Moggridge, *British Monetary Policy*, thinks that a 10 per cent devaluation would have been reasonable (pp. 233, 245–50). For sympathetic modern discussions of the policy adopted in 1925, see A.J. Youngson, *The British Economy, 1920–1966* (1967), pp. 23–35 and 171ff; and B. Williams, 'Montagu Norman and Banking Policy in the Nineteen Twenties', *Yorkshire Bulletin of Economic and Social Research*, 11 (1959–60).

exchange standard which would help to take the pressure off the pound.[87] The Belgian stabilisation of 1926 was successfully handled by London with Federal Reserve support.[88] But the attempts to steer countries such as Romania and Poland towards sterling fell foul of an increasingly assertive France, whose central bankers were not afraid to accuse the British of 'financial imperialism', a charge which seemed to leave the British genuinely hurt and rather baffled.[89] The French were supported in this by an increasingly suspicious United States, and Britain's endeavours came to very little.[90]

The restabilisation of the French franc at an undervalued rate in 1928 increased the pressure on London by making Paris as well as New York an attractive home for international funds. Bank Rate remained high in Britain, growth was below the world average and exports were sluggish. Discontent with the gold standard increased steadily in business circles though, again, it had few effective outlets and was muted by fear of labour unrest in the wake of the General Strike.[91] The pressure for government action to reduce unemployment was also mounting, as the Keynesian-inspired Liberal plan of 1929 and Mosley's imaginative initiative of 1930 for increasing public expenditure both show.[92] Neither proposal made much impact on policy. The official line, known as the 'Treasury View', was that public works merely diverted expenditure from private to public channels;[93] as budget deficits began to appear in the world depression after 1929, the financial authorities pressed for deflation and budget balancing. The aim was to impress upon foreigners the fact that $4.86 was safe in London's hands and to steer government away from the temptation to spend its way

---

87. Dayer, *Sir Charles Addis*, pp. 179, 181–2; Costigliola, *Awkward Dominion*, pp. 200–5.

88. Sayers, *Bank of England*, I, pp. 191–2.

89. Note the pained tone of Henry Clay, one of the Bank of England's advisers: 'For some years past it had been more than current comment in Europe, both in political and banking circles, that Governor Norman desired to establish some sort of dictatorship over the central banks of Europe and that I was collaborating with him'. Sir Henry Clay, *Lord Norman* (1957), p. 265.

90. Richard Hemmig Meyer, *Banker's Diplomacy: Monetary Stabilization in the Nineteen Twenties* (1970); J.L. Kooker, 'French Financial Diplomacy: the Inter-War Years', in Benjamin M. Rowland, ed. *Balance of Power or Hegemony* (New York, 1976); Sayers, *Bank of England*, I, pp. 191–5; Boyce, *British Capitalism at the Crossroads*, pp. 141–9, 158–66.

91. Boyce, *British Capitalism at the Crossroads*, pp. 90–5.

92. The classic text here is Robert Skidelsky, *Politicians and the Slump: The Labour Government of 1929–31* (1967). See also Alan Booth and Melvyn Pack, *Employment, Capital and Economic Policy: Britain, 1918–1939* (1985).

93. Donald Winch, *Economics and Policy* (1970), pp. 112–15, 118–22; Skidelsky, *Politicians and the Slump*, pp. 451–6; G.C. Peden, *Keynes, the Treasury and British Economic Policy* (1988), pp. 11, 27–9.

out of the crisis. In this the Treasury was supported by the Bank of England and by a wide spectrum of opinion. Beleaguered businessmen, conscious of falling profits, linked deficit financing with punitive taxation and inflation. Labour voters, on the other hand, were either terrified of inflation or criticised welfare spending and other government handouts as being an encouragement to 'spongers'.[94] If, as De Cecco claims, Keynes's historic achievement was to purge the English polity of its rentier assumptions on economic policy, his task had only just begun in 1930.[95]

THE FINANCIAL CRISIS, 1929–31

The major beneficiary of the 1925–9 boom, which accompanied Britain's return to gold, was the United States. Stabilisation under the gold standard offered American capital and trade the chance to begin an economic invasion of Europe.[96] Brief and unstable though it was, this stream of American goods, capital and institutions across the Atlantic was, in a sense, a trial run for the much greater and more permanent extension of the economic power of the United States in Europe after 1945. The transatlantic flow soon aroused fear and hostility:[97] a sense of the imminent Americanisation of the world, mingled with resentments about war debt repayments and American tariffs, lay behind the bitter Anglo-American naval disputes of 1927–8, for example.[98] The pressure of a high exchange rate and severe American competition also helped to stimulate demand for protectionism in Britain. Similar pressures were being felt across the continent. One reaction to the rise of the United States was the awakening of an interest in European economic union, and this was being actively canvassed by 1930. When the screw of American protectionism was given a further twist in 1929–30, a debate was sparked off across Europe on the iniquities of the huge American balance of payments surplus, its resolution via foreign investment and the resulting 'com-

94. Skidelsky, *Politicians and the Slump*, esp. pp. 406–9.

95. M. De Cecco, 'The Last of the Romans', in Robert Skidelsky, ed. *The End of the Keynesian Era* (1977), pp. 18–24.

96. M.D. Goldberg, 'Anglo-American Economic Competition, 1920–1930', *Economy and History*, 16 (1973) provides a useful background.

97. Boyce, *British Capitalism at the Crossroads*, pp. 106–18, 176–84; Holland, *Britain and the Commonwealth Alliance*, p. 37.

98. Cameron Watt, *Succeeding John Bull*, pp. 56–7; B.J.C. McKercher, *The Second Baldwin Government and the United States, 1924–1929: Attitudes and Diplomacy* (Cambridge, 1984).

mercial imperialism'. The French premier suggested a European Economic Union and the British were faced with the possibility, however remote, of being squeezed between two huge protected economic empires in North America and on the continent – foreshadowing their eventual fate in the 1960s.[99]

In 1930 a European accord on economic policy seemed remote. Besides, the British had an alternative available if the cosmopolitan economy should fail: empire unity, last seriously considered in the 1916–18 wartime emergency. As exports began to decline rapidly and the world economy started to disintegrate, the clamour for protection and for a retreat into empire increased. By then, not only much of industry but also large sections of organised labour were looking to the empire to save them from chaos.[100] More significantly, the City of London was also moving swiftly in the same direction, its cosmopolitanism worn down by competition from New York. The empire offered a safe haven, and 'protection was the price the City was prepared to pay to maintain sterling as a world currency'.[101] Thus for industry, unions and even finance, 'empire unity' provided an escape hatch down which they hoped to disappear in order to avoid the agonies of modernisation and restructuring as competition increased.[102] 'For many of its advocates an Empire strategy was attractive precisely because it was anti-development, a policy which protected the domestic industrial structure from new conditions in the world economy'.[103] Joining Europe was not an acceptable option; Britain's living standards might have had to fall to the continental level in order to compete. As Neville Chamberlain put it, succinctly and threateningly in 1929: 'If we do not think imperially, we shall have to think continentally'.[104] By the end of the decade, City and industrial interests were probably closer than at any time in their history, comrades in adversity as the world economy collapsed in ruins. If, by 1931, they could no longer manage a world economy, the British still aspired to run an empire.

As the groundswell of opinion in favour of protection increased, it spilled over into the centre of political life. In 1930 the Labour Cabinet

99. This is one of the main themes of Boyce, *British Capitalism at the Crossroads*.

100. Ibid. esp. pp. 232–3, 250–7. See also Forrest Capie, *Depression and Protectionism: Britain between the Wars* (1983), pp. 40–76.

101. Boyce, *British Capitalism at the Crossroads*, p. 253. On financial interests in protection see also Dayer, *Sir Charles Addis*, p. 217.

102. Michael Dintenfass, '"The Politics of Producers' Co-operation": the FBI–TUC–NCEO Talks, 1929–33', in Turner, *Businessmen and Politics*, pp. 84–7.

103. Holland, *Britain and the Commonwealth Alliance*, pp. 26–7.

104. R.W.D. Boyce, 'America, Britain and the Triumph of Imperial Protectionism in Britain, 1929–30', *Millennium*, 3 (1974), p. 63.

was having to cling grimly to its traditional free trade beliefs as rank-and-file opinion changed rapidly, though it was strong enough to resist the white empire's call for preferences at the Imperial Conference of 1930.[105] The transformation on the Conservative side was more complete. In 1923, when the Ruhr crisis appeared to threaten the collapse of order in Europe, Baldwin had reacted by trying to sell protectionism and imperial preference to the electorate and had been roundly defeated.[106] But by 1930, with a virtual alliance on the back-benches between financiers and industrialists, the party could opt for a tariff with much greater confidence.[107]

The increased favour with which protection and empire policies were viewed in financial circles between 1929 and 1931 did not mean that orthodoxy had been abandoned. The Bank of England and the Treasury still regarded it as their duty – something far above the grubby game of party politics – to cajole, bully and even bounce governments, of any political stripe, into deflationary policies once budget deficits began to appear.[108] Discipline had to be maintained: foreign help was refused at times to ensure that pressure to deflate remained acute.[109] The gold standard had also to be defended *à outrance* for the sake of the 'honour' upon which the City placed such great store.[110] It may be, however, that by late 1930 or early 1931, the Bank had recognised that holding on to the standard would be impossible if New York and Paris continued to absorb gold and force deflation on the world economy. For a while Norman and his colleagues put their faith in the Bank of International Settlements, created in 1929, to act as a new way of extending the authority of sterling and of bringing about the informal central bank cooperation which was so dear to the Bank of England.[111] But, as this hope faded,

105. Boyce, *British Capitalism at the Crossroads*, pp. 257–66, 272–5.

106. Holland, *Britain and the Commonwealth Alliance*, p. 110. On the electoral politics of tariffs in the 1920s see C. Cook, *The Age of Alignment* (1971), pp. 140–78. For the imperial preference element see W.K. Hancock, *Survey of British Commonwealth Affairs*, Vol. II, Pt. I, (Oxford, 1940), pp. 143–7, and Drummond, *British Economic Policy and the Empire*, pp. 60–64.

107. Williamson, 'Financiers, the Gold Standard and British Politics, 1925–1931', pp. 119–20.

108. Ibid. pp. 120–9. See also his article, 'A "Banker's Ramp"? Financiers and the British Political Crisis of 1931', *Eng. Hist. Rev.*, XCIX (1984); Boyce, *British Capitalism at the Crossroads*, pp. 348–55.

109. Boyce, *British Capitalism at the Crossroads*, pp. 346–8.

110. See the comment of Keynes in *Collected Works*, IX, p. 245.

111. On the Bank of International Settlements (BIS) and its connection with the Young Plan of 1929 dealing with reparations see Dayer, *Sir Charles Addis*, pp. 352–8. There were some in the City who worried about the BIS as a 'super-bank' which might challenge London. See Boyce, *British Capitalism at the Crossroads*, p. 196; Burk, *Morgan Grenfell*, pp. 144–5.

they concentrated upon trying to force the Americans and French to recognise their 'responsibilities', while keeping a tight hold on the money supply in Britain. In this way they hoped both to demonstrate that they had played the game to the end, as gentlemen should, and also to ensure that, if gold was abandoned, financial discipline at home would not be relaxed.[112] In practice, the financial authorities felt they had been let down, not only by foreigners who would not play by the rules, but also by British industry, which had failed to respond to the stimulus of competition and thus to strengthen the balance of payments.[113]

The abandonment of the gold standard in September 1931 was a defeat for the City, for gentlemanly capitalism and for cosmopolitanism. But the impact of the depression was even greater in the United States, and her international economic sphere shrank markedly in the 1930s. As the United States retreated into economic isolationism, leaving wreckage strewn across the world, the British were left with the freedom to strike out on their own and to try to regain, within the confines of the empire and the Sterling Area, the power they had exercised before 1914 but which had eluded them in the 1920s.

---

112. See the argument in Dayer, *Sir Charles Addis*, pp. 217–30. Addis had been seriously worried by the deflationary consequences of the United States' thirst for gold in the late 1920s and had begun to recognise that the return to gold might have had adverse consequences for Britain (see pp. 199, 210–12).

113. Williamson, 'Financiers, the Gold Standard and British Politics', pp. 113, 117–18; Boyce, *British Capitalism at the Crossroads*, pp. 288–91. For a recent analysis of the causes of the 1931 crisis see Forrest Capie, Terrence E. Miller and Goeffrey E. Wood, 'What Happened in 1931?', in Forrest Capie and Geoffrey E. Wood, *Financial Crises*; and, for an extended treatment, Diane B. Kunz, *The Battle for Britain's Gold Standard in 1931* (1987). See also Burk, *Morgan Grenfell*, pp. 148–56.

CHAPTER FIVE

'A Latter-Day Expression of Financial Imperialism': The Origins of the Sterling Area, 1931–9[1]

FINANCIAL CRISIS AND ECONOMIC ORTHODOXY

The pre-1913 international financial system, which the British strove mightily to reintroduce in the 1920s, depended on Britain's ability to maintain the convertibility of sterling at a fixed rate, to lend liberally and to maintain a free market for imports.[2] In the 1930s the pound went off gold, the balance of payments on current account lapsed into deficit and overseas lending was severely limited. Free trade was abandoned in 1932, and was replaced by a tariff on manufactured imports and by a system of imperial preference supported by quotas and other bilateral arrangements with empire and foreign countries. Did this mean that Britain's traditional policies had been fully overthrown, and that the Tariff Reform dream of an imperial system supporting a revived industrial Britain had come fully into its own? The main purpose of what follows is to suggest that the answer to this question must be in the negative. The gold standard was abandoned in 1931 with extreme reluctance; tariffs were introduced in support of time-honoured monetary and financial policies both at home and overseas; and the Ottawa negotiations and the other trade arrangements of the 1930s make more sense if they, too, are considered as part of an attempt to salvage as much as possible of the traditional financial arrangements from the disasters of 1929–32.

The introduction of a tariff on manufactured imports in 1932 was

1. The quotation is from A.W.F. Plumptre, *Central Banking in the British Dominions* (Toronto, 1940), pp. 191–2.
2. Robert Skidelsky, 'Retreat from Leadership: the Evolution of British Economic Foreign Policy, 1870–1939', in Benjamin M. Rowland, ed. *Balance of Power or Hegemony* (New York, 1976).

not primarily, as historians have sometimes argued, a device designed to stem the growth of industrial unemployment as export values collapsed after 1929.[3] The central preoccupation of governments from 1929 was to maintain the external value of the pound; its defence was undertaken with the traditional complex of objectives in mind.[4] Without a stable currency, Britain's international leadership and her invisible earnings would be jeopardised.[5] Of equal importance was the recognition, as strong in the 1930s as in the run-up to the restoration of the gold standard in 1925, that a commitment to defending the pound would require severe monetary discipline: with no gold standard to defend, governments might easily give in to the temptation to spend their way out of a crisis. Even in the midst of the deflationary whirlwind of 1931, officials at the Bank of England were worried about inflation if the currency was allowed to float. One of Norman's advisers drew the obvious moral: 'with a floating rate control of domestic credit conditions must be even stricter than it is when the danger signal of weak exchange automatically compels credit restrictions'.[6] Financial discipline meant balanced budgets: the Treasury welcomed the cheap money policy made possible by falling interest rates in the wake of Britain's abandonment of the $4.86 rate chiefly because it allowed for a conversion of part of the national debt to the lower interest rates, cut government expenditure, made fewer demands on the taxpayer and made it easier to avoid deficits. By 1930 a tariff had other great attractions for those who stood by orthodoxy: it could, for example, help to restore confidence in sterling by improving the trade balance and increasing government revenue when other sources were drying up in a contracting economy.[7]

For the Labour Party, many of whose supporters strongly favoured free trade in the consumer's interest, the prospect of tariffs, like the

3. 'The National Government itself believed that it was following an anti-unemployment policy': Ian M. Drummond, *Imperial Economic Policy 1917–39: Studies in Expansion and Protection* (1974), p. 179.
4. Most of what follows in the next three paragraphs is based upon B.J. Eichengreen, 'Sterling and the Tariff, 1929–32', (Princeton Studies in International Finance, No. 48, 1981), reprinted in idem, *Elusive Stability: Essays in the History of International Finance* (Cambridge, 1990).
5. This was why Keynes, the most persistent critic of the authorities' financial policy over the years, thought in 1931 that the $4.86 rate should be defended for as long as possible. Eichengreen, 'Sterling and the Tariff', p. 9.
6. Sir Henry Clay, *Lord Norman* (1957), p. 436.
7. Alan Booth, 'Britain in the 1930s: a Managed Economy?', *Econ. Hist. Rev.*, 2nd ser. XL (1987), pp. 503–10. On cheap money see Susan Howson, 'Cheap Money and Debt Management in Britain, 1932–51', in P.L. Cottrell and D.E. Moggridge, eds. *Money and Power: Essays in Honour of L.S. Pressnell* 1988).

prospect of deflation, proved disastrously divisive. The National Government, largely staffed by Conservatives, which took over in August 1931 had no such scruples. Support for the tariff was strong in sections of the Conservative Party and had been growing in the 1920s, as we have seen. What was new in 1931 was the call for a tariff on grounds of 'financial stability'.[8]

The National Government was formed to forestall devaluation. When, six weeks later, this proved impossible and Britain left gold in September 1931, fundamental policy objectives did not undergo radical change. Both government and officials adjusted rapidly to the idea that some devaluation of the pound against the dollar and other currencies had its advantages in making Britain more industrially competitive; the Exchange Equalisation Account, created under the auspicies of the Bank of England to manage the currency, at first aimed at keeping sterling low against the dollar and the franc.[9] But a stable currency remained a priority. Although there was considerable disagreement initially about the most acceptable rate, all those in authority were determined to prevent a steady slide in the pound's value. Continuous depreciation would have increased the competitiveness of industrial exports but it would also have pushed up import prices, lowered real wages and, it was feared, set off a wage–price spiral ending in runaway inflation with the same consequences as in Europe in the early 1920s. Besides this, it was well understood that a government without a commitment of any kind to particular rates or bands of rates for the currency might give in to the eternal temptation to spend more money than it gathered in revenue, with similar inflationary consequences.[10] Insofar as tariffs, by cutting down manufactured imports in particular, helped to restore the trade balance and, therefore, to support the value of sterling, they were an aid to 'sound' finance. This was principally the reason why they were introduced, in emergency in 1931 and permanently the year after. The relative insignificance of the claims of industrial exports in the

8. Eichengreen, 'Sterling and the Tariff', p. 22. The shift in opinion was symbolised by the replacement of Snowden, an ardent free-trade Labourite, with Neville Chamberlain, heir to his famous father's tariff campaign, as Chancellor of the Exchequer in the National Government which was formed in August 1931.

9. Susan Howson, *Sterling's Managed Float: The Operation of the Exchange Equalization Account, 1932–9* (Princeton, NJ, 1980).

10. In a memorandum for the government, written in August 1931, Henry Clay pointed to 'The vicious circle of inflation, to which the departure from the Gold Standard lays us open' via import price increases and reckless government expenditure. 'The only way to stop it is to balance the Budget'. Quoted in Robert Skidelsky, *Politicians and the Slump; The Labour Government of 1929–31* (1967), pp. 414–15.

crisis can be gauged from the fact that the government believed, rightly or wrongly, that by raising the exchange rate tariffs would exacerbate the unemployment problem in the short run.

After devaluation, it was hoped that 'sterling would depreciate relative to the currencies of Britain's industrial competitors but [the British] encouraged the principal raw material suppliers to link their currencies to the pound at the traditional parity'.[11] Out of the last concern came the Sterling Area, a group of countries which were heavily dependent on the British market (Tables 5.1 and 5.2), did most of their trade in sterling, fixed their own currencies in relation to the pound, and held some or all of their reserves in sterling. Membership of the area in the 1930s included not only the territories of the British Empire (except for Canada and British Honduras, which were in the dollar bloc) but also a large group of countries economically dependent on Britain, some of them in Europe.[12]

The holding of sterling as a reserve asset as well as for transactions purposes had begun well before 1913, as Lindert has shown,[13] and the Imperial Economic Conference of 1923 recommended that empire governments should increase the practice,[14] no doubt as part of Britain's attempt to follow up her Genoa proposals. So, there is something in the claim of Henry Clay, an adviser to the Bank of England, that the suspension of gold payments in 1931 'brought out the true nature of the Sterling Area'.[15] Apart from the dependent parts of the empire, which had no option, the rest of the countries which followed sterling after September 1931 were theoretically free to resist incorporation but, in practice, were forced into it because of a heavy dependence on British trade, or British credit, or both.[16]

11. Eichengreen, 'Sterling and the Tariff', p. 26.

12. For the overlap between trade dependence and sterling bloc membership see Tables 5.1 and 5.2. The criteria for membership of the bloc are also listed by Brinley Thomas, 'The Evolution of the Sterling Area and its Prospects', in Nicolas Mansergh et al., *Commonwealth Perspectives* (Durham, NC, 1958), p. 180. Thomas has a slightly different list of countries and excludes Argentina. For De Vegh's detailed criteria for including countries in his list, see Table 5.1. The list of 15 principal sterling countries given by F.V. Meyer, *Britain, the Sterling Area and Europe* (Cambridge, 1952), p. 40, also excludes Argentina.

13. P.H. Lindert, *Key Currencies and Gold, 1900–13* (Princeton Studies in International Finance, no. 24, 1969).

14. Ian M. Drummond, *British Economic Policy and the Empire, 1919–39* (1972), p. 119.

15. Although he went on to say that 'observers may be pardoned for thinking that what they saw was something new and not something which had existed before without being apparent'. Sir Henry Clay, 'The Sterling Area', in Institute of Bankers, *Current Financial Problems and the City of London* (1949), p. 213.

16. League of Nations, *International Currency Experience: Lessons of the Inter-War Period* (1944), p. 48.

Table 5.1 British trade with the Sterling Area, 1929 and 1937 (£m.)

	Exports to	Net imports from	Trade balance	Trade balance as % of exports
1929				
European Sterling Area[a]	36.8	116.2	−79.4	−215.8
Argentina	29.1	81.9	−52.8	−181.6
British empire[b]	289.3	293.8	−4.5	−1.6
Rest of the Sterling Area[c]	21.0	29.0	−8.0	−42.9
Total Sterling Area[d]	376.2	520.9	−144.8	−38.5
Non-sterling trade	353.2	590.2	−237.0	−67.1
Total trade	729.4	1,111.1	−381.8	−52.4
1937				
European Sterling Area[a]	49.7	104.7	−55.0	−110.7
Argentina	20.0	59.5	−39.5	−196.9
British empire[b]	224.2	305.1	−80.9	−36.1
Rest of the Sterling Area[c]	14.5	22.1	−7.6	−52.4
Total Sterling Area[d]	308.4	491.4	−182.9	−59.3
Non-sterling trade	212.9	461.3	−248.4	−116.8
Total trade	521.3	952.7	−431.3	−82.7

Source: Trade figures are from B.R. Mitchell and P. Deane, *Abstracts of British Historical Statistics* (Cambridge, 1962) and *Statistical Abstracts for the United Kingdom* (HMSO). Total Sterling Area is the sum of European Sterling Area, Argentina, British empire and Rest of the Sterling Area. The list of Sterling Area countries is taken from De Vegh, *The Pound Sterling*, pp. 7–9. De Vegh defined three groups: first, 'those which hold all official international assets as sterling balances or securities, i.e. Australia, the British colonies (except Hong Kong, British Honduras, British Malaya) the British mandates, Eire and Siam. Second, 'countries which hold sterling but which feel free to alter their holdings', e.g. British Malaya, Denmark, Egypt, Estonia, Hong Kong, India and Burma, Iraq, Latvia, Lithuania, New Zealand, Portugal and South Africa. Third, those 'which hold official gold and/or other currency reserves as well as sterling reserves, but in actual practice peg their currencies to the pound sterling', e.g. Argentina, Finland, Norway and Sweden. De Vegh regarded the inclusion of Argentina and Sweden in this list as 'debatable', although this may be because he was writing at a time when the flight from sterling was becoming pronounced.

Notes: [a] The European Sterling Area consists of Norway, Sweden, Denmark, Finland, Latvia, Lithuania and Estonia. Iceland is omitted.
   [b] The British empire total includes Eire but excludes Canada and British Honduras.
   [c] The Rest of the Sterling Area includes Portugal, Iraq, Egypt and Thailand (Siam).

Table 5.2 Share of United Kingdom in the foreign trade of some Sterling Area countries, 1929, 1933 and 1937 (per cent)

	Exports			Imports		
	1929	1933	1937	1929	1933	1937
Australia	45	54	52	41	42	42
Denmark	56	64	53	15	28	38
Egypt	34	41	31	21	23	22
Eire	92	94	91	78	70	50
Estonia	38	37	34	10	18	17
Finland	38	46	43	13	21	19
India	21	30	32	42	41	32
Latvia	27	43	38	8	22	21
Norway	27	20	25	21	23	18
New Zealand	74	86	76	49	51	50
Portugal	23	22	22	27	28	18
Sweden	25	26	23	17	18	12
South Africa	66	78	79	43	50	43

Source: League of Nations, *International Currency Experience: The Lessons of the Inter-war Period* (Geneva, 1944), p. 48.

> Not only would [these countries] have been faced with a serious loss [in their own currency] on the reserves they held in sterling, if they had refused to depreciate their own currency with sterling: they could not face the obstruction to their exports (and stimulus to imports) which an appreciation of their currency on sterling would have involved.[17]

The emergence of the Sterling Area marks an important stage in the decline of sterling from its position of 'Top Currency' before 1913 to the 'Master Currency' status within the empire that it held after World War II.[18] Its emergence had been anticipated by Keynes as early as August 1931 when, in giving up $4.86 for dead, he had urged the Labour government to take the initiative in forming a sterling bloc on the basis of a devalued pound. 'Many people in the City', he

17. Clay, 'The Sterling Area', pp. 213–14. Some indication of the relationship between trade with Britain and national output levels for various sterling countries can be found in Ingvar Svennilson, *Growth and Stagnation in the European Economy* (Geneva, 1954), p. 198.

18. A 'Top Currency' is defined as 'the preferred medium of the international economy', something which derives from 'the issuing state's position of economic leadership', which 'inspires monetary confidence even amongst political opponents'. A 'Master Currency' is one imposed by an imperial or hegemonic state on countries which rely upon it, though whether the currency is forced on its subordinates or not depends upon the economic strength of the issuing state. See Susan Strange, *Sterling and British Policy: A Political Study of an International Currency in Decline* (Oxford, 1971), pp. 4–5.

claimed, 'far more than might be expected . . . are now in favour of something of this sort'.[19] London had accepted that its orbit of operations was permanently reduced and was ready to make the best of it. After devaluation, the Treasury soon appreciated the value of creating conditions which

> make it easy for as many as possible of the unstable currencies to base themselves on sterling so that we may become leaders of a sterling block which, pending our stabilization on gold, would have the best opportunities for mutual trade and would give sterling a new force in the world.[20]

The necessary prerequisite was a stable pound, albeit at a lower parity than $4.86. If Britain could retain financial stability she would also retain the confidence of sterling-holders and 'the leadership of the block will be ours and the vital commercial business which it carries with it'.[21] Balanced budgets and the sterling bloc were intertwined from the beginning.[22] Throughout the 1930s the Treasury was worried about retaining the allegiance of sterling-holders, especially non-empire ones, and used this to hammer home its views on the need for financial restraint at home.[23]

In economic policy terms there was little change in fundamentals during the 1930s. Governments were not even Keynesian in drift, let alone philosophy. There was a great deal of intellectual debate, involving enlightened, younger members of both Conservative and Labour Parties, about the need for public works, redistribution of income and a new role for the state in regenerating depressed regions, where unemployment remained very high even at the height of the boom in 1937. But this discussion had little impact on the National Government which, under Treasury guidance, stuck firmly to the view that modernisation and recovery depended upon increased

19. Susan Howson, *Domestic Monetary Management in Britain, 1919–38* (Cambridge, 1975), p. 79, n. The City's interest is confirmed by Ian M. Drummond, *The Floating Pound and the Sterling Area, 1931–1939* (Cambridge, 1981), p. 14. For FBI support see Michael Dintenfass, '"The Politics of Producers' Co-operation": the FBI–TUC–NCEO Talks, 1929–1933', in John Turner, ed. *Businessmen and Politics: Studies in Business Activity in British Politics, 1900–1945* (1984), pp. 87–8.

20. Drummond, *The Floating Pound*, p. 10.

21. Ibid. p. 22. Strong support for the area also came from the government's own economic advisers. See Susan Howson and Donald Winch, *The Economic Advisory Council, 1930–1939* (Cambridge, 1974), pp. 257–8.

22. On this theme see also Roberta Allbert Dayer, *Finance and Empire: Sir Charles Addis, 1861–1945* (1988), pp. 238, 247, 292–3.

23. Ibid. p. 16.

efficiency in the private sector and that the best aid the government could give was to keep taxation down and balance its books.[24]

FINANCIAL IMPERIALISM WITHOUT GOLD

For most of the 1930s the countries of the sterling bloc were building up their reserves, so the demand for sterling was higher than was justified by current transaction needs.[25] The result of this additional demand for sterling was to offset, to some degree, the efforts of the Exchange Equalisation Account, created at the Bank of England, to keep the sterling rate below its pre-1931 level against other major currencies. Consequently, the terms of trade between Britain and the rest of world moved in Britain's favour, imports were encouraged and exports discouraged. Cheaper imports certainly raised real wages and living standards in Britain; however, it has been estimated that the use of sterling to build reserves rather than to purchase goods from Britain may have reduced British exports by between 6 per cent and 10 per cent between 1932 and 1938 and deepened the unemployment problem in the severely depressed export areas. The tendency to import more from, and export less to, sterling bloc countries was also reinforced by the decision of important members, such as Australia and New Zealand, to link their currencies with sterling at a devalued rate compared with the 1920s. In addition, by an intricate process, demand for sterling as a reserve reduced the money supply in Britain. The rise in sterling balances increased competition for Treasury bills between British and overseas banks, and reduced the British banks' supply of liquid assets as well as keeping Treasury bill rates low.[26]

As we have seen, industrial exports did less well out of the sterling system of the 1930s than invisibles, and this invites comparisons with experience before 1913. In saying this, it must be remembered that

24. There is a vast and growing literature on this subject. Particularly useful here are the summaries of the literature given in G.C. Peden, *Keynes, the Treasury and British Economic Policy* (1988); Scott Newton and Dilwyn Porter, *Modernization Frustrated: The Politics of Industrial Decline in Britain since 1900* (1988), pp. 78ff. See also W.R. Garside, 'The Failure of the "Radical Alternative"': Public Works, Deficit Finance and British Interwar Unemployment', *Journal of European Economic History*, 14 (1985); and idem, *British Unemployment, 1919–39: A Study in Public Policy* (Cambridge, 1990).

25. Much of the next paragraph depends upon Meyer, *Britain, the Sterling Area and Europe*, pp. 36–46.

26. League of Nations, *International Currency Experience*, p. 61.

the overvaluation of sterling would have been reduced once sterling countries had built up sufficient reserve levels and that, in 1938, the shedding of sterling resources in the trade depression of that year pushed down the sterling rate and helped to cushion the impact of the depression on export values.[27] Moreover, the creation of the sterling bloc was valuable in maintaining liquidity in the crisis after 1929 and was an important element in the hesitant recovery of the world economy in the 1930s, thus making a considerable contribution to the growth of exports from their low point in 1932. Nonetheless, the reasoning behind the encouragement of the sterling bloc, like the argument for a tariff, shows how the defence of orthodox finance (and the assumption that the fortunes of industrial exports and the economic health of the older industrial areas were a direct consequence of this defence), was almost a reflex action among the political elite and their advisers.[28] As we shall see, these presuppositions about maintaining Britain's economic role in the world had a marked influence upon her trade negotiations with the empire countries after 1932 and with other sterling-bloc members.

When the tariff was permanently established in 1932, the crown colonies were exempted from its provisions; but the Dominions and India were granted free entry only pending negotiations with Britain at the Ottawa Conference about reciprocal concessions in their markets. At Ottawa the British hoped initially to persuade the Dominions to lower their tariffs and allow empire free trade. According to the British, this policy would stimulate exports, increase demand for Dominion produce in Britain and, by encouraging growth in Britain, allow for foreign investment.[29] In practice, no Dominion was willing to lower tariffs significantly and all of them decided instead to give Britain preferences in their markets in return for similar concessions for themselves in the British market.

As a result of Ottawa and subsequent negotiations, and despite taking measures to protect her own farmers from Dominion as well as foreign competition, Britain made more generous trade concessions to the Dominions than they made to her and received fewer benefits in return. Exports to the Dominions (including Canada, which

27. Meyer, *Britain, the Sterling Area and Europe*, p. 44.
28. Meyer notes that, had Britain joined the dollar bloc, stockpiling dollars would have reduced imports and lowered real incomes, 'though there might have been some stimulus to employment, especially in the export trades' (ibid. p. 44). Joining another bloc with all its implications for Britain's role in the world was, of course, unthinkable in the 1930s.
29. R.F. Holland, *Britain and the Commonwealth Alliance, 1918–39* (1981), pp. 130, 141.

received the benefit of empire status without being a member of the sterling bloc) averaged £143m. in 1925–9 and had fallen to £111m., or by 22 per cent, by 1934–8. Even when set against an overall fall in export values of 38 per cent in this period, the result was disappointing for British exporters. Against this, while net imports as a whole fell by 29 per cent, net imports from the Dominion rose from £183m. in 1925–9 to £189m. in 1934–8. Trade with India and the crown colonies showed the same trend. Exports from Britain were actually 44 per cent lower in 1934–8 than in 1925–9, while imports from them were only 15 per cent down on 1920s levels in the mid-1930s. This evidence fits with Drummond's rough estimate that, by 1937, the concessions won by Britain at Ottawa pushed up her exports to the Dominions by about 5 per cent, whereas the concessions she made may have added 10 per cent to her imports from the Dominions in the same year.[30] One result of this trend was that Britain's balance of trade deficit with her empire widened considerably.

The preferential system created as a result of the Ottawa Conference did not, of course, come up to the expectations of the Dominions.[31] Leaving aside permanent irritants such as Britain's determination, inexplicable to the Dominions, not only to support her own farmers but also to preserve some of the home market for foreigners like the Argentines and the Danes, the Dominions began to realise that the British market was not big enough, or growing fast enough, to ensure a level of export-led growth sufficient to solve their massive unemployment problems.[32] But the new arrangements were an even greater disappointment to British industrial exporters: it is worth asking why.

There are a number of obvious reasons why empire countries should have done better out of the preferential system than Britain. The collapse in empire primary produce prices in the depression was catastrophic, and recovery very slow, so that demand for British industrial goods was bound to suffer badly. On the other hand, Britain's national income fell relatively little in 1929–32, and was much higher in 1937 than in 1929, thus keeping import demand reasonably buoyant when compared with, for example, that of the

30. Drummond, *British Economic Policy and the Empire*, p. 102.
31. The literature on the Ottawa conference and its implications, on which the next two paragraphs are based, is now considerable. Chapters 5–8 of Drummond's *Imperial Economic Policy* are very thorough, and there is a useful summary in his earlier book, *British Economic Policy and the Empire*, pp. 92–119. There are also excellent summaries and critical accounts in Skidelsky, 'Retreat from Leadership', pp. 178–83, and Holland, *Britain and the Commonwealth Alliance*, Ch. 8.
32. Holland, *Britain and the Commonwealth Alliance*, p. 145.

United States. Given the persistence of balance of payments problems in the 1930s, and an inability to borrow as British overseas investment dried up, it is not surprising that recovery in the Dominions included a significant degree of import-substituting manufactures. The British underestimated the growing manufacturing interests in the Dominions, especially the power of the industrial lobbies in Canada and Australia and, in doing so, were grievously mistaken about the extent of the complementarity between the white settlement areas and the mother country. The British originally went to Ottawa believing that they could obtain tariffs on their exports to the Dominions and India low enough to allow them into empire markets on equal terms with domestic industry. Instead, after much haggling, they were given preferences which resulted from a further rise in Dominion tariffs on foreign goods.[33]

Besides this, however, there was also a wider sense in which it was necessary to the furtherance of the sterling system that Britain should accord the Dominions – and some other members of the Sterling Area – more generous treatment than they gave to her. In January 1932 H.D. Henderson, a prominent member of the Economic Advisory Committee, made the point that the relationship between a British balance of trade deficit and the strength or weakness of sterling was not an obvious one: a big deficit need not necessarily imply a steadily falling pound. If, for example, Britain increased imports from the empire the deficit would increase too, but this would not put a strain on the sterling exchange rate because it would mainly result in an addition to the empire's London sterling balances

> with the result that the governments of India and Australia would find it easier to meet their sterling obligations without recourse to fresh borrowing. So far from weakening sterling, this would actually tend to strengthen it, by diminishing fears of eventual financial default by those countries, which form an intimate part of the British financial system.

He went on to say immediately:

> Conversely and for the same reasons, it would do nothing to strengthen sterling but something to weaken it, if we were to reduce our imports from India and Australia, whether by consuming less or by replacing these imports by home consumption.[34]

33. Drummond, *British Economic Policy and the Empire*, pp. 97, 100–1.
34. Hubert D. Henderson, 'Sterling and the Balance of Trade', in idem, *The Inter-War Years and Other Papers* (Oxford, 1955), p. 87. For a similar recognition of the importance of the sterling and debt questions in the Ottawa equation, see the comments by William Graham at the end of H.V. Hodson's article, 'Imperial Economic Policy', *International Affairs*, 14 (1935), pp. 542-3.

Empire countries were already good customers for British exports, and Britain's balance of trade with them was more favourable than it was with most other countries. Since the empire countries were often considerable borrowers and were dependent on British financial services and shipping, they had heavy bills to meet for invisible items. In the circumstances of the 1930s some of them would have had considerable difficulty in meeting their debt obligations and in building up sterling reserves unless access to sterling was improved. Default or repudiation could have destabilised sterling and might even have led to the collapse of the sterling bloc. Generous provision for the empire in British markets, and an adverse movement in the balance of her trade with the empire, were the price Britain had to pay for a smoothly functioning sterling bloc. Before 1913, Britain not only kept an open market which allowed debtors to acquire sterling, but also lent considerable amounts abroad and thereby allowed debtors to increase steadily their demands for British goods. In the 1920s the system still worked, though more sluggishly, as British overseas investment began to decline. In the 1930s overseas new issues declined to an average of only £33m. per year between 1932 and 1939 (of which £27m. per year went to the empire) and were tiny in comparison with repayments every year from 1933 onwards.[35] Faced with both a shrinking world market and a drying up of loans, the chief colonial debtors needed preferential treatment in the British market to obtain sterling, while simultaneously keeping tight control on imports of British goods. If, at Ottawa, the British had negotiated a better settlement for their industrial exporters in the Dominions, this 'success' could have imperilled the latter's ability to meet their sterling obligations.

Over the years, empire countries had been very important customers for British exporters and, from 1870 onwards, had often compensated the older industrial areas of Britain for declining markets elsewhere. But in the 1930s they could not keep up their demand for British commodities without threatening the whole sterling system. Some other members of the sterling bloc were, however, not quite in the same position. Some non-empire sterling holders had benefited as much as the others from the openness of the British market in the past, but lack of kinship relations and their independence of British capital markets had restricted their demand for Britain's exports. Unlike the empire countries, many of them had run heavy balance of payments surpluses

---

35. Howson, *Domestic Monetary Management*, p. 105. See also Alfred E. Kahn, *Britain and the World Economy* (1946), pp. 188–95.

with Britain in the 1920s. Given their dependence on the British market – which increased as other major markets contracted faster than Britain's after 1929 – and given that British exports to them could be increased substantially without precipitating balance of payment crises there, it was possible for Britain to make vigorous attempts to promote her industrial exports. In the 1930s it was relatively easy, too, for her to restrict their imports in favour of British farmers and those of the Dominions without fear of retaliation, and also to use the threat of further cuts to force these countries to take more British exports.

Immediately after Ottawa, for example, Britain signed an agreement with Denmark, 64 per cent of whose exports came to Britain in 1933 (Table 5.2). The agreement, signed in 1933, gave certain quotas for Danish produce in return for reduced duties on British exports to Denmark and an undertaking by the Danes to purchase specified quantities of certain industrial commodities, especially coal. As a result, the ratio between British imports of Danish produce and British exports to Denmark fell from 5.4:1 in 1932 to 2.2:1 in 1937.[36] Similar agreements were made with a number of other European countries including some, like the Soviet Union, which were not within the sterling group, but which had a large balance of trade surplus with Britain. These bilateral agreements were favourable to British exporters simply because the authorities could squeeze the European sterling-holders without precipitating a sterling crisis. Even here, though, success was limited. The share of the European sterling-holders in British exports rose from 5 per cent to 9.5 per cent between 1929 and 1937, but their share had already increased in the depression, reaching 7.2 per cent in 1932,[37] so the subsequent agreements confirmed a trend rather than established an entirely new one. Britain's gains were also limited because, in pushing her exports in these markets, she often displaced foreigners who found compensation by cutting into Britain's share of trade in the non-sterling world.[38]

---

36. B.N. Thomsen and B. Thomas, *Anglo-Danish Trade, 1661–1963*, (Aarhus, 1963), pp. 364ff and esp. Table XV, p. 367. For a detailed study see T.J.T. Rooth, 'Limits of Leverage: the Anglo-Danish Trade Agreement of 1933', *Econ. Hist. Rev.*, 2nd ser. XXXVIII (1984).

37. Political and Economic Planning, *Report on International Trade* (1937). The data are derived from Table 1, p. 288.

38. The best study of the trade relations between Britain and the European sterling countries is T.J.T. Rooth, 'Tariffs and Trade Bargaining: Anglo-Scandinavian Economic Relations in the 1930s', *Scandinavian Economic History Review*, XXXIV (1986). Also useful is the P.E.P. cited in n. 37, App. III. There are good sections in Carl Kreider, *The Anglo-American Trade Agreement: A Study of British and American Commercial Policies, 1934–1939*, (Princeton, NJ, 1943), pp. 57–67; and J.H. Richardson, *British Economic Foreign Policy* (1936), pp. 101f. Most of the contemporary studies suggest

Not all the non-empire countries dependent upon Britain were in this rather helpless position. There is no doubt, for example, that, despite her desperate need for markets for her beef, Argentina's debt position, her threat to hinder repayments and her operation of exchange controls, had some influence on commercial relations with Britain.[39] It is also worth noting that those countries, including Germany, which had frozen payments for British exports in the financial crisis, were treated by Britain in a very similar manner. In negotiating agreements with them, the main objective of the British government was to collect debts rather than to maximise trade flows; if necessary, imports from the debtors were encouraged and British exports suppressed in order to achieve this goal.[40]

Table 5.1 helps to confirm these findings. In those countries in the sterling bloc which, in 1929, were already good customers for British industrial exports – the empire countries – Britain had to offer entry into her market on easy terms but had to be restrained in pushing her own exports. Britain's share of the empire's markets rose but not as rapidly as did the empire's share of the British market, and Britain's balance of trade deficit with this imperial group increased significantly.[41] In those areas where export performance had been less satisfactory in the past, and where the countries concerned had strong balance of trade or balance of payments surpluses with Britain, imports could be restricted and there was some leeway for export promotion. Argentina, which had borrowed large amounts of British capital, could retain more or less the status quo in relative terms. The

---

how hard these countries were squeezed; but they did considerably better than non-sterling foreign countries in the British market. Drummond has noted, in passing, that in the bilateral agreements made from 1933 onwards, Britain 'in effect . . . promised not to squeeze the Argentinians, the Danes and the Swedes merely to make more room for the Dominions' foodstuffs' (*Imperial Economic Policy*, p. 311). The whole area of trade and financial policy towards Europe is the subject of a detailed study based on official documentation to be published eventually by Dr T.J.T. Rooth.

39. Argentina is dealt with in Chapter 7 in this volume. See the comment made by Robert Menzies, the Australian politician, on the fact that 'the Board of Trade . . . appears to be more pro-Argentinian than pro-Australian', in Drummond, *British Economic Policy and the Empire*, p. 224. Lord Beaverbrook also complained about 'the granting of Dominion status to the South American republic'. See F.C. Benham, *Great Britain under Protection* (New York, 1941), p. 136.

40. Henry Joseph Tasca, *World Trading Systems: A Study of American and British Commercial Policies* (Paris, 1939), pp. 94–6, 122–3, 146–51.

41. South Africa is an exception which proves the rule. Her gold exports - not included in the trade statistics – were very high in the 1930s, giving her a comfortable balance of payments surplus with Britain and allowing the latter to increase the value of her commodity exports to South Africa by nearly 30 per cent between 1929 and 1937.

European members of the sterling bloc, who were more vulnerable because they were not heavy debtors, had their import share stabilised but also had to take a much larger share of British exports, and their trade deficits with Britain were sharply reduced.

Emphasising the importance of sterling and the sterling bloc in the eyes of the British authorities in the 1930s alters some of the judgements made in the past about Britain's loss of economic influence within the empire in the 1930s. The use of tariffs to hamper British trade in India and the Dominions has led some scholars to wonder whether the British had any imperial authority at all,[42] whereas, as we have shown, concessions on tariffs were often a key part of the strategy for maintaining international financial stability. Within the orbit of the sterling bloc, Britain's power was still impressive. The creation of the bloc is a tribute to that; most members joined because they simply could not survive outside it. Hence South Africa, although keen on the retention of a gold standard because of her own exports of gold, was forced into line with sterling in 1933. This is hardly surprising considering that 78 per cent of her imports came from Britain in 1933 and 50 per cent of her own exports went to Britain in return (Table 5.2).[43]

Britain still aspired, and with considerable success, to maintain a high degree of financial authority within the sterling camp. Tariffs and trade were negotiable matters, but the British always took it for granted that finance was too important a matter to be left to mere colonials, even white ones. Imperial preference was in many ways Britain's substitute for the inability to lend – what meagre loans were available in the 1930s usually went to area members, often to help them build up sterling balances[44] – and a means of helping her own recovery, and that of the empire, without recourse to high government spending and other inflationary strategies in Britain and in the colonies.[45]

Throughout the 1930s the Bank of England was unceasing in its pursuit of central bank 'co-operation' within the empire, with the same ends in view. Central banking in the Dominions had begun in the 1920s in South Africa and Australia, and had been recommended

42. Drummond, *British Economic Policy and the Empire*, p. 140, asks rhetorically, after examining Dominion and Indian tariff policies, who was exploiting whom.
43. See Table 5.2. See also Brinley Thomas, 'The Evolution of the Sterling Area', in Nicoles Mansergh, *Commonwealth Perspectives* (Durham, NC, 1958), p. 180.
44. R.B. Stewart, 'Instruments of British Policy in the Sterling Area', *Political Science Quarterly*, 52 (1937), pp. 184–91.
45. R.S. Sayers, *The Bank of England, 1891–1944* (Cambridge, 1976), II, pp. 449, 451.

for India. In the 1930s, as the search for economic stability intensified, central financial institutions in these countries were strengthened and Canada and New Zealand also felt the need for similar bodies. The Bank of England had always wished to shape these institutions in its own image and pressed, with varying degrees of success, for private central banks whose freedom from competition with other banks and independence from government would enable them to manage the money supply on sound principles in the way that gentlemanly capitalists in Britain had long taken for granted.[46] In the 1930s, when the Bank's European plans had been shattered and when the Dominions began to emerge as the core of the overseas Sterling Area, Anglo-Dominion financial relations reached a new level of importance.[47] As one prominent Bank of England director, Sir Josiah Stamp, put it in 1934: 'the flow of capital funds' from London had once been the chief means of empire development but 'that great chapter may be regarded as closed' and 'the time has gone by when the Empire finance can be represented by the great financial institution in London' and their agencies abroad. With the rise of central banking, the Dominions were asserting 'an internal financial sovereignty', and doing it for reasons of domestic management.[48] It was vital to the future of the Sterling Area that these new institutions should learn to look outwards as soon as possible:

> We have perhaps hitherto looked upon co-operation between the foreign central banks as the first essential, to which co-operation between the Dominion Central Banks may be a useful auxiliary. But actually the priority should be reversed. The Dominions on a sterling exchange standard are critically interested in the fortunes of sterling and must join with Britain as custodians of the validity of sterling values especially if, as trade relations make most probable, the chief external reserves are in sterling. The Dominion banks as a whole even if not individually, at any moment are certain to hold large funds in London, and if they are moved and operated independently of each other and the Bank of England, then the difficulties of managing sterling must be all the greater. If the 'unknown' seller of sterling were a Dominion Bank, we might well find the resources of the Exchange Equalization Account being unnecessarily invoked to maintain sterling values, whereas fuller knowledge, by

46. See Norman's 'General Principles of Central Banking', as listed in Lyndhurst Faulkiner Giblin, *The Growth of a Central Bank: The Development of the Commonwealth Bank of Australia, 1924–45* (Melbourne, 1951), p. 40.

47. Sayers, *The Bank of England*, II, p. 513. For a contemporary recognition of the importance of imperial financial cooperation, see Howson and Winch, *The Economic Advisory Council*, pp. 258–60.

48. Sir Josiah Stamp, *Central Banking as an Imperial Factor* (Cust Foundation Lecture, Nottingham University, 1934), pp. 1–2, 7.

planning requirements correctly on a time basis, would obviate action in the dark.[49]

Stamp was at pains to stress that cooperation would not involve Bank of England dictatorship.[50] Nevertheless, the Bank did assume a right to leadership and did its best via advice, the recommendation of personnel and other means, to influence financiers in the Dominions to its own way of thinking. In Britain the Bank's own strivings for independence were part of its determination to keep financial management as far as possible out of the political arena and prevent overspending. Similarly, as the Dominions began inevitably to exercise a greater conscious control over their economies, the temptation for governments, free of gold standard restrictions, would be to embark upon a course of monetary inflation which would eventually endanger trading and financial relations with Britain, make debt payment more difficult and perhaps imperil the stability of sterling. If, for example, rapid inflation should lead to a balance of payments problem in a Dominion, its sterling reserves would be run down, perhaps at a time when the pound was under severe pressure for other reasons. The more that Norman and other prominent Bank directors could persuade overseas governments to leave their central bankers alone, the more likely the latter were to resist these pressures and to remain 'dependent on traditional financial prospects, upon the trend of opinion in financial and business circles and upon the advice of the Bank of England itself'.[51]

What 'central banking co-operation' meant to the Bank of England in practice was the reinforcing of those export-oriented, London-facing trading and financial interests in the Dominions and other satellites which had thrived upon the old monetary orthodoxies in the past and which would automatically support the Sterling Area and hold out against economic nationalism in the colonies,[52] in the same way that the Bank, the Treasury and the traditional nexus of internationally minded economic interests were holding out against economic nationalism and the interventionist state in Britain. One Dominion economist with extensive governmental experience did not hesitate at the time to call this 'a latter-day expression of financial imperialism . . . the maintenance and extension of London's influence and control'.[53]

49. Ibid. pp. 21–2.
50. Ibid. pp. 22–3.
51. Plumptre, *Central Banking in the British Dominions*, pp. 191–2.
52. Ibid. pp. 196–7.
53. Ibid. p. 193.

British politicians, and those who advised them, gave first priority to the restoration of the gold standard in the 1920s and defended their position until the last in the crisis of 1931. When they had to admit defeat they did not turn to a different set of objectives, but resurrected the old financial system on a reduced scale within what came to be known as the Sterling Area. Tariffs were broached in the first place to defend the gold standard and then to underpin the financial stability upon which the new sterling system, like the old, depended. Imperial preference, which was decisively rejected in 1930 at the Imperial Economic Conference before sterling fell, and then turned to in a panic when the collapse of the world economy was clearly apparent,[54] also found its chief significance in the 1930s as a part of the strategy for maintaining the viability of sterling as an international currency.[55] After 1931, as before, the preoccupations and prejudices of the British financial establishment were the base upon which British economic foreign policy was built. Like the gold standard regime which preceded it, the Sterling Area was controlled by traditional financial criteria and judgements which had an automatic, almost subconscious, priority. Industry, disappointed again, was already looking beyond Ottawa and towards a more multilateral trading world as early as 1936.[56]

THE COMING OF THE *PAX AMERICANA*

The Sterling Area conferred many benefits on Britain, helping both to cushion her from some of the worst effects of the world depression and to retain her share of world trade after decades of relative decline. It also offered the City of London an international standing and influence which must have seemed unattainable in the desperate days of 1931. But the area was a spontaneous piece of crisis management

54. Holland, *Britain and the Commonwealth Alliance*, pp. 120–2. There is a detailed treatment in Drummond, *Imperial Economic Policy*, Ch. 4, and a shorter one in his *British Economic Policy and the Empire*, pp. 67–9.

55. Drummond, in his early work, appreciates this to some degree when he argues that imperial policy was about 'sterling, debt service, the budget and unemployment', but he puts rather too much weight on the last of these and the discussion of the financial aspects does not come out fully in the body of the work. See *Imperial Economic Policy*, pp. 422–5.

56. R.F. Holland, 'The Federation of British Industries and the International Economy, 1929–39', *Econ. Hist. Rev.*, 2nd ser. XXXIV (1981), pp. 287–300, which charts the growing interest of industrial lobbyists, like the FBI, in markets outside the empire, especially after 1936.

aimed at salvaging as much of the old economic order as possible: it was simply not big enough or influential enough to offer a cure for an ailing world economy in the 1930s. Nor could it provide solutions to Britain's own fundamental foreign trade crisis stemming from the low demand for uncompetitive, old-fashioned labour-intensive exports in the regions, and the continuing lack of international competitiveness of the new industries of the Midlands and the south-east. Rapid growth in these areas, together with the concessions to the Dominions in particular which made the Sterling Area viable, meant that imports, including manufactures, recovered very quickly from depression despite protection in 1932. So, although invisible income rose steadily between 1932 and 1937 as the City reaped the benefits of the stable financial order in the Sterling Area, the current account of the balance of payments began to show persistent deficits from the mid–1930s onwards. Britain's inability to lend in the 1930s was the most potent sign of her weakening ability to influence the pace of change in the world economy.

Full international recovery, as the authorities began to recognise, now depended on what happened in the United States, the nature of her demands upon the world economy and whether or not American foreign investment would recover the levels reached in the 1920s. Moreover, the balance between the Sterling Area as a whole and the dollar bloc was precarious and could easily be disrupted. From the mid-1930s onwards, the steadily increasing threat of war with Germany pushed up the dollar imports of the Sterling Area significantly. This development, together with the nervousness induced in some sterling-holders by the threat of war, eventually led to capital flight and a falling pound. The international financial hegemony which had potentially been within the reach of the United States since 1918 was now achieved as Britain made the disagreeable, but inevitable, choice in favour of economic dependence upon the United States rather than military conquest by Germany.

The gentlemanly elite's perception of Britain's domestic and international economic weakness had a marked effect upon what was called 'appeasement' in the 1930s.[57] If appeasement means that a trading nation recognises its dependence on the world economy and tries to prevent the economic disruption arising from war by concili-

---

57. The literature on British diplomacy in the run up to the war is massive. For a short bibliographical guide see R.J. Overy, *The Origins of the Second World War* (1987). Interesting interpretations from our perspective can be found in Paul Kennedy, *The Realities Behind Diplomacy: Background Influences on British External Policy* (1980), Chs. 5 and 6; and Bernard Porter, *Britain, Europe and the World, 1850–1986* (1987), Ch. 4.

ating its potential enemies, then the British had been appeasers for generations.[58] But in the 1930s exceptionally heavy pressures were pushing the British in this direction to a much greater extent than in the past. It was widely recognised, in government and among the armed services, that Britain was 'overstretched' in the 1930s.[59] She had a huge burden of imperial defence commitments which had to be met from an economy relatively less powerful than before 1914, a less secure currency and small reserves of gold and foreign currencies. At the same time, Britain's enemies were numerous – Germany, Japan and Italy made a formidable list – and she had few plausible allies. France was in a state of internal economic and political disorder, and the Soviet Union was perceived to be both unreliable and ideologically unpalatable. In the run-up to the war, too, the prospect of military support from the United States was non-existent while, as we shall see, Britain was loath to rely on the Americans financially for fear of losing her economic independence.

This concentration of adverse circumstances meant that it was sensible for the authorities in Britain to try to solve their diplomatic problems by conciliating their enemies and avoiding all-out war. Besides this, it is clear that successive British governments in the 1930s were sympathetic to some of Germany's territorial claims. The policy of uniting as many Germans as possible within the Third Reich was not particularly offensive to many officials and politicians in key positions in Britain who still felt guilty over the supposed harshness of the Versailles settlement and were willing to accommodate Germany at the expense of some of the smaller nations created in 1918.[60] Moreover, an aggressive policy towards Germany, and towards Japan, was ruled out to some degree by the need to placate opinion in the empire. The Dominions in particular were adamant for appeasement right up until Munich and beyond; there is some plausibility in the argument that, in the event of war, Britain could be sure of their support, which was vital especially in relation to raw material and food imports, only when she had convinced them that every avenue for peace had been explored.[61]

58. On this issue see the suggestive article by P.M. Kennedy, 'The Tradition of Appeasement in British Foreign Policy, 1865–1939', *Brit. Jour. Internat. Stud.*, 2 (1976).

59. This is one of the themes of Paul Kennedy's major work, *The Rise and Fall of the Great Powers* (1988).

60. Norman Medlicott, 'Britain and Germany: the Search for Agreement, 1930–37', in David Dilks, ed. *Retreat from Power: Studies in British Foreign Policy in the 20th Century*, Vol. I, 1906–39 (1981).

61. Richie Ovendale, *Appeasement and the English-Speaking World: Britain, the United States, the Dominions and the Policy of Appeasement, 1937–39* (Cardiff, 1975); and idem,

The point at which economics and foreign policy most clearly converged, however, was on the question of rearmament. Financial orthodoxy had survived after 1918 only because the growing demands for expenditure on social services and education were compensated by severe cuts in defence, both naval and military. Rearmament had to be undertaken once Hitler seemed capable of launching Germany into war. At the same time, there was a pervasive fear in financial, administrative and political circles in Britain that a too rapid rate of rearmament would produce inflation, destroy the economic and social stability of the nation and wreck the Sterling Area by precipitating a financial crash equal to, or greater than, that of 1931. At the Treasury, the assumption was that rearmament diverted savings and industrial capacity from productive employment, provoked inflation, and reduced investment by pushing up taxes.[62] Inflation posed a threat to real wage levels and threatened an industrial relations crisis[63] that would not only affect output but also reduce Britain's image abroad as a strong and stable nation.[64] Moreover, assuming the ever-present need to balance budgets, it was feared that if government expenditure on defence rose too quickly welfare benefits would suffer, and this prospect had alarming implications for social order and morale.

Rapid rearmament also had deleterious effects upon Britain's balance of payments and put the existence of the Sterling Area in jeopardy. Rearmament widened the balance of payments deficit, putting downward pressure on sterling and opening the possibility of severe drains of gold and dollar reserves if a high rate of exchange was maintained. Given the need to import vital supplies in wartime, the Treasury was convinced that war readiness required that sterling remained strong.[65] This priority increased the emphasis upon tempering the arms build-up. The authorities hoped that enough would be

---

'Britain, the Dominions and the Coming of the Second World War, 1933–9', in Wolfgang J. Mommsen and Lothar Kattenacker, eds. *The Fascist Challenge and the Policy of Appeasement* (1983).

62. G.C. Peden, *British Rearmament and the Treasury, 1932–9* (Edinburgh, 1979), pp. 64–7, 71–92; F. Coghlan, 'Armaments, Economic Policy and Appeasement: Background to British Foreign Policy, 1931–7', *History*, 57 (1972); Robert Paul Shay, *British Rearmament in the Thirties: Politics and Profits* (Princeton, NJ, 1977), Chs. I and 4.

63. R.A.C. Parker, 'British Rearmament, 1936–39: Treasury, Trades Unions and Skilled Labour', *Eng. Hist. Rev.*, XCVI (1981).

64. On this complex theme see Gustav Schmidt, 'The Domestic Background to British Appeasement Policy', in Mommsen and Kattenacker, *The Fascist Challenge*.

65. R.A.C. Parker, 'Economics, Rearmament and Foreign Policy: the United Kingdom before 1939. A Preliminary Study', *Journal of Contemporary History*, 10 (1975), pp. 637–9. On government sensitivity to City opinion see Peden, *British Rearmament and the Treasury*, p. 95; Sayers, *Bank of England*, II, pp. 567–71.

done to deter Hitler and other potential enemies, and to interest them in some reasonable settlement of differences short of war, without having to accelerate the arms race to a point where a collapse of sterling and a flight from the currency undermined Britain's international economic position.

The rearmament programme was strongly influenced at all stages by these considerations, and foreign and military policy were shaped accordingly. The concentration on air power reflected the belief that this was the most cost-effective deterrent; the emphasis on economy meant that expenditure on the army and navy was limited. The services had been victims of economies ever since 1919, and the state of the army in the mid-1930s, for example, made it practically impossible for the British to produce any show of force on the continent. Similarly, naval economies meant that the policing of the empire in the Far East became an increasingly cosmetic affair.[66] In a more general perspective, there was a powerful link between economies in defence and foreign policy as a whole up until 1938:

> Based on the Treasury's firm belief that a continuance of the existing rate of rearmament would destroy Britain's economy and consequently her ability to defend herself, the Government's programme sought to limit the nation's expenditure on armaments while pursuing a foreign policy that would diminish the need for them. The policy by which defence spending was to be limited was known as rationing. The policy by which the nation's enemies were to be conciliated was known as appeasement.[67]

Deeply unsatisfied by the outcome of the Ottawa agreements, British industrialists were eager by the late 1930s for European-wide market sharing agreements with Germany and were actively encouraged in this endeavour by the National Government.[68] The City, too, had an active interest in loosening the economic restrictions of Hitler's Germany: many acceptance credits had been frozen in the depression and could be released only if Germany opened up her economy and earned more foreign exchange.[69] But appeasement was far more than an attempted rapprochement between sinister capitalist interests,

66. Shay, *British Rearmament in the Thirties*, Ch. 2; P.M. Kennedy, '"Appeasement" and British Defence Policy in the Inter-War Years', *Brit. Jour. Internat. Stud.*, 2 (1976); Lawrence Roy Pratt, *East of Malta, West of Suez: Britain's Mediterranean Crisis, 1936–1939*, (Cambridge, 1975).
67. Shay, *British Rearmament in the Thirties*, pp. 195–6.
68. Holland, 'The Federation of British Industries and the International Economy', pp. 296–9.
69. On this problem see Sayers, *The Bank of England*, II, pp. 503–12; and Neil Forbes, 'London Banks, the German Standstill Agreements and "Economic Appeasement" in the 1930s', *Econ. Hist. Rev.*, 2nd ser. XL (1987).

encouraged by those who believed that Germany, like Italy, was a natural ally against Bolshevik Russia. Basically, it was an attempt to pull Germany away from autarky and warlike preparations and propel her towards economic liberalism and peace. The main target of the British appeasers were the German 'moderates' – including some of Hitler's senior aides – who, supposedly, were more interested in raising living standards than in building a war machine and who might produce a force within Germany sufficient to make war impossible if they received adequate support from outside. To this end, the British were willing to offer a range of economic concessions and benefits if the Germans would agree on disarmament and on a return to the liberal fold.[70] Many of these schemes were aimed at liberalising Anglo–German trade, including the 1934 Clearing Agreement (renewed annually thereafter), which left the Germans considerable freedom to use sterling to buy goods other than those produced in Britain or the empire.[71] Between 1935 and 1938, too, the British government actively considered making some colonial concessions to Germany and floated the idea of a central African consortium in which Germany would participate with other colonial powers in the exploitation of Africa's wealth.[72] When this failed to tempt Hitler, the British shifted the emphasis to south-east Europe, offering loans and trade agreements to help Germany achieve her economic objectives in that region without the need for force.

Nonetheless, the policy of economic appeasement had strict limits. Some elements in the Foreign Office, for example, put the blame for Germany's aggression on the growth of protectionism which followed the 1929–31 crisis, and saw a return to freer trade as being crucial to peace. But the majority view was that the Ottawa system must be preserved and that concessions could only be made in that context. There was also resistance to the idea that economic concessions should be handed out *gratis*: they were to be traded against concrete political guarantees on Germany's part.[73] Viewed in the round, the policy was intended to steer a course between either abandoning the Sterling Area and protection in an attempt to mollify the enemy, or embarking on a Churchillian policy of matching Hitler

70. C.A. MacDonald, 'Economic Appeasement and the German "Moderates", 1937–1939', *Past and Present*, 56 (1972); Berndt-Jürgen Wendt, '"Economic Appeasement" – a Crisis Strategy', in Mommsen and Kattenacker, *The Fascist Challenge*, pp. 163–4.
71. Wendt, '"Economic Appeasement"', pp. 168–9.
72. See pp. 227–8 and the references given there.
73. Gustav Schmidt, *The Politics and Economics of Appeasement: British Foreign Policy in the 1930s* (Leamington Spa, 1986), pp. 137–46, 195–225.

bomb for bomb, since it was widely believed that both policies would produce economic disaster and weaken Britain drastically should war be forced upon her. Following this cautious course put the British in a position where they felt sufficiently well-armed in 1939 to face the prospect of war with some military confidence.[74]

One other, very unwelcome, effect of rearmament was an increased dependence upon the United States both politically and economically.[75] Until the German menace became tangible, following Hitler's invasion of the Rhineland in 1936, Britain relished her freedom within the Sterling Area and resisted attempts by the United States to restore the gold standard. In an ideal world the British monetary authorities would have liked to return to gold;[76] but they were determined not to adopt a fixed rate of exchange for fear that it would have to be defended by high interest rates, thus losing the benefits of cheap money. So, at the World Economic Conference of 1933, when both France and the United States argued that Britain should return to gold at the 1925–31 rate, the British agreed – provided certain conditions were met. France and the United States, which had large balance of payments surpluses, would have to inflate their economies and lower their tariffs so as to increase their imports, raise commodities prices and release gold. Both were also expected to agree on measures for economising on gold, showing that the British still hankered after the gold exchange standard they had vainly pursued in the 1920s.[77] The proposals were put forward largely in the knowledge that neither France nor the United States would consider them, since both were wedded to deflation. The British had, anyway, already pre-empted the possibility of a cosmopolitan settlement of the world crisis by moving to the Ottawa system; Roosevelt gave the World Economic Conference its final and fatal blow by devaluing the dollar before the proceedings had begun. Nonetheless, the insistence on the need for American reflation as a prerequisite of any restored fixed exchange-rate regime meant that Britain had tacitly recognised that the future of the liberal world economy was at the mercy of the United States.

74. Overy, *The Origins of the Second World War*, p. 67.
75. For an excellent overview of the changing relationship see B.M. Rowland, 'Preparing the American Ascendency: the Transfer of Economic Power from Britain to the United States', in Rowland, *Balance of Power or Hegemony*, and idem, *Commercial Conflict and Foreign Policy: A Study in Anglo-American Relations, 1932–1938* (New York, 1987).
76. Sayers, *Bank of England*, II, p. 450.
77. Clarke, 'The Reconstruction of the International Monetary System', pp. 19–40. See also Drummond, *The Floating Pound and the Sterling Area*, Chs. 6 and 7.

The devaluation of the dollar in 1933 brought the pound–dollar rate back to roughly the same level as under the old gold standard and the British authorities kept it there until 1938,[78] when the crisis began to overwhelm them, for fear that the United States would retaliate if the pound fell significantly. By 1936, with the German problem intensifying, the British also began to weaken slightly in response to persistent American demands that they should stabilise the pound on gold again. In the Tripartite Agreement of 1936 Britain came together with the Americans and the French to agree on the extent and timing of a devaluation of the franc and to refrain from any competitive devaluation in response to French action.[79] Together with the French, Britain and the United States also agreed to settle central bank balances in gold on a 24-hour basis at a price based on the going exchange rate of their currencies relative to the dollar, the only currency which now had a fixed value in relation to gold: the dollar was becoming slowly, but effectively, the *numéraire* of the system.[80] The Agreement was the smallest concession to American demands the British felt they could decently make; they were still determined to avoid committing themselves to a fixed rate of exchange for fear that this might have to be defended by high interest rates, and so ruin the cheap-money policy.

By 1938 rearmament and the fear of war were seriously affecting the balance of payments and inducing a flight from sterling to the dollar. Even in the mid-1930s, the balance of payments of the Sterling Area with the Dollar Area was rather precarious. Britain's own large deficit with the United States was offset by the dollar earnings of the mainly underdeveloped parts of the empire and by exports of South African gold to an apparently insatiable American Treasury. This balance could easily be disturbed, as in 1937–8, when a recession in

78. On exchange-rate policy see Howson, 'Sterling's Managed Float', passim, and Sayers, *Bank of England*, II, pp. 474–5. The advantages of the 1931 devaluation against the dollar were lost by early 1934 but, measured against all other currencies, the pound stayed below its 1929–30 level until 1936. John Redmond, 'An Indication of the Effective Exchange Rates of the Pound in the Nineteen Thirties', *Econ. Hist. Rev.*, 2nd ser. XXXIII (1980).

79. Blow-by-blow accounts of the origins of the Tripartite Agreement can be found in Drummond, *The Floating Pound and The Sterling Area*, Chs. 8 and 9; and idem, 'London, Washington and the Management of the Franc, 1936–9', (Princeton Studies in International Finance, No. 45, 1979). See also Stephen V.O. Clarke, 'Exchange Rate Stabilization in the Mid-1930s: Negotiating the Tripartite Agreement', (Princeton Studies in International Finance, No. 41, 1977); and Sayers, *The Bank of England*, II, pp. 475–81 and III, App. 28.

80. H. van B. Cleveland, 'The International Monetary System in the Inter-war Period', in Rowland, *Balance of Power or Hegemony*, pp. 53–6.

the United States led to a sharp cut-back in imports of empire commodities and put pressure on the sterling exchange rate.[81] Borrowing, together with rumours of war and the effects of preparations for war, which included heavy imports of supplies for the United States, meant dollar shortages and a recognition that, if war did break out, Britain's survival could well depend on her ability to borrow in the United States.[82] This could not be taken for granted: in Washington, Congress refused to allow loans to any nation which was in deficit on war debt – and Britain had stopped payment in 1934 – or any nation which was judged to be a belligerent in war.[83]

A need to keep on the right side of the American administration was the chief reason why Britain signed the Anglo-American reciprocity treaty in 1938.[84] Signing it did not imply that the British authorities had lost interest in the Ottawa agreements and were ready to dismantle the preferential system. Few concessions were made to American demands for entry into the British market and even these were made feasible only because Canada was willing to surrender some of her privileges in Britain in return for easier entry into the American market. Without Canada's flexibility, it is unlikely that a treaty would have been signed.[85] Britain stood by the preferential system and the delicate network of financial relations which held it together because, in the event of war, the system would be vital for survival. The direct benefits from easier trade conditions in the United States were few and the chief value of the agreement to Chamberlain and his government was political. The hope was that the agreement would signal to Hitler the unity of the democracies and deter him from further aggression, as well as increasing the chances of borrow-

81. Kreider, *The Anglo-American Trade Agreement*, pp. 69–70.

82. For an interesting contemporary analysis of this see Imre de Vegh, *The Pound Sterling: A Study of the Balance of Payments of the Sterling Area* (New York, 1939), pp. 69–70, 107–12.

83. The modification of the last-named restrictions in the Neutrality Act of 1937, which allowed for sales of armaments to belligerents on a 'cash and carry' basis, may be seen as a bid by the United States to capitalize on Britain's dependence. See Warren F. Kimball, 'Lend Lease and the Open Door: the Temptations of British Opulence, 1937–1942', *Political Science Quarterly*, LXXXVI (1971), p. 239.

84. A useful study of the 1938 Agreement, which places it in the context of Anglo-American relations in the 1930s, is R.N. Kottman, *Reciprocity and the North Atlantic Triangle, 1932–1938* (Ithaca, NY, 1958).

85. Kreider, *The Anglo-American Trade Agreement*, pp. 104–7; Ian M. Drummond and Norman Hillmer, 'A Shaft of Baltic Pine: Negotiating the Anglo-American-Canadian Trade Agreement of 1938', in Cottrell and Moggridge, *Money and Power*, p. 204. For a more detailed study see Ian M. Drummond and Norman Hillmer, *Negotiating Freer Trade: The United Kingdom, the United States, Canada and the Trade Agreements of 1938* (Waterloo, 1989).

ing in the United States.[86] It certainly implied no real trust in the Roosevelt administration, since the British authorities were well aware that the American campaign for reciprocity was rooted in a virulent hostility to the preferential system and to the imperialism which supposedly lay behind it.[87]

The lack of any real understanding or sympathy between the two great liberal powers was made plain during the sterling crisis which began early in 1938, even before Hitler's invasion of Austria. As sterling began to fall, the United States' reaction was to assume that the British were deliberately pushing down the rate in order to gain a competitive edge in export markets: it was hard for them to understand that the empire that they always believed was bursting with wealth, was actually chronically short of foreign exchange. Faced with the threat of retaliatory devaluation and worried about creating a bad impression in the United States when war seemed imminent, the British opted to hold the exchange rate up and allow their gold reserves to run down. Between the beginning of 1938 and the early months of 1939, Britain lost about half of her foreign exchange reserves to the United States.[88] By then, facing problems of inflation and labour unrest provoked by rearmament, and fearful that stringent controls would soon have to be placed on foreign exchange, there was a strong feeling in government circles that if Britain had to go to war at all, it were better sooner than later.[89]

Given the mutual suspicion and even hostility which existed between Britain and the United States, and the clear recognition in London that American help might be forthcoming only at the cost of emasculating the Sterling Area and accepting the 'open door' and the United States' economic supremacy,[90] it is no surprise that Chamberlain should have continued to put his efforts into reaching a settlement with Germany.[91] The exact rationale behind British foreign policy in

86. Drummond and Hillmer, 'A Shaft of Baltic Pine', pp. 205, 209. For a different perspective see Hans-Jürgen Schröder, 'The Ambiguities of Appeasement: Great Britain, the United States and Germany, 1937–9', in Mommsen and Kattenacker, *The Fascist Challenge*.

87. For an insight into the philosophy behind the American drive for reciprocity in the 1930s see A.W. Schatz, 'The Anglo-American Trade Agreement and Cordell Hull's Search for Peace', *Journal of American History*, 57 (1970–1).

88. R.A.C. Parker, 'The Pound Sterling, the American Treasury and British Preparations for War, 1938–9', *Eng. Hist. Rev.*, XCVIII (1983).

89. Parker, 'The Pound Sterling', p. 277; G.C. Peden, 'A Matter of Timing: the Economic Background to British Foreign Policy, 1938–1939', *History*, 69 (1984).

90. Callum A. MacDonald, *The United States, Britain and Appeasement, 1936–9* (1981), pp. 180–1.

91. For the 1938–9 discussions with German business circles and others, see Mac-Donald, 'Economic Appeasement and the German "Moderates", 1937–39', pp. 114–131.

1938–9 is not easy to determine. After the absorption of Austria – a move with which he had no particular quarrel – Chamberlain stressed that Britain would go to war if the empire were attacked or if the territory of France, Belgium, Portugal, Iraq or Egypt were violated. Of the last three, Portugal had a certain strategic naval significance; Iraq was important for oil; and Egypt was also of strategic and economic value and under strong British informal influence. All three were members of the Sterling Area and this connection with Britain was bolstered by loans.[92] On eastern and south-eastern Europe, the British clearly felt they could find some *modus vivendi* with the Germans. Subsequent events are open to an interpretation based on traditional concerns about the balance of power. Although Czechoslovakia was dismembered at Munich in return for solemn guarantees of peace from Hitler, this seemed 'reasonable' in London because British interests in Europe were affected only marginally; but further aggression in eastern Europe was unacceptable to Britain because it would give the Germans control over resources large enough to allow them to dominate Europe. On this reading, British policy in 1938–9 was similar to that of pre-1914.[93] Other historians stress that, even after Munich, the British were quite willing to see Germany acquire further territory as part of a general settlement, but finally had to oppose Hitler's use of force.[94]

Whatever interpretation is favoured, it remains true that after Munich, and right up until the outbreak of war, the British carried on trying to deter Germany from war by offering trading and financial concessions in return for political guarantees. It is very likely that Chamberlain's ultimate ambition was to secure a settlement which would stimulate European growth and keep Britain free from dependence on the United States: 'behind Chamberlain's idea for economic negotiations in 1938–9 may be seen the idea of a European Four-Power Directorate (Britain, France, Germany and Italy), serving to assure the continued prosperity and power of Europe in the face of

92. Holland, *The Commonwealth Alliance*, p. 201. On Britain's policy towards foreign loans to these countries and to other sensitive areas, including Greece, Turkey and China, see Simon Newman, *March 1939: The British Guarantee to Poland. A Study in the Continuity of British Foreign Policy* (Oxford, 1976), Chs. 3 and 4.

93. Newman, *March 1939*, pp. 107. This is compatible with the evidence concerning Britain's forceful policy in Romania, where control of oil was involved. See Philippe Marguerat, *Le IIIe Reich et le pétrole roumain, 1938–1940* (Geneva, 1977). For the considerable economic stake built up by Britain in south-east Europe after 1918 see Alicia Teichova, *An Economic Background to Munich* (Cambridge, 1974).

94. This is the view of David E. Kaiser, *Economic Diplomacy and the Origins of the Second World War: Germany, Britain, France and Eastern Europe* (Princeton, NJ, 1980).

the emerging superpowers',[95] that is, the United States and the Soviet Union. The United States certainly reacted with great alarm to these negotiations: Roosevelt believed that Chamberlain was 'attempting to engineer an Anglo-German money and trade deal . . . which would . . . exclude American trade from Europe, Africa and Latin America'.[96] Others in Washington spoke of the 'selfish City interests' intent upon carving up Europe at America's expense.[97]

Appeasement failed: the British assumed that German demands were rational and limited, whereas they proved to be irrational and boundless. As Chamberlain feared, war brought with it a severe challenge to the economic and social status quo. The war of 1914–18 had shaken gentlemanly capitalism in Britain; another war might extinguish it altogether by putting into question the whole social order on which gentlemanly capitalism had flourished. War also raised again, in a more menacing form, the prospect of a shift in the locus of economic power from the City to industry and organised labour, because when national survival was at stake, the role of the 'producing' part of the nation was much enhanced, as it had been during World War I.[98] At the same time, war would also bring the United States the economic dominance foreshadowed, but not fully achieved, between 1916 and 1918. In the early days of the war, the Chamberlain government did as much as it could to preserve the status quo. Mass mobilisation was deferred in the vain hope that it would not be necessary, and a fully fledged war economy was slow to appear. At the same time, exports were strongly encouraged in order to build up exchange reserves. The sudden fall of France in 1940 brought this phase of semi-commitment to an end. From then on the 'national interest' had, inevitably, to be defined in terms of full employment of all productive resources rather than financial orthodoxy regarding the position of sterling.[99] As early as 1940, Britain was desperately short of dollars and dependent upon American

95. Newman, *March 1939*, p. 7. See also John Charmley, *Chamberlain and the Lost Peace* (1989).

96. Watt, *Succeeding John Bull*, p. 81.

97. MacDonald, *The United States, Britain and Appeasement*, pp. 72–5; and idem, 'The United States, Appeasement and the Open Door', in Mommsen and Kattenacker, *The Fascist Challenge*, pp. 403–4.

98. There are some perceptive ideas on these themes in Schmidt, *The Politics and Economics of Appeasement*, and Maurice Cowling, *The Impact of Hitler* (1975).

99. On the coming of a war economy see Newton and Porter, *Modernization Frustrated*, pp. 90ff.

generosity for her survival.[100] By then she had fallen back on her 'special relationship' with the United States, preferring economic dependence upon her to military subjugation by Germany. This decision was

> essentially a response to weakness. Ever since the 1890s, the United States had seemed the least threatening of her competitors and, therefore, cutting her losses, the most attractive potential ally against the rest, especially given the similarities of language and culture.[101]

In 1939 the *Pax Britannica* was replaced by the *Pax Americana* and British gentlemanly capitalists had to adapt themselves once again, this time to serve under new masters. As they did so, however, they kept in view the prospect of 'educating' their dominant ally, and their determination to reinstate sterling and retain the empire remained strong, as we shall see.

100. Kimball, 'Lend Lease and the Open Door', pp. 240–3. Also idem, '"Beggar My Neighbour": America and the British Interim Financial Crisis, 1940–1941', *Jour. Econ. Hist.*, XXIX (1969).
101. David Reynolds, 'Competitive Co-operation: Anglo-American Relations in World War Two', *Hist. Jour.*, 23 (1980), p. 245.

PART THREE
The Wider World

CHAPTER SIX
Maintaining Financial Discipline: The Dominions, 1914–39

One of the best known themes in the history of the British empire between the wars is the steady movement of the white Dominions towards political independence.[1] The Balfour Report of 1926 gave birth to, and the Statute of Westminster in 1931 legally enshrined, the concept of equality of status between Britain and the major settlement colonies. But in many ways the notion of equality was no more than a polite fiction. All the white Dominions, save Canada, relied ultimately upon the power of Britain and her ability to defend them; Canada escaped this dependence only because she was protected by proximity to the United States.[2] In matters economic, the Dominions were similarly placed. Between the wars all of them were highly dependent for their prosperity on trade, despite tariff-aided import substitution during World War I and in the depression of the 1930s. Britain remained easily the most important trading partner of the Dominions throughout the period, the only exception being Canada, whose trade with the United States was of great importance (Table 6.1). The importance of the British market for Dominion exports diminished somewhat in the 1920s as the world struggled back to multilateralism and Britain made slow progress in comparison with her rivals. With the exception of South Africa, Britain's share increased again, dramatically, in the 1930s when depression struck

1. Good general histories include: R.F. Holland, *Britain and the Commonwealth Alliance, 1918–39* (1981); D. Judd and P. Slinn, *The Evolution of the Modern Commonwealth, 1902–1981* (1982); P.N.S. Mansergh, *The Commonwealth Experience* (1969); W.K. Hancock, *Survey of British Commonwealth Affairs*, Vol. I (Oxford, 1936) and Vol. II, Pt. I (Oxford, 1940), is also excellent despite being fifty years old.
2. J.G. Darwin, 'Imperialism in Decline? Tendencies in British Imperial Policy between the Wars', *Hist. Jour.*, 23 (1980), pp. 665–7. In this context see also the classic text by A.P. Thornton, *The Imperial Idea and its Enemies* (1959), pp. 196ff.

Table 6.1 Britain's share of Dominion trade, 1913–38 (per cent)

	1913	1929	1933	1938
Exports from				
Canada	49.8	25.3	39.6	39.1
Australia	45.4	38.1	47.4	56.2
New Zealand	84.1	75.0	87.3	84.7
South Africa	78.8	48.4		38.8
Imports into:				
Canada	21.3	15.1	24.3	17.5
Australia	52.3	39.7	41.3	42.1
New Zealand	61.1	46.1	51.3	47.8
South Africa	56.7	43.9		43.9

Sources: F. Capie, *Depression and Protectionism: Britain between the Wars* (Manchester, 1983), Table 2.9, p. 30; *Statistical Abstracts of the United Kingdom* (HMSO).

and the Ottawa system was set in place. Similarly, while reliance on British manufactured goods in the Dominions was weakened after the war, especially in Canada, the 1930s saw a modest reversal of the trend.

Behind trade lay finance: if anything, Dominion dependence on Britain in this sphere was greater than in the case of trade, although this has not been well recognised by historians. As we have already seen, the money supply in Australia, New Zealand and South Africa before 1914 was determined largely by the state of the London balances of their banks which depended, in turn, upon the level of exports and the ability to borrow. Borrowing from Britain had, of course, played a crucial part in the development of these colonies before the war. During the conflict, the London money market tap was turned off to a considerable degree; in the 1920s capital exports were low by pre-war standards, though the Dominions absorbed a larger share of them; in the 1930s they were reduced to a trickle. As a result, the Dominions were forced to rely more on their own savings for investment and growth, and local money markets developed accordingly.[3]

There is no doubt that after 1914 the Dominions became steadily aware of their own financial identity, not only because of greater self-reliance in terms of investment, but also because, for most of this period, Britain was not on the gold standard. Before 1914 the link

3. A.W.F. Plumptre, *Central Banking in the British Dominions* (Toronto, 1940), pp. 9–13.

between Australasian and South African currencies and London sterling, via the gold standard, was so close that it was difficult for the colonists to distinguish between them.[4] The floating of sterling from 1919 to 1925, and again after 1931, allowed for divergence; the precise relations between Dominion and British exchange rates became, for the first time, a matter of conscious management.[5] The Bank of England was quick to recognise the problem. In response, it encouraged the Dominions to establish central banks, which the Bank hoped would help to coordinate monetary policy in the empire, prevent embarrassing divergencies in exchange rates and make it easier for the Dominions to follow London if and when the gold standard was abandoned. Ideally, these peripheral central banks would be made in the Bank's own image, that is as essentially private institutions, free of government interference and independent in judgement, and able to exercise monetary control through their position as holders of the accounts of the government and of the local commercial banks. The Bank's great, if unspoken, fear was that, with 'automatic' discipline no longer possible and with increasing self-confidence in the Dominions, the role of the state in economic management on the white periphery would swell to intolerable proportions. In the worst case, radical governments might seize on central banks as ideal instruments for printing money to finance Utopian schemes. Inflation and economic collapse would be the inevitable result and the British trader and investor, whom the Bank had a duty to protect, would bear a considerable share of the burden. An independent status for central banks in the Dominions was thus regarded by the Bank as being a guarantee of sound money.

For their part, the Dominions recognised the importance of central banking in an age of managed currencies, and they were willing to take advice and even personnel from Threadneedle Street. On the other hand, in countries where the role of the state in economic development had been so much greater than was the case in Britain, it proved difficult to create effective central banking institutions by slavishly imitating the Bank of England. Moreover, Dominion governments and other interested parties were wary of imperial dominance and resented too much interference from London. Not surprisingly, what looked like independence to the Bank could seem like an arrogant metropolitan imposition when viewed from a colonial perspective.[6] In

4. G.R. Hawke, 'New Zealand and the Return to Gold in 1925', *Austral. Econ. Hist. Rev.*, XI (1971), p. 49.
5. Plumptre, *Central Banking in the British Dominions*, p. 13.
6. Ibid. Chs. VI and VII.

practice, this incipient clash between imperial and nationalist impulses did not matter much. With the exception of New Zealand in the late 1930s, Dominion governments followed an orthodox financial path. London balances remained of overwhelming importance to the money supply in all the Dominions save Canada. In the 1920s most governments still saw the ability to borrow in Britain as being vital to their country's development, and power remained in the hands of those who recognised the importance of the British economic connection and the need to satisfy London's criteria for sound financial management. After 1929, what bound the Dominions to London most effectively was the crushing weight of accumulated debt, when exports had collapsed and fresh loans were few and small. It has been noted that 'the Imperial Conference of 1930 resembled nothing so much as an interview between a bank manager and his improvident clients'.[7] The link connecting this crisis with the Ottawa preferential arrangements was a strong one for it was 'the prospect of a chain of defaults triggered in the first instance by primary producers overseas [which] seized the British of the need to shore up artificially the agricultural incomes of their closest partners'.[8]

The problems of the 1930s thus reinforced the financial dependence of the Dominions. We can see this most obviously in our first case study of Australia, the heaviest borrower in the 1920s and the most desperately indebted in the following decade. Then we look briefly at South Africa, whose dependence on British trade actually declined markedly in the inter-war period, but who could not shake off the dominance of London finance. Next, we examine New Zealand's belated and ultimately futile attempt, in the late 1930s, to break free of the restrictions imposed by membership of the Sterling Area. Lastly, we consider why it was that Canada, whose banking system did not depend on London sterling balances even before the war and who fell increasingly within the financial orbit of the United States in the 1920s, was tempted to join the Sterling Area in the worst years of depression.

THE AUSTRALIAN DEBT CRISIS

After 1914 the symbiotic relationship between London funds and the Australian money supply still held:

7. Darwin, 'Imperialism in Decline?', p. 664.
8. R.F. Holland, 'Imperial Collaboration and Great Depression: Britain, Canada and the Wheat Crisis, 1929–35', *Jour. Imp. and Comm. Hist.*, XVI (1988), p. 115.

London funds appear to be the barometer of the system: if they rose to unusually high levels, this was the signal for an expansion of credit, if they fell to unusually low levels, this was the signal for a contraction of credit.[9]

All the major Australian banks, like their counterparts in South Africa and New Zealand, were heavily engaged in the London market. Funds built up rapidly in London at certain times of the year because of the seasonality of pastoral and agricultural exports to Britain and drained back only slowly to Australia only to pay for the steadier flow of imports. In the mean time, the funds could be usefully employed either on the London Stock Exchange or in the discount market, with the result that the Australian banks were often responsive more to shifts in monetary policy and interest rates in Britain than they were to domestic conditions.[10] The banks tried to offset the effects of normal export seasonality on Australian credit and did not automatically respond to upward or downward shifts in metropolitan balances, but major changes in the latter were registered in Australia.[11] In 1921, for example, when imports rose with unusually rapidity, London balances fell sharply and the result was a severe, if temporary, contraction of credit in Australia.[12]

Despite the strength of the link between London finance and Australian credit – and the link was just as strong in the case of New Zealand and South Africa[13] – the British monetary authorities were anxious in the early 1920s to bring about a more conscious cooperation between themselves and Dominion bankers because, as we have seen, once sterling was floated after 1919, Dominion currencies and British sterling could diverge from each other more easily than in the past. At the 1923 Imperial Conference, the Dominions were urged to build up sterling balances in London, rather than hold gold reserves, in line with the Genoa proposals; the Bank of England also stressed the importance of monetary coordination and tried to promote central banking on traditional lines.[14] In the Australian case, this meant

9. F.D. Guiney, 'Money Supply and Australian Trading Banks, 1927–39', *Austral. Econ. Hist. Rev.*, XI (1971), p. 165. See also J.S.G. Wilson, 'The Australian Trading Banks', in R.S. Sayers, ed. *Banking in the British Commonwealth* (Oxford, 1952), pp. 20–2, 27–8.

10. A.J.S. Baster, *The Imperial Banks* (1929), pp. 215–17, 243–50.

11. Guiney, 'Money Supply and the Australian Trading Banks', p. 166.

12. A.H. Tocker, 'The Monetary Standards of Australia and New Zealand', *Econ. Jour.*, 34 (1924), p. 570.

13. On South Africa in this context see S.H. Frankel, 'The Situation in South Africa', *Economic Journal*, 43 (1933), p. 106.

14. Lyndhurst Falkiner Giblin, *The Growth of a Central Bank: The Development of the Commonwealth Bank of Australia, 1924–1945* (Melbourne, 1951), pp. 17–18.

encouraging the view that the Commonwealth Bank should take on wider responsibilities.

The Commonwealth Bank had begun life in 1911 as a state bank, promoted by the Labour Party, trade unionists and other nationalists who were distrustful of the trading banks and their London connections and wished to see the new bank offer cheap credit as a challenge to the traditional 'money power'. But by the early 1920s the Commonwealth Bank's influence rested mainly upon its position as banker to the federal government, a role much enhanced during the war.[15] Despite its origins, the Bank was also fierce in its devotion to orthodoxy, sometimes to an extent which even London found uncomfortable to live with. In 1923–4, with Australian exports riding high and the banks flush with funds in London, the Bank used its newly won control over the note issue to slow down the expansion of credit in Australia. Its main aim was to keep the Australian pound high with a view to an early return to the gold standard, which the Australians had abandoned in 1919 along with Britain. Since, at that time, London sterling was under pressure and falling against gold, a gap emerged between the value of the Australian pound and sterling. This development was embarrassing to the British, who were still extolling the virtues of a gold-exchange standard and who expected colonials to follow London's financial lead at all times.[16] But the outcome of the crisis was satisfactory to Britain. In 1924 new legislation prompted the Commonwealth Bank to allow a greater flexibility in the note issue. At the same time it received some of the powers of a central bank, including a measure of control over the reserves of the commercial banks and the right to discount their bills. The control over bank reserves was very limited and the Australian bill market small and immature, so the gain in authority was more theoretical than real: the trading banks still relied on London as the only market liquid enough to place their spare funds. But the 1924 regulations did indicate that politicians on the right of centre in Australia, who valued the British connection highly, were eager to

15. For the early history of the Bank see Peter Love, *Labour and the Money Power* (Melbourne, 1984), Ch. 2; R. Gollan, *The Commonwealth Bank of Australia: Origins and Early History* (Canberra, 1968); Giblin, *The Growth of a Central Bank*, pp. 2–6; Baster, *The Imperial Banks*, pp. 145ff; Plumptre, *Central Banking in the British Dominions*, pp. 86–8.

16. Giblin, *The Growth of a Central Bank*, pp. 6–13; Gollan, *The Commonwealth Bank of Australia*, p. 157; Geoffrey Blainey, *Gold and Paper: A History of the National Bank of Australia* (Melbourne, 1958), p. 313.

try to model their own system of monetary management on London practice.[17]

In the late 1920s liaison between the Commonwealth Bank and the Bank of England was close and the latter was not slow to offer advice.[18] The Commonwealth Bank was too competitive with the trading banks for the Bank of England's taste, but it did show a pleasing independence of government, despite governmental influence on its directorate, and demonstrated the same deep suspicions of politically motivated financial extravagance as animated the Old Lady herself.[19] This was not, perhaps, too surprising in a country where wealth based on primary export, and its commercial and banking connections, was such a dominant force.[20]

Australian exports suffered during the war, which had drastic effects on shipping space and freights.[21] Government and banks had to help out with loans and in some cases, especially wool, the British authorities were content to buy up Australia's produce and let her set the price; but these were unusual circumstances.[22] The decline in exports was the chief reason for a wartime fall in Australian income,[23] but exports recovered in the post-war boom and, in the 1920s, the traditional assumption 'for which in the post-war period there was almost a national consensus', that the British market remained the key to Australian economic success was not disturbed.[24] Economic

17. Giblin, *The Growth of a Central Bank*, pp. 13–23; Gollan, *The Commonwealth Bank of Australia*, Ch. 10; Baster, *The Imperial Banks*, pp. 162–5; J.S.G. Wilson, 'The Commonwealth Bank of Australia', in Sayers, *Banking in the British Commonwealth*, pp. 39–44; Plumptre, *Central Banking in the British Dominions*, pp. 88–91; Love, *Labour and the Money Power*, esp. pp. 84–7.

18. Giblin, *The Growth of a Central Bank*, pp. 37–46. See also the article by Sir Ernest Harvey, Comptroller of the Bank of England, in the *Economic Record*, 3 (1927). Harvey visited Australia to give advice in that year.

19. On the conservatism of bankers in general in Australia see C.B. Schedvin, *Australia and the Great Depression: A Study of Economic Development and Policy in the 1920s and 1930s* (Sydney, 1970), pp. 76–87. On independence from government see Giblin, *The Growth of a Central Bank*, pp. 50–1.

20. W.D. Rubinstein, 'The Top Wealth Holders of New South Wales, 1817-1939', *Austral. Econ. Hist. Rev.*, XX (1980), esp. pp. 148–50.

21. N.G. Butlin, Alan Barnard and J.J. Pincus, *Government and Capitalism: Public and Private Choice in Twentieth-Century Australia* (Sydney, 1982), p. 76.

22. Kosmas Tsokhas, 'W.M. Hughes, the Imperial Wool Purchases and the Pastoral Lobby, 1914–20', *Jour. Imp. and Comm. Hist.*, XVII (1989), tries to generalise about Anglo-Australian economic relationships, and in particular to deny the imperial element in them, on the basis of the wartime experience of wool sales without sufficiently considering the uniqueness of the times.

23. Stuart McIntyre, *Oxford History of Australia, 1901–1942*, Vol. IV (Oxford, 1986), p. 155.

24. W.H. Richmond, 'S.M. Bruce and Australian Economic Policy', *Austral. Econ. Hist. Rev.*, XXIII (1983), pp. 239–40. For interpretations of the 1914–29 period see M.

development in the 1920s was very much on pre-war lines. Resources were concentrated on extending the agrarian frontier to make space for a larger population and, simultaneously, to improve Australia's export performance. Rising incomes on the frontier would provide the stimulus to industry and services in the cities and guarantee balanced growth.[25] To implement this ambitious programme, the Australians required large-scale immigration and a considerable inflow of new capital to create the infrastructure needed on the new frontiers. In the event, export growth was slow in the 1920s: the world market for primary produce was sluggish and Britain's own tardy progress limited the expansion of demand.[26] Despite enthusiastic support for the Empire Settlement Act, the flow of immigrants never reached pre–1913 proportions.[27] Moreover, rapid development led to rising imports, a rise only marginally slowed by the progress of heavily protected, high-cost Australian industry.[28]

To pay for these imports Australians borrowed extensively in Britain;[29] overseas debt repayment rose from 17 per cent of export

Dunn, *Australia and the Empire: From 1788 to the Present* (Sydney, 1984); Peter Cochrane, *Industrialization and Dependence: Australia's Road to Economic Development, 1870–1939* (St Lucia, 1980), and Barrie Dyster and David Meredith, *Australia in the International Economy in the Twentieth Century* (Cambridge, 1990), Ch. 5.

25. W.A. Sinclair, *The Process of Economic Development in Australia* (1976), pp. 175–81; McIntyre, *Oxford History of Australia*, Vol. IV, Chs. 9 and 10; Richmond, 'S.M. Bruce and Australian Economic Policy', *passim*. Compare this with the import-substitution phase during the world war described by Sinclair on pp. 172–4.

26. E.A. Boehm, 'Australia's Economic Depression of the 1930s', *Economic Record*, 49 (1973), p. 609.

27. D.H. Pope, 'The Contours of Australian Immigration, 1901–30', *Austral. Econ. Hist. Rev.*, XXI (1981), esp. Table 1. For the imperial context see Ian M. Drummond, *British Economic Policy and the Empire, 1919–39* (1972), Ch. 2, and above p. 56.

28. Schedvin, *Australia and the Great Depression*, pp. 51–62; but cf. Boehm, 'Australia's Economic Depression of the 1930s', pp. 615–21. See also Butlin, Barnard and Pincus, *Government and Capitalism*, pp. 88–9.

29. The Commonwealth government also borrowed heavily in Britain during the war. See Dyster and Meredith, *Australia in the International Economy*, Table 5.3, p. 92. After 1914 Australians were just beginning to think in terms of borrowing elsewhere, but very little was achieved in this regard. During the war there was some talk, at both state and Commonwealth levels, of tapping the New York market. The Commonwealth government tried hard to suppress this initiative because it feared that, if the states could find new sources of finance, the Commonwealth government's fight against wartime inflation would be made more difficult. It is also doubtful whether money could have been raised on Wall Street at the time. See Bernard Attard, 'Politics, Finance and Anglo-Australian Relations: Australian Borrowing in London, 1914–1920', *Australian Journal of Politics and History*, 35 (1989), pp. 152–6. In 1921 the Queensland Labour government went further. It came to London to borrow but found the City hostile because Queensland pastoralists, who objected to local Labour Party legislation, had managed to convince the City that the proposed loans were risky. Labour responded by successfully raising funds in New York. But this proved an expensive

Table 6.2 Balance of payments: Australia, 1909–39 (quinquennial averages, £m.)[a]

	Balance of trade	Overseas debt payments	Other invisibles	Current account balance[b]	Overseas debt as % of exports
1909–13	+17.8	−15.0	−3.1	−0.3	19.3
1919–20/1923–24	+18.4	−27.8	−8.6	−18.0	20.3
1924–25/1928–29	+6.9	−36.1	−10.6	−39.8	25.1
1929–30/1933–34	+29.9	−40.1	−6.4	−16.6	38.7
1934–35/1938–39	+35.7	−38.4	−9.6	−12.3	27.6

Source: I.W. McLean, 'The Australian Balance of Payments on Current Account, 1901 to 1964–5', *Australian Economic Papers*, 7 (1968), pp. 83–6. For similar estimates see Butlin, *Australian Domestic Product, Investment and Foreign Borrowing*, Pt. IV, Ch. XXXI.

Notes: [a] We have included gold production in exports throughout and not treated it as an invisible item.

[b] Balance of trade plus overseas debt repayments plus other invisibles.

income in 1920 to 28 per cent by the end of the decade (Table 6.2).[30] Between 1925 and 1928 Australian borrowings accounted for over two-fifths of all overseas flotations in London;[31] Australian 'extravagance' – often involving state rather than federal spending – was the talk of the City of London. In 1929 the Bank of England was urging moderation on the Australians, much to the annoyance of local politicians of all shades of opinion, who felt that the Bank already had too much

business: by 1924 the government had compromised with its wool barons and it then found the City more obliging. On this episode, see: Gollan, *The Commonwealth Bank of Australia*, pp. 151–2; McIntyre, *Oxford History of Australia*, IV, pp. 231–2; B.C. Schedvin, 'G. Theodore and the London Pastoral Lobby', *Politics*, 6 (1971); Love, *Australia and the Money Power*, pp. 78–91. There were some successful attempts to organise state borrowings in New York in the late 1920s. On this see Dyster and Meredith, *Australia in the International Economy*, p. 119.

30. These figures are based upon statistics gathered by I.W. McLean, 'The Australian Balance of Payments on Current Account, 1901 to 1964–5', *Australian Economic Papers*, 7 (1968), pp. 84–7, and summarised in Table 6.2. Similar figures are given in Schedvin, *Australia and the Great Depression*, Table 13, p. 73, and in Dyster and Meredith, *Australia in the International Economy*, Table 5.10, p. 108. D. Clark, 'The Closed Book? The Debate on Causes', in Judy Mackinolty, ed. *The Wasted Years: Australia's Great Depression* (Sydney, 1981), offers rather lower ratios but they follow similar trends over time (p. 23). Dyster and Meredith show that public authorities' foreign debts rose from £364m. in 1918 to £631m. in 1929, with the states being the chief borrowers (Table 5.3, p. 93).

31. Schedvin, *Australia and the Great Depression*, Table 15, p. 100 and Ch. V. passim.

influence.[32] By the time of the Wall Street crash, the Australians were effectively borrowing to pay interest on previous loans, and the problem was compounded because a great deal of the borrowing was on overdraft and other forms of short-term credit and was difficult to roll over in a crisis.[33] Little wonder that the Australians were at the forefront of demands that Britain should offer the Dominions preferences in their markets for, without this particular boon, the development strategy of the 1920s was incomplete and potentially disastrous.

Disaster struck in 1929, when a mild upswing in the economy from a low point in 1926–7 was completely aborted by the rapid drop in export prices, which fell by 23 per cent between 1929 and 1930 and continued to fall heavily for the next three years.[34] The collapse in export income, combined with an inability to borrow, caused a drastic shrinkage in London funds and, after an interval,[35] a severe credit squeeze, a slump in imports and a cut in output, though, in real terms, the fall in the latter was not as severe as in the 1890s.[36] One immediate outcome of the collapse in the export sector was a crisis in overseas loan repayments, which was made much more acute by the short-term nature of much of the debt (Table 6.2).[37]

The problem of the floating debt was sufficiently serious in 1930 to attract the attention of the Bank of England, which was still fighting to keep Britain on the gold standard and feared the effect of default or deferment of debt payment on the position of sterling. The Labour

32. Richmond, 'S.M. Bruce and Australian Economic Policy', pp. 247–8; Clark, 'The Closed Book?', pp. 19–21; Schedvin, *Australia and the Great Depression*, pp. 103–4.

33. Schedvin, *Australia and the Great Depression*, p. 7; W.K. Hancock, 'Forty Years On', *Aus. Econ. Hist. Rev.*, XXII (1972–3), p. 73.

34. T.J. Valentine, 'The Course of the Depression in Australia', *Explorations in Economic History*, 24 (1987), p. 47. Besides Valentine and Schedvin there are valuable studies of the depression in: Boehm, 'Australia's Economic Depression of the 1930s'; W.A. Sinclair, 'Economic Development and Fluctuations in Australia in the 1930s', *Economic Record*, 51 (1975) (together with a reply by Boehm); Clark, 'The Closed Book?', and idem, 'Fools and Madmen', in Mackinolty, *The Wasted Years*. See also R.G. Gregory and N.G. Butlin, eds. *Recovery from the Depression: Australia and the World Economy in the 1930s* (Cambridge, 1989), and Dyster and Meredith, *Australia in the International Economy*, Ch. 6. There is an excellent discussion of the political economy of the crisis in McIntyre, *Oxford History of Australia*, IV, Ch. 11, and Love, *Australia and the Money Power*, Ch. 5.

35. Hancock, 'Forty Years On', p. 78. See also Schedvin, *Australia and the Great Depression*, pp. 204–10, which indicates the extent to which the banking system tried to delay the impact of falling London balances on Australian credit.

36. For G.D.P. figures see N.G. Butlin, *Australian Domestic Product, Investment and Foreign Borrowing, 1861–1938–9* (Cambridge, 1962), Table 13, p. 33. For comparisons with other countries' experiences, see Dyster and Meredith, *Australia in the International Economy*, Table 4.1, p. 84.

37. Schedvin, *Australia and the Great Depression*, pp. 90–1, 112–15.

government in Australia, elected to federal power in 1929, was also anxious to secure Bank of England aid in the immediate crisis,[38] and to help discipline state governments whose loan expenditures had been high in the previous decade. The outcome was a visit to Australia in 1930 by one of the Bank's leading figures, Sir Otto Niemeyer.[39] His recommendations were frigidly orthodox: Australia must deflate to keep imports down and take a cut in living standards in order to improve competitiveness in world markets and retain financial credibility which, in his view, also meant adhering to free trade and staying on gold.[40] But, in 1930, higher tariffs and quota restrictions to reduce imports, and a heavy devaluation of the Australian pound against sterling, proved inevitable.[41] Nonetheless, the banks, including the Commonwealth Bank – grateful for Niemeyer's moral backing, which it had actively sought[42] – hesitated over devaluation, were wholeheartedly in favour of meeting the crisis through deflation and balanced budgets, and were keen to head off any attempt by Labour to mitigate it by a wholesale creation of domestic credit.[43] The urge to strive for a solution to the monetary crisis which London would approve stemmed from the fact that 'it was important to impress Niemeyer with the financial orthodoxy of both the government and the banks, for assistance from the Bank of England and the future of Australian credit in London depended on his report'.[44]

38. Ibid. pp. 132–5.
39. We have learned a great deal about the origins of the Niemeyer visit from Bernard Attard, 'The Origins of the Niemeyer Mission: Anglo-Australian Financial Relations, 1921–1930', a paper read at the Sir Robert Menzies Centre for Australian Studies in the Institute of Commonwealth Studies, 24 May 1989. See also Schedvin, *Australia and the Great Depression*, pp. 134–7. Niemeyer's activities in South America are noted below, pp. 160, 166.
40. For Niemeyer's recommendations see Schedvin, *Australia and the Great Depression*, pp. 181–5. Also Peter Love, 'Niemeyer's Australian Diary and other English Records of his Mission', *Historical Studies*, 20 (1982–3), p. 261; Giblin, *The Growth of a Central Bank*, pp. 83–4; Love, *Australia and the Money Power*, pp. 100–1; Dyster and Meredith, *Australia in the International Economy*, pp. 135–6; E.D.G. Shann and D.B. Copland, eds. *The Crisis in Australian Finance, 1929–31* (Sydney, 1931), pp. 18–29.
41. On devaluation see Schedvin, *Australia and the Great Depression*, pp. 155–68, and on tariffs, pp. 141–4. The latter are also discussed in Butlin, Barnard and Pincus, *Government and Capitalism*, pp. 89–92.
42. Schedvin, *Australia and the Great Depression*, p. 135. The banks with London head offices resisted devaluation because they disliked 'the prospect of incurring substantial capital losses on their Australian assets'. The major 'local' bank, the Bank of New South Wales, was more worried about the effects of a high exchange rate on their customers. See M.W. Butlin and P.M. Boyce, 'Monetary Policy in Depression and Recovery', in Gregory and Butlin, *Recovery from the Depression*, pp. 201–4.
43. Ibid. pp. 183–4.
44. Ibid. p. 161. On this issue see also Neville Cain, 'Recovery Policy in Australia,

In the event, the Bank of England did not offer the Australians immediate assistance to overcome their funding problem, but this only gave the representatives of orthodoxy, particularly the Commonwealth Bank, even greater cause to urge on the federal and state governments the need for monetary discipline of the kind finally espoused in the Premiers' Plan of 1931.[45] In the course of the crisis, the Commonwealth Bank's authority grew significantly. Its control over the trading banks increased greatly in 1930, when the Mobilisation Agreement brought their gold reserves under Commonwealth Bank control as part of the attempt to ensure that Australia's obligations in London were met.[46] The Bank also took on a much more strategic position within Australian finance in the early 1920s through its issue of Treasury bills, which helped the federal government over its immediate financial problems and produced an asset which the Commonwealth Bank could use to influence the liquidity and credit-creating power of the trading banks.[47] It was strong enough, too, with help both from the trading banks and the Bank of England, to see off an attempt, by Labour in 1930, to turn the Commonwealth Bank into a simple commercial concern and to hand over its main public functions to a new state-controlled bank;[48] and it led the chorus of complaint which ruled out the possibility of a mildly reflationary economic package being adopted by Labour in 1931.[49]

The pursuit of deflation provoked immense antagonism especially

1930–2: Certain Native Wisdom', *Austral. Econ. Hist. Rev.*, 23 (1987), p. 202; and the statement by the Chairman of the Loan Council in February 1930, printed in Shann and Copland, *The Crisis in Australian Finance*, p. 10.

45. On the Premiers' Plan see Schedvin, *Australia and the Great Depression*, pp. 7–9, 244ff; Love, *Australia and the Money Power*, pp. 124–6. For recent debates on policy see Butlin and Boyce, 'Monetary Policy in the Depression and Recovery', and J. Pincus, 'Australia's Budgetary Policy in the 1930s', both in Gregory and Butlin, *Recovery from the Depression*. Dyster and Meredith claim that the premiers were 'overawed by the crisis [and] by the authority of the Bank of England'. See *Australia in the International Economy*, p. 137.

46. Ibid. pp. 8, 136–9; Giblin, *The Growth of a Central Bank*, pp. 69–70.

47. Giblin, *The Growth of a Central Bank*, pp. 121ff; Schedvin, *Australia and the Great Depression*, pp. 196–201; Dyster and Meredith, *Australia in the International Economy*, pp. 139–40.

48. Giblin, *The Growth of a Central Bank*, pp. 107–15; Schedvin, *Australia and the Great Depression*, pp. 172–6.

49. On Theodore's proposal and the opposition it aroused see Love, 'Niemeyer's Australian Diary', pp. 263–4; idem, *Australia and the Money Power*, pp. 114ff; Schedvin, *Australia and the Great Depression*, pp. 226–7, 239–43.Clark, 'Fools and Madmen', pp. 185ff, sees the plan in the context of other criticisms of orthodoxy. See also Cain, 'Recovery Policy in Australia', passim, and T.J. Valentine, 'The Battle of the Plans: A Macroeconomic Model of the Inter-War Economy', in Gregory and Butlin, *Recovery from the Depression*.

from organised labour, which saw Niemeyer as 'the Jewish bailiff from the Bank of England who had been sent to force down Australian living standards so that foreign bondholders might get their pound of flesh',[50] and regarded the Australian bankers as evil collaborators in this process. In New South Wales the Labour government went so far as to threaten to reschedule overseas debts and reduce interest payments unilaterally, and there was angry, if vague, talk of default.[51] But these forces could not hold out against the enormous range of interests, political and economic, which looked to Britain and the international economy as the main support for Australian development. The Labour government, torn between imperial and nationalist ideologies, collapsed in 1931, with one section joining more conservative political groupings to form a national government devoted, among other things, to sound money.[52] Just as disputes over financing government broke Labour in Britain and led to the formation of a National Government, so similar disputes, based on competing ideologies, shattered a Labour government in Australia and put in power those who still saw Australia's relationship with Britain as a central fact of policy. As the leading authority on the depression has argued, 'the struggle to avoid default on public obligations underpins the entire history of the depression'.[53]

Economic policy followed traditional lines in the 1930s and the Commonwealth Bank, which was more or less in tune with the Bank of England in the crises of 1929–32,[54] used its enhanced influence to ensure that an internationalist frame of reference was retained in economic and financial affairs. In the 1930s the Commonwealth Bank had greater influence over the exchange rate than hitherto and even

50. Love, 'Niemeyer's Australian Diary', p. 262. See also Schedvin, *Australia and the Great Depression*, pp. 186–7, 191–2. For trade union reactions see Shann and Copland, *The Crisis in Australian Finance*, pp. 58–61.

51. Clark, 'Fools and Madmen', p. 188; Schedvin, *Australia and the Great Depression*, pp. 186–8, 233–5, 269–70, 251–4; Love, *Australia and the Money Power*, pp. 104–7, 115–16; also Shann and Copland, *The Crisis in Australian Finance*, p. 182.

52. Schedvin, *Australia and the Great Depression*, esp. Ch. XIII. Lang's radical government in New South Wales was defeated at the polls in 1932. See Love, *Australia and the Money Power*, pp. 129–31; and Dyster and Meredith, *Australia in the International Economy*, pp. 143–4. For some insight into the tensions within the Labour Party in Australia see Shann and Copland, *The Crisis in Australian Finance*, pp. 61–5.

53. Schedvin, *Australia and the Great Depression*, p. 3. See also Butlin and Boyce 'Monetary Policy in Depression and Recovery', pp. 205–7. It has recently been argued that the defeat of even mildly reflationary measures demonstrates 'how much more important than elected ministries a determined coalition of domestic and foreign investors could be'. Dyster and Meredith, *Australia in the International Economy*, p. 140.

54. The Bank of England's approval of its Dominion counterpart is clear from Sayers, *The Bank of England*, I, p. 207.

hankered after restoring parity between the Australian pound and sterling, although it had, in practice, to accept that the Australian currency was actually pegged to sterling at the rate of £A125 to £100 sterling.[55] It is noticeable too, that in occasional moments of difficulty, the Bank of England was willing to help the Australians to maintain this rate, in contrast to its rigid policy in 1929–30, when Australia was wrestling with its short-term debt problem.[56] The Commonwealth Bank was also keen to phase Treasury bills out of the system once the worst of the depression was over because it saw them as being inflationary.[57] In doing this, it was, consciously or not, probably hindering the development of a separate Australian money market and enhancing the influence of London on the Australian financial system. It was, in short, offering just the sort of cooperation Norman, Stamp and other prominent money men in England hoped to elicit from the maturing Dominions once sterling had to be managed.[58]

In their struggle to retain the status quo in political economy and to fend off nationalist solutions to the depression, Australia's outward-looking and British-oriented elites were significantly helped by the Ottawa system. This gave the Australians a secure niche in the British market, especially for meat, fruit and dairy produce;[59] in return, Australia made relatively few concessions to British exporters. Faced with shrinking world markets and a drying up of loans, Australia needed significant help in the British market while keeping a tight control of imports because, as the chief colonial debtor, she had few other ways of generating the export surplus

55. Schedvin, *Australia and the Great Depression*, pp. 359–65. See also Giblin, *The Growth of a Central Bank*, pp. 136–50; Cain, 'Recovery Policy in Australia', pp. 209–11.

56. Giblin, *The Growth of a Central Bank*, pp. 142–3.

57. Ibid. pp. 159ff; Schedvin, *Australia and the Great Depression*, pp. 330–7. Schedvin notes that the funding of deficits meant that the funding policy succeeded in stabilising the amount of Treasury bills on the market only from 1932 (p. 337). See also Plumptre, *Central Banking in the British Dominions*, pp. 249–50, 322–14; and Butlin and Boyce, 'Monetary Policy in Depression and Recovery', pp. 208–11.

58. It is worth noting here that officials of the Commonwealth Bank tried to insist on the trading banks keeping a fixed proportion of their reserves with the Bank. This arrangement might have given the Commonwealth Bank greater indirect control over the London balances because these would have had to be run down to build up reserves with the Bank. But the Bank's policy was part of an internal power struggle with the commercial sector rather than a device to reduce the power of the London market over Australian finance. See Plumptre, *Central Banking in the British Dominions*, pp. 272–7.

59. Besides Drummond's comprehensive studies, see also R. Duncan, 'Imperial Preference: the Case of Australian Beef in the 1930s', *Economic Record*, 39 (1963), and Forrest Capie, 'Australian and New Zealand Competition in the British Market, 1920–1939', *Austral. Econ. Hist. Rev.*, XVIII (1978).

necessary to pay her obligations. In 1928 exports and imports of goods were both equal to about 18 per cent of Australia's national income, and her additional invisible payments, for debt-service and invisibles such as shipping, could be met only by borrowing. By 1937, when income per head had recovered the 1928 level, exports were still equivalent to 18 per cent of national income. Ottawa probably had a lot to do with this: Australian exports to Britain were higher in value terms in 1934–8 than they had been in 1925–9 despite heavy falls in the prices of primary produce (Table 6.3). In contrast, imports in 1937 were equivalent to only 13 per cent of national income and the rise in the trade surplus, together with some further borrowing, gave Australia the means to meet her invisible commitments more easily (Table 6.3). In Australia itself, the gap created by the suppression of imports was filled by domestic manufactures, aided by high tariffs and the devalued Australian pound.[60] The chief losers here were British manufacturers: Britain's exports to Australia were much lower in 1934–8 than they had been in the late 1920s (Table 6.3). Keeping Australia as a fully functioning member of the Sterling Area in the 1930s meant that her industrialisation was encouraged at

Table 6.3 British trade with the Dominions, 1909–38 (quinquennial averages, £m.)

		1909–13	*1925–29*	*1934–38*
Canada	Exports[a]	24.5	34.3	25.2
	Imports	27.2	60.6	72.3
	Balance of trade	−2.7	−26.3	−47.1
Australia	Exports[a]	33.8	61.1	23.4
	Imports	36.9	59.2	61.8
	Balance of trade	−3.1	+1.9	−38.4
New Zealand	Exports[a]	10.2	22.1	16.6
	Imports	19.4	47.9	43.8
	Balance of trade	−9.2	−25.8	−27.2
South Africa	Exports[a]	21.3	33.0	37.1
	Imports	10.7	22.7	14.3
	Balance of trade	+10.6	+10.3	+22.8

Source: B.R. Mitchell and P. Deane, *Abstract of British Historical Statistics* (Cambridge, 1962).
Note: [a] Exports include re-exports.

60. Schedvin, *Australia and the Great Depression*, p. 377; Mark Thomas, 'Manufacturing in Economic Recovery in Australia, 1932–1937', in Butlin and Gregory, *Recovery from the Depression*.

Britain's expense. Had the Australians not been able to meet the crisis in this way, the landed exporters, and the commercial and financial interests in the urban areas to which they were tied, might have lost faith in the British connection and would have found it extremely difficult to resist the claims of those who demanded a more radical and a more inward-looking solution to Australia's economic difficulties.[61]

Antipodean politicians were always inclined to adopt an over-confident attitude towards the parent concern and frequently assumed, in the most aggressive manner, a right to favourable economic treatment.[62] They often claimed that preferences were no more than their due: had they not been offering Britain preferences in their market for years? They were also adept at identifying their own interests with imperial ones. At the time of Ottawa, 'the dominant feature was the conviction of Australian governments that their own interests were equivalent to imperial interests and that, since it was the duty of British governments to uphold imperial interests, it should do what Australian governments told it to do'.[63] In reality, of course, Australia was only one element, albeit an important one presenting special problems, within a complex, and still cosmopolitan, British financial and trading system. Once Ottawa had been put in place, the Australians were reminded, sometimes rudely, of the limits of their position. In 1933, for example, the federal government demanded a massive conversion of its loans to lower rates of interest, once cheap money had been established in Britain, and vague threats that default or unilateral reductions of interest payments might take place if Australian needs were not met were uttered, sometimes by prominent and respected men. The British response was cool: they had their own conversion operations under way and these took priority. They also knew that Australia was too dependent to take drastic action. The Dominion continued to borrow in London, though at a much reduced rate, throughout the 1930s. This facility, and the conversion operation, were possible only because Australians were seen in

61. Schedvin, *Australia and the Great Depression*, pp. 373–5, for some general reflections on Australian financial orthodoxy. It may be worth noting here that, if the effects of devaluation are added to the tariff change of the early 1930s, protection against British imports was higher in 1939 than in 1930, despite Ottawa. Butlin, Barnard and Pincus, *Government and Capitalism*, p. 91.
62. J.D.B. Miller, 'An Empire that Don't Care What You Do', in F.W. Madden and W. Morris-Jones, eds. *Australia and Britain: Studies in a Changing Relationship* (1980), pp. 92–4.
63. Ibid. p. 99.

London to have responded to the crisis in the correct manner.[64] Conversion duly took place, but at a pace dictated by the British.[65] It brought much needed relief: annual debt payments fell from £28.4m. in 1930 to just over £20m. by 1939.[66]

On the trade front the Australians also found, in the latter half of the decade, that Britain was unwilling to give them the special place in the British market that they felt they deserved. Danes and Argentines were found seats at the British table, as well as the true sons of empire. Worse still, in 1936, when the Australians diverted trade from Japan and the United States towards Britain in the hope of winning further concessions from London, all they received was retaliation from an angry Japan.[67] No other episode in Anglo-Australian relations in the 1930s reveals better the essentials of the economic relationship between them:

> What seems to have lain behind the trade diversion policy was a numb fear in official quarters in Australia that if they allowed Japan to rout Lancashire in the sale of textiles to Australia, then they would be subjected by the government of the United Kingdom to a further substantial contraction of the British market for all types of agricultural produce.[68]

Lancashire was pleased, but the Australians accorded cotton too much importance. Seen from London, it was necessary for Australia to maintain her trade with Japan because this had a significant bearing on Australia's financial relations with Britain:

64. Pincus, 'Australian Budgetary Policy in the 1930s', p. 177. In this context, Keynes's comments on the Australian debt problem in 1932 are worth remembering. He admitted that 'Australia has heavily overborrowed in the past and I have often advised that her securities be avoided'. But now, he claimed, London 'profoundly appreciates' the Australian determination 'to fulfil her bond'. In the coming era of 'ultra-cheap money', he felt that London would soon resume her position as an overseas lender and that 'respectable borrowers will be greatly sought after. . . .'. And why should not Australia be one of these? It lies within her power'. *Collected Works of John Maynard Keynes*, XXI (Cambridge, 1982), pp. 99–100.
65. Neville Cain and Sean Glynn, 'Imperial Relations under Strain: the British–Australian Debt Contretemps of 1933', *Austral. Econ. Hist. Rev.*, XXV (1985); see also Drummond, *The Floating Pound and the Sterling Area*, pp. 115–18.
66. Pincus, 'Australian Budgetary Policy in the 1930s', p. 184.
67. John B. O'Brien, 'Australia–British Relations during the 1930s', *Historical Studies*, 22 (1987), pp. 582–3; D.C.S. Sissons, 'Manchester v Japan: the Imperial Background of the Australian Trade Diversion Dispute with Japan, 1936', *Australian Outlook*, 30 (1976).
68. N.F. Hall, '"Trade Diversion" – An Australian Interlude', *Economica*, new ser., 5 (1938), p. 7. The episode is also treated by K.H. Burley, *British Shipping and Australia, 1920–1939* (Cambridge, 1968), pp. 135–44, and is seen from an Australian domestic perspective in Kosmas Tsokhas, 'The Wool Industry and the Trade Diversion Dispute with Japan', *Hist. Stud.*, 23 (1989).

> Whatever might be the resentments of British manufacturers at the advance of competitors in the Australian market, British bondholders and the financial guardians of the British balance of payments had a desire that Australia should not default on her debt. And it was only by maintaining reasonable relations with her foreign trading partners that Australia could accumulate with some of them (and notably with Japan) the surpluses which she must thereafter transfer to London.[69]

Equally humbling to Australian pride was the Anglo-American Trade Agreement of 1938. To facilitate the Agreement, Australia was forced to give up a few privileges in Britain and to loosen restrictions on imports from the United States. In this respect, Australia was a 'sacrificial lamb' making an accord possible: 'she had surrendered preferences in the British market, ended trade diversions and made concessions to Canada and in return received nothing except faint praise for aiding the cause of world peace'.[70] By then, the Australians were grudgingly recognising that the intricate network of British overseas commitments made it impossible for the latter to go to endless lengths to satisfy the needs of Australian exporters.[71] By the mid-1930s the financial crisis which had given Australia her particular importance in the early days of world depression, had been mitigated through a combination of financial orthodoxy and the Ottawa agreements. From then onwards, Australia needed no special treatment from Britain and received none. Her role thereafter was to play her part in the Sterling Area, whose strength and stability depended on trading and financial relations ranging far beyond the bounds of empire.

DISCIPLINING THE AFRIKANER

In Australia, despite the hostility of a large section of the Labour movement to British finance, there was never any real possibility that governments would adopt policies which threatened essential British interests. In South Africa the collaborative forces were weaker and anti-British nationalism was more politically overt and strident.

---

69. Hancock, *Survey of British Commonwealth Affairs*, Vol. II, Pt. I, p. 253.
70. Ruth Megaw, 'Australia and the Anglo-American Trade Agreement, 1938', *Jour. Imp. and Comm. Hist.*, III (1975), p. 204.
71. For a revisionist approach to Anglo-Australian economic relations which is consistent with our line of argument see O'Brien 'Australia–British Relations', pp. 583–6; also Hancock, *Survey of British Commonwealth Affairs*, Vol. II, Pt. I, pp. 256–7.

Nonetheless, between the wars, British economic and financial power remained formidable and nationalist governments were forced to come to terms with it.[72]

Between 1902 and 1910, when the Union came into existence, an uneasy bargain was struck in South Africa whereby local freedoms were traded against an acceptance of British paramountcy in the region.[73] Afrikaner concerns centred on the maintenance of harmonious relations among the disparate groups making up the white population and on the question of white supremacy and the economic security needed to underpin it. This, in turn, depended on the prosperity and growth of the mining industry, which had a determinant influence on the rest of the economy, including agriculture, and also provided the state with the bulk of its revenues. The progress of mining itself required large supplies of cheap African labour, much of it found through sub-imperialist activity beyond the borders of the Union.[74] Mining's future was also, to a considerable degree, in British hands. Britain was South Africa's dominant trading partner and the City was the channel through which vital foreign investments flowed into mining and the rest of the South African economy. This became obvious during World War I, when Britain virtually commandeered South Africa's supplies of gold.[75] In the inter-war period, South African prosperity remained heavily dependent upon gold exports[76] and the colony's trade was still tied to Britain, though the latter's

72. For a general introduction to South African history see T.R.H. Davenport, *South Africa: A Modern History* (1977). Very useful surveys include A.P. Walshe and A.D. Roberts, 'Southern Africa', in the *Cambridge History of Africa*, Vol. 7 (Cambridge, 1986), and D.H. Houghton, 'Economic Development, 1865–1965', in Monica Wilson and Leonard Thompson, eds. *The Oxford History of South Africa*, Vol. II (Oxford, 1971).

73. The sizeable literature on this subject is surveyed by Deryck Schreuder, 'Colonial Nationalism and Tribal Nationalism: Making the White South African State', in John Eddy and Deryck Schreuder, eds. *The Rise of Colonial Nationalism* (Sydney, 1988). See also Ronald Hyam, 'The Myth of the "Magnanimous Gesture": the Liberal Government, Smuts and Conciliation, 1906', in Ronald Hyam and Ged Martin, *Reappraisals in Imperial History* (1976).

74. Alan H. Jeeves, *Migrant Labour in South Africa's Mining Economy: The Struggle for the Gold Mines' Labour Supply, 1890–1920* (Montreal, 1985); David Yudelman and Alan Jeeves, 'New Labour Frontiers for Old; Black Migrants to the South African Gold Mines, 1920–85', *Jour. Southern African Stud.*, 13 (1986). On South African sub-imperialism see Ronald Hyam, 'The Politics of Partition in South Africa, 1908–61', in Hyam and Martin, *Reappraisals in Imperial History*; and P.R. Warhurst, 'Smuts and South Africa: a Study in Sub-Imperialism', *South Afr. Hist. Jour.*, 16 (1984).

75. R. Ally, 'War and Gold – The Bank of England, the London Gold Market and South Africa's Gold, 1914–19', *Jour. Southern Afr. Stud.* 17 (1991).

76. Bruce R. Dalgaard, *South Africa's Impact on Britain's Return to Gold, 1925* (New York, 1981), Table 7, p. 28.

importance diminished somewhat over the period as a whole (Table 6.3). Britain was also an important source of foreign capital, which accounted for two-fifths of net investment in the economy in the 1920s. Dependence on imported capital fell sharply in the 1930s, when external public borrowing ceased and some loans were repaid, but the private sector continued to rely on foreign investment, and the balance of payments showed a persistent deficit on current account.[77] In addition, the South African banking scene was dominated by two firms with headquarters in London, the Standard Bank and Barclays DCO, which, in 1926, took over the only 'local' bank of substance, the National.[78]

Falls in mining income, or a slowing down of overseas investment flows, could create white unemployment and cause outbursts of resentment against mining capitalists and the British connection behind them. Within the limits set by the need to maintain white political and economic hegemony, Smuts's South Africa Party was sympathetic to mining capitalists rather than to trade unions, and proud of the imperial link;[79] but one feature of the inter-war period was the rise of the National Party under Hertzog's leadership, which was much less openly collaborative. National Party politicians often took advantage of Afrikaner sentiment to demand greater local autonomy, but they had to take care not to scare off the capital which made white prosperity possible, and they also had to live with continued British trading and financial dominance. After 1918, one way that Nationalists could secure both white votes and room for manoeuvre internationally was by giving active support to a policy of rapid industrialisation under protection. As a result, employment opportunities grew rapidly, white living standards rose and import substitution reduced South Africa's dependence on British trade. It

77. S.H. Frankel and H. Herzfeld, 'An Analysis of the Growth of the National Income of the Union in the Period of Prosperity before the War', *South African Journal of Economics*, 12 (1944), Table 8, p. 128 and Appendix I, p. 138.

78. On duopoly in South African banking see Stuart Jones, 'The Apogee of Imperial Banks in South Africa: Standard and Barclays, 1919–39', *Eng. Hist. Rev.*, CIII (1988). This development is put in the wider context of the growth of corporate banking and the increasing integration of Imperial and local banks within the empire in Baster, *The Imperial Banks*, pp. 223–243. See also A.C.L. Day, 'The South African Commercial Banks', in Sayers, *Banking in the British Commonwealth*, pp. 353–9.

79. The war against Germany was unpopular in many Afrikaner circles and the decision to invade German South-West Africa provoked a rebellion in sections of the army in 1914. Although this episode underlined the strength of local nationalist feeling in South Africa, it is important to note that the rebellion was suppressed by Afrikaner generals, including Smuts. See N.G. Garson, 'South Africa and World War I', in Norman Hillmer and Philip Wigley, eds. *The First British Commonwealth* (1980).

proved impossible, however, to shake off British financial imperialism before World War II broke out. Indeed, as was the case with other white colonies, the development of industry, insofar as it made it possible for South Africa to run a trade surplus, improved her ability to service returns on capital raised in London and took some of the strain out of financial dependence.

The hesitant world economic recovery of the early 1920s made it harder to underwrite the political compromise which held the Union together. Gold-mining was beset by rising costs and declining profitability, while agriculture made only a partial recovery from the postwar slump of 1920–1.[80] In these circumstances, nationalist demands, linking economic autonomy with political independence, had an increasing appeal. The first serious test of this platform came in 1919–20, when sterling was allowed to float. The banks adjusted their exchange rates for the South African pound so as to follow sterling. The price of gold rose in terms of paper currency, but since the banks were legally obliged to convert paper into gold on the old terms it became profitable to export gold from South Africa. There was a rapid gold drain and a contraction of credit which aggravated an already difficult economic situation in 1920. There were many calls in South Africa for a unilateral revaluation of the South African pound and a break in the link with sterling. But the opinion of the commercial bankers, including the South African-based National Bank, was that revaluation would ruin South Africa's trade with Britain, precipitate a balance of payments crisis and induce a capital flight from South Africa. These views prevailed: in 1920, South Africa left the gold standard and the pound was made inconvertible.[81]

One other outcome of the crisis was the creation of the first central bank in the Dominions, the South African Reserve Bank.[82] The Reserve Bank, like the Bank of England, was a private institution with sole rights of note issue, some control over the reserves of the commercial banks and the power to rediscount. Its first governor was

80. Maryna Fraser and Alan Jeeves, *All That Glittered: Selected Correspondence of Lionel Phillips, 1890–1924* (Cape Town, 1977), pp. 9, 284.

81. Dalgaard, *South Africa's Impact on Britain's Return to Gold*, pp. 45–50; J.A. Henry, *The First Hundred Years of the Standard Bank* (1963), pp. 176–84; also E. Cannan, 'South African Currency', *Econ. Jour.*, 30 (1920).

82. On the origins and original constitution of the Reserve Bank see G. de Kock, *A History of the South African Reserve Bank* (Pretoria, 1954); Dalgaard, *South Africa's Impact on Britain's Return to Gold*, pp. 51–2; Plumptre, *Central Banking in the British Dominions*, esp. pp. 59–60; H. Strakosch, 'The South African Reserve Bank', *Econ. Jour.*, XXXI (1921); E.H.D. Arndt, *Banking and Currency Development in South Africa, 1652–1927* (Cape Town, 1928); A.C.L. Day, 'The South African Reserve Bank', in Sayers, *Banking in the British Commonwealth*, pp. 373–7.

a Bank of England man, and the Reserve Bank was clearly intended to be an institution with an independent voice in South Africa[83] which would cooperate with London in the novel and difficult task of ensuring that the South African pound did not get out of line with sterling. In practice, the Reserve Bank had little influence. Originally, it did not even hold the government's account and, as South Africa had only a rudimentary money market, the commercial banks still took most of their investment business to the City, where the Bank of England's influence was all-pervasive.[84]

Britain's decision to float sterling also weakened the demand for gold and increased the pressure on the mining industry to cut costs. Falling wages for white workers and reductions in the prices paid for supplies of foodstuffs alienated miners and farmers and led in 1922 to the Rand Revolt, a major strike of white miners which was crushed by the joint action of the government and the mining companies. The association between the pro-imperial South Africa party and mining capitalists during the strike lost Smuts the support of the electorate;[85] in 1924, Hertzog's Nationalists came to power with a mandate to improve the living standards of white workers and to reduce South Africa's dependence on Britain.[86] Hertzog's success was not welcomed in London: the National Party still had its roots in Afrikaner rural culture and there were fears that the new government would be anti-capitalist as well as anti-British.

Hertzog's administration undoubtedly felt an instinctive sympathy towards its agricultural constituency, but it also had a shrewd awareness of the need to work with and, if possible, to harness the forces of modernisation in South Africa.[87] Dependence on revenues

83. The commercial banks urged the need for the central bank to be independent. 'Those who gave this excellent advice in South Africa could scarcely be expected to realize how thoroughly the new Governor had been indoctrinated to the same effect in London': Henry, *The First Hundred Years of the Standard Bank*, p. 188.

84. Jones, 'The Apogee of the Imperial Banks in South Africa', pp. 894–5, 897, 907; Day, 'The South African Reserve Bank', pp. 373, 386; Plumptre, *Central Banking in the British Dominions*, p. 61.

85. On Smuts's attitudes towards mine-owners and mine-workers see Donald Denoon, *Settler Capitalism: The Dynamics of Dependent Development in the Southern Hemisphere* (Oxford, 1983), pp. 197–9.

86. Relations between government and workforce are dealt with by David Yudelman, *The Emergence of Modern South Africa: State, Capital and the Emergence of Organised Labour on the South African Gold Fields, 1902–1939* (Westport, Conn., 1983).

87. On Afrikanerdom's relationships with capitalism see Dan O'Meara, *Volkscapitalisme: Class, Capitalism and Ideology in the Development of Afrikaner Nationalism, 1934–1948* (Cambridge, 1983); and for a broad view of the politics of rural development, Timothy Keegan, 'The Dynamics of Rural Accumulation in South Africa: Comparative and Historical Perspectives', *Comp. Stud. in Soc. and Hist.*, 28 (1988).

from gold-mining ensured that the government cooperated with the mining firms in maintaining the flow of migrant labour; reliance on the London money market (despite the fact that new capital was in short supply in the 1920s) guaranteed that existing foreign debts would be serviced punctually. At the same time, the government pursued a vigorous and successful campaign of industrialisation. Tariffs, though limited by an obligation (inherited from before 1914) to give preferential treatment to Britain, were used to create manufacturing employment for whites; aspirations to economic independence were symbolised by the establishment of a prestigious state-sponsored enterprise, the Iron and Steel Corporation, in 1928.[88]

Perhaps the most telling illustration of the Nationalists' ambitions and limitations with respect to Britain in the 1920s was the attempt to wrest control of monetary policy from London. By 1924, pressure to take South Africa back to gold was building up again. With the British still uncertain about the date of return, the new Hertzog government decided to go it alone, despite Britain's clear preference for continuing the link with sterling.[89] Hertzog took advice from Kemmerer, the American 'money doctor', widely known as a champion of the gold standard, and from a Dutch central banker: the opinion of the City of London was deliberately unsought.[90] Again, the commercial banks protested that South Africa was too dependent on Britain to return to gold before her, and the English governor of the Reserve Bank was, generally speaking, in favour of South Africa retaining her link with sterling.[91] But, in this case, the banks were ignored for reasons that were primarily ideological and political: going back to gold alone would undermine British imperial power and broadcast South Africa's ability to survive outside the imperial circle.[92] South Africa's action also had wider implications, for 'when a Dominion broke from the fold Britain was in a poor position to

88. W.G. Martin, 'The Making of an Industrial South Africa: Trade and Tariffs in the Interwar Period', *Int. Jour. African Hist. Stud.*, 23 (1990); Nancy Clark, 'South African State Corporations: the Death Knell of Economic Colonialism?', *Jour. Southern African Stud.*, 14 (1987).

89. Dalgaard, *South Africa's Impact on Britain's Return to Gold*, pp. 76, 158. For a general discussion of the anti-imperial element in monetary thinking see ibid. pp. 12–19.

90. Ibid. p. 86. For the Kemmerer-Vissering Commission's recommendations in detail see ibid. pp. 93–4, 102–4, and C.S. Richards, 'The Kemmerer-Vissering Report and the Position of the Reserve Bank of South Africa', *Econ. Jour.*, 35 (1925). Kemmerer's role in South America is noted below, p. 151.

91. Dalgaard, *South Africa's Impact on Britain's Return to Gold*, pp. 99–100; Richards, 'The Kemmerer-Vissering Report', p. 561.

92. Dalgaard, *South Africa's Impact on Britain's Return to Gold*, pp. 127–30.

expand its financial radius of power through infiltrating Central Europe'.[93] So, the South African decision – which the City of London met with profound silence in the hope of reducing its impact[94] – may, as already suggested, have had some influence on Britain's decision to return to gold in 1925, though the concurrent German stabilisation was of at least equal significance. In any event, Britain's return robbed the nationalists of their victory and left unanswered the anxious enquiries of the commercial banks as to whether or not South Africa was really able to strike out independently.

The world slump after 1929 and the financial crisis of 1931 gave added impetus to nationalist forces in South Africa, as elsewhere. Hertzog was a leading influence on the discussions which led to the Dominions being accorded 'equality of status' with Britain in 1931,[95] and legislative changes at home meant that, by the mid-1930s, South Africa had achieved a considerable degree of constitutional freedom. However, it proved more difficult to free the economy from its reliance on Britain. By the late 1930s, external trade was much more diversified than before 1914 and, contrary to the experience of other dominions, trade dependence on Britain continued to decrease in the depression decade (Table 6.1). However, as we have pointed out elsewhere, diversification of trade was consistent with (and often supported) continued financial dominance. Although the share of capital supplied to the gold-mining industry from local sources grew substantially during the 1930s,[96] the City's contribution to investment remained crucial.

The decisive test of South Africa's ability to manage its own economic affairs occurred after Britain left the gold standard in 1931.[97] Hertzog decided not to follow suit. Again, nationalist motives were prominent, but the government also genuinely feared that the rush to leave gold would prove the ruin of South Africa's most important industry. The consequences were disastrous. Agricultural exports, already hit by the world depression, suffered grievously from a high South African pound. There was also a considerable flight of capital as speculators anticipated that South Africa would devalue. The commercial banks' London balances fell, and they responded in time-

93. Ibid. p. 157.
94. Ibid. p. 153.
95. Holland, *Britain and the Commonwealth Alliance*, pp. 54–5, 59.
96. Alan Jeeves, 'Migrant Labour and South African Expansion, 1920–1950', *South Afr. Hist. Jour.*, 18 (1986).
97. What follows is based largely on Drummond, *The Floating Pound and the Sterling Area*, Ch. 4. See also Henry, *The First Hundred Years of the Standard Bank*, Ch. 18; Plumptre, *Central Banking in the British Dominions*, pp. 398–402.

honoured fashion by squeezing credit in South Africa. This was deemed unpatriotic,[98] but the government, which tried vainly to counter capital flight by raising funds in New York and Amsterdam,[99] and the Reserve Bank, now firmly under Afrikaner influence, could do little to prevent it.

The Kemmerer-Vissering Commission which, in 1924–5, had advised the South African government to return to gold, had argued that the Reserve Bank's powers should be increased by allowing it to compete commercially, by giving it the government's account and by taking steps to create a bill market in South Africa.[100] All these reforms were attempted. However, no short-money market of significance developed in South Africa; acting as the government banker did not confer as much authority as it did in Australia or New Zealand because the role of the state in the South African economy was less significant. So, although the Reserve Bank proved helpful in lending to government at the height of the crisis, it had not the power to determine the money supply or to influence radically the exchange rate.[101] The country was still relatively small and underdeveloped. Despite her abundance of gold, South Africa was forced to accept in 1933 that she must allow her currency to go off gold and float with sterling: 'she was in fact on a sterling exchange standard and her gold exports were a means of keeping up her sterling reserves'.[102] South Africa was becoming more assertive in her relations with Britain but 'economic control outlived political control', and this was intimately connected with the hold which British financial institutions had on the country – a hold which, if anything, actually tightened in the inter-war years.[103]

Failure to remain on the gold standard had repercussions on domestic economic policy. The crisis weakened the Nationalists, who were forced into a coalition with Smuts's party, one consequence of which was to halt the further extension of protectionist tariffs.[104] Despite this, when the sharp rise in world gold prices after 1933

98. See Henry, *The First Hundred Years of the Standard Bank*, pp. 237–8.

99. Drummond, *The Floating Pound and the Sterling Area*, pp. 79–80. In 1931 the Reserve Bank appointed a new governor who lacked sympathy with Britain. See ibid. p. 78, and Henry, *The First Hundred Years of the Standard Bank*, pp. 241–2.

100. Dalgaard, *South Africa's Impact on Britain's Return to Gold*, pp. 94–6, 104.

101. Plumptre, *Central Banking in the British Dominions*, pp. 63–6, 403–5; Jones, 'The Apogee of the Imperial Banks', p. 899; Frankel, 'The Situation in South Africa', pp. 106–7.

102. Brinley Thomas, 'The Evolution of the Sterling Area' in Nicolas Mansergh et al., *Commonwealth Perspectives* (Durham, NC, 1958), p. 180.

103. Jones, 'The Apogee of the Imperial Banks', pp. 893, 915.

104. Martin, 'The Making of Industrial South Africa', pp. 82–4.

triggered off a boom in South Africa, industry prospered as much as mining. The latter, however, stayed at the centre of government concerns partly because, in the 1930s, it provided a rising proportion of state revenues; ensuring a steady flow of African labour for the mines thus remained a matter of great official concern. The coalition's alliance with mining interests, and its espousal of a 'practical' form of apartheid, was viewed with unease by purists who favoured absolute segregation and an almost equivalent degree of autonomy from foreign business.[105] But they had little influence at the time: in the 1930s the nationalist coalition worked with the mining companies, remained in the Sterling Area and paid its overseas debts without fuss. Its political independence was also problematic: the outbreak of World War II split the coalition, but it was Smuts, who supported Britain, who triumphed, and Hertzog, who wanted South Africa to remain neutral, who was defeated.

The settlement which shaped the Union of South Africa was a compromise between British and Afrikaner interests. Afrikaner politicians did not become merely servants of foreign business but, as in other settler colonies, political advance was associated with continued economic subordination, and nowhere more so than in matters of banking, capital investment and monetary policy. Profound though it was, the gulf between Briton and Afrikaner was spanned by the realisation that dependence with high wages was preferable to independence at lower standards of living. Acting on this appraisal was greatly helped by the fact that a large part of the costs of economic development and political stability could be transferred to the African labour force, which was both cheap and disenfranchised. This congenial formula worked for several generations: the accumulated bill is now being presented.

NEW ZEALAND BREAKS THE SHACKLES

The Afrikaner population was always big enough and influential enough to insert a strongly anti-imperial strand into South Africa's relations with the rest of the British empire. By contrast, New

105. For an introduction to the literature on this theme see Shula Marks and Stanley Trapido, eds. *The Politics of Race, Class and Nationalism in Twentieth-Century South Africa* (1987).

Zealand was traditionally the most docile of the Dominions.[106] Yet the strains imposed upon her by the depression of the 1930s eventually led her to challenge the basic premises upon which the Sterling Area was founded.

Of all the Dominions, New Zealand was the most trade dependent throughout the period (Table 6.1) and, with interest on debt running at twice the level of the export surplus in the 1920s, she was a persistent borrower throughout the decade.[107] Despite this, when international trade in primary products collapsed after 1929, New Zealanders were not faced with such an overwhelming balance of payments difficulty as beset their Australian neighbours because they did not have Australia's acute short-term debt problem and, probably as a result, found London more accommodating. Exports fell by two-fifths in value between 1929 and 1932 but this was more than balanced by a 50 per cent cut in import values in the same period. Only in 1930 and 1931 did New Zealand have to run down its balances in London, and then a certain amount of aid from the Bank of England was required. After 1932, exports started to recover, aided by the Ottawa concessions (Table 6.3), and New Zealand again began to run the balance of trade surpluses which had been characteristic of her economy since the 1890s.[108]

Nonetheless, export values did not regain their 1929 levels until 1936. To maintain her trade surplus and a healthy position as regards London funds, New Zealand had to suppress imports through devaluation, higher protection and a deflationary economic policy. National income fell by roughly three-tenths between 1929 and 1932.[109] It did not recover the 1929 level until the late 1930s,[110] and unemployment remained high throughout the decade. The fact that the mother country had failed to solve New Zealand's economic difficulties, and had even seen fit to put quota restrictions on New Zealand's exports in the 1930s, dealt a blow to the imperial sympathies of the remotest of Britain's 'children'. Unlike Australia, where those most hostile to the 'money power' were kept from political office, bitterness at the supposed iniquity of the bankers and rentiers resulted

106. A very useful general history of New Zealand for our purposes is Sinclair's *History of New Zealand*.
107. Rosenberg, 'Capital Imports and Growth, the Case of New Zealand: Foreign Investment in New Zealand, 1840–1958', *Econ. Jour.*, 71 (1961), pp. 97–8; Sinclair, *History of New Zealand*, pp. 254–5.
108. Hawke, *The Making of New Zealand: An Economic History* (Cambridge, 1985), pp. 128, 133–5.
109. Sinclair, *History of New Zealand*, p. 255.
110. Hawke, *The Making of New Zealand*, Figure 4.5, p. 77.

in the election, in 1935, of a radical government which made a gallant, even imprudent, attempt to assert the right to decide the country's economic future without reference to Britain's own economic priorities.[111]

Part of the new strategy of the late 1930s involved a radical use of the recently formed central bank, the Reserve Bank of New Zealand, whose origins lay in the early days of the world depression. Commercial banking in New Zealand and Australia was so closely related that, during the Australian exchange crisis of 1930, it seemed possible that the New Zealand pound might be devalued along with the Australian though, at that time, New Zealand's balance of payments problem was not so acute.[112] On a brief visit during his Australian trip, Niemeyer advised the New Zealanders that the solution lay in creating a central bank to manage their currency and credit, thus reducing the influence of the Australian banks and preventing a fall in the New Zealand pound. The Reserve Bank, built on lines approved by the Bank of England and with a Governor imported from Threadneedle Street, finally appeared in 1933, though too late to achieve its mission of preventing the devaluation of the New Zealand pound.[113]

In its earliest days, the Reserve Bank was the handmaiden of a government determined to adhere to monetary orthodoxy.[114] However, with the coming of a Labour government, this cautious and conservative institution was nationalised and used as one of the main instruments of a policy devoted to reducing unemployment, improving welfare and diversifying the economy, all of which required unprecedented levels of government expenditure.[115] By 1938 the policy was running into severe balance of payments constraints. Exports, which had risen rapidly in the world boom of 1937, fell sharply in the subsequent depression of 1938. Imports rose quickly as incomes increased in 1936–7 and marked time in 1938.[116] The balance

111. Sinclair, *History of New Zealand*, pp. 260–2, 265–6.
112. This was first recognised by B.C. Ashwin, 'Banking and Currency in New Zealand', *Economic Record*, VI (1930). See also G.R. Hawke, *Between Government and Banks: A History of the Reserve Bank of New Zealand* (Wellington, 1972), pp. 18–22.
113. G.R. Hawke, *Between Government and Banks*, esp. Ch. 3; idem, 'The Government and the Depression of the 1930s in New Zealand: an Essay Towards a Revision', *Austral. Econ. Hist. Rev.*, XIII (1973), pp. 75–84; idem, *The Making of New Zealand*, pp. 151–2; Plumptre, *Central Banking in the British Dominions*, pp. 115–22, 185–7.
114. See Hawke, 'The Government and the Depression of the 1930s in New Zealand', pp. 86–7, and idem, *The Making of New Zealand*, pp. 150–1.
115. Hawke, *Between Government and Banks*, pp. 101–10; Sinclair, *History of New Zealand*, pp. 265–9.
116. Hawke, *The Making of New Zealand*, p. 128.

of trade surpluses shrank with alarming speed and reserves held in London began to fall heavily in 1938-9. The position was greatly aggravated by a flight of capital as propertied New Zealanders took fright at 'socialism'.[117] Exchange and import controls had to be applied in 1938: exchange reserves in London fell by £34m. between 1935 and 1939,[118] and the government found it needed credit in London despite having come to power pledged to avoid making any more commitments to the 'bloodsuckers' of the City.

The British reaction to the crisis revealed the depths of gentlemanly distaste for those who refused to play the financial game by the normal rules.[119] In the Treasury, New Zealand's policy was described as 'a dreadful business' involving 'a degree of government control and of regimentation of industry which is intolerable except in a totalitarian system'.[120] However, given the mess that New Zealand was in by 1938, the Treasury preferred exchange controls to devaluation, which might have stoked up inflation in the Dominion and further threatened her ability to meet her obligations in London. When New Zealand applied for assistance in 1939, the Treasury was disinclined to help and made it clear to the colonial emissaries that there was little sympathy for antipodean socialism in the City. New Zealand responded by hinting at default. In normal times the British might well have called the New Zealanders' bluff. But in 1939 times were not normal, and it was recognised that Britain could not let default become an issue when sterling was under immense pressure. In the end, the New Zealanders got their loan, though on rigorous terms and in return for a promise to remove some of the more obnoxious restrictions placed on imports. The Bank of England did its best to ensure a successful flotation to the extent of taking up about two-fifths of the loan itself. Had it not been for the imminence of war, New Zealand would most probably have been left, as Australia had been in 1930, to pay the price for its financial innovations without support from London.

117. Plumptre, *Central Banking in the British Dominions*, p. 97. See also Hawke, *The Making of New Zealand*, pp. 163–6.

118. Hancock, *Survey of British Commonwealth Affairs*, Vol. II, Pt. I, pp. 283–4; Rosenberg, 'Capital Exports and Growth', pp. 98–9.

119. Drummond, *The Floating Pound and the Sterling Area*, p. 115. Our account is based largely on pp. 103–15 of this work, though Hancock, *Survey of British Commonwealth Affairs*, Vol. II, Pt. I, pp. 271–84, is still well worth reading.

120. The quotations are from Phillips, a leading British Treasury official, cited in Drummond, *The Floating Pound and the Sterling Area*, pp. 109, 107.

CANADA AND STERLING

If Australia, New Zealand and South Africa all presented Britain with a complex sum of financial problems, each one with its unique features, they had one quality in common: they were all more or less willing members of the Sterling Area. Canada, the oldest and most economically developed of the white Dominions, was not.[121] Canadian banks habitually kept their reserves in New York rather than in London. In the nineteenth century New York was favoured at least partly for its proximity. After 1900, though, the preference reflected the brute fact that the United States began to overtake Britain as Canada's chief economic partner. During the war and in the 1920s, the United States substantially increased her lead over Britain as a provider of Canadian imports and overtook her as a market for the Dominion's exports (Table 6.4). More fundamentally, the United States became Canada's chief source of imported capital after 1914.

Table 6.4 Trade of Canada with various countries, 1911–39 (per cent)

	United States	*UK*	*Other Sterling Area*	*Others*
Imports				
1911	60.8	24.3	4.4	10.5
1926	66.3	16.3	5.0	12.4
1929	68.8	15.0	4.8	11.4
1937	60.7	18.2	11.0	10.1
1939	66.1	15.2	10.0	8.7
Exports				
1911	38.0	48.2	6.1	7.7
1926	36.3	36.4	7.6	19.7
1929	42.8	25.2	9.1	22.9
1937	36.1	40.3	10.4	13.2
1939	41.1	35.5	11.1	12.3

Source: H.G.J. Aitken et al., *The American Economic Impact on Canada* (Durham, NC 1959), Table 6, p. 155.

In 1914, Britain still owned three-quarters of all the foreign investment in Canada and the United States one-fifth.[122] By 1930 the British

121. A useful general introduction to Canadian history in this period is provided by Robert Bothwell, Ian M. Drummond and John English, *Canada, 1900–1945* (Toronto, 1989). On Canadian economic history see the appropriate sections in Richard Pomfret, *The Economic Development of Canada* (Toronto, 1984): and William L. Marr and Donald G. Paterson, *Canada: An Economic History* (Toronto, 1980).

122. K.H. Buckley and M.C. Urquhart, eds. *Historical Statistics of Canada* (Cambridge, 1965), p. 169.

share had fallen to one-third and the American had risen to two-fifths. During the war, when Canadian exports to Britain rose sharply and Britain's exports to her fell, Canada was effectively exporting capital to Britain; when Britain left gold in 1919 and the Canadians stuck firmly to it, the fall in sterling gave Canada a chance to repatriate substantial amounts of British–held Canadian securities.[123]

Canada had its Anglophiles and others who, although not devoted to the imperial ideal, viewed the growth of American influence in Canada with alarm and hoped, as did metropolitan imperialists, that improved relations with Britain would act as a counterweight. In the 1920s common ground was hard to find. Canada wanted preferences but Britain hung on grimly to free trade. On the other side, the Canadians were unenthusiastic about granting further preferences to British manufacturers and were lukewarm on imperial emigration schemes.[124] The economic catastrophe of the early 1930s, however, forced Canada and Britain into a greater interdependence. The collapse of American demand after 1929 hit Canada extremely hard:[125] the Ottawa agreements provided partial compensation. Perhaps the worst hit group in Canada, the western prairie wheat farmers, received little advantage from the preferential system since Britain had little control over the price of wheat, or wool, and a number of other commoditites exported by the empire.[126] But other Canadian exports, including manufactures, did well. Canada's exports to Britain fell from £57m. in 1929 to £35m. in 1931, but then rose rapidly again to £92m. by 1937 (Table 6.4). Britain's exports to the Dominion did much less well, hindered as they were by the depressed state of the Canadian economy and by high tariffs designed to protect local manufacturers.[127]

The overall effect of the depression and of the Ottawa agreements

---

123. Hancock, *Survey of British Commonwealth Affairs*, Vol. II, Pt. i, p. 187; John Archibald Stovel, *Canada in the World Economy* (Harvard, Mass., 1959), p. 240.

124. Norman Hillmer, 'Personalities and Problems in Anglo-Canadian Economic Relations between the Two World Wars', *Bulletin of Canadian Studies*, III (1979), pp. 8–11; see also Holland, *Britain and the Commonwealth Alliance*, pp. 107–8; Drummond, *British Economic Policy and the Empire*, pp. 84–6.

125. On the depression see A.E. Safarian, *The Canadian Economy in the Great Depression* (Toronto, 1959), and Alan G. Green and Gordon R. Sparks, 'A Macro-Economic Interpretation of Recovery: Australia and Canada', in Gregory and Butlin, *Recovery from Depression*.

126. R.F. Holland, 'The End of the Imperial Economy? Anglo-Canadian Disengagement in the 1930s', *Jour. Imp. and Comm. Hist.* (1983), and idem, 'Imperial Collaboration and Great Depression'.

127. T.J.T. Rooth, 'Imperial Preference and Anglo-Canadian Trade Relations in the 1930s – the End of an Illusion', *British Journal of Canadian Studies*, 1 (1986), provides a comprehensive review of the statistical evidence.

was to reverse the tendency for the American share of Canadian trade to increase. Not only did trade with Britain grow, but also the share of the rest of the Sterling Area in Canadian trade rose. Since Canada was not a member of the area, her inclusion in the preferential system was a sign that 'imperial' and sentimental factors had their place in British economic foreign policy in the 1930s. At the same time, it is probably the case that, if Canada was ever to be tempted to join the Sterling Area, something like the Ottawa system, and the shift it confirmed in Canadian trading patterns, was a necessary preliminary. Moreover, it was quickly recognised, both in Britain and Canada, that the weakening of the tie with the United States and the beginnings of the preferential system did open up the possibility of Canada joining the sterling bloc.

The Canadians left the gold standard in 1929, and unhinged their own dollar from that of the United States, though the abandonment was not recognised officially until 1932.[128] When sterling went off gold in 1931, Canada was thus left with the problem of whether to re-attach her currency to the dollar or to peg it to sterling. The alternative was to pursue an independent line of policy because Canada's money market was developed enough to allow some limited degree of independence. There were strong pleas from imperial enthusiasts in Britain, and a measure of support in banking circles in Canada, for a sterling peg system. Following sterling in 1932 and 1933 was tempting because it would have meant a significant devaluation against the American dollar and would have had beneficial effects on Canada's balance of trade with the United States, which was heavily adverse. But there was also a widespread fear that devaluation would have inflationary effects; that it would increase the already heavy weight of repayments on American debt; and that it would reduce Canada's credibility in New York, the money market that really mattered to her, since loans from London were unlikely in the 1930s. These arguments were ultimately decisive in keeping Canada out of the sterling area, but she also avoided a fixed link with the American dollar and tried to steer an independent course on exchange rates throughout the 1930s.[129]

128. The following paragraph depends heavily on Drummond, *The Floating Pound and the Sterling Area*, esp. pp. 64–71. See also Douglas H. Fullerton, *Graham Towers and his Times* (Toronto, 1986), pp. 28–31.

129. On the Canadian management of exchange rates see Michael D. Bordo and Angela Redish, 'Credible Commitment and Exchange Rate Stability: Canada's Interwar Experience', *Canadian Journal of Economics*, XXIII (1990); E.P. Neufeld, *Bank of Canada Operations, 1935–54* (Toronto, 1955), pp. 50–2; Plumptre, *Central Banking in the British Dominions*, pp. 408–21.

The question of managing the exchanges and the wider problem of dealing with the depression brought the issue of central banking into focus in Canada, and a Royal Commission was appointed in 1933 to investigate whether such a bank was necessary.[130] Two of the five members were British, including Sir Charles Addis, a Bank of England director and a confidant of its Governor. Under their influence, the Commission argued for a private institution similar to the Bank of England.[131]

These views were largely accepted when the Bank of Canada was formed in 1935,[132] with the express intent of keeping it free of political interference.[133] In their Report, the Commissioners explained that the most pressing task facing a Canadian central bank would be the exchanges since 'the need for international monetary co-operation is urgent and constant'. Order could be restored for the international economy only through 'the introduction of central banks working to harmonize national policy with the needs of the international situation'. The establishment of central banks in the empire was a key part of the process since they were 'the instrument of imperial monetary co-operation'. The whole Report was, in short, as clear an expression of the Bank of England's philosophy as could be wished, right down to the stress upon the primacy of the central banks' external role and the cautionary statement that a Canadian central bank 'would not be a source of unlimited credit for all borrowers on all occasions; indeed its operations might as often be restrictive as expansive'.[134]

The Bank of Canada's first Governor was on record as being

130. Fullerton, *Graham Towers and his Times*, pp. 33–9.

131. On Addis, see Dayer, *Finance and Empire: Sir Charles Addis, 1861–1945*, pp. 248–9; on Norman's influence in canvassing the idea of central banking, see Fullerton, *Graham Towers and his Times*, p. 42. The other English member of the Commission was Lord Macmillan, former chairman of the famous Macmillan Committee of 1930. See also Sayers, *Bank of England*, II, p. 514–15.

132. For a wide-ranging discussion of the origins of the Bank in the Canadian context see Michael D. Bordo and Angela Redish, 'Why Did the Bank of Canada Emerge in 1935?', *Jour. Econ. Hist.*, XLVII (1987); Craig McIvor, *Canadian Monetary, Banking and Fiscal Development* (Toronto, 1958), Ch. VII; Irving Brecher, *Monetary and Fiscal Thought and Policy in Canada, 1919–1939* (Toronto, 1957), Pt. III; G.S. Watts, 'The Origin and Background of Central Banking in Canada', *Bank of Canada Review* (1972); and R.B. Bryce, *Maturing in Hard Times: Canada's Department of Finance through the Great Depression* (1986), pp. 124–30, 135–44.

133. Plumptre, *Central Banking in the British Dominions*, p. 145–7. It should be noted that one Bank of England adviser to the Committee was happy to accept the idea of public ownership of a Canadian central bank, but Macmillan insisted on recommending a private company. Fullerton, *Graham Towers and his Times*, p. 44, 45–7.

134. All quotations are from the *Report of the Royal Commission on Banking and Currency in Canada*, Ch. V, (Ottawa, 1933), as reprinted in E.P. Neufeld, ed. *Money and Banking in Canada* (Toronto, 1964), pp. 234–46.

sympathetic to the idea of Canada joining the Sterling Area;[135] the Bank's deputy governor was from the Bank of England. Furthermore, there is no doubt that the English members of the Royal Commission hoped that a Bank of Canada would serve as manager of a monetary system based on sterling. Addis, who described Canada in 1934 as 'an important component of the sterling group . . . which has not yet linked its currency to the pound',[136] and who saw the Royal Commission as a way 'to ensure that Canada was not wooed away from sterling by her American neighbour',[137] argued that a floating Canadian dollar could easily spark inflation. A return to gold would be ideal but, that apart, Canada's best option was to become part of 'an Imperial Sterling Union in which other countries might be invited to join' so that she could 'take part in an Imperial monetary policy in which every unit in the British empire might be called upon to co-operate as a means of defence against the menace to the whole Empire of the rapid economic nationalism of other countries'. Addis did not see Canada's mounting indebtedness to the United States as forming a barrier to her membership of the Sterling Area. Canada could get all the American dollars she needed in London in exchange for 'surplus sterling', and any difficulties could be overcome 'if a Canadian Central Bank, acting as a member of the Sterling Union and in full knowledge of the movement of other currencies', took appropriate action. But to ensure this the Bank would have to be independent not only of governments – always likely to be hijacked by special interest groups promoting dangerous schemes involving 'funny money' – but also of the commercial banks, which could easily behave in a monopolistic and self-interested fashion.[138]

Needless to say, the extent of British influence on central banking in its early days generated much anxiety and hostility in Canada. This was particularly so on the prairies, the area worst affected by depression, where it was hoped that a central bank might be used to cheapen and extend credit. In 1934 one western politician, later to become a director of the Bank of Canada, wanted anxiously to know: 'Are we to have a Norman Conquest of Canada?'[139] The private

135. Fullerton, *Graham Towers and his Times*, pp. 31–2; Drummond, *The Floating Pound and the Sterling Area*, p. 65.
136. Dayer, *Sir Charles Addis*, p. 247.
137. Ibid. p. 133.
138. C.S. Addis, 'Canada and Its Banks', *Quarterly Review*, 263 (1934), quotations are from pp. 51 and 53.
139. Fullerton, *Graham Towers and his Times*, pp. 48–9. On the prairie theme see T.D. Regehr, 'Banks and Farmers in Western Canada, 1900–1939', in John E. Foster, ed. *The Developing West: Essays in Canadian History* (Edmonton, 1983).

nature of the original Bank certainly offended many in Canada: what looked like independence to Addis appeared as a dangerous freedom to many North Americans,[140] who had a more benign and positive view of the state's role in banking than did most Bank of England directors. With a change of government in 1936 came nationalization.[141] However, this made no perceptible difference to the Bank's policy, which continued to be cautious and in line with government insistence on balanced-budget orthodoxy.[142] Nor did the Bank revive the opportunity to lead Canada into the Sterling Area: in exchange policy an independent course was steered between New York and London, a course made possible by the relatively advanced nature of the Dominion's money market.

After the disturbances of 1929–33, the British share of Canadian imports began to decline again. Despite Ottawa, Canadian exports to Britain did not expand rapidly enough to fill the gap left by the loss of exports to the United States and, by the mid-1930s, the Canadians were again looking south in the hope of improvement.[143] A liberalising agreement was made in 1935, and in 1938 came the Anglo-American trade agreement which, as we have already seen, was made possible because Canada was willing to forgo some of her privileges in the British market in order to make further inroads into that of the United States. Moreover, the Canadians began to run a balance of payments surplus with Britain in the late 1930s, partly as a result of the Ottawa agreements. Consequently, Canada was running an overall balance of payments surplus by the late 1930s and becoming a net exporter of capital.[144] The brief moment when Canada could have been enticed into the British financial camp had passed.

140. Ibid. pp. 49–50.

141. Ibid. p. 67–70; Plumptre, *Central Banking in the British Dominions*, pp. 147–9. See also Neufeld, *Bank of Canada Operations*, pp. 3–15, on the attempt to define a degree of independence for the Bank in the late 1930s.

142. On Bank policy in general see Neufeld, *Bank of Canada Operations*, Ch. IV, and Fullerton, *Graham Towers and his Times*, pp. 71–86.

143. Holland, 'The End of the Imperial Economy?', p. 172.

144. Her deficit on the balance of payments current account with the United States was more than offset by a large surplus with Britain. See H.G.J. Aitken et al. *The American Economic Impact on Canada* (Durham, NC, 1959), Table 13, p. 161; Stovel, *Canada in the World Economy*, Table 15, pp. 233–4; and Buckley and Urquhart, *Historical Statistics of Canada*, p. 160.

IMPERIAL PREFERENCE AND BRITISH FINANCE

In many ways the Ottawa preferential system was the logical outcome of decades of lending to the white dominions. While the world economy was buoyant, obligations could be met if Britain retained free trade; but once international trade ran into difficulties in the 1930s, free trade had to go because some degree of discrimination in favour of major debtors was necessary to prevent massive defaults. Even so, the preferential system proved inadequate to Dominion needs and its limitations provoked disappointment, even bitterness. By the late 1930s the pro-British elites on the white periphery, accustomed to treating Britain as a bottomless market for their produce and as an endless source of capital and migrants, were facing the hard truth that the mother country no longer had the strength and size to ensure rapid growth and full employment in the Dominions.

> In Canada, Australia, South Africa and even in gentle New Zealand the 1930s were characterised by moves to unscramble all those neat little imperial 'packages' which for decades had been an essential foundation of 'natural development'; they were rebound in ways that were internally more secreted and only loosely meshed into imperial networks, however relatively important the British remained as conventional trading partners.[145]

However, this process of 'ideal prefabricated decolonization'[146] had not gone far in 1939 and, from the international financial viewpoint, Britain still had a massive authority which was only just beginning to be questioned when war broke out again. The appearance of central banking in the Dominions registered both the beginning of the Dominions' attempts to further their own autonomy and Britain's determination to keep financial control in changing circumstances. If the Bank of England was only partially successful in ensuring that Dominion central banks would be created in its own image, the colonists remained, on the whole, orthodox in their monetary policies; the power of London balances and the money market of the City was still of overwhelming significance for most of the white periphery.[147] Indeed in the early 1930s, as the financial power of the United States waned, Britain seemed set to recover some of the ground lost

145. Holland, 'Imperial Collaboration and Great Depression', p. 124.
146. Ibid.
147. For an effective summing up on this see Plumptre, *Central Banking in the Dominions*, pp. 422–5. See also P. Aldaheff, 'Public Finance and the Economy in Argentina, Australia and Canada during the Depression of the 1930s', in D.C.M. Platt and Guido Di Tella, eds. *Argentina, Australia, Canada: Studies in Comparative Development, 1870–1965* (1985).

by her in the previous twenty years, so much so that Canada was tempted to join the sterling group. Perhaps overwhelmed by the pressing nature of her debt problems, Australia was the most obedient Dominion in financial terms. A more aggressive nationalism in South Africa could not prevent conformity to the dictates of sterling; New Zealand's late surge of radicalism was a little more successful but in special circumstances. By the late 1930s impending world war and the resurgence of the United States meant that the problem for the Sterling Area was not so much expansion as survival: it is doubtful if New Zealand's cheeky attempt to buck the system would have been tolerated to the same degree if Hitler had not been ready to strike against Poland.

If the Dominions were beginning to take their first, rather hesitant steps towards economic self-determination the process was, paradoxically enough, aided in the long run by the structure of the Sterling Area itself. The area could function properly only if the dependent members were able to meet their debt obligations and maintain adequate London balances. Now that British lending had virtually ceased, the main way of ensuring this was to produce, or increase the size of, Dominion balance of trade surpluses with Britain. This could be achieved through preferences in the British market. But, given the limitations on the size of the British market and the number of claimants to be satisfied, Dominion surpluses of a sufficient scale could be acquired only through the introduction of a fairly rigorous programme of import substitution which affected, most of all, British manufactured exports. Asymmetry in the mutual preferences given, with Britain getting the worst of the deal, was probably essential if the Sterling Area was to work. The growth of industry on the white periphery was necessary to the functioning of the imperial economy, increasing the complexity of Dominion economies and hastening the time when they would become self-supporting enough to detach themselves from Britain's financial leading strings. British gentlemanly capitalism was steadily, if unwittingly, sowing the seeds of its own destruction at the very centre of the empire where its power was strongest.

CHAPTER SEVEN

'A New Era of Colonial Ambitions': South America, 1914–39[1]

With the outbreak of World War I, South America sinks beneath the horizon of imperial history. Its disappearance, having won silent support with the passage of time, is now scarcely noticed. The elimination of a whole continent undoubtedly eases the task of historians of empire who are fully occupied in grappling with colonial nationalists after 1914, and it accords with the definition of the terms of the trade which confines empire to its constitutional parts. But the excision, being so radical, also fits oddly with the prominence given to South America in the debate on informal rule in the nineteenth century, and thus raises the question of whether the invisible empire (assuming that it existed) was simply destroyed in the upheaval brought by World War I, or whether it survived in some as yet unacknowledged form during the inter-war period.

To examine Britain's ties with South America after 1914 is therefore to peer into the outer space of imperial studies, and the results must be considered prospective rather than definitive. Fortunately, however, specialists on the history of the continent have produced important research on subjects which are closely related to the main theme of the present work. In drawing on this literature, we hope to make it known to a wider audience as well as to incorporate it into an argument for reintegrating South America into the study of British imperialism after 1914.[2] Specifically, we shall suggest that

1. The quotation is borrowed from Oswaldo Aranha: see below, pp. 152–3. We deal here, as in Volume I, Chapter 9, with the continental mainland and not with the larger entity, Latin America.
2. The basic reference is now Leslie Bethel, ed. *The Cambridge History of Latin America*, Vols. IV and V, *1870–1930* (1986). Future volumes will cover the period after 1930.

Britain's priority, after 1913 as before, was to maintain her position as banker to the world. During the 1920s this aim manifested itself in a series of determined efforts to steer South America back to pre-war conditions of normality; in the 1930s the banker turned debt collector while also trying to keep the republics 'sterling minded'.[3] Britain's exports of manufactures had a place in this strategy, but it was usually second place, and in the 1930s the old staples came to be regarded as more of a handicap than an asset. As the almost instinctive affinities which had smoothed relations in the pre-war era came under strain in the turbulence of war and depression, so Britain leant heavily on the republics, where and when she could, to try to hold them in their allotted place. These ambitions brought the British into conflict with rival powers, and helped to set the scene for a renewed scramble for influence in South America at the close of the 1930s which, we suggest, ought to command much greater attention from historians of imperialism than it has done so far.

A CONTINENTAL PERSPECTIVE

South America remained one of Britain's major trading partners between 1914 and 1939, accounting for about 9 per cent of her exports in 1928 and 7 per cent in 1937, and for about 9 per cent of her imports in the same years.[4] As in the pre-war era, British trade had a marked regional bias: Argentina, Brazil and (to a diminishing extent) Chile were responsible for no less than 80 per cent of Britain's exports to South America and for over 85 per cent of her imports from the continent in the inter-war period. As in the nineteenth century, too, Argentina was of overwhelming importance, receiving 49 per cent of all Britain's exports to South America in 1928 and 54 per cent in 1937, and supplying 67 per cent and 65 per cent of her imports from the continent in the same years. A more detailed view is provided by Svennilson's data on Britain's trade with her two principal partners (Table 7.1). Britain's exports staged a partial recovery in the 1920s,

3. Marcelo de Paiva Abreu, 'Anglo-Brazilian Economic Relations and the Consolidation of American Pre-eminence in Brazil, 1930–1945', in Colin Lewis and Christopher Abel, eds. *Latin America, Economic Imperialism and the State* (1985), p. 388.
4. The trade data are based primarily on the *Statistical Abstract for the United Kingdom, 1899–1913* (1914) and the *Statistical Abstract for the United Kingdom, 1913 and 1924 to 1937* (1948), and are best regarded as being no more than approximate measures of magnitude.

Table 7.1 Exports to Argentina and Brazil, 1913, 1928 and 1938 (millions of US dollars at 1938 prices)

	Exports to Argentina from			Exports to Brazil from		
	UK	*Germany*	*USA*	*UK*	*Germany*	*USA*
1913	131	87	48	72	65	45
1928	121	77	127	55	42	65
1938	80	57	76	21	58	50

Source: Ingvar Svennilson, *Growth and Stagnation in the European Economy* (Geneva, 1954), p. 190.

following the disruption caused by World War I, but suffered again in the 1930s, as a result of the slump, and by 1938 were well below the levels of 1913, as was trade to Argentina and Brazil as a whole. In default of a sustained growth in export values, the period was marked by an intense struggle for market shares. Britain lost ground in this contest mainly because she still relied on traditional lines, such as textiles and railway equipment, which were experiencing problems of secular decline, but also because exports were hit at a critical moment of recovery by the overvaluation of sterling following the return to gold in 1925.

After 1914 Britain also faced serious problems in South America, as elsewhere, because she was unable to muster the capital needed to run the international economy at its pre-war level.[5] Investment in Argentina and Brazil (the principal recipients of British capital in the continent after 1914, as before) continued to expand slowly during the 1920s, but the rate of return was generally lower than it had been in the pre-war era, and most of the new investment entering the republics in the 1920s was supplied by the United States. Once the world slump put an end to the modest recovery of the 1920s, inflows of capital from all sources virtually ceased until the close of the 1930s. Since income from shipping and insurance also suffered from falling profitability and reduced market shares after 1914, Britain could no longer rely on surpluses from South America to settle deficits with other parts of the world, and she even began to experience difficulties in balancing her payments with Argentina, her principal trading

5. The basic source for this period remains the pioneering study by J. Fred. Rippy, *British Investments in Latin America, 1822–1949* (Minneapolis, Minn., 1959). As this is now regarded as being unreliable in a number of respects, it has been used with caution and checked against recent research on individual countries. Investments made by the United States are well covered by Barbara Stallings, *Banker to the Third World: U.S. Portfolio Investment in Latin America, 1900–1986* (Berkeley, Calif., 1987).

partner.[6] Nevertheless, and despite the advance of the United States, Britain remained the largest foreign investor in South America down to 1939. The continent still accounted for a sizeable share of the total stock of British capital placed abroad, and, in consequence, it continued to be an important source of overseas investment income. If the 1920s were spent preparing the ground for a resumption of foreign lending, the 1930s were devoted to safeguarding the capital that had already been invested.

World War I eliminated one of Britain's leading rivals, Germany, but it also presented opportunities to another, the United States.[7] As Britain's own plans for taking over Germany's share of South American trade were frustrated by the demands of the war effort in Europe, the United States was able to increase her economic influence in the continent by strengthening her commercial and financial ties with the republics.[8] The growing concern, shared by the Foreign Office and the City, that the dollar would replace sterling lay behind the de Bunsen trade mission, which showed the flag in South America in 1918, and also prompted a number of schemes, at once devious and optimistic, for mobilising funds from other countries to support British interests.[9] Far from being isolated by the disruptive effects of hostilities, South America, like China, became an arena for a fierce, if still pacific, power struggle which saw Britain's dominance in the large southern republics challenged, though not yet displaced, by the United States.[10]

The long-term significance of Anglo-American rivalry was revealed during the 1920s. Britain gave notice of her intention of

6. Roger Gravil, *The Anglo-Argentine Connection, 1900–1939* (Boulder, Col., 1985), p. 164, but also Michael Hilton, 'Latin America and World Trade', in Mark Abrams, ed. *Britain and her Export Trade* (1946), p. 178.

7. The definitive work is now Bill Albert, with the assistance of Paul Henderson, *South America and the First World War: The Impact of the War on Brazil, Argentina, Peru and Chile* (Cambridge, 1988). See also Juan Ricardo Couyoumdjian, *Chile y Gran Bretaña durante la Primera Guerra Mundial y la postguerra, 1914–1921* (Santiago, 1986). A seminal study for the wider context is Carl Parrini, *Heir to Empire: United States Economic Diplomacy, 1916–1923* (Pittsburgh, Pa, 1965).

8. Two case studies of particular relevance to our main theme are: Robert Mayer, 'The Origins of the American Banking Empire in Latin America: Frank A. Vanderlip and the National City Bank', *Journal of Inter-American Studies and World Affairs*, 15 (1973), and Emily S. Rosenberg, 'Anglo-American Economic Rivalry in Brazil during World War I', *Diplomatic History*, 2 (1978), pp. 143, 150–1. See also C. Marichal, *A Century of Debt Crises in Latin America: From Independence to the Great Depression, 1820–1930* (Princeton, NJ, 1989), pp. 180–1.

9. Gravil, *Anglo-Argentine Connection*, pp. 142–3; Rosenberg, 'Anglo-American Economic Rivalry', pp. 136–9.

10. Albert, *South America and the First World War*, p. 308.

resuming her pre-war role in South America, and the two largest banks operating in Argentina and Brazil strengthened their capital base to meet the testing uncertainties of the day.[11] But Britain's long-term goal also called for measures which, in the short run, proved counter-productive. Foreign lending was restrained in the early 1920s to assist the return to gold, and interest rates were raised in 1925 to support the chosen parity, with the result that the capital available for overseas loans was offered on terms which were less competitive than they had been before the war. In the absence of a sizeable stream of overseas finance from London, Britain found herself relying on funds raised in the United States to maintain the Atlantic triangle of trade and payments.[12] In the 1920s it was capital flows from New York that enabled the South American republics to pay their debts in London and thus helped Britain to settle her deficit with the United States.

The interest of the United States, on the other hand, lay less in acting as a spear-carrier in a great British epic than in managing the Atlantic triangle to her own advantage.[13] That this required the destruction of the financial dominance of London was fully appreciated in the United States, and it found concrete expression in the increasingly concerted efforts of the New York banks to capture South American business from the mid-1920s.[14] As British diplomacy pondered the delicate task of re-establishing the supremacy of London through the medium of New York, the financial power of the United States began to cut into the market share and the profits of British banks and commercial services at the close of the 1920s.[15] Surveying the casualty list in 1929, the British Ambassador in Argentina commented that 'the United States under Hoover means to dominate this continent by hook or by crook. It is British interests that chiefly stand in the way. These are to be bought out or kicked out'.[16]

11. Couyoumdjian, *Chile y Gran Bretaña*, p. 214.

12. Marichal, *A Century of Debt*, pp. 187–8.

13. Joseph S. Tulchin, *The Aftermath of War: World War I and United States Policy Toward Latin America* (New York, 1971), pp. 101–7.

14. Burton I. Kaufman, 'United States Trade and Latin America: the Wilson Years', *Journal of American History*, 58 (1971), pp. 345, 353, 355; Rosenberg, 'Anglo-American Economic Rivalry', pp. 136–7; Marichal, *A Century of Debt*, p. 182. Banking competition had been limited during the war by the fact that Morgan, the leading investment bank in the United States, had respected Britain's sphere of influence. See Parrini, *Heir to Empire*, p. 55.

15. Rosenberg, 'Anglo-American Economic Rivalry', pp. 144–6, 150; Roger Gravil, 'British Retail Trade in Argentina, 1900–1940', *Inter-American Economic Affairs*, 29 (1970), pp. 8–10, 23; idem, *Anglo-Argentine Connection*, pp. 159–63.

16. FO memo. 25 October 1929. Quoted in Gravil, *Anglo-Argentine Connection*, p. 163. On the ambassador, Robertson, see ibid. p. 175, n.41.

It is important to recognise that this rivalry went far beyond the cut and thrust of normal business relationships, and became a battle for the 'hearts and minds of men' as well as for their pockets. The highly publicised visits of the eminent Princeton economist, Edwin Kemmerer, to South America in the 1920s acquired almost missionary status.[17] Animated by a spirit of scientific optimism, the 'money doctor' (as he became known) toured the Andean republics dispensing persuasive prescriptions for the ills of the time. The fact that his advice, which centred on fiscal reform and the adoption of the gold standard, was highly orthodox is less significant than his recommendation that the medicine should be bought from the United States, a prospect that caused a good deal of anxiety in London.[18] The gravitational pull of the United States also began to be felt at the level of popular culture through the spread of cinema, radio and newspaper services, a trend symbolised by the growing influence of Hollywood and by the creation of South America's first international superstar of light entertainment in the person of Carlos Gardel.[19]

With the onset of the world slump, the advance of the United States lost a good deal of its momentum. Capital flows dried up and renewed protectionism (installed by the formidable Hawley-Smoot Tariff of 1930) reinforced the ramparts of fortress America.[20] The transition from 'dollar diplomacy' to Roosevelt's Good Neighbor policy was not a straightforward shift from informal expansion to effective isolation. But in the early 1930s the United States was temporarily less of a threat to Britain than was the renascent presence of Germany. Excluded from the British and French empires by a network of discriminatory measures, and grappling with a balance of payments deficit that was rapidly depleting her gold reserves, Germany pushed into neutral areas such as South America, seeking exclusive bilateral links, bartering exports for essential imports, where possible, and making striking gains in Brazil and some of the smaller

---

17. Paul W. Drake, *The Money Doctor in the Andes: The Kemmerer Missions, 1923–1933* (Durham NC, 1989). As we have seen (p. 131), Kemmerer's presence and influence extended beyond South America with consequences that prompted remedial action from Britain's own itinerant money doctors.

18. Drake, *Money Doctor*, Ch. 1. For the wider context of Anglo-US financial rivalry during this period see Roberta Allbert Dayer, *Finance and Empire: Sir Charles Addis, 1861–1945* (1988), pp. 109–17. Kemmerer's visit to South Africa in 1924 was greatly resented by the Bank of England (ibid. p. 168).

19. Tulchin, *Aftermath of War*, pp. 206–33; Simon Collier, *The Life, Music, and Times of Carlos Gardel* (Pittsburgh, Pa, 1986).

20. On the cessation of foreign lending see Stallings, *Banker to the Third World*, App. A.

republics.[21] The prospect that a string of fascist colonies might materialise in South America, combined with anxieties that membership of Britain's new sterling club might also be extended to the republics, prompted the United States to take a renewed interest in the continent at the close of the 1930s.[22] The passage of the Reciprocal Trade Agreements Act in 1934 and the creation of the Export-Import Bank in the same year were early signals of this intent.[23] As international rivalry intensified, it also took on a new aspect during this period, spreading beyond trade and finance to the control of airways and airwaves, as fascist propaganda, beamed initially at German and Italian immigrant communities, challenged the battered and still underfunded forces of liberalism.[24] As far as South America was concerned, World War II was very largely a continuation of these conflicts by other means, which suggests that more emphasis ought to be given to its imperialist origins.[25]

The leaders of South American states had no doubt that they were under threat from contending imperialist forces. It was commonly accepted by Brazilian commentators in the 1930s that the world was divided between 'colonizing peoples and colonizers', and that there was no room for intermediate categories.[26] Oswaldo Aranha, Brazil's

21. There is considerable literature on Germany's relations with South America during this period. An accessible overview is Alton Frye, *Nazi Germany and the American Hemisphere, 1933–1941* (New Haven, Conn. 1967). More recent literature is cited in Jean-Pierre Blancpain, 'Des visées pangermanistes au noyautage hitlérien: la nationalisme allemand et l'Amérique latine (1890–1945)', *Revue Historique*, 281 (1989). On the important military connection see Frederick M. Nunn, *Yesterday's Soldiers: European Military Professionalism in South America, 1890–1940* (Lincoln, Nebr., 1983).

22. This re-entry is dealt with by David B. Haglund, *Latin America and the Transformation of U.S. Strategic Thought, 1936–1940* (Albuquerque, 1984).

23. Stanley E. Hilton, *Brazil and the Great Powers, 1930–1939* (Austin, Texas, 1975), pp. 39, 48–9, 71; Frederick C. Adams, *Economic Diplomacy: The Export-Import Bank and American Foreign Policy, 1934–1939* (Columbia, Miss., 1976).

24. Frye, *Nazi Germany*. Case studies include: Ricardo Silva Seitenfus, 'Ideology and Diplomacy: Italian Fascism and Brazil, 1935–38', *Hisp. Am. Hist. Rev.*, 64 (1984); Orazio A. Ciccarelli, 'Fascist Propaganda and the Italian Community in Peru during the Benvides Regime, 1933–39', *Jour Latin Am. Stud.*, 20 (1989), pp. 361–8. See also Fred. Fejes, *Imperialism, Media, and the Good Neighbor: New Deal Foreign Policy and the United States Shortwave Broadcasting to Latin America* (Norwood, NJ, 1986); William A. Burden, *The Struggle for Airways in Latin America* (New York, 1943); and Alfred Padula, 'Pan Am in the Caribbean: the Rise and Fall of an Empire', *Caribbean Review*, 12 (1983), pp. 24–7, 49–51.

25. The starting point for this subject, which has attracted a good deal of research in recent years, is now R.A. Humphreys, *Latin America and the Second World War*, Vol. I (1981), Vol. II (1982). For one of many case studies see Graham Taylor, 'The Axis Replacement Program: Economic Warfare and the Chemical Industry in Latin America, 1942–44', *Dip. Hist.*, 8 (1984).

26. Hilton, *Brazil and the Great Powers*, p. 183.

astute Minister of Finance, predicted in 1935 that 'a new era of colonial ambitions, determined more by economic factors than strictly political ones, is going to take charge of universal destinies.'[27] Survival was seen to depend on manipulating these menacing expansionist forces by using one power to fend off another without allowing protection to become captivity – a dangerous game but one without alternatives.

While juggling with weighty foreign interests, South American governments also had to grapple with serious domestic problems, especially in the aftermath of the world slump, which brought widespread economic distress and caused a rash of defaults on foreign loans and a matching set of political and military coups.[28] Moreover, it became clear in the 1930s that these upheavals were not merely products of a temporary, if severe, crisis in the world economy, but were also connected to underlying long-run developments, notably the closing of the agricultural frontier and the continuing expansion of population, which posed acute problems of future sources of economic growth and employment, and also called into question the established alliance between export-interests and foreign firms.[29]

These developments and their policy implications have rightly been given considerable attention by specialists of the period who have examined the rise of radical nationalism, state intervention, and the growth of import-substituting industries. Yet, as recent work has also shown, powerful continuities survived amidst manifest signs of change, especially in the area of international economic policy, where liberal orthodoxy retained remarkable influence in unpropitious circumstances.[30] Admittedly, the fulsome pro-British proclamations of a Pellegrini or a Nabuco were rarely issued by their successors, but

27. Quoted in ibid. p. 11.
28. Overviews include: Carlos F. Diaz Alejandro, 'Latin America in the 1930s', in Rosemary Thorpe, ed. *Latin America in the 1930s: The Role of the Periphery in World Crisis* (New York, 1984); Michael Twomey, 'The 1930s Depression in Latin America: a Macro Analysis', *Explorations in Economic History*, 20 (1983); and Marichal, *A Century of Debt*, Ch. 8.
29. Contemporary discussion of these questions is dealt with by Guido Di Tella, 'Economic Controversy in Argentina from the 1920s to the 1940s', in Guido Di Tella and D.C.M. Platt, eds. *The Political Economy of Argentina* (1986).
30. There is now a developing revisionist literature on this theme. See, for example, A. O'Connell, 'Free Trade in One (Primary Producing) Country: the Case of Argentina in the 1920s', in Di Tella and Platt, *Political Economy*; Peter Alhadeff, 'The Economic Formulae of the 1930s: a Reassessment', in ibid.; Steven Topik, *The Political Economy of the Brazilian State, 1880–1930* (Austin, Tex., 1987); and Winston Fritsch, *External Constraints on Economic Policy in Brazil, 1889–1930* (1988). Fascinating insights by a contemporary and participant are given by Raúl Prebisch, 'Argentine Economic Policies since the 1930s', in Di Tella and Platt, *Political Economy*.

the appeal of liberal doctrines had always been pragmatic and was no less effective for being shorn of some accompanying rhetoric, however genuine. Open economies were maintained as far as possible and for as long as possible; debt service was continued to the point where default was a necessity rather than a matter of choice; and the republics generally cooperated in the various schemes put forward by foreign missions to reorder their fiscal and monetary policies. If the state became interventionist, it was largely to safeguard the existing division of labour, not to overthrow it, and the steps taken to promote local industries were motivated partly by the need to economise on imports so that foreign debts could be serviced. The new authoritarian regimes harnessed populism, but they also aimed to control radicalism. By the end of the period, the old export alliance had been jolted but not unseated, and some of the partners looked forward to riding again after World War II.

ARGENTINA

Argentina remained by far the most important of Britain's commercial partners in South America after the war, as before, and indeed accounted for an increasing share of Britain's trade with that continent.[31] The republic took 42 per cent of Britain's exports to South America in 1913, 48 per cent in 1928–9, and 53 per cent in 1936–7. Imports from Argentina represented an even higher proportion, amounting to 58 per cent, 68 per cent and 63 per cent respectively of the value of goods shipped to Britain from the continent in the same years. In addition, well over half the stock of British capital in South America was held in Argentina, and at its peak in 1929 amounted to about £435m., which generated approximately 12 per cent of Britain's income from overseas investments.[32] Argentina was clearly a weighty

31. The data are derived from the sources given in n. 4 above, from Laura Randall, *An Economic History of Argentina in the Twentieth Century* (New York, 1978), pp. 224–5, and from Colin Lewis, 'Anglo-Argentine Trade, 1945–1965', in David Rock, ed. *Argentina in the Twentieth Century* (1975), p. 115.

32. See David Rock, *Argentina, 1516–1982* (1986), p. 192, and Rippy, *British Investments*, p. 161. However, it has to be said that this remains a very grey area. See also the estimates given in Albert, *South America and the First World War*, p. 147 (for 1913), Gravil, *Anglo-Argentine Connection*, p. 183 (for 1930), and Humphreys, *Latin America and the Second World War*, I, p. 30 (for 1936). There is at present no work on British investment during the period after 1914 to compare with Irving Stone's *The Composition and Distribution of British Investment in Latin America, 1865–1913* (New York, 1987).

commercial partner, ranking on a par with Canada, Australia and India, and not therefore one to be given up lightly.

Britain responded to the problems thrown up by World War I by subjecting Argentina to a degree of ungentlemanly pressure which infringed the republic's sovereignty and limited her freedom of choice.[33] Although Argentina refused to depart from neutrality, Britain tightened her grip on the direction of overseas trade by insisting that ties with Germany were cut and by contracting various purchasing agreements which committed the republic to supply the Allied powers with essential items. In some cases, these agreements were extended into the immediate post-war period – a helping hand which Vestey Bros, for example, used to improve their position in the meat trade.[34] The election of the Radical Party in 1916 was no more welcome in London than the accompanying anti-foreign rhetoric of the new President, Hipolito Yrigoyen, but these developments proved to be portents of a distant future rather than signals of immediate change. The essential planks of the Anglo-Argentine relationship survived the strains of war: the dividends of British firms continued to be remitted freely, and interest on the national debt was paid punctually, despite the hardship this caused in Argentina.[35]

Britain's plans for restoring the pre-war order were also shared by the most influential circles in Argentina after 1918.[36] Yrigoyen never pressed his attacks on British interests to the point where a major confrontation took place. His most publicised success was in preventing the British railway companies from increasing their rates in 1919; his less well publicised concession, in one of his last acts as president in 1922, was to allow the rise to take place.[37] His successor, Marcelo Alvear, was keen to maintain the Anglo-Argentine alliance, partly to secure a market for the republic's exports of foodstuffs at a time when over-supply in world markets was becoming a problem, and partly to have a counterweight to the growing influence of the United

33. Gravil, *Anglo-Argentine Connection*, Ch. 5; Albert, *South America and the First World War*, pp. 61–77, 143–56.
34. Gravil, *Anglo-Argentine Connection*, p. 133; but see also Albert, *South America and the First World War*, pp. 68–9.
35. Albert, *South America and the First World War*, pp. 155–6; Marichal, *A Century of Debt*, pp. 175–7.
36. This is not to underestimate the influence of the war in stimulating discussion of possible alternative paths of economic development. See Javier Villanueva, 'Economic Development', in Mark Falcoff and Ronald H. Dolkart, eds. *Prologue to Peron: Argentina in Depression and War* (Berkeley, Calif., 1975), pp. 58–9; and Randall, *Economic History*, p. 220.
37. Winthrop R. Wright, *British-Owned Railways in Argentina: Their Effect on Economic Nationalism, 1854–1948* (Austin, Tex., 1974), pp. 119–23.

States. Consequently, in the 1920s Argentina adhered to open, free-trading policies which fitted with Britain's interests.[38] Tariffs remained low, foreign debts continued to be serviced, and relations between the Argentine government and the railway companies returned to congenial normality.[39]

The real threat to Britain's design at this time came from the advance of the United States rather than from the rise of Argentine nationalism. During the 1920s the United States began investing in Argentina on a sizeable scale for the first time, buying into public utilities and financing sales of new products, such as electrical goods and motor vehicles.[40] In 1929, when concern in London reached the point of alarm, the Foreign Office tried to stem the tide by dispatching a high–level trade mission to South America under the leadership of Edgar Vincent (metamorphosed as Lord D'Abernon), whose early career had been spent in the deep waters of Ottoman finances.[41] In a second metamorphosis, Yrigoyen, who had returned to office in 1928, kept his name but changed his opinions, and issued a series of reassuring, pro-British messages. Britain's railway investments, he declared, were 'sacred'. 'We have worked with the English and with English capital for fifty years. We know them and what they are. I see no reason of exchanging old friends for new'.[42]

The D'Abernon mission played on the president's fear of the United States and hinted that Argentina might be excluded from the various schemes for imperial preference then under discussion. In the hope of keeping the door open for Argentina's exports, Yrigoyen agreed to buy an additional £9m. worth of British manufactures, which was the equivalent of Britain's balance of trade deficit with Argentina at that time. To confirm the alliance, Britain allowed a loan of £5m. to be issued through Barings (though the arrangement was kept secret because the Treasury had just reimposed its curb on overseas loans). The agreement was regarded as a triumph for the British negotiators, though it is now clear that it also suited the

38. O'Connell, 'Free Trade'.

39. The principal tariff increase (in 1923) was for revenue rather than for protectionist purposes. See O'Connell, 'Free Trade', p. 90. On the railways see Wright, *British-Owned Railways*, pp. 126–30.

40. Stallings, *Banker to the Third World*, pp. 125, 131, 134, 164, 170; Marichal, *A Century of Debt*, pp. 182–91; Gravil, *Anglo-Argentine Connection*, Ch. 6.

41. See Volume I, pp. 406–7. On the D'Abernon Mission see Gravil, *Anglo-Argentine Connection*, pp. 163–72; Wright, *British-Owned Railways*, pp. 130–5; and Paul B. Goodwin, 'Anglo-Argentine Commercial Relations: a Private Sector View', *Hisp. Am. Hist. Rev.*, 61 (1981), pp. 37–41.

42. Quoted in Wright, *British-Owned Railways*, p. 133.

interests of the Argentine government.[43] In the event, D'Abernon was denied his success. Yrigoyen was overthrown by a military coup in 1930, following the trade depression and ensuing revenue crisis, and his successor, General Uriburi, began his presidency by favouring the United States.[44] One of his first acts was to bury the D'Abernon agreement – much to the satisfaction of United States' business interests in Argentina.[45]

The D'Abernon mission had no practical significance, but it stands as a reaffirmation of Britain's determination to prevent the United States from taking over Argentina, and it can also be seen both as a holding operation pending the re-establishment of free trade and as an anticipation of the bilateral agreements which Britain deployed in constructing a smaller trading world in the 1930s. Either way, Britain's claim to enjoy a special relationship with Argentina remained unqualified. As the British ambassador in Buenos Aires put it: 'Without saying so in as many words, which would be tactless, what I really mean is that Argentina must be regarded as an essential part of the British empire'.[46]

Uriburu's expectations of the United States were rapidly disappointed by the abrupt cessation of foreign lending and by the revival of protectionism in 1930. Uriburu himself was quickly dispatched, and his successor, General Agustin Justo, who took office in 1930, reasserted the influence of the large landowners who had traditionally benefited from the Anglo-Argentine alliance. By this time, however, Britain was already moving towards a system of imperial preference, and Argentina faced the prospect that this door, too, would soon close. The republic still hoped to be treated as an 'honorary dominion', but the paid-up members, especially Australia, made sure that she was excluded from the Ottawa agreements, with the result that her exports to Britain came up against increased duties and quantitative restrictions.[47] These developments were particularly serious for the beef industry, which relied almost exclusively on the British

---

43. Goodwin, 'Anglo-Argentine Commercial Relations', pp. 39–40.

44. David Rock, 'Radical Populism and the Conservative Elite, 1912–1930', in Rock, ed. *Argentina*, pp. 84–7; Anne Potter, 'The Failure of Democracy in Argentina, 1916–1930: an Institutional Perspective', *Jour. Latin Am. Stud.*, 13 (1981).

45. Though the charge that Standard Oil played an important part in the coup is not supported by the evidence. See Rock, 'Radical Populism', p. 84, and Gravil, *Anglo-Argentine Connection*, p. 172.

46. Robertson to Henderson, 17 June 1929, FO 37/13460. Quoted in Wright, *British-Owned Railways*, p. 135.

47. Ian M. Drummond, *Imperial Economic Policy, 1917–1939* (1974), pp. 254–66; Gravil, *Anglo-Argentine Connection*, pp. 179–86.

market and which also formed the economic basis of the political power of the ruling elite.

These problems led to a series of discussions which produced the Roca–Runciman Pact in 1933 and set the course of Anglo-Argentine commercial relations for the rest of the decade.[48] The Pact was controversial at the time and it remains a lively issue among specialists today. On the one hand, it has been seen as an imposition which sacrificed Argentina's national development, especially the prospects for autonomous industrial growth, to the interests of a privileged minority; on the other, it has been regarded as a negotiated deal which was crucial to the economic recovery of the republic during the 1930s. The exploration of these questions stretches beyond the direct concern of this study. However, it is relevant to observe that the debate has suffered from a tendency to overemphasise the role of commodity trade; recent research, in revealing the importance of the financial aspects of the Pact, suggests that the priorities of the British side were those which, as we argued earlier, also underlay the Ottawa agreements.[49]

There seems little doubt that the Pact saved the Argentine beef industry by allowing meat exports access to the British market. Although the terms of entry were less generous than in the days of unrestricted free trade, the share of Argentine exports sent to Britain nevertheless rose from 28 per cent in 1927 to 36 per cent in 1939.[50] In return, Argentina reduced tariffs on goods imported from Britain, though with results that were not quite so clear cut. Britain's staple exports held on to business they would otherwise probably have lost, and her share of the import market increased, mainly at the expense of the United States. But the rise was modest (from 19 per cent in 1927 to 22 per cent in 1939),[51] and it is significant that local importers did not regard the Pact as giving Britain's traditional manufactures a

48. See Gravil, *Anglo-Argentine Connection*, pp. 186–203; Marcelo de Paiva Abreu, 'Argentina and Brazil during the 1930s: the Impact of British and American Economic Policies', in Thorpe, *Latin America*; Arturo O'Connell, 'Argentina into the Depression: Problems of an Open Economy', in ibid.; Peter Alhadeff, 'Dependency, Historiography and Objections to the Roca Pact', in Christopher Abel and Colin Lewis, eds. *Latin America, Economic Imperialism, and the State* (1985); idem, 'Economic Formulae', in Di Tella and Platt, *Political Economy*. Roca was Vice-President and 'an anglophile and a gentleman' (Wright, *British-Owned Railways*, p. 167); Runciman, the President of the Board of Trade, was a gentleman above most gentlemen. The Pact was renewed in 1936 and lasted until 1956.

49. See pp. 84–90.

50. Colin Lewis, 'Anglo-Argentine Trade, 1945–1965', in Rock, ed. *Argentina*, p. 115.

51. Ibid.

new lease of life.[52] On the contrary, the members of the British Chamber of Commerce in Buenos Aires were beginning to move into local industries in the 1930s, and their interest in the old staples was steadily diminishing.[53]

The financial aspects of the Pact were much more significant from the British point of view and were an important consideration for the Argentine side too.[54] The financial crisis in 1931 had compelled Argentina to impose exchange controls to prevent the value of the peso from collapsing.[55] Blocking the repatriation of profits created serious difficulties for British firms and for an estimated 20,000 British investors who depended, to a greater or lesser degree, on incomes derived from capital placed in Argentina.[56] However, exchange controls could not be lifted without external financial assistance to support the peso. The problem was solved by a loan of £11m., known as the Roca Funding Loan, which was raised in London by Barings in 1933. Once the Funding Loan had been agreed, both sides were free to sign the more publicised Roca–Runciman Pact. Seen in this context, the Pact was significant less as an agency promoting British manufactures than as an instrument of debt collection which provided Argentina with the means of earning sufficient sterling to meet her foreign obligations.[57] Taken together, the Loan and the Pact were vital to maintaining Argentina's credit-worthiness, and to creating the conditions which enabled her, remarkably, to service her debts without interruption throughout the 1930s.[58]

It is clear that Argentine governments adopted a consistently orthodox response to the economic crisis and that they did so to preserve their markets and credit in Britain. Moreover, fiscal and monetary orthodoxy continued to characterise policy throughout the 1930s. Public expenditure was contained, import tariffs (and internal taxes) were raised when necessary to balance the budget, and the money supply was closely controlled to hold the value of the peso, as

52. Goodwin, 'Anglo-Argentine Commercial Relations', pp. 32, 47.

53. Ibid. p. 49.

54. See especially Abreu, 'Argentina and Brazil', and Alhadeff, 'Dependency, Historiography'.

55. In 1929, the economic crisis had forced Argentina to close the Conversion Office and to suspend automatic convertibility, though gold exports were allowed so that the public foreign debt could continue to be serviced.

56. Board of Trade data published in the *South American Journal*, 4 March 1933, and cited in Alhadeff, 'Dependency, Historiography', p. 371.

57. Abreu, 'Argentina and Brazil', pp. 154–6; Alhadeff, 'Dependency, Historiography', pp. 369–71.

58. Alhadeff, 'Dependency, Historiography', p. 373; idem, 'Economic Formulae', pp. 109–11.

this was crucial to maintaining the confidence of external investors.[59] It was these considerations, rather than plans for wider development, that underlay the creation of the Central Bank in 1935, following advice from one of Britain's own money doctors, Sir Otto Niemeyer, a director of the Bank of England and a former senior Treasury official.[60] The Central Bank, one of several established during the 1930s in the empire and associated countries with strong ties to Britain, was in many respects an agent of British policy. Barings (who still acted as official advisers to the Argentine government) had well-placed contacts within the Bank itself, and representatives of British banks in the republic were on the Board of Directors.[61] Besides overseeing domestic monetary orthodoxy, the Bank was important in strengthening Argentina's ties with the emerging sterling bloc by pegging the peso to sterling and by holding the republic's currency reserves in London.[62]

The priority given by Britain to protecting existing investments during this period was implemented with notable tenacity in the case of the railways.[63] The railway companies, many of which were still British-owned, ran into serious difficulties in the 1930s as profits fell in the depression. When the companies tried to shore up their position by pressing for special concessions from the Argentine government, they met a hostile response. Given that the railways accounted for a very sizeable share of all British investment in Argentina, the Foreign Office did what it could to assist them, though in the event without much success. However, the outcome was not a defeat for British policy or for British investors. By 1935 the Foreign Office had reached the conclusion that the railways were becoming a lost cause, partly because of their managerial deficiencies, but mainly because of competition from motor transport, which developed rapidly in the 1930s following an aggressive marketing drive by US companies.[64] Moreover, by provoking a nationalist reaction, the railways were

59. Alhadeff, 'Economic Formulae'; idem, 'Public Finance and the Economy in Argentina, Australia and Canada during the Depression of the 1930s', in D.C.M. Platt and Guido Di Tella, eds. *Argentina, Australia, and Canada: Studies in Comparative Development, 1870–1965* (1985).

60. Alhadeff, 'Economic Formulae', pp. 112–13.

61. Randall, *Economic History*, pp. 64–5; Jorge Fodor, 'The Origins of Argentina's Sterling Balances, 1939–43', in Di Tella and Platt, *Political Economy*, p. 158.

62. Philip W. Bell, *The Sterling Area in the Postwar World* (Oxford, 1956), p. xxiv.

63. Raúl García Heras, 'Hostage Private Companies under Restraint: British Railways and Transport Coordination in Argentina during the 1930s', *Jour. Latin. Am. Stud.*, 19 (1987); Wright, *British-Owned Railways*, Chs. 10–11.

64. Raúl García Heras, *Automotores noteamericanos, caminos y modernizacíon urbana en la Argentina, 1918–1939* (Buenos Aires, 1985).

jeopardising wider financial interests as well as their own position.[65] With these considerations in mind, and with the cooperation of the companies, the Foreign Office began to negotiate the transfer of the railways to the Argentine government. Agreement was reached in principle in 1936, though the terms remained in dispute. However, following the outbreak of World War II, Argentina accumulated large sterling balances which Britain effectively blocked in London until 1948, when they were finally released to enable the republic to buy the railways outright in a deal which met both the claims of popular nationalism and the interests of foreign investors.[66] Since Peron's government also used the occasion to pay off all outstanding bonds held in Britain, the date can be said to mark the end of a century of Anglo-Argentine relations which began with the outflow of capital from London and ended with its repatriation.[67]

BRAZIL

Britain's relations with Brazil in the period after 1914 deserve more attention than they have received, despite the appearance of some familiar signs of decline, because they illustrate with particular clarity the continuing priority attached to finance at a time of developing rivalry with the United States. The value of Anglo-Brazilian commerce fell steadily, and Britain's share of the republic's total overseas trade also dropped – in the case of the import market from 25 per cent in 1913 to 10 per cent in 1938 and in the case of exports from 13 per cent to 9 per cent during the same period.[68] By the close of the 1930s the United States and Germany had become Brazil's leading overseas trading partners. It is also true that most of the new foreign capital entering Brazil in the 1920s came from the United States, and that in the 1930s Britain was disinvesting, with the result that the total stock of British capital held in the republic dropped from about

65. Heras, 'Hostage Private Companies', pp. 50–1, 60–1.
66. Raúl García Heras, 'World War II and the Frustrated Nationalization of the Argentine British-Owned Railways, 1939–1943', *Jour. Latin Am. Stud.*, 17 (1985); Wright, *British-Owned Railways*, Chs.11–13; Fodor, 'Origins of Argentina's Sterling Balances', pp. 164–78; Lewis, 'Anglo-Argentine Trade', pp. 131–2.
67. Marichal, *A Century of Debt*, p. 217.
68. The data are derived from sources given in n. 4 above. See also Peter Uwe Schliemann's neglected study, *The Strategy of British and German Direct Investors in Brazil* (1981), pp. 104–5.

£291m. in 1929 to about £160m in 1938.[69] Nevertheless, Britain was still the largest foreign investor in Brazil in 1929, and possibly even in 1939 too. The British may have abandoned hopes of raising their share of commodity trade, but they mounted a spirited defence of their financial stake, while at the same time trying to keep the lid on the rising influence of the United States.

Initially, Britain expected to benefit from the elimination of Germany's trade with Brazil during World War I, though in the event the principal gains went to the United States.[70] British finance, however, was not so easily dislodged.[71] At the close of 1914, the long-standing connection with Rothschilds enabled Brazil to raise a large foreign loan (of £14.5m.), which made it possible for the republic to reschedule existing debts and hence to continue repayment, albeit at a reduced level. Two years later, opposition from the Rothschilds was sufficient to prevent Brazil from encouraging the United States to develop closer financial links with the republic.[72] As Britain's own financial position deteriorated, however, the United States made greater progress, and towards the end of the war the financing of the coffee trade began to shift from sterling to dollars and so from London to New York.[73] This development raised anxiety levels in London, but it was nevertheless seen as a trend that could be reversed once peacetime conditions had been restored.

The struggle to return to normality continued throughout the 1920s. Brazil's problems were intensified by the post-war slump of 1920–1, which pushed her into greater reliance on loans from the United States, initially to refinance existing obligations and subsequently to fund broader development projects, especially the expansion of public utilities and the purchase of foreign-owned railways.[74] As a result of these inflows, Brazil became by far the largest borrower in South America in the 1920s.[75] At the same time, the continuing fragility of Brazil's export sector and the uncertainties of a world which had yet to return to the gold standard prompted a set of

---

69. Albert, *South America and the First World War*, p. 309; Hilton, 'Latin America and World Trade', pp. 178–9; Rippy, *British Investments*, Ch. 13. Given the present state of research, these figures are best read as broad indicators of what is generally agreed to have been the main trend.

70. Albert, *South America and the First World War*, pp. 77–94, 130–43.

71. Fritsch, *External Constraints*, Ch. 3.

72. Ibid. p. 45.

73. Rosenberg, 'Anglo-American Economic Rivalry', pp. 131–2.

74. Marichal, *A Century of Debt*, pp. 173, 184, 197–9; Steven Topik, *The Political Economy of the Brazilian State* (Austin, Tex., 1987), pp. 127–8.

75. Marichal, *A Century of Debt*, pp. 184–5.

reforms, beginning in 1921, which widened the powers of the Banco do Brasil and in particular authorised it to increase the money supply.[76] These changes were the outcome of considerable debate in academic and political circles in Brazil, and they followed similar experiments undertaken during the war. They were intended to bail out the republic at a critical time rather than to launch a drive for economic independence, but they were nevertheless departures which placed the principles of sound finance at risk.

Britain responded to these twin challenges by using her leverage over the funding of Brazil's scheme for supporting coffee prices. This was a crucial issue, both because coffee still accounted for about 50 per cent of the value of all Brazil's exports during the early 1920s and remained vital to the republic's ability to service its debts,[77] and because of the continuing political weight of coffee interests, which Britain had traditionally supported. Moreover, Britain's influence in this sensitive area of finance was enhanced by the fact that the United States refused to lend for this purpose on the ground that subsidies for coffee producers had to be paid for by American consumers (and voters).[78] The City used its advantage to the full. In 1922 a group headed by Schroder, Barings and Rothschilds raised a loan of £9m. to fund the coffee support scheme, and attached strings to it which greatly reduced Brazil's control over the market by placing sales in the hands of a committee of City bankers (as had happened in 1908).[79] Similar loans were made later in the 1920s, after the federal government had transferred responsibility for supporting coffee to São Paulo, and ensured that London's influence continued to be felt at a particularly sensitive point of juncture between the economy and political authority.[80]

An opportunity arose for London to take a firm grip on Brazil's finances in 1923, when continuing economic difficulties led the republic to approach Rothschilds for a substantial loan of £25m.[81] The City used the occasion to send a high-level mission, led by Edwin

76. Principally by issuing fiat bank notes against short-term trade bills. See Fritsch, *External Constraints*, Ch. 4.
77. Fritsch, *External Constraints*, pp. 63, 70.
78. Marichal, *A Century of Debt*, pp. 195–6; Fritsch, *External Constraints*, p. 81.
79. Fritsch, *External Constraints*, pp. 67–8, 84.
80. Ibid. pp. 126–8, 154–7.
81. We are particularly indebted at this point to research by Winston Fritsch, who has rescued the Montagu Mission from undeserved obscurity. See 'The Montagu Financial Mission to Brazil and the Federal Economic Policy Changes of 1924', *Brazilian Economic Studies*, 9 (1985), and the slightly more compressed version in *External Constraints*, pp. 84–107.

Montagu, a prominent banker and former Secretary of State for India, to curb government expenditure and put an end to the Banco do Brasil's experiments with inflationary finance by imposing 'some palatable form of control or advice'.[82] Not a man for half measures, Montagu sought to halt the development of the Brazilian steel industry, control railway policy and take over the Banco do Brasil.[83] While pressing the Brazilian government to sell its shares in the Bank, Montagu asked Rothschilds if they 'or their friends' would be interested in buying them, a proposal that was appreciated but wisely declined on the grounds that 'it would be most unpopular in Brazil for the national bank to be owned by foreigners'.[84] Nevertheless, as well as drawing up a package of stern measures for the public sector, the final deal incorporated a device for separating the Banco do Brasil from the government, and in June the loan was cleared for flotation.[85] However, Montagu was denied his triumph at the last moment by the embargo on foreign loans which the Bank of England had just requested. Although his mission failed, it stands as a very clear (and little-known) example of Britain's continuing imperialist ambitions in a country where they are generally supposed to have withered away.

On this occasion, however, the message survived the departure of the medium. Driven by the continued deterioration of the economy, and by the consequent need to attract foreign lenders, Brazil adopted a deflationary policy in 1924 and also freed the federal budget of an encumbrance by transferring the responsibility for supporting coffee prices to the state of São Paulo.[86] These reforms, culminating in Brazil's return to gold in 1927, fell short of Montagu's requirements, but they were sufficient to re-establish the republic's credit-worthiness and they enabled the federal government to approach both the United States and Britain (once the embargo on foreign loans was lifted at the end of 1925) for new finance. In the intense competition between London and New York which followed, London retained control

82. Montagu to Rothschild, 26 December 1923. Quoted in Fritsch, *External Constraints*, p. 90. As noted below (pp. 182–3) Montagu's constitutional innovations while Secretary of State were designed to strengthen Britain's grip on India. His team included Sir Charles Addis, the peripatetic Chairman of the Hongkong and Shanghai Bank, who watched over Britain's financial interests in the Far East. (See below, pp. 241–2).
83. Fritsch, *External Constraints*, pp. 89–90. It is worth noting that Montagu's opposition to Brazil's proposed steel industry was prompted not by concern for British exports but by anxiety about the consequences of increased public expenditure for the republic's ability to pay its external debts.
84. Ibid. pp. 90–1.
85. Ibid. pp. 94–100.
86. Ibid. pp. 104–11, 114.

over the funding of the coffee support scheme, now guaranteed by São Paulo, while the much larger federal loan, which was supposed to be shared between the two financial centres, went to New York. This outcome was the result of a fortuitous diplomatic complication which led the Foreign Office to ask the City to withdraw from the loan at the last moment, and it provides an interesting example of how special interests could be called upon to defer to higher priorities which were in the long-term interest of all parties concerned.[87] The British bankers pointed out that 'we have financed Brazil since her independence and to allow her to go to America would be a great loss to this country'.[88] The Foreign Secretary replied that his request was in the interests of 'peace, which I take to be the first of British interests and especially the first interest of the City of London'.[89] Following this appeal, the bankers agreed 'to respect his wishes loyally'.[90]

In Brazil, as in Argentina, these unsteady and protracted attempts to return to pre-war normality were destroyed by the world slump. As export prices collapsed and the flow of foreign capital ceased, Brazil faced a serious balance of payments crisis, mounting domestic discontent, and heightened political tension.[91] Yet, even as the international economic order broke up, the Brazilian government still held on to the gold standard, serviced its debts and allowed remittances to be made freely.[92] At the same time, the federal government approached Rothschilds, cap in hand, for a major loan to support the gold standard.[93] The City responded by laying down conditions which were essentially those sought by the Montagu mission; the Brazilian representatives twisted and turned, but in the end they accepted. Once again, the City was close to taking hold of Brazilian finances; once again it was frustrated, this time by the coup that brought Getulio Vargas to power at the close of 1930.

The central question now became the protection of British investments in a world which was beginning to take to the idea of default.

87. The problem arose because Brazil's claim to be permanently represented on the Council of the League of Nations conflicted with Poland's application, which Britain supported. See Fritsch, *External Constraints*, p. 116.

88. Memo. by Wellesley, 19 April 1926, FO 371/11115, A2075/G. Quoted in Fritsch, *External Constraints*, p. 117.

89. Minute by Chamberlain, 16 April 1926, FO 371/11115, A2075/G. Quoted in ibid. p. 117.

90. As n. 88.

91. Fritsch, *External Constraints*, pp. 138–59.

92. Marichal, *A Century of Debt*, p. 203.

93. Fritsch, *External Constraints*, pp. 157–9; Marichal, *A Century of Debt*, p. 221.

Britain's immediate response was to dispatch Sir Otto Niemeyer to Brazil in 1931 to remind the government of the need to keep to the rules of the game. His report repeated the now standard British prescription in recommending tax increases, administrative reforms, a balanced budget, adherence to the gold standard, and the creation a central bank to maintain convertibility.[94] The medicine, however, was no longer acceptable: Vargas reacted by suspending payments on the foreign debt. Rothschilds, showing an impressive turn of speed, moved swiftly to limit the potential damage and (with the assistance of Niemeyer) managed to negotiate preferential treatment for the oldest and best secured loans, which were held principally by British investors.[95] When the Brazilian foreign debt was restructured in 1934, the partnership of Rothschilds and Niemeyer again succeeded in winning privileged treatment for British investors.[96]

In 1937, however, a further default occurred, this time in circumstances which revealed the extent to which foreign finance and foreign influence had become caught up in the gathering international rivalries of the immediate pre-war years.[97] From 1934 Germany had begun to make sizeable inroads into Brazil's overseas trade, principally by means of bilateral trade agreements. By ceasing to repay Brazil's existing debts, Vargas could afford to build up his 'new state' by diverting scarce foreign exchange to purchases of German capital goods and military supplies.[98] This strategy was possible only because Brazil's creditors were unwilling or unable to apply sanctions. The

94. Marichal, *A Century of Debt*, p. 220; Abreu, 'Anglo-Brazilian Economic Relations', pp. 381–2. Niemeyer also recommended a programme of economic diversification. See Fiona Gordon-Ashworth, 'Agricultural Commodity Control under Vargas in Brazil, 1930–1945', *Jour. Latin Am. Stud.*, 12 (1980), pp. 87–8. This was significant because it recognised the need to modify the pattern of specialisation established in the nineteenth century.

95. Marcelo de Paiva Abreu, 'Brazilian Public Debt Policy, 1931–43', *Brazilian Economic Studies*, 4 (1978), pp. 112–18.

96. Between 1932 and 1937 Brazil paid £6m. to £8m. per year (about 20 per cent of the import bill) in public debt service, mainly to British creditors: Abreu, 'Brazilian Public Debt', p. 115.

97. The best guide is Hilton's valuable study, *Brazil and the Great Powers*. See also Ricardo A. Silva Seitenfus, 'Le Brésil de Getulio Vargas et la formation des blocs, 1930–1942' (Ph.D. thesis, University of Geneva, 1981.)

98. Abreu, 'Brazilian Public Debt', pp. 138–9. It is now acknowledged that Vargas made dextrous use of international rivalries to secure Brazil's interests; but this is not to say that Brazil was able to become independent of the major powers. See Hilton, *Brazil and the Great Powers*, Chs. 5–6, and, for the end of the story, idem, 'The Overthrow of Getulio Vargas in 1945: Diplomatic Intervention, Defense of Democracy or Political Retribution', *Hisp. Am. Hist. Rev.*, 67 (1987). On the 'new state' see, for example, Stanley Hilton, 'The Armed Forces and Industrialisation in Modern Brazil: the Drive for Military Autonomy (1889–1954)', *Hisp. Am. Hist. Rev.*, 62 (1982).

United States exercised restraint over debt collection mainly because she was trying to turn Brazil into a political ally. Britain had no such larger motives but no leverage either: she could neither tempt Brazil by dangling the prospect of fresh supplies of capital nor threaten her export trade, which did not depend on the British market and had in any case already suffered from imperial preference.[99] If Britain's frustration was evident, so was her purpose: by the late 1930s the Foreign Office had abandoned the defence of Britain's trade with Brazil, while the City was pressing the republic to cut back on imports and to move further into import-substitution so that more foreign exchange would be available for debt service.[100]

Prospects for repayment did not brighten until 1939, when the United States adopted a more active policy towards Brazil to counter the spread of Nazi influence.[101] With the outbreak of war, Brazil lost her German connection and was drawn further into the embrace of the United States. In these changed circumstances, it is not surprising that Brazil came to terms with her creditors or that the settlement favoured bond-holders in the United States rather than those in Britain.[102] Although this deal confirmed the emergence of the United States as the leading foreign power in Brazil, it did not signal the immediate eclipse of British influence. In fact, British finance, though not British trade, was rescued by the exigencies of war: Brazil's need for export markets led in 1940 to the Anglo-Brazilian Payments Agreement, which gave Brazil an outlet for her exports in exchange for sterling credits in London.[103] The improvement in Britain's bargaining position ultimately enabled her to reach a satisfactory settlement of the debt problem, as in Argentina, by transferring British-owned assets to the Brazilian government. As in Argentina, too, Britain hoped to keep Brazil 'sterling minded', and made plans to recapture her position in South America once the war had ended.[104]

99. Hilton, *Brazil and the Great Powers*, pp. 133–9; Abreu, 'Anglo-Brazilian Economic Relations', pp. 381–3; idem, 'Brazilian Public Foreign Debt', pp. 134, 138–9.

100. Abreu, 'Anglo-Brazilian Economic Relations', pp. 382–3; idem, 'Argentina and Brazil', p. 149; idem, 'Brazilian Public Foreign Debt', pp. 115, 120–1.

101. Marichal, *A Century of Debt*, pp. 387–8; Abreu, 'Brazilian Public Foreign Debt', pp. 121–3; Hilton, *Brazil and the Great Powers*, pp. 195–7.

102. Abreu, 'Anglo-Brazilian Economic Relations', p. 387; idem, 'Brazilian Public Foreign Debt', pp. 122–5.

103. Abreu, 'Anglo-Brazilian Economic Relations', p. 387.

104. Ibid. p. 388; idem, 'Brazilian Public Foreign Debt', pp. 126–30. As Abreu has also shown, Britain manipulated Brazil's sterling balances to her own advantage: 'Brazil as a Creditor: Sterling Balances, 1940–1952', *Econ. Hist. Rev.*, 2nd ser. XLIII (1990). See also Hilton, *Brazil and the Great Powers*, p. 216.

CHILE

Chile was far less important from Britain's perspective than were Argentina and Brazil, and the decline of British interests there was also much more precipitate. World War I damaged Britain's dominance of trade and finance in Chile to a far greater extent than in Argentina and Brazil.[105] Exports from the United States filled the space left by Germany's enforced withdrawal, and US capital and technology began to develop Chile's resources of copper, the export of the future. The United States continued its advance during the 1920s, buying up public utilities and supplying most of the capital which funded the development policies promoted by President Ibanez, the self-styled 'Chilean Mussolini', at the close of the decade.[106] Britain's interests, on the other hand, remained concentrated on the nitrate industry, which began to suffer from the development of synthetics in the 1920s and declined precipitously during the 1930s.[107] With the advent of the slump, Chile, like Argentina and Brazil, maintained debt service for as long as possible, but the removal of Ibanez in 1931 also brought down financial orthodoxy, and default quickly followed.[108] The republic became caught up in the revived imperialism of the late 1930s, as the resurgence of German influence first alarmed the United States and then prompted an economic and diplomatic reaction which continued throughout World War II. Britain's involvement in these increasingly weighty developments was both limited and diminishing. She gave up any hope of enlarging her share of Chile's import market in the 1930s, and concentrated on looking after her investments. A series of protracted negotiations ensued, beginning in 1932, when Chile redeemed part of the external debt, and continuing until 1948, when a final settlement was reached.[109]

105. Albert, *South America and the First World War*, pp. 95–105, 156–65; Couyoumdjian, *Chile y Gran Bretaña*, pp. 247–8.

106. Michael Montéon, *Chile in the Nitrate Era: The Evolution of Economic Dependence, 1880–1930* (Madison, 1982), Ch. 5; Thomas F. O'Brien, 'Rich Beyond the Dreams of Avarice: the Guggenheims in Chile', *Bus. Hist. Rev.*, 63 (1989); Marichal, *A Century of Debt*, pp. 173, 181–91; Humphreys, *Latin America and the Second World War*, I, p. 23.

107. Albert, *South America and the First World War*, pp. 98, 105.

108. Marichal, *A Century of Debt*, p. 212.

109. Humphreys, *Latin America and the Second World War*, I, pp. 6, 24–6; Marichal, *A Century of Debt*, p. 212.

DEBT-COLLECTING AND CONTROL IN SOUTH AMERICA

Far from giving up her claim to be the predominant foreign power in South America, Britain made a sustained attempt to retain her grip on Argentina and Brazil, the most important republics, after 1914. In the 1920s her paramount concern was to reassemble the pre-war international economic order, with London conducting the orchestra, and to this end strenuous efforts were made to strengthen the British connection, as the Montagu Mission to Brazil and the D'Abernon Mission to Argentina demonstrate. The shortage of capital also highlighted the importance, for balance of payments reasons, of holding on to markets for manufactures. In the 1930s policy became centred more or less exclusively on the defence of existing, and still very substantial, investments. This priority was bound up with the aim of keeping the republics, as far as possible, solvent and 'sterling minded', and it found concrete expression in the central banks promoted by Britain's travelling 'money doctors', and in the quasi-imperial ties which joined Argentina to Britain after 1933.

While it is correct to say that the Roca-Runciman Pact was negotiated rather than imposed, it is also apparent that Britain used Argentina's dependence on the British market to extract favourable treatment for her investments. This point becomes clear from a comparison with Brazil. There, Britain's bargaining position was much weaker because none of Brazil's exports relied on the British market.[110] The result was that the republic was able to treat her creditors with less deference than Argentina dared risk. From this perspective, the Pact should be seen primarily as a means of debt-collecting: Argentina, like the Dominions, had to be allowed space in the British market so that she could earn the exchange needed to meet her foreign obligations. This aim would have been frustrated if Britain had negotiated better terms for her exports of manufactures. In fact, as we have seen, Britain's old staple exports were being jettisoned in the 1930s by the Foreign Office, the City and the British Chamber of Commerce in Buenos Aires in favour of working with nationalist demands instead of against them. Moving into local manufacturing was beginning to make sense on economic as well as on political grounds, and to the extent that it held out the promise of assisting debt payments it found favour in the City too.

110. The Peruvian case was very similar. See Bill Albert, 'Sugar and Anglo-Peruvian Trade Negotiations in the 1930s', *Jour. Latin Am. Stud.*, 14 (1982).

It is equally clear that the period after 1914 was characterised by intense imperialist rivalries over the 'unclaimed' regions of the world, the two outstanding examples being South America and China. This theme is bypassed by standard approaches to British imperialism which focus on the management of nationalism within the formal empire after World War I. As we have seen, the period witnessed a fierce struggle for financial control of the South American republics and for the markets that would fall to the successful power. The fact that the new conquistadors mobilised techniques of informal influence which made use of film, radio, cinema and the press, while also deploying tangible capital assets and the products of the second Industrial Revolution, adds to the distinctiveness as well as to the importance of this neglected phase of imperialist rivalry.

Britain's role in this contest was no more reactive than it was before 1914. She had sizeable commitments in South America which had to be developed as well as defended because they were integral both to her international system of trade and payments and, through this, to the structures of power and privilege at home. Consequently, Britain vigorously promoted her own interests as well as responded to the claims of Germany and the United States. Chile is one example of a number (especially among the smaller republics) where the takeover by the United States was comprehensive and seemingly irreversible soon after 1914, and it therefore showed the face of the future to contemporaries, even if they did not always recognise it. Elsewhere, however, Britain scored considerable success in looking after her interests in a world which no longer observed the rules of the game either instinctively or sometimes at all. If Argentina is the best example of a reliable (if sometimes reluctant) ally, it is also by far the most important one. It ought to be added, too, that Britain's performance in Brazil can be seen to have been much more impressive than is usually assumed, once attention is shifted from commodity trade to finance. Nor should the endless web-spinning diplomacy of the time be regarded as a rearguard action in the long retreat from empire. The descendants of the artificers who had galvanised Africa in the late nineteenth century did not see it that way, and in World War II, amidst the sound and debris of what might easily have become defeat, they held yet more meetings to design their re-entry in the post-war world. The timetable had slipped, but the plan remained intact.

CHAPTER EIGHT

'Financial Stability and Good Government': India, 1914–47[1]

After 1914, the study of India's history becomes increasingly preoccupied with political events and especially with charting the route to independence in 1947.[2] An older Whig tradition, invented to accompany the landmarks it described, purported to show that the transfer of power was the culmination of a sequence of well-judged constitutional reforms that set India on a progressive path toward liberal democracy. In more recent years, this interpretation has given way to an alternative which rejects the view that the road to independence consisted of a series of ordered steps, whether designed on high by imperial masterminds or hewn at ground level by dedicated nationalist leaders, and stresses instead the complexity of relationships among diverse political interests in Britain and India, and the uncertainty of their trajectory. In reaction to the element of uncritical self-approval that marked the older tradition, the newer approach emphasises the hard-headed bargaining that lay behind the idealised version of a stately procession towards independence; in harmony with the 'excentric' theory of imperialism, current thinking also allows room for the role of independent or semi-independent influences on the periphery.

1. The quotation is taken from a statement made by the Prime Minister (MacDonald) to the House of Commons in June 1931, and cited in B.R. Tomlinson, 'Britain and the Indian Currency Crisis, 1930–2', *Econ. Hist. Rev.*, 2nd ser. XXXII (1979), pp. 94–5: 'It will not be possible to introduce the proposed constitutional changes if financial stability is not assured and His Majesty's Government are determined not to allow a state of affairs to arise which might jeopardise the financial stability and good government of India'. We are grateful to Dr G. Balachandran for his helpful comments on this chapter. The forthcoming publication of his important research on inter-war monetary and fiscal policy will greatly advance our knowledge of these subjects.
2. Introductions to the recent literature are provided by John Gallagher and Anil Seal, 'Britain and India between the Wars', *Modern Asian Studies*, 15 (1981), and Sumit Sarkar, *Modern India, 1885–1947* (Delhi, 1983).

This aspect of recent historiography can be seen in the work produced by the school of 'subaltern studies', which has questioned perceptions of India's vast diversity formulated and represented by elites in Delhi and London, and has explored the many alternative worlds that existed in the provinces, underlining in the process the distinction between the ideals of policy and the realities of everyday practice.[3]

The contribution made by revisionist historians is rich and illuminating, and fits a broader trend in the study of 'late' colonialism in other parts of the British empire.[4] At the same time, the perspective remains predominantly political, even if much of the attention has shifted from officers to other ranks; and in some formulations it has posited an unnecessarily sharp distinction between interest and ideology. Accordingly, there remains room for a different kind of revisionism, one that seeks to reconsider the objectives of those who ran the Indian empire by relating economic to political considerations and by reappraising the metropolitan perspective on imperial management. This undertaking is not an attempt to turn the clock back by refurbishing an older-style of imperial history; nor is it in conflict with the view from the periphery. It simply suggests that questions relating to the direction of imperial policy towards India are historically significant, have become, in important respects, unfashionable, and need to be readvertised. The aim, however, is more easily formulated than executed because much of the work undertaken by economic historians, valuable though it is, has been inspired by a concern with economic development rather than with imperial purpose, and it, too, has tended to stay within sub-disciplinary boundaries. Nevertheless, sufficient research has been published in recent years to enable some of the links to be joined and for the following outline to be sketched.[5]

Our interpretation of the period after 1914 is essentially an extension of the argument we developed to explain Britain's purpose in India in the nineteenth century. Britain's traditional manufacturing interests, which were already beginning to suffer from free trade and from their inability to alter the priorities of policy-makers in London, underwent a marked decline in India after World War I. As we have

3. The best guide to the subject is Ranajit Guha, ed. *Subaltern Studies*, I–VI (Delhi, 1982–9). The approach can be compared to the literature on resistance in colonial Africa.
4. See also chapter 9.
5. It will become apparent that we are particularly indebted to research undertaken by Dr B.R. Tomlinson, whose work has transformed as well as enlarged our understanding of the period.

seen in other contexts, evidence of industrial decay has conventionally been used as an index of imperial decline too, and it forms the background to current debates about the management of Indian nationalism. This reasoning, as we have already argued, is misleading because it bypasses or underestimates a more important measure of value, that provided by fiscal priorities and the associated need to safeguard India's ability to fund her external financial obligations. These imperatives were determined not by a conspiracy of bond-holders but by a concern for the probity of public finance, though this had the additional and congenial effect of providing security for private investors. As we shall see, fiscal priorities exerted a powerful influence on economic policy after 1914, as before. The doctrine of the balanced budget inhibited an expansionist development pro-gramme and was a target of nationalist criticism. But it also sought to maximise export earnings and to increase revenue by taxing imports and by promoting local industries, and these measures aroused opposition from British manufacturers, who became increas-ingly frustrated with policies that favoured Indian interests above their own. Amidst these cross-currents, policy-makers held steadily to their purpose: in the 1920s India was drawn into Britain's efforts to reconstruct the pre-war international economic order; and in the 1930s, when hopes of world recovery financed by new investment were replaced by strategies of debt-collecting, India was ordered into the sterling bloc on terms dictated by London.

These priorities had wide-ranging political ramifications. The choice of political alliances in India was determined largely by the need to promote groups that would support the government's fiscal and monetary policies. At the outset of the period under review, when the land tax was still the most important source of state revenue, the Government of India continued to regard the large land-holders as being its principal allies.[6] However, as customs and excise duties assumed greater significance, Delhi attempted to win support from Indian representatives of the 'modern' economy in the hope that, by offering them a stake in the Raj, they could be detached from the nationalist movement. Limited constitutional reforms were intro-duced with the aim of controlling and redirecting opposition, not for the purpose of helping it on its way; radical political advance was constrained by the fear that the transfer of power would enable an

---

6. On the land tax see Dharma Kumar, 'The Fiscal System', in idem, ed. *The Cambridge Economic History of India*, Vol. II, *c.1757-c.1970* (Hyderabad, 1984), pp. 916–19, 928–9. Land revenues accounted for 50 per cent of total revenues in 1850–9, for 23 per cent in 1920–1, and for 21 per cent in 1940–1.

independent government to renege on its external financial obligations. While these conditions held, Britain did not relax her grip on
India any more than she did in the case of other debtor countries.
Independence was eventually conceded when India became ungovernable, but the transition was greatly eased by the fact that, in 1947, the
case for 'staying on' was no longer compelling. By then, India had
ceased to be one of Britain's largest debtors and had joined the ranks
of her creditors instead, while Britain's newer interest in joint ventures
in manufacturing and other economic activities pointed to the wisdom
of working with the nationalists rather than against them.

PATTERNS OF TRADE AND INVESTMENT

We can begin to expand this argument by considering the data on
foreign trade and investment.[7] After 1914, Britain's visible trade with
India underwent a secular decline that extended throughout the period
under review. On the eve of World War I, Britain still supplied about
two-thirds of India's imports, but this figure dropped to about half in
the 1920s, fell to nearly one-third in the 1930s (when Manchester
cottons were virtually eliminated from the Indian market), and sank
to one-quarter in 1940–41. Looked at from the perspective of the
metropole, India accounted for about 13 per cent of all visible exports
from the United Kingdom in 1913, about 11 per cent in the 1920s, 9
per cent in the 1930s and 8 per cent in the 1940s. In the 1920s the
value of British exports achieved a measure of stability, though at
levels that were approximately one-third lower than in the decade
before World War I; but export values were cut by more than half
between 1929 and 1937, and Britain's competitive position declined
to a greater extent in India than in the world as a whole.

The corollary of Britain's loss of exports was the penetration of
the Indian market by foreign rivals and the development of import-
substituting industries. The combined share of the import market

7. The summary which follows is derived from: the *Statistical Abstract for the British
Empire*, the *Statistical Abstract for the United Kingdom* (relevant years), K.N. Chaudhuri,
'Foreign Trade and the Balance of Payments (1757–1947)', in Kumar, *Cambridge
Economic History*, Ch. X, and B.R. Tomlinson, 'Imperial Power and Foreign Trade:
Britain and India, 1900–1970' (forthcoming). J.D. Tomlinson, 'Anglo-Indian Econ-
omic Relations, 1913–1928 with Special Reference to the Cotton Trade' (Ph.D. thesis,
University of London, 1977) contains valuable data on its particular subject. The
statistics are not robust enough to permit fine tuning but the broad trends are likely to
be accurate. The underlying figures include Burma until 1937.

taken by Britain's main competitors, Japan, Germany and the United States, rose from just under 10 per cent in 1914 to just over 33 per cent in 1936–7. The advance of foreign rivals was particularly marked in the 1930s, when Japan became the leading supplier of cotton goods. At the same time, Britain took an increasing proportion of India's exports, especially following the trade agreements of the 1930s, and in 1938–9 her share rose to just over one-third of the total. The development of import-substitution was even more telling: in 1900 imports accounted for about 63 per cent of the market for cotton textiles, and virtually all of them were British; by 1936 only about 12 per cent of the market was supplied by imports, of which a mere 4 per cent came from Britain. The remaining 88 per cent came from domestic sources: nearly two-thirds of this total were produced by modern textile mills. If benefits were conferred by British rule, very few of them found their way to Manchester during this period; and if the industrial bourgeoisie really did pull the wires of government, it is curious that they should have been so ineffective in defending their interests in India, which had long been one of their major markets, and was fully under British control.

British investment experienced a modest increase during the inter-war period as a whole, though the rise was very limited and occurred mainly in the early 1920s, when there was a temporary revival of government borrowing.[8] Thereafter, decline set in: lack of growth in the Indian economy limited its attractions to British investors as the 1920s advanced; lack of revenue, combined with political unrest, made them positively wary in the 1930s. Nevertheless, the composition of foreign investment experienced an important qualitative change which we have observed in other parts of the world: in the 1930s and 1940s, when much of the infrastructure of state-building had been laid down, there was increase in the proportion of private foreign investment and a corresponding decline in public-sector loans. This shift was associated with the beginnings of structural change in the economy, as opportunities for developing import-substituting activities drew in multinational corporations and encouraged joint-ventures by private entrepreneurs. Despite the failure to generate substantial new flows of foreign capital, India remained one of the

---

8. Evidence of the scale of private investment is fragmentary, but see A.K. Bagchi, *Private Investment in India, 1900–1939* (Cambridge, 1972), B.R. Tomlinson, 'Foreign Private Investment in India, 1920–1950', *Mod. Asian Stud.*, 12 (1978), and idem, 'Foreign Investment in India and Indonesia, 1920–1960', *Itinerario*, 10 (1986).

principal recipients of British foreign investment, and Britain still had a large stake to defend in the sub-continent.[9]

The full significance of these trends can be appreciated by looking at the balance of payments. Before 1914, Britain ran a surplus on her visible trade with India, and India settled the deficit through her exports to continental Europe and other parts of Asia.[10] This pattern of exchange survived in the 1920s, though in a less robust form, but it underwent a fundamental change in the 1930s, when India developed a surplus on her visible trade with Britain. The fact that Britain could no longer call upon substantial earnings from her commodity trade with India to settle her deficits with Europe and the United States was both a symptom and a contributory cause of her growing balance of payments problems in the inter-war period. To this extent, there is some truth in the view that India was less valuable to Britain in the 1930s than she had been before World War I. At the same time, however, India became a large net exporter of gold in the 1930s, and this item boosted her current account surplus and helped to service her foreign debt, pay the Home Charges and settle the deficit on the rest of her invisible trade. From this perspective, India remained highly prized: remittances from the sub-continent accounted for 15–16 per cent of Britain's total net invisible earnings in the 1930s and made a vital contribution to the stability of sterling and the balance of payments at a particularly difficult time.[11]

Transfers from India increased during the 1920s as a result of new government borrowing, and became more burdensome in the 1930s, when revenues were affected by the slump. Whereas in the late nineteenth century, debt service and the Home Charges accounted for about 16 per cent of India's current revenues, in 1933 they reached a peak of just over 27 per cent.[12] By then, India's surplus on her commodity trade with Britain had become increasingly necessary, both to pay for the growing proportion of imports drawn from other countries (notably Japan) and to meet her traditional obligations on her invisible account with Britain.[13]

The statistics on overseas trade and payments, fragmentary though they are in some respects, confirm that Britain's commodity exports

9. Tomlinson, 'Foreign Private Investment', p. 660.

10. See Volume I, pp. 178–80, 324, 341–3.

11. B. Chatterji, 'Business and Politics in the 1930s: Lancashire and the Making of the Indo-British Trade Agreement, 1939', *Mod. Asian Stud.*, 15 (1981), p. 529; Sarkar, *Modern India*, pp. 258–60.

12. Kumar, 'Fiscal System', pp. 937–9; B.R. Tomlinson, *The Political Economy of the Raj, 1914–1947* (1979), p. 90.

13. Tomlinson, *Political Economy*, pp. 45–6.

were indeed of diminishing importance in her trade with India after 1914, whether measured by absolute value or by their contribution to the balance of trade and balance of payments. In the embattled commercial world of the 1930s, India remained a sizeable market for British goods, and it was not one to be given up lightly. But the collapse of sales of Manchester cottons further reduced the national significance and political influence of British manufacturers trading to the sub-continent. Invisible earnings and transfers of capital, on the other hand, became relatively more important and acquired greater weight in Britain's stake in India. This evidence suggests two hypotheses. One is that the Government of India was likely to have been preoccupied by the need to ensure that payments to Britain continued to flow smoothly, and that fiscal and monetary policy remained central to Britain's imperial purpose. The other is that financial priorities raised delicate issues of political control: they had to be applied without provoking discontent on a scale that would imperil the authority structures that were vital to the functioning of the imperial economy.

THE GENTLEMEN OF THE RAJ

The argument derived from these hypotheses will be developed in the remaining part of this chapter. Before doing so, however, brief consideration needs to be given to the social background and cultural values of the men who managed India during the period under review. We have already suggested that the transition from Company to crown rule in 1858 created wider employment opportunities for members of professional families in the Home Counties, and is not to be seen as marking the triumph of the industrial bourgeoisie.[14] These recruits were either gentlemen or gentlemen in the making: accordingly, they tended to despise industry as well as to fear the spread of its influence, and they took more readily to activities that produced a means of support that was both substantial and virtually unseen. By upbringing and education, they had closer affinity with invisible income than with commodity trade, and they were enthusiastic agents of the fiscal and financial priorities of government as they emerged in India during the second half of the nineteenth century.

These values survived the decimation inflicted by World War I and

14. See Volume I, pp. 319–20, 327–33.

continued to infuse policy in India (as in Africa and Malaya) down to the point where British rule was withdrawn, and in some respects they survived its passing. The pessimism that weighed upon intellectuals as they brooded over 'the decline of the West' in the inter-war period did not in general burden members of the Indian Civil Service (ICS). They remained men with a purpose united by shared values. If these had been challenged during World War I, they were reinvigorated thereafter. The imperial mission continued to be a global advertisement for liberal capitalism and constitutional means of effecting change; as such, it had to be vigorously promoted to counter the powerful alternatives envisaged by Bolshevism, fascism and the pan-Islamic movements which appeared in different parts of the empire. In these circumstances, possessing an empire and defining a role were complementary, even inspirational, aims.

Gentlemanly norms continued to predominate: the ideal of the leisured amateur who undertook activities that had a general impact on the public mind remained unquestioned, as did the snobbery that was integral to the definition of social class in Britain and, when exported, turned members of the ICS into a caste in India. But gentlemen also aligned themselves to a code that stressed the virtues of honour, duty and public service, and they brought a moral certainty to the task of government that ought not to be discounted or treated as a disguise for material motives. This morality was derived from a particularly clear and sometimes militant brand of Christianity of the kind associated with the Round Table group and Exeter Hall.[15] Sir Arthur Hirtzel, the most important official in the India Office during the 1920s, was steeped in both the classics and Christian theology.[16] He believed, even after World War I, that the British empire was a greater, Christian version of the Roman imperial ideal, and that India's destiny under the Raj was bound up with her spiritual progress. An imperialist, he explained, was animated by the belief that 'the race to which he belongs is the noblest, and the civilization and ideals for which it stands are the highest – are, in fact, so high that all the world must needs accept them. Now, this is an

15. Gerald Studdert-Kennedy's illuminating study, *British Christians, Indian Nationalists and the Raj* (Delhi, 1991), provides an important corrective to accounts of British policy that concentrate on the process of bargaining and minimise the role of ideals and ideology.

16. Studdert-Kennedy, *British Christians*, Ch. 2. Hirtzel (1870–1937) was educated at Dulwich and Oxford, and was Assistant Under-Secretary of State at the India Office, 1917–21, Deputy Under-Secretary, 1921–4, and Permanent Under-Secretary, 1924–30.

outlook upon life that is at once familiar to the Christian'.[17] This vision does not merely qualify a crude, materialist interpretation of the imperial purpose, whether couched in political or economic terms, but suggests, more interestingly, ways in which principle and interest were joined. Both Sir Basil Blackett and Sir George Schuster, successively Finance Members of the Council of India during 1922–8 and 1928–34, were Christian exponents of economic rationality: financial management was for them an instrument of Christian rule, the balanced budget was the realisation of a state of spiritual harmony, and taxation was a powerful force for moral progress as well as a means of funding the Raj.[18] For such men, Christian faith and faith in the empire were spiritual and temporal dimensions of one integrated and superior system of belief.

As the values survived, so did the pattern of recruitment that supported them.[19] Members of the Indian Civil Service continued to be drawn overwhelmingly from upper- and middle-class families with professional backgrounds. With few exceptions, they were educated at public schools, and three-quarters of them had been to Oxford or Cambridge. The service was lifted from the depression that passed across it at the close of World War I, revitalised by a new sense of mission, and boosted by improvements in pay and conditions.[20] In the 1930s the ICS, having dealt firmly with Congress 'agitators', adapted to Congress governments; it also adjusted to a process of Indianisation, not least by assimilating Indian recruits to gentlemanly ideals.[21] The decline came during World War II, when lack of manpower allied to lack of will-power brought the machinery

17. Quoted in Studdert-Kennedy, *British Christians*, pp. 46–7.
18. Ibid. pp. 150–1, p. 240, n.16, pp. 226–7, n.33. Lugard held very similar views. Blackett (1882–1935), the son of a Nottingham vicar, was educated at Marlborough and Oxford. He was a leading City figure, and his directorships included the Bank of England, De Beers, and Cable and Wireless. Schuster (1881–1982) was educated at Oxford and enjoyed a successful career in the City before entering government service (in the Sudan) after World War I. Such men would repay further attention, not only for the interest of their Christian banking principles, but also because their advice and direction were felt in other parts of the empire besides India.
19. David C. Potter, *India's Political Administrators* (Oxford, 1986); T.H. Beaglehole, 'From Rulers to Servants: the I.C.S. and the Demission of Power in India', *Mod. Asian Stud.*, 11 (1977).
20. Ann Ewing, 'The Indian Civil Service, 1919–1924: Service Discontent and the Response in London and Delhi', *Mod. Asian Stud.*, 18 (1984).
21. Some fascinating records of this process have been set down by those who experienced it: Roland Hunt and John Harrison, *The District Officer in India, 1930–1947* (1980); Raj K. Niga, *Memoirs of Old Mandarins* (New Delhi, 1985); and S.Y. Krishnaswamy's gentle and self-deprecating *Memoirs of a Mediocre Man* (Jayanagar, 1983).

of government close to breakdown.[22] By 1945, however, Britain's interest in India had already begun to change; before then the gentlemen of the Raj did their duty effectively, as we shall now see.

THE IMPACT OF WORLD WAR I

World War I seriously disrupted India's international trade and payments.[23] Britain's exports were badly affected by shipping shortages, foreign competition (especially from Japan) and local import-substituting industries, and her surplus on visible trade with India disappeared.[24] British officials were alive to the threat posed by Japan, but recognised that she had to be allowed unfettered entry into India, even at the expense of Lancashire's textile exports.[25] Some inducement was needed to persuade Japan to acquiesce in the imperial presence in India at a time when she was tempted to encourage anti-colonial movements in Asia, and to bolster the Anglo-Japanese alliance, which was crucial to Britain's position in the Far East.[26] The war also dislocated India's gold exchange standard by severing the link between the level of currency in circulation and the value of the rupee.[27] Liquidity problems led to a growth in the money supply without a corresponding rise in India's reserves of silver bullion, and an increase in the world price of silver caused the bullion value of the rupee to rise above its established exchange rate. Consequently, the exchange rate became dependent on the sterling price of silver, while the level of currency in circulation was influenced by the government's financial needs. These needs mounted rapidly after 1914, principally because of the massive cost of stoking the British military

22. David C. Potter, 'Manpower Shortage and the End of Colonialism: the Case of the Indian Civil Service', *Mod. Asian Stud.*, 7 (1973).

23. The most valuable (and also curiously neglected) study is De Witt C. Ellinwood and S.S. Pradhan, eds. *India and World War I* (Manohar, 1978). Specialists on India might profit from Bill Albert, *South America and the First World War* (Cambridge, 1988).

24. See, for example, J.D. Tomlinson, 'The First World War and British Cotton Piece Exports to India', *Econ. Hist. Rev.*, 2nd ser. XXXII (1979).

25. See Thomas G. Fraser, 'India in Anglo-Japanese Relations During the First World War', *History*, 63 (1978).

26. Don Dignan, *The Indian Revolutionary Problem in British Diplomacy, 1914–1919* (New Delhi, 1983), Ch. 9.

27. B.R. Tomlinson, 'Monetary Policy and Economic Development: the Rupee-Ratio Question, 1921–1927', in K.N. Chaudhuri and Clive Dewey, eds. *Economy and Society: Essays in Indian Economic and Social History* (Delhi, 1979), pp. 200–1.

machine.[28] India supplied over 1.5 million men for war service between 1914 and 1918; the expense placed a heavy burden on the Indian taxpayer and pushed the budget into deficit.[29]

Economic problems led readily to civil disorder and provided popular support for a new brand of assertive nationalism which drew inspiration variously from the Irish Home Rule movement, the Japanese economic miracle and the Russian Revolution, as well as from its own indigenous roots. [30] This heady mixture, stirred by German support, solidified as the war progressed into demands for self-government and for a new deal for India's economy. This was a formative time for a whole generation of nationalist leaders, from Argentina to China. It saw the emergence of Gandhi as the leader of the Indian National Congress, and it set the political agenda until independence was achieved in 1947.[31] Gandhi displaced the moderate leadership of Congress, and drew upon popular support to an extent that transformed the nature as well as the size of the political arena.[32] The non–cooperation movement of 1921–2, for example, was the first of a succession of similar popular protests, and the fact that it was launched after Germany had been defeated indicated that settling the peace was going to be an even more difficult task than winning the war.

Britain's response to these challenges provides a good guide to her priorities and a sound measure of her commitment to holding the Indian empire. The budgetary crisis was met in 1917 by allowing the Government of India to increase the tariff on imported cotton goods from 3.5 to 7.5 per cent (without also raising the countervailing excise on Indian textiles).[33] Manchester's opposition was fierce but unsuc-

28. On the role of the Indian army see Jeffrey Greenhut, 'The Imperial Reserve: the Indian Corps on the Western Front, 1914–19', *Jour. Imp. and Comm. Hist.*, 12 (1983); Keith Jeffrey, *The British Army and the Crisis of Empire, 1918–22* (Manchester, 1984), Ch. 6; and S.D. Pradhan, 'Indian Army and the First World War', in Ellinwood and Pradhan, *India and World War I*.

29. Tomlinson, *Political Economy*, pp. 106–10.

30. On protest movements see Sakar, *Modern India*, pp. 147–64, Dignan, *The Indian Revolutionary Problem*, and (for a non-politicised example) David Arnold, 'Looting, Grain Riots and Government Policy in South India, 1919', *Past and Present*, 84 (1979).

31. Judith M. Brown, *Gandhi's Rise to Power: Indian Politics, 1915–1922* (Cambridge, 1972).

32. Judith M. Brown, 'War and the Colonial Relationship: Britain, India and the War of 1914–18', in Ellinwood and Pradhan, *India and World War I*; Stanley A. Wolpert, 'Congress Leadership in Transition: Jinnah to Gandhi, 1914–20', in ibid.

33. The key study here is Clive Dewey, 'The End of the Imperialism of Free Trade: the Eclipse of the Lancashire Lobby and the Concession of Fiscal Autonomy to India', in Clive Dewey and A.G. Hopkins, eds. *The Imperial Impact: Studies in the Economic History of India and Africa* (1978).

cessful, and the Government of India's independence in matters of tariff policy was confirmed by the Fiscal Autonomy Convention of 1919. The action taken in 1917 eased India's fiscal problems, assisted Bombay's cotton mills, and mollified nationalist feeling. Taken as a whole, the episode symbolised the waning power of the Lancashire lobby, and indeed of the provinces in British political life, and the growing influence on policy of forces within India; but it also emphasised the paramountcy of sound money principles, and hence of Treasury orthodoxy.[34]

Re-connecting the rupee to sterling proved to be a delicate and protracted operation, especially while sterling itself was floating against other currencies. But the aims of policy were quite clear from the report of the Babington-Smith Committee, which was appointed in 1919 to recommend a solution to the problem, even if their application was frustrated by the post-war slump of 1920–1.[35] The Committee was preoccupied by the need to conserve Britain's gold reserves and increase her credit in preparation for returning to pre-war normality. Accordingly, it recommended a high exchange rate for the rupee against sterling in the hope of attracting silver to India rather than gold. This strategy was also deflationary, and it complemented the Government of India's efforts in the immediate post-war period to reduce the volume of currency in circulation and to regain budgetary stability. As Manchester was sacrificed to help balance India's budget, so India was drawn into a strategy for regaining Britain's pre-eminence in international finance.

Fiscal orthodoxy was accompanied by political concessions which were designed to win over moderate nationalist opinion.[36] Constitutional reforms were recommended by the Montagu-Chelmsford Report in 1918 and embodied in the Government of India Act in the following year. The principal concession centred on the devolution of various administrative functions to elected legislative assemblies in the provinces. Ostensibly, this was a step on the road to 'responsible' government, and was treated as such by a generation of liberal historians; but it is currently interpreted as being a device to perpetuate British power by dispersing opposition from the centre and by

34. Arthur Redford, *Manchester Merchants and Foreign Trade*, II, *1850–1939* (Manchester, 1956), Ch. 22, charts the demoralisation and failures of the Manchester lobby from its own Chamber of Commerce records.

35. G. Balachandran, 'India in Britain's Liquidity Crisis: the Stabilization of 1920', *Occasional Papers in Third World Economic History*, No. 1 (SOAS, 1990); Tomlinson, 'Monetary Policy', pp. 199–201.

36. P.G.Robb, *The Government of India and Reform, 1916–1921* (Oxford, 1976); and for the longer period R.J. Moore, *The Crisis of Indian Unity, 1917–1940* (Delhi, 1974).

giving a larger number of Indians in the provinces a political stake in the Raj.[37] The reforms certainly did not imply any weakening of imperial resolve. As Montagu pointed out in the House of Commons in 1922, constitutional advance depended on continuing 'good conduct', and marks could be scored only by cooperating with the imperial mission.[38] Moreover, vital areas of policy, such as foreign affairs, defence and finance (including the most important sources of revenue) remained firmly in the hands of the Viceroy.[39] The need to maintain political stability was the proximate cause of constitutional reform,[40] but it is also important to recognise that in 1919, as in 1857, civil order sustained the credit as well as the credibility of the Raj.

THE ATTEMPT TO RETURN TO NORMALITY: THE 1920s

The Montagu-Chelmsford reforms reinvigorated the imperial mission by giving it a renewed sense of purpose. In the 1920s the revitalised agents of the Raj set about 'nation-building' in the provinces, and they used the new constitution to reinforce their alliance with conservative land-holders and princes and to divide moderate nationalists from those who were not prepared to accept the new rules of the game.[41] This strategy rested on techniques of collaboration that have engaged much historical research, but it also involved coercive and other means of control that were not found in the liberal handbook. Current historiography may well underestimate this facet of British rule. Despite the fact that only a small number of white officials were present to hold the 'imperial facade' in place,[42] steps

37. Gallagher and Seal, 'Britain and India', pp. 400–6; Sarkar, *Modern India*, pp. 165–8. The conservative features of the reforms are well brought out in David Page's study of the Punjab and the United Provinces: *Prelude to Partition: The Indian Muslims and the Imperial System of Control, 1920–1932* (Delhi, 1982).

38. Quoted in Tomlinson, *Political Economy*, p. 111. Edwin Montagu (1879–1924), the second son of the first Lord Swaythling, was educated at Clifton and Cambridge, and was Secretary of State for India from 1917 to 1922.

39. Neil Charlesworth, 'The Problem of Government Finance in British India: Taxation, Borrowing, and the Allocation of Resources in the Inter-War Period', *Mod. Asian Stud.*, 19 (1985), pp. 523, 530–6, 542–3.

40. As argued by Gallagher and Seal, 'Britain and India'.

41. On the conservative alliance see: Barbara N. Ramusak, *The Princes of India in the Twilight of Empire: Dissolution of a Patron–Client System, 1914–1939* (Columbus, Ohio, 1976); S.E. Ashton, *British Policy Towards the Indian States, 1905–1939* (1982); and Page, *Prelude to Partition*.

42. Judith Brown, 'Imperial Facade', *Transactions of the Royal Historical Society*, 26 (1976).

were taken to repress unconstitutional opposition and to censor subversive influences by blocking the inflow of anti-imperialist ideas, including American democratic republicanism as well as soviet social-ism.[43] It is interesting to note that Mazzini's autobiography (which was translated into Marathi in 1907) was banned in India shortly after it had been published and had sold out there, and it remained on the imperial index until 1947.[44] Mazzini had become a hero in England not least as a result of the writings of the Whig historian, George Macaulay Trevelyan.

These observations are made not to pass judgement on British rule but to underline Britain's determination to remain in charge of India's destiny. Early in 1922, Lloyd George informed the Cabinet that 'we were now masters in India, and we should let it be understood that we intend to remain so'.[45] Shortly afterwards, Montagu stamped on the belief that 'we regard our mission in India as drawing to a close, that we are preparing for a retreat. If such an idea exists', he added, 'it is a complete fallacy'.[46] These were not empty words: they marked a conscious commitment to re-establishing Britain's position as a world power, and matched similar statements of intent made about the South American republics, China and the African colonies. As the war had heightened public consciousness of the importance of the empire,[47] so the peace held out the prospect of taking out imperial insurance for the British way of life and of demonstrating its superiority over the alternatives that threatened it, both at home and abroad.[48]

Economic reconstruction in the 1920s was concerned, above all, with re-establishing India's place in the international payments system based on sterling. Accordingly, priority was given to balancing the Indian budget after the exigencies of war and to stabilising the

43. David Arnold, *Police Power and Colonial Rule: Madras, 1859–1947* (Delhi, 1986); S.T. Bashkaran, 'Film Censorship and Political Control in British India', *Journal of Indian History*, 54 (1976).

44. Dignan, *Indian Revolutionary Problem*, pp. xiv-xv.

45. Cabinet minute, 10 October 1922, quoted in Algernon Rumbold, *Watershed in India, 1914–1922* (1979), p. 279.

46. Quoted in Keith Jeffrey, '"An English Barrack in the Oriental Seas?" India in the Aftermath of the First World War', *Mod. Asian Stud.*, 15 (1981), p. 385.

47. John M. Mackenzie, *Propaganda and Empire: The Manipulation of British Public Opinion, 1880–1960* (Manchester, 1984).

48. The most important threat at this time was revolutionary socialism. The Indian dimension is covered by S.D. Gupta, *Comintern, India and the Colonial Question, 1920–37* (Calcutta, 1980), and Sada Nand Talwar, *Under the Banyan Tree: The Communist Movement in India, 1920–1964* (New Delhi, 1985). The Indian Communist Party, founded in 1920, followed Comintern directives and was strikingly unsuccessful, though this did not prevent it from being banned in 1934.

exchange rate of the rupee. Sharp increases in taxation and severe retrenchment corrected budget deficits in 1918–19 and 1922–23 and enabled the Government of India to restore its credit-worthiness.[49] By then, however, it was apparent that the budget had to be expanded as well as balanced in order to fund the 'nation-building' projects that flowed from the Montagu-Chelmsford reforms. Given the prevailing monetary orthodoxy, there could be no big push for development, though some observers had begun to suggest that Britain's interests were ceasing to be served by India's backward agrarian economy, and even that they might gain from promoting local industry.[50] The only alternative was to increase the revenue from taxation. In practice, this meant augmenting the receipts from customs duties because the traditional source, the land tax, could not readily be expanded. Consequently, the general tariff on imports was increased from 7.5 per cent in 1917 to 11 per cent in 1921, and eventually reached 25 per cent in 1931.[51] Although this was a revenue tariff, it had a protective effect, and thus mollified Indian manufacturers while simultaneously increasing public revenues.

The main cost of this solution was borne by companies exporting to India. British firms were particularly hard hit because their Japanese rivals, besides having the advantage of high productivity, were also helped by the depreciation of the yen during the 1920s. Lancashire, the most notable casualty of the Government of India's tariff policy, was dealt a further blow in 1925, when the excise duty on Indian cotton goods was removed.[52] Officials had long resisted Indian demands for the abolition of the cotton excise on grounds of fiscal need, but finally gave way when agitation in Bombay threatened to turn an economic grievance into a political cause. The government had no wish to abandon Manchester's manufacturers, but the outcome was a damaging blow to their declining cause, and they were left with no more than a vague hope that they might benefit from imperial preference at some indeterminate point in the future.

In the 1920s, however, imperial preference had more appeal to

---

49. Tomlinson, 'Monetary Policy', pp. 200–1.

50. Lloyd George, for example, argued that: 'We must increase the wealth of India if we are going to make a success of a new system of government'. Quoted in John Gallagher, *The Decline, Revival and Fall of the British Empire* (Cambridge, 1982), p. 103. See also the Report of the Industrial Commission of 1916, cited in Dileep M. Wagle, 'Imperial Preference and the Indian Steel Industry, 1924–39', *Econ. Hist. Rev.*, 2nd ser. XXXIV (1981), p. 121.

51. Tomlinson, *Political Economy*, p. 62.

52. Basudev Chatterji, 'The Abolition of the Cotton Excise in 1925: a Study in Imperial Priorities', *Indian Econ. and Soc. Hist. Rev.*, 17 (1980).

Britain's ailing staple industries than to orthodox free traders in the City, who were bent on reconstructing the pre-war system of multilateral settlements, or to the Government of India, which was concerned about the budgetary consequences and political implications of trade restrictions. As a result, in 1924 India opted for 'discriminating protection' for a few industries rather than for imperial preference.[53] This policy gave a further boost to import-substituting industries, especially iron and steel, and also helped the budget by economising on imports.[54] Adjustments were made to incorporate differential duties on imports of iron and steel in 1927 and cotton goods in 1930, in response to pleas from British industry, but these were modest breaches of free trade which neither retarded the development of Indian manufactures nor checked the flow of imports from Japan.[55] The pursuit of fiscal objectives and the need to placate Indian opinion not only pushed the claims of British manufacturers down the list of policy priorities, but also induced the gentlemen of the Raj to overcome their distaste for industry to the extent of promoting it in India.

Stabilising the rupee was a more protracted and controversial process.[56] Fluctuations in the exchange rate during the immediate post-war period brought considerable uncertainty to commercial and official transactions, and involved the government in contentious problems of money management. Fixing the sterling value of the rupee was therefore a matter of high priority, though success ultimately depended on sterling's return to the gold standard. After a period when the exchange was allowed to float, the Government of India fixed the sterling rate at 1*s*. 6*d*. in 1924. This rate was endorsed

53. Basudev Chatterji, 'The Political Economy of "Discriminating Protection": the Case of Textiles in the 1920s', *Indian Econ. and Soc. Hist. Rev.*, 20 (1983).

54. Tomlinson, *Political Economy*, pp. 61–4. Britain's exports of textiles and iron and steel were particularly badly affected. The only gains went to suppliers of machinery. See Colin Simmons, Helen Clay and Robert Kirk, 'Machinery Manufacture in a Colonial Economy: the Pioneering Role of George Hattersley and Sons Ltd. in India, 1919–43', *Indian Econ. and Soc. Hist. Rev.*, 20 (1983).

55. Wagle, 'Imperial Preference', pp. 120–31; Chatterji, 'Political Economy', pp. 268, 270.

56. See B.R. Tomlinson, 'Monetary Policy', and J.D. Tomlinson, 'The Rupee/Pound Exchange Ratio in the 1920s', *Indian Econ. and Soc. Hist. Rev.*, 15 (1978). Both authors, writing independently, reach broadly similar conclusions about the motives behind British policy towards this forbidding but important issue. Readers will recall that Miss Prism advised Gwendolen to omit the chapter on the Fall of the Rupee as it was 'somewhat too sensational'; she would probably have regarded its rise as going quite beyond the bounds of good taste and comprehension. On the other hand, it will also be remembered that Gwendolen was not very good at taking advice. Oscar Wilde, *The Importance of Being Earnest* (1895), Act II.

by the Hilton-Young Commission of Inquiry in 1925; it was operative when sterling rejoined the gold standard, and it held until 1931.

The long haul back to a fixed exchange rate underlined the Government of India's determination to play its part in reviving the pre-war sterling system. The chosen rate, 1s. 6d., was unpopular in India because it was thought to be too high. The result, so it was argued, was to boost the import trade and cheapen remittances to London, while also deflating the domestic economy.[57] It is now apparent, however, that Lancashire had no influence on the rupee rate and gained little if anything from the decision to fix it at 1s. 6d.[58] It is equally clear that, while the Bombay textile interest was able to secure concessions in the area of tariffs (not least because they suited the goverment's budgetary policy), it had no effect at all on monetary policy, despite vociferous lobbying. On the other hand, the rate undoubtedly assisted the payment of the Home Charges because fewer rupees were required to settle sterling debts. However, specific advantages such as this have to be set in the broader context of re-establishing sound money principles.[59] This meant restoring not only a stable exchange rate but also the automaticity of the monetary system and hence the confidence of external creditors. It was with this aim in mind that the Hilton-Young Commission (1925–6) recommended establishing a reserve bank to oversee the operation of the monetary system. Whether or not the rupee exchange rate was overvalued, the intention was to fix it at a level that would suit London's interests. A high exchange rate meant that India would continue to absorb silver rather than gold. Any deflationary consequences were the price that India had to pay for upholding monetary orthodoxy and avoiding the political effects of unbridled inflation. Sound money, a stable polity and moral order were an indivisible trinity. Britain had no intention of reproducing the experience of Weimar Germany either at home or in India.

By 1926 Britain had returned to the gold standard and silver prices had fallen. A high exchange rate for the rupee no longer implied that India would absorb silver rather than gold, and policy-makers in Whitehall reverted to pre-war techniques of managing India's gold exports, principally through exchange intervention. The high sterling exchange rate of the rupee now served a different purpose: it meant that India's gold import point was less likely to be reached and,

57. Tomlinson, 'Monetary Policy', pp. 204–5, 207.
58. Tomlinson, 'The Rupee/Pound Exchange Ratio', p. 145.
59. Tomlinson, 'Monetary Policy', pp. 208–9; Tomlinson, 'The Rupee/Pound Exchange Ratio', pp. 139, 147–9.

accordingly, that a larger share of the empire's gold reserves could be placed at London's disposal. In this way, policy towards India continued to reflect Britain's wider purpose in seeking to reconstruct the pre-war international order based on the gold standard and the supremacy of sterling.

ECONOMIC CRISIS AND POLITICAL ADVANCE: THE 1930s

In India, as elsewhere, the sustained effort to reconstruct the pre-war international economic order was brought to a halt by the onset of the world slump in 1929. Research on the impact of the slump on India and on imperial policy is comparatively recent, but the evidence now accumulating suggests that the predominantly political accounts which have dominated the historiography of the period, and particularly of the Government of India Act in 1935, need to be revised to give greater weight to economic influences on imperial policy.[60]

The most obvious manifestations of the slump in India were falling export prices, declining terms of trade, reduced profits in the overseas trade sector, and renewed budgetary problems for the government. These conditions heightened discontent in India, fuelled the nationalist movement and gave considerable impetus to the demand for constitutional progress.[61] The civil disobedience campaign led by Gandhi in 1930–1 included a boycott of British goods, and it unnerved expatriate business, caused a flight of capital from India and placed a question mark over the government's ability to maintain order. Since Congress was explicit in declaring that it would devalue the rupee and repudiate

60. Recent surveys include: Dietmar Rothermund, 'The Great Depression and British Financial Policy in India, 1929–34', *Indian Econ. and Soc. Hist. Rev.*, 18 (1981); idem, 'British Foreign Trade Policy in India During the Great Depression, 1929–39', in ibid.; O. Goswami, 'The Depression, 1930–1935: its Effects on India and Indonesia', *Itinerario*, 10 (1986); and Colin Simmons, 'The Great Depression and Indian Industry: Changing Interpretations and Changing Perceptions', *Mod. Asian Stud.*, 21 (1987).

61. See, for example, Christopher Baker, 'Debt and the Depression in Madras, 1929–1936', in Dewey and Hopkins, *Imperial Impact*; Arvind N. Das, 'Peasants and Peasant Organisations: the Kisan Sabha in Bihar', *Journal of Peasant Studies*, 9 (1982); Arvind Kumar Sharma, 'A Study of the Agrarian Discontent in the United Provinces, 1930–31, *Quarterly Review of Historical Studies*, 23 (1983); Sugata Bose, 'The Roots of "Communal" Violence in Rural Bengal: a Study of the Kishoreganj Riots, 1930', *Mod. Asian Stud.*, 16 (1982); David Baker, '"A Serious Time": Forest Satyagraha in Madhya Pradesh, 1930', *Indian Econ. and Soc. Hist. Rev.*, 21 (1984); and the general survey in D.N. Dhanagare, *Peasant Movements in India, 1920–1950* (Oxford, 1983).

India's foreign debt, the alarm felt in London was well founded. But just as nationalist demands compelled attention, so pressures to balance the budget, to meet imperial financial obligations and to support British business mounted too. These contradictory claims concentrated the official mind, and the outcome provides as good a guide to official priorities as the imperfect historical record will allow. Once again, the Government of India gave first priority to sound money policies, and prescribed further bouts of retrenchment and deflation to maintain the external value of the rupee, to ensure the smooth flow of remittances and to guarantee India's international credit-worthiness. The measures that followed were carried through in the face of strenuous opposition both from nationalist opinion in India, which claimed that the government's monetary policy harmed the local economy, and from British exporters, whose interests were severely damaged by increased import duties.

Official priorities first expressed themselves during the rupee crisis of 1930–2.[62] As economic depression and political uncertainty exerted pressure on the exchange rate, the Government of India sought approval in 1931 for a modest devaluation of the rupee (to 1s. 4d.). But London turned down the proposal, fearing that the move would increase the rupee costs of meeting India's sterling obligations and would also turn out to be a short step on the road leading to more serious devaluation and even to bankrupcy. Default was unthinkable, given that India's sterling debt stood at over £350m. and the Home Charges at about £30m. a year. Commitments of this order had serious implications for the stability of sterling, which was itself becoming increasingly vulnerable. After much agonising at the Treasury and the India Office, it was eventually conceded that Britain would have to pick up the bill if India failed to meet her debt payments. As the India Office observed in 1931: 'There is no escape from the conclusion that as long as the British Government retains obligations which absorb so large a proportion of the total revenue of India, it must retain a direct interest in the financial administration of the country'.[63] Accordingly, Britain imposed a deflationary emergency budget on India in 1931 and made heavy calls on India's gold reserves to hold the exchange rate at 1s. 6d. When Britain left the gold standard in September of that year, London decreed that India should

---

62. B.R. Tomlinson, 'Britain and the Indian Currency Crisis'. Carl Bridge, 'Britain and the Indian Currency Crisis, 1930–2: a Comment', *Econ. Hist. Rev.*, 2nd ser. XXXIV (1981), raises interesting questions of emphasis but does not disturb the main point made here. See also B.R. Tomlinson's 'Reply', ibid.
63. Quoted in Tomlinson, *Political Economy*, p. 127.

follow, and the rupee was placed on a sterling standard at the existing rate of 1s. 6d.

The integration of the rupee into the Sterling Area, combined with renewed gold flows to London following the depreciation of sterling and the rupee, restored confidence among investors and enabled India to meet her traditional financial commitments.[64] Only then was Britain prepared to consider further constitutional advance for India. Even so, the Government of India Act in 1935 gave the Viceroy final control over fiscal and monetary matters, committed the government to holding the exchange rate at 1s. 6d., and ensured that currency reserves were ear-marked for sterling obligations.[65] The interesting development at this point was the decision to delegate key aspects of monetary policy to the new Reserve Bank of India, which had been founded in 1934.[66] The establishment of a Central Bank had been recommended by the Hilton-Young Commission in 1925, but it was not acted upon until the redivision of power contemplated in the Government of India Bill caused Whitehall and the City to reconsider ways of safeguarding Britain's financial interests. The Reserve Bank of India, like its counterparts in the Dominions, was designed to remove monetary policy from the political arena, or, to be precise, to prevent nationalists from tampering with monetary orthodoxy. Here, as elsewhere, the Governor of the Bank of England, Norman, played a key role in promoting the idea and implementing it.[67] Norman selected the first governor, Sir Osborne Smith, and groomed him for the position; when Smith was tempted into flirting with a lower exchange rate for the rupee, he was forced to resign in 1936. His successor, Sir James Taylor, had spent his career in the Indian Civil

64. Ibid. pp. 137–8; Basudev Chatterji, 'Lancashire Cotton Trade and British Policy in India, 1919–1939' (Ph.D. thesis, Cambridge University, 1978), p. 521. An interesting sidelight on imperial financial cooperation is provided by Frank H.H. King, *History of the Hongkong and Shanghai Bank*, Vol.III (Cambridge, 1988), pp. 195–6. Towards the close of 1931, when Britain was desperately trying to repay short-term credits advanced by Washington and Paris, the Bank of England made a secret deal (via the ubiquitous Sir Charles Addis) which authorised the Hongkong and Shanghai Bank to locate and buy gold in India and then ship it to London. This was duly done.

65. Tomlinson, *Political Economy*, pp. 128–31; idem, *The Indian National Congress and the Raj, 1929–1942* (1976), pp. 21–4. Sir James Grigg (1890–1964), who was Finance Member of the Council of India from 1934 to 1939 (in succession to Schuster), was deliberately chosen for his unwavering adherence to fiscal and monetary orthodoxy and for his well-known commitment to Britain's imperial mission.

66. See S.L.N. Simha, *All the Bank's Men: Management of the Reserve Bank of India* (Madras, 1975); E.P.W. de Costa, *Reserve Bank of India: Fifty Years (1935–85)* (New Delhi, 1985); Rajul Mathur, 'The Delay in the Formation of the Reserve Bank of India: the India Office Perspective', *Indian Econ. and Soc. Hist. Rev.*, 25 (1988).

67. R.S. Sayers, *History of the Bank of England*, I (1963), p. 204.

Service and was a man of proven loyalty: the exchange rate was held at 1s. 6d., and there it remained until after India had been granted independence. From the British point of view, the results of these measures were wholly satisfactory: the confidence of overseas creditors was restored, the repatriation of capital was halted, the flow of remittances was maintained, and India's credit-rating remained at a level that enabled her to attract long-term private investment in the second half of the 1930s.

If the monetary policy imposed on India aroused intense opposition from Congress, the tariff policy adopted by the Government of India was much closer to nationalist demands. Even in tariff matters, however, the Government of India exercised the freedom of action it had won in 1919 in ways that supported Britain's financial priorities. As in the 1920s, deflationary budgets were accompanied by increased import duties, which hit Britain's manufactured exports and protected Indian industry.[68] Indeed India's import-substituting manufactures experienced a decisive advance during the 1930s as a result of government support, indigenous enterprise, and the appearance of subsidiaries of transnational companies (such as Metal Box, Dunlop, Unilever and ICI).[69] Revenue imperatives were also a powerful motive for encouraging India's exports, as the international trade agreements of the 1930s clearly showed.[70] The crucial issue throughout these negotiations was the need to guarantee a market for India's exports so that she could continue to make remittances to London. This consideration ensured that India was treated on the same terms as the dominions at the Ottawa Conference in 1932. The labyrinthine negotiations that followed (leading to the Lees–Mody Pact on cotton goods in 1933, the Supplementary Agreement on steel in 1934 and the Anglo-Indian Trade Agreement of 1939), could scarcely conceal the fact that Britain was being forced to bargain with a dependent

68. Charlesworth, 'The Problem of Government Finance', p. 525.
69. Rajar K. Ray, *Industrialisation in India: Growth and Conflict in the Private Sector, 1914–47* (Delhi, 1979), Ch. 6; Simmons, Clay and Kirk, 'Machinery Manufacture in a Colonial Economy'; B.R. Tomlinson, 'Continuities and Discontinuities in Indo-British Economic Relations: British Multinational Corporations in India, 1920–1970', in Wolfgang Mommsen and Jürgen Osterhammel, eds. *Imperialism and After: Continuities and Discontinuities* (1986), p. 163; idem, 'Foreign Investment', p. 148; and, for a longer perspective, idem, 'British Business in India, 1860–1970', in R.P.T. Davenport-Hines and Geoffrey Jones, eds. *British Business in Asia Since 1860* (Cambridge, 1989).
70. Ian M. Drummond, *British Economic Policy and the Empire, 1919–1939* (1972), pp. 121–40; Tomlinson, *Political Economy*, pp. 123–44; Chatterji, 'Business and Politics', pp. 550–1, 572–3.

part of her empire or that India was the chief beneficiary.[71] In the course of the 1930s India achieved a visible trade surplus with Britain and also repaid much of the capital raised in the 1920s to promote provincial development.[72] Meanwhile, Lancashire's exports to India dwindled to insignificance, despite strenuous efforts to reserve a place for them in their former domain.[73]

The political implications of these trends unwound as the decade advanced. When it became clear at the close of the 1920s that further constitutional advances were needed to hold the loyalty of moderate nationalists and to amputate support from the 'extremists', the British goverment formulated a plan in 1931 for conceding a greater measure of self-government but containing it within a federal structure.[74] As we have seen in other cases (notably Canada and South Africa), federation was a well-tried imperial device for grouping territories that would otherwise be 'unviable', that is to say unable to raise the foreign loans needed to fund their development, without at the same time creating a powerful central government that might jib at continuing external management of important aspects of economic policy. The idea in the Indian case was to stop Congress from controlling the centre by drawing the princely states into a federal arrangement. This proposal ran into fierce opposition in India, and it also threatened to split the Conservative Party in Britain. In the early 1930s the constitutional concessions envisaged for India were opposed by a coalition consisting of about 50 Conservative MPs, led by Churchill, a band of Christian idealists, who believed that the British government was abandoning its historic mission, and leading representatives of Manchester's manufacturers, who thought that the country's industrial interests were being cast aside.[75] Encouraged by this unusual degree of political recognition, Manchester made an exceptional effort to present its case, notably by founding the Cotton Trade League in 1933, by pressing for the repeal of the Fiscal

71. Tomlinson, *Political Economy*, pp. 132–5; Chatterji, 'Business and Politics', pp. 550, 566–73.

72. Bagchi, *Private Investment*, pp. 438–9.

73. Chatterji, 'Political Economy', pp. 270, 274–5; idem, 'Business and Politics', pp. 560–5; Redford, *Manchester Merchants*, Ch. 22.

74. Carl Bridge, *Holding India to the Empire* (Delhi, 1986), Chs. 3–4 provides an excellent account of these developments. We should note here that we refer to the British government in a generic sense because there was a broadly bipartisan approach to India and indeed to colonial questions as a whole at this time. In the case of India, the only significant division occurred within the Conservative Party over the Government of India Bill.

75. Studdert-Kennedy, *British Christians*, Ch. 7; Redford, *Manchester Merchants*, pp. 283–90.

Autonomy Convention of 1919, and by opposing further constititional concessions. The most significant result of this movement was its total failure. The die-hards, the idealists and the Lancashire lobby were comprehensively defeated, and Hoare's plan for salvaging British finance on a raft of constitutional reform was launched as the Government of India Act in 1935.[76]

The British scheme did not emerge without modification, but it was adjusted to fit Indian realities rather than pressures from Manchester manufacturers and their allies. The Government of India Act offered a large measure of self-government in exchange for financial and other safeguards, and it also made provision for a federation of Indian states. The federation, however, failed to materialise. The slump weakened the rural pillars of British rule by destroying the prosperity of agriculture and shifting the locus of development to the towns.[77] By the close of the 1930s, agrarian distress and criticism from Congress had cost the 'landed interest' and the princes much of their popular support, while their reluctance to cooperate in Britain's scheme for federation caused the agents of the Raj to question their value as political allies.[78] Casting about for durable alternatives, the Government of India tried to build up the Muslim League as a conservative counterweight to radical nationalism, and to attract Indian business interests by offering them protection against imports and by frightening them with the bogey of left-wing Congress socialism.[79] This strategy, in turn, had to be rethought in 1937, when elections set in train by the Government of India Act resulted in the defeat of the League and the installation of a Congress government.

Even at this stage, fortune or, as some imperialists would have put it, providence, lent a hand to the imperial cause. Once in power, Congress began to reach an understanding with Indian business by muting its proposals for nationalisation, and by controlling labour unrest in exchange for political and financial support.[80] At the same

76. Sir Samuel Hoare (1880–1959): Harrow, Oxford; Secretary of State for India, 1931–35; Secretary of State for Foreign Affairs, 1935.

77. See, for example, C.J. Baker, *An Indian Rural Economy, 1880–1955* (Oxford, 1984), pp. 525–6.

78. Ashton, *British Policy*, Ch. 6. See also I.A. Talbot, 'Deserted Collaborators: the Political Background to the Rise and Fall of the Punjab Unionist Party, 1923–1947', *Jour. Imp. and Comm. Hist.*, 11 (1982); and Karen Leonard, 'Aspects of the Nationalist Movement in the Princely States of India', *Quarterly Review of Historical Studies*, 21 (1981–2).

79. Page, *Prelude to Partition*, Ch. 4; Ayesha Jalal and Anil Seal, 'Alternative to Partition: Muslim Politics between the Wars', *Mod. Asian Stud.*, 15 (1981); Claude Markovits, *Indian Business and Nationalist Politics, 1931–39* (Cambridge, 1985), Chs.3–4.

80. Markovits, *Indian Business*, Chs. 5–6.

time, British firms also adopted a more cooperative attitude towards Congress, following the growth of joint ventures with Indian companies in the 1930s.[81] The short period of Congress government, from 1937 to 1939, was important for the shape of future political alliances because it showed that 'responsible government' did not necessarily have to be in British hands. The Government of India itself saw the experience as producing a new set of indigenous allies who could still be shaped to the imperial purpose. The Viceroy, Lord Linlithgow, gave little indication, even in his private correspondence, that he was in India to manage a retreat:

> After all, we framed the constitution as it stands in the Act of 1935 because we thought it the best way . . . of maintaining British influence in India. It is no part of our policy, I take it, to expedite in India constitutional changes for their own sake, or gratuitously to hurry the handing over of the controls to Indian hands at any rate faster than that which we regard as best calculated, on the long view, to hold India to the Empire.[82]

WAR, FINANCE AND INDEPENDENCE

The outbreak of World War II derailed Britain's plans for training a new team of political allies. Despite windfall gains for parts of the economy, notably the import-substituting industries, the war had a generally adverse effect on India, bringing price inflation and famine, and causing heavy loss of life at the front.[83] India's international trade was disrupted, customs revenues suffered, and the government faced renewed budgetary problems. Discontent once again fed into powerful, though often conflicting, political forces, as Indian leaders tried to gauge the outcome of the war and to lay their bets accordingly. But Congress held together and became more militant, and Britain's plans for a federal India sank beyond the point where they could be salvaged. Britain's immediate reaction to these developments reflected her determination to retain control of India and with it her leadership of the empire. Although attempts were made to buy off Indian opposition with constitutional concessions, culminating in the much-

81. Chatterji, 'Business and Politics', pp. 540–2.
82. Linlithgow to Zetland, 21 December 1939, quoted in Bridge, *Holding India*, p. 153.
83. Tomlinson, *Political Economy*, pp. 92–100, 140–1, 160–1; Paul Greenough, 'Indian Famines and Peasant Victims: the Case of Bengal in 1943–44', *Mod. Asian Stud.*, 14 (1980).

publicised Cripps mission in 1942, the evidence now suggests that these were ploys approved by Churchill to gain time for Britain and to soothe anti-colonial feeling in the United States.[84] The main aim, championed by Churchill and the Viceroy, Linlithgow, was to use the opportunities presented by the war to reassert British paramountcy in both India and Burma.[85] The Government of India took advantage of its wartime emergency powers to suppress opposition, following the Quit India campaign of 1942–3, and coupled this with a further attempt to promote the Muslim League, which was regarded as being a more congenial associate than Congress.[86]

Britain's assertiveness failed to survive the war and Churchill's defeat in the general election of 1945. Repression could not be sustained indefinitely; nor, in the event, could the imperial mission be revived in India. By the end of the war, there was a loss of purpose at the very centre of the imperial system. The gentlemanly administrators who managed the Raj no longer had the heart to devise new moves against increasing odds, not least because after 1939 the majority of the Indian Civil Service were themselves Indian.[87] In 1945 the new Viceroy, Wavell, commented on the 'weakness and weariness of the instrument still at our disposal in the shape of the British element in the Indian Civil Service'.[88] The towns had been lost to opponents of the Raj; the countryside had slipped beyond control. Widespread discontent in the army was followed in 1946 by a mutiny in the navy. It was then that Wavell, the unfortunate messenger, reported to London that India had become ungovernable.[89] The days

84. This episode is covered by R.J. Moore, *Churchill, Cripps and India, 1939–1945* (Oxford, 1979), and idem, *Escape from Empire: The Attlee Government and the Indian Problem* (Oxford, 1983), Chs. 1–2. Gary Hess, *America Encounters India, 1941–47* (Baltimore, Md, 1971), suggests that, while Roosevelt was sympathetic towards Indian nationalism, he also felt that the nationalists should earn US support by demonstrating their loyalty during the war. This qualification removed much of the pressure that Britain would otherwise have experienced.

85. Moore, *Churchill, Cripps and India*, pp. 122–47. Linlithgow's stance is dealt with by Gowher Rizvi, *Linlithgow and India* (1978). On Britain's plans for Burma see Nicholas Tarling, 'A New and Better Cunning: British Wartime Planning for Post-War Burma, 1942–3', *Jour. South-East Asian Stud.*, 13 (1982), and idem, '"An Empire Gem": British Wartime Planning and Post-War Burma, 1943–44', ibid. The final phase of British rule is covered in an important article by Hugh Tinker, 'Burma's Struggle for Independence: the Transfer of Power Thesis Re-Examined', *Mod. Asian Stud.*, 20 (1986).

86. Sarkar, *Modern India*, pp. 388–405.

87. Potter, 'Manpower Shortage', pp. 68–9.

88. Quoted in Epstein, 'District Officers in Decline', p. 514.

89. See A.P. Thornton, 'With Wavell on to Simla and Beyond', in Norman Hillmer and Philip Wigley, eds. *The First British Commonwealth* (1980).

when 'every white skin automatically extracted a salute'[90] were now to be written about rather than experienced.

Yet to explain the transfer of power solely or even mainly in terms of personalities and the collective pyschology of the bureaucracy is to miss a train of causation that began before the war and ran through to the terminal point at independence. By 1947 Britain ceased to have substantial economic motives for retaining India. The war destroyed what was left of India's value as a repository for Britain's old, staple manufactures. At the same time, it encouraged foreign investment to shift further into local manufacturing, with the result that by 1947 capital goods accounted for nearly half of Britain's exports to India.[91] The signals were clear: the future of British exports and investment lay in cooperating with Indian business interests and, through them, with Congress. As the Labour government rapidly discovered, cooperation meant conferring independence as soon as possible.[92] More important still, the war transformed Britain's financial stake in India as a whole: from being one of Britain's major debtors, India emerged in 1945 as her largest single sterling creditor. When Britain decided to rearm in the late 1930s, she reluctantly agreed to meet the expense of using the Indian army outside the sub-continent.[93] This cost and that of importing material supplies from India were settled during the war by means of paper credits, which were held as sterling balances in London. By 1945 India's balances amounted to approximately £1,300m.[94] Consequently, constitutional advance in India was no longer constrained by fear of default, as it had been in the 1930s.

In Britain's changed and desperate economic situation in 1945, India had ceased to be an imperial asset.[95] As far as visible trade was concerned, India was now in deficit with the United States and was no longer a net contributor to the Sterling Area's hard currency pool. Moreover, the British authorities were reluctant to promote exports to India partly because overseas demand for capital goods was thought to hamper domestic reconstruction, and partly because exports had to be directed to areas where they could earn dollars. The sterling balances were undoubtedly a problem because India, as the principal

90. Epstein, 'District Officers in Decline', p. 496.

91. B.R. Tomlinson, 'Indo-British Relations in the Post-Colonial Era: the Sterling Balances Negotiations, 1947–49', *Jour. Imp. and Comm. Hist.*, 13 (1985), p. 156.

92. Gallagher, *Decline, Revival and Fall*, pp. 144–5; Tomlinson, *Political Economy*, p. 149.

93. Tomlinson, *Political Economy*, pp. 138–41.

94. Ibid. p. 140.

95. Tomlinson, 'Indo-British Relations', unravels Anglo-Indian economic relations in the period immediately after World War II.

claimant, held no less than one-third of the total. The balances had to be freed because Britain was committed to restoring convertibility. However, if India drew on them at will, Britain's reserves would be depleted and an unacceptably large proportion of her exports would be drawn to the sub-continent. Moreover, if India left the Sterling Area, the damage would extend beyond Britain's hard currency position to the credibility of the area as a whole. The solution was found in an agreement that kept India in the Sterling Area and phased the withdrawal of the balances over a period that, in the event, extended to the close of the 1950s. In this way, the financial settlement acquired a political complement because agreement on the balances and on India's continuing membership of the sterling club greatly eased the transition to independence and to dominion status.[96]

HOLDING INDIA TO THE EMPIRE

The evidence currently available suggests that the history of British rule in India does not fit easily into the conventional theory of imperial decline. The most general version of this theory is based on an implicit acceptance of an organic metaphor of growth, and is therefore readily inclined to trace the decay apparent in ancient states to defects accompanying their birth, to excesses of youth and to intimations of mortality appearing in middle age. Since this insight is a property of the historical model itself, it is unfortunate that it has often been treated as solving the problem rather than as revealing the important questions, which concern the definition of power, the measurement of decline, and the appropriateness of the life cycle of unnamed organisms for the study of human behaviour. These methodological issues extend far beyond the case of India and therefore cannot be explored here. But we have considered two specific and well-favoured illustrations of the thesis, and found them to be unconvincing. Socio-psychological arguments couched in terms of faltering will-power are not generally applicable to the Indian case until the very eve of the transfer of power, at which point they were also symptoms as well as causes of the termination of British rule. Explanations which draw on observations about Britain's economic

96. On the diversification of India's external economic links after independence see Michael Lipton and John Firn, *The Erosion of a Relationship: India and Britain Since 1960* (Oxford, 1976).

decline are open to a different objection: signs of decline can indeed be found during the period under review and even before 1914; but, to the extent that they rest on the performance of Britain's staple manufactured exports, they are an imperfect measure of economic strength and a poor guide to the purposes of imperial policy.

Our own assessment agrees with the revisionist argument, referred to at the outset of this chapter, that policy-makers were much more concerned with perpetuating Britain's presence in India than with preparing themselves for immolation. However, the revisionist approach tends to emphasise the study of high politics in London and Delhi and to exclude or minimise wider considerations of the kind discussed here. This is partly a matter of specialisation, but it may also reflect a concern that giving weight to economic aspects of causation might be seen to offer too much to Marxist or Marxisant arguments. The account we have tried to construct describes the economic dimension of the imperial purpose and the policies it promoted without, we hope, being either narrow or deterministic.

From this perspective, it appears that British rule in India cannot be understood on the assumption that the agents of the Raj represented the executive arm of the industrial bourgeoisie. Despite its importance, the manufacturing lobby in Britain never came to direct policy towards India and it was rarely able to divert it from the path marked out to accommodate Britain's wider aims. Any argument to the contrary has to explain a formidable list of failures, from the Fiscal Autonomy Convention in 1919 to the Government of India Act in 1935, and it must also come to terms with the painful irony that policies adopted by the British Government of India often favoured Bombay more than Manchester. After 1914, Britain did indeed direct her energies and formidable manipulative skills to the task of retaining her grip on the sub-continent, not to loosening it. But policy remained firmly in the hands of gentlemen whose representation of the national interest gave first place to financial considerations. The exchange rate of the rupee was held at levels that were intended to assist debt service and to manage bullion movements; its deflationary consequences induced gold flows which helped to support Britain's balance of payments and sterling. When choices had to be made between competing claims, as was increasingly the case, Lancashire took second place to London because preserving textile exports was less important than defending sterling. The Indian budget was bent to this purpose, and political alliances were shaped to reinforce it. This priority reflected a power much greater than that exercised by a mere conspiracy of bond-holders: it stood for a form of capitalist enterprise that gave money-making social acceptability among the British elite; it upheld an interest that had become vital to the success of Britain's management of the global economic system; and it inspired and elevated the imperial mission by linking sound money with sound morality and joining both in a high-minded and therefore justificatory vision of human progress under the imperial aegis.

Accordingly, India can be placed in a broader imperial perspective rather than being sealed in its own historiography. The upsets caused by World War I, and Britain's determined reaction to them, were very similar to those found in other parts of the world, both within the empire (as in the case of Africa) and outside it (as in the cases of Argentina and China). As the war helped to revive the imperial mission, so the period of post-war reconstruction in the 1920s showed how India was expected to assist Britain's return to pre-war normality. The performance of this role explains the otherwise impenetrable wrangle over the exchange rate of the rupee, and it also accounts for the use made of tariff autonomy to balance the budget and, effectively, to create barriers to Britain's manufactured exports. Here, too, policy towards India was very similar to that adopted elsewhere. The closest comparison is probably with the Dominions, which used their tariff autonomy for much the same purpose, and tropical Africa, where monetary policy (as well as tariffs) was still tightly regulated by London. In this respect, India was a hybrid: a Dominion as far as tariffs were concerned, but a colony in monetary affairs.

When the world slump and the financial crisis of 1931 aborted the return to the pre-war cosmopolitan order, Britain concentrated on constructing a smaller version, which became the Sterling Area, and on salvaging her overseas investments by devising new techniques of debt collection. India was again representative of most of the empire in being attached to the sterling bloc: like tropical Africa, India entered on terms dictated by London whereas the dominions were able to negotiate a modest devaluation of their currencies against sterling; but these were variations along a continuum that still represented British control. Similarly, India's tariffs rose to protect the budget, import substituting manufactures were developed, and exports were given a favoured place in British markets – all with the aim of ensuring that debt service and other external remittances continued to flow. As Britain's exports went into steep decline, so British control was tightened.

The 1930s emerge as a period of particular interest because they mark the demise of old, nineteenth-century complementarities and the beginnings of a new economic relationship. The slump destroyed rural incomes, reduced the importance of revenues from land and cast doubt on the political value of the alliance between the Raj and the landed magnates, in much the same way as the merits of indirect rule in Africa came to be questioned at the close of the 1930s. At the same time, the growth of modern manufacturing, of joint ventures between expatriate and Indian entrepreneurs, of the proportion of deposits held in indigenous banks, and of a pragmatic alliance with Congress all pointed in a direction that was already being taken by the Dominions and was just being embarked upon by countries such as Argentina and China. The main obstacle to political independence remained India's indebtedness: fear of repudiation caused the Government of India Act to be hedged with restrictions and proscribed further constitutional advance. When, as a result of the war, the financial and monetary imperatives which had long underpinned the imperial mission were removed, the imperial presence quickly followed.

The role of powerful personalities, the failure of techniques of control, and the loss of confidence in London and Delhi must all have their place in any full assessment of the transfer of power. But if the analysis fails to identify the underlying purpose of policy and the ways in which changes in the relationship between Britain and India fulfilled that purpose or made it redundant, it will miss a central theme of causation – and one, moreover, that is not confined to the case of India.

CHAPTER NINE
'Playing the Game' in Tropical Africa, 1914–40[1]

The study of African history has been transformed in the thirty years which have passed since the end of colonial rule. The history of the pre-colonial era has been extensively rewritten, and there is now a considerable literature on the diverse experience of Africans under colonial rule. To this novel history from below has been added, more recently still, a renewed interest in colonial policy – a history from above which went out of fashion in the immediate aftermath of independence.[2] Two large themes of relevance to the present study

1. The quotation is from F.D. (Lord) Lugard, *The Dual Mandate in British Tropical Africa* (1922, 3rd edn. 1926), p. 132. Referring to the qualities exhibited by the colonial service, Lugard observed that the public schools and universities had 'produced an English gentleman with an almost passionate conception of fair play, of protection of the weak, and of "playing the game".' The term 'tropical Africa' is used here in a broad sense to include Nigeria, the Gold Coast, Sierra Leone, the Gambia, the Anglo-Egyptian Sudan, Kenya, Uganda, Nyasaland, Northern Rhodesia, the mandated territories of Tanganyika, Togo and Cameroun, and, stretching a point, Southern Rhodesia. Although their formal status varied, these territories were all effectively under direct control apart from Southern Rhodesia, which became self-governing in 1923. The main exclusions, therefore, are Egypt and the Union of South Africa.
2. Comprehensive guidance can be found in A.D. Roberts, ed. *The Cambridge History of Africa, 1905–1940*, Vol. 7 (Cambridge, 1986), Michael Crowder, ed. *The Cambridge History of Africa, 1940–1975*, Vol.8 (Cambridge, 1985), and L.H. Gann and Peter Duignan, eds. *Colonialism in Africa, 1870–1960*, 5 vols. (Cambridge, 1969–75). Cyril Ehrlich, 'Building and Caretaking: Economic Policy in British Tropical Africa, 1890–1960', *Econ. Hist. Rev.*, 2nd ser. XXVI (1973), offers an illuminating interpretation; Terence Ranger, ed. 'White Presence and Power in Africa', *Jour. African Hist.*, 20 (1979), brings together a number of detailed studies; J. Forbes Munro, *Britain in Tropical Africa, 1880–1960* (1984) provides a concise account of economic relationships. All historians of colonial policy are indebted to W.K. Hancock's classic, *Survey of British Commonwealth Affairs*, Vol. II, Pts. 1 and 2 (1940 and 1942), and to Ian M. Drummond's important study, *Imperial Economic Policy, 1917–1939* (1974). A.D. Roberts, 'The Earlier Historiography of Colonial Africa', *History in Africa*, 5 (1978), draws attention to the work of an earlier generation of scholars whose contributions have been neglected in recent years, despite their high quality.

have emerged from this new historiography.[3] One treats colonial rule after 1914 as being a study in the management of imperial retreat in the face of nationalist advance; the other, influenced largely by Marxist and dependency theories, focuses on the relationship between capitalism and the 'colonial state' in Africa.[4] We shall comment on these themes here but not be led by them because our own analysis of the colonial presence starts from different assumptions. As will be apparent by now, we doubt whether the conventional hypothesis about imperial decline can carry the weight placed upon it, and we have reservations, too, about approaches which treat capitalism in an undifferentiated way or suppose that its relationship with either development or underdevelopment is unlinear.

We shall begin, instead, by identifying two qualities which set the tropical African colonies apart from the other cases we have examined and make them a particularly interesting test of our argument. From a political standpoint, the fact that the colonies were under direct control from London allowed impositions of will which were impossible in the self-governing parts of the empire and in regions of informal influence. Of course, all governments labour under constraints, and the formulation and implementation of colonial policy were no exception in being clouded by compromise and diluted by circumstance. Nevertheless, the colonial case is still the clearest available guide to the intended priorities of imperial policy. From an economic perspective, tropical Africa provides an example of a region where private finance lagged behind political control. Once again, this is a generalisation which requires qualification with respect to specific territories, sectors and periods. But the central point remains: the City was not prepared to pour money into tropical Africa, and no amount of rhetoric from imperial enthusiasts could conjure opportunities to compare with those available in South Africa and in other parts of the world.

It might be thought that these considerations call for an explanation which departs from our general interpretation, perhaps by stressing the independence of political issues from financial pressures or possibly by allowing the manufacturing lobby more scope in influencing policy. Neither departure, however, is necessary. On the contrary, we shall suggest that the appropriate model for Africa is one of

3. And others which are not our concern, notably the question of the costs and benefits of colonial rule.

4. Although this designation is now widely used, it is often ill-defined. Older terms, such as 'colony' and 'colonial government', are more appropriate where the context allows specific meanings to be assigned.

colonial rule with limited supplies of capital. The need for external loans and the search for revenue ensured that fiscal problems had a permanent place at the centre of policy and made colonial governments more, not less, dependent on financial considerations. The City's caution was not, in these circumstances, industry's gain. Manufacturing interests made more noise than headway, and the few concessions they won were on the whole consistent with fiscal priorities. Moreover, financial discipline was infused with moral purpose. Injections of both invigorated the civilising mission and stiffened the imperial will, and in this way exercised a pervasive influence on all aspects of policy, including the doctrine of trusteeship. Thus sustained, Britain demonstrated her determination not merely to keep her empire but also to enlarge it; and, in the course of the fierce international rivalries that affected Africa between 1914 and 1945, she gained ground rather than surrendered it.

TRADE, FINANCE AND ECONOMIC POLICY: AN OVERVIEW

Our explanation of the partition of Africa stressed the fact that Britain's main interests lay in parts of the continent which were relatively well endowed with human and natural resources. The subsequent development of Africa, as measured by commercial and financial flows, confirms that Britain received the lion's share of the gains from colonial rule.[5] Nevertheless, it is important to recognise that these did not amount to very much when placed in a global context. In 1920 Britain's possessions throughout tropical Africa (including the newly acquired mandates) accounted for little more than 2 per cent of her total exports; although the share (but scarcely the value) increased, it was still not much over 3 per cent at its peak in 1938.[6]

5. Between 1907 and 1935, about 85 per cent of the value of exports from sub-Saharan Africa as a whole came from British territories, which also received about 77 per cent of all foreign capital invested in the region between 1870 and 1935. South Africa was pre-eminent in both trade and investment; but British territories were still predominant, even within tropical Africa. The starting point for this subject remains S. Herbert Frankel, *Capital Investment in Africa* (1938).

6. Calculated principally from *Statistical Abstract for the United Kingdom, 1913 and 1923–36* (1937); *Statistical Abstract for the British Empire, 1913 and 1924–29* (1931); *Statistical Abstract for the British Empire, 1929–38* (1939); and *Statistical Abstract for the British Commonwealth, 1933–39 and 1945–47* (1950). We should also like to acknowledge our indebtedness to F.V. Meyer's pioneering study, *Britain's Colonies in World Trade* (1948). It should be pointed out that the underlying data are fragile and that our summary statements are intended to provide orders of magnitude only.

Moreover, Britain had a continuing interest in preserving free trade for her colonies so that they could maintain export earnings and service their debts. Consequently, though Britain remained their most important trading partner, the tropical African colonies conducted just over half of their overseas trade with other countries at the close of the 1930s, despite the rise of protectionism. British finance and commercial services, on the other hand, exercised a near monopoly of colonial business throughout the period under review.[7] Britain accounted for virtually all foreign investment in her tropical African colonies, limited though it was; she had almost complete control of banking; and she continued to dominate shipping services, even though foreign rivals cut into the re-export trade in the inter-war period.

Clearly, the economic significance of the African colonies is not to be found by measuring the absolute or even the relative value of their connection with the metropole. It lay, instead, in the contribution they made to Britain's balance of payments and to meeting the needs of special interest groups. Britain still ran a surplus on her visible trade with tropical Africa, and this was enhanced by returns on investment and by other invisible earnings. Taken together, the two made a useful, if still modest, contribution to settling Britain's international accounts. The colonies in tropical Africa also offered a refuge for Britain's older staples, such as textiles and metal goods, which had been pushed out of more attractive markets elsewhere; and they provided a haven for investors (especially larger investors in the Home Counties) who put their money and their faith in the empire because colonial government loans were backed by an imperial guarantee, which was implied where it was not also formally stated.[8] However, it is important to distinguish between these interests: manufacturers were given opportunities but few privileges; investors were singled out for favourable treatment. This difference was partly a reflection of the general bias of British policy, but it also recognised that the whole colonial enterprise would founder unless overseas investors could be persuaded to put their money into the Dark Continent.

The fundamental and persistent difficulty faced by colonial officials in tropical Africa was how to generate taxable resources in territories

7. Frankel, *Capital Investment*, pp. 193, 210; Peter Svedberg, 'Colonial Enforcement of Foreign Direct Investment', *Manchester School*, 50 (1981); Kathleen M. Stahl, *The Metropolitan Organization of British Colonial Trade* (1951), pp. 145, 204–6, 292–3, 295–6; Charlotte Leubuscher, *The West African Shipping Trade, 1909–1959* (Leiden, 1963), pp. 32–4, 55–6, 81–2.
8. John M. Atkin, 'British Overseas Investment, 1918–1931', (Ph.D. thesis, University of London, 1968), pp. 115–17, 120–1, 125.

which were generally poor and rarely came with a ready-made tax base.[9] The fact that revenue was essential to pay for the colonial administration, the largest single item of expenditure, no doubt concentrated the minds and ordered the priorities of successive generations of officials. But it has also to be remembered that colonial governors were engaged in a large state-building exercise involving long-term capital investment.[10] To make the sovereignty they had acquired effective, the colonial authorities were obliged to build an infrastructure as well as to extend the machinery of state. An undertaking of this magnitude depended on foreign loans, and these could be raised only if revenues were available for debt-service and if investors were confident that there would be no wavering over repayment. The link between revenues and borrowing-power prompted the colonial authorities to take a keen interest in promoting exports because overseas trade was the most promising source of revenue and could be tapped efficiently by means of tariffs.[11] The poorer colonies were, by definition, those which failed to generate a sizeable taxable trade. There, colonial rule laboured on the harder and more contentious task of levying direct taxes, and borrowing-power was consequently severely constrained.

Although policy issued from the Colonial Office, commercial, monetary and fiscal matters were all subject to rules laid down by the Treasury, whose guiding principle remained that enunciated by Earl Grey in 1852: 'the surest test for the soundness of measures for the improvement of an uncivilised people is that they should be self-sufficing'.[12] Broadly speaking, the African colonies adhered to these

9. In contrast to India, where land taxes made a fundamental contribution to government revenues. The history of taxation in colonial Africa remains a neglected subject. For a rare case study see Tijjani Garba, 'Taxation in Some Hausa Emirates, 1860–1939', (Ph.D. thesis, University of Birmingham, 1986); and for a comparison of tax burdens, David Fieldhouse, 'The Economic Exploitation of Africa: Some British and French Comparisons', in Prosser Gifford and William Roger Louis, eds. *France and Britain in Africa* (New Haven, Conn., 1971). Some long-run considerations are discussed by A.G. Hopkins, 'The World Bank in Africa: a Historical Perspective', *World Development*, 14 (1986).

10. This point is clearly brought out by John Lonsdale, 'The Conquest State of Kenya', in J.A. de Moor and H.L. Wesseling, eds. *Imperialism and War: Essays on Colonial Wars in Asia and Africa* (Leiden, 1989).

11. Frankel, *Capital Investment*, p. 188, appears to understate revenue from customs duties. Compare E.A. Brett, *Colonialism and Underdevelopment in East Africa: The Politics of Economic Change, 1919–1939* (1973), p. 192.

12. Quoted in Allan McPhee, *The Economic Revolution in British West Africa* (1926), p. 208. The two departments had their disputes, but kept them within the family. See Ronald Hyam, 'The Colonial Office Mind, 1900–1914', *Jour. Imp. and Comm. Hist.*, 8 (1979); and John M. Carland, *The Colonial Office and Nigeria, 1898–1914* (Stanford, Calif., 1985), pp. 199–200.

principles: they maintained open economies to enable trade potential to be maximised, designed tariffs primarily to raise revenue rather than to encourage discrimination or protection, and were generally successful in balancing their budgets. It is true, of course, that policies of free trade were modified in the 1930s, but, as far as tropical Africa was concerned, the modifications were not very significant. The colonies were also expected to complement the British economy by exchanging raw materials for manufactured goods, but here, too, commercial policy was not fashioned to produce this result. Colonial officials offered minimal concessions to Manchester's demands for special treatment and they made few serious efforts to block the development of manufacturing in Africa, though they were equally reluctant to promote it.[13] If this measure of impartiality found its justification in the high doctrine of trusteeship, it also owed a good deal to the lower calculus of the budget, for officials were alert to the revenue costs of the trade distortions sought by special interests and to the fiscal implications of protecting infant industries in unpromising circumstances.

Financial policy, on the other hand, was tightly controlled. The orthodoxy which the Treasury and its allies hoped to spread throughout the world was most fully realised in the tropical colonies, which functioned as compliant subsidiaries of the sterling system.[14] The monetary regime was supervised by Currency Boards, which issued coin and paper currencies through the agency of authorised expatriate banks in the colonies and kept reserves (at reassuringly high levels) in London. Colonial currencies, though visually distinct from sterling, were held at parity with it and were freely convertible. Money supply was determined not by the colonial administration but by the balance of payments, and in essence by export earnings. A rise in earnings increased the supply of money by an amount which matched effective demand; a decline had the opposite effect. The Currency Boards were

13. See, for example, Marion Johnson, 'Cotton Imperialism in West Africa', *African Affairs*, 73 (1974), pp. 178–87, and David Meredith, 'The British Government and Colonial Economic Policy', *Econ. Hist. Rev.*, 2nd ser. XXVIII (1975), pp. 495–7.

14. See, in particular, J. Mars, 'The Monetary and Banking System and Loan Market of Nigeria', in M. Perham, ed. *Mining, Commerce, and Finance in Nigeria* (1948); W.T. Newlyn and D.C. Rowan, *Money and Banking in British Colonial Africa* (Oxford, 1954); and Barbara Ingham, 'Colonialism and the Economy of the Gold Coast, 1919–45', in B. Ingham and C. Simmons, eds. *Development Studies and Colonial Policy* (1987). Additional historical detail is given in A.G. Hopkins, 'The Creation of a Colonial Monetary System: the Origins of the West African Currency Board', *African Historical Studies*, 3 (1970); and Jan S.Hogendorn and Henry A. Gemery, 'Cash Cropping, Currency Acquisition and Seignorage in West Africa, 1923–50', *African Economic History*, 11 (1982).

thus passive instruments, mediating as official money-changers between colonial currencies and sterling. These arrangements, combined with the principle of the balanced budget, produced a paradise of sound money in a wilderness of colonial backwardness, and ensured that the 'rules of the game' imposed by London were not bent by colonial politics or even by colonial governments. Devaluation was as unthinkable as it was impossible; the exchange rate was eternally predictable; deficit financing was unknown; and fiscal autonomy was as distant a prospect as political independence.

The strict regulation of monetary and fiscal affairs was vital in giving investors confidence in a region that was otherwise generally unattractive. The link with sterling ensured that colonial business continued to be financed through London and also helped Britain to retain a large proportion of the trade itself.[15] Private investment was encouraged by holding royalties at low levels, by excusing company profits from colonial taxation, and by excluding the colonies from the embargoes which the Treasury imposed on overseas loans at critical times in the inter-war period.[16] In the public domain, the financial orthodoxy guaranteed by the imperial connection induced the City to raise money for colonial government loans, thus completing the link with revenue-gathering efforts in the colonies. Further assistance came from the Colonial Loans Act (1899), which enabled the colonies to borrow from the imperial government instead of from the open market, and from the Colonial Stock Act (1900), which allowed them to raise money on favourable terms by granting colonial loans trustee status.[17] Both measures departed from the ideal of non-intervention by calling upon taxpayers to provide incentives for investors, even though in practice their scope was limited.[18] In all of these measures of support, the Treasury and the Bank of England were intimately associated with the City and with the expatriate banks, which, in turn, were joined to the colonial administration by holding the government account and by acting as agents of the Currency Boards.[19]

15. Stahl, *Metropolitan Organization*, pp. 296–6.
16. Atkin, 'British Overseas Investment', p. 76.
17. Atkin, 'British Overseas Investment', pp. 14–15, 76, 83, 86; Sir Alan Pim, 'Public Finance', in Perham, ed. *Mining, Commerce, and Finance*, p. 245.
18. Joseph Chamberlain's efforts to direct public funds towards the empire were severely curtailed by the Treasury. See Richard M. Kesner, *Economic Control and Colonial Development: Crown Colony Financial Management in the Age of Joseph Chamberlain* (Oxford, 1981); and, more generally, R.V. Kubicek, *The Administration of Imperialism: Joseph Chamberlain at the Colonial Office* (Durham, NC, 1969).
19. Newlyn and Rowan, *Money and Banking*, p. 74; L.H. Gann and Peter Duignan,

TRUSTEESHIP AND THE TRUSTEES

These financial imperatives were fed into the machinery of formal rule and emerged, synthesised, in the concept of trusteeship.[20] As a term of imperial art, trusteeship had few rivals. In authorising both conservation and amelioration, it combined a respect for tradition with a commitment to progress: the former gave it a past; the latter held out the promise of a future. The idea that imperial rulers were trustees provided them with a validation as custodians of civilisation which stood above their own particular purposes. As Lugard, the leading imperial propagandist of the day, put it: 'We hold these countries because it is the genius of our race to colonise, to trade and to govern'.[21] The colonial contract could be justified by referring to abstract principles of legitimation, 'good government' could take the place of self-government, and taxation could be levied without representation on the eighteenth-century principle that the disenfranchised were 'virtually represented' by their betters. Trusteeship was not only firm of purpose, but also malleable with respect to time and circumstance, and this was an asset which the defenders of empire mobilised in response to domestic criticism of colonial rule. By updating and redefining the civilising mission, they were able to transform hostile forces, including Labour governments, into imperial trustees who found themselves improving the empire rather than trying to abolish it.[22]

To reduce trusteeship to economic motives is to mistake a part for the whole; but to translate the concept into forms of colonial rule without recognising the powerful influence of financial imperatives is

---

The Rulers of British Africa, 1870–1914 (1978), pp. 48–53, 68–9; Richard Fry, *Bankers in West Africa: The Story of the Bank of British West Africa Ltd.* (1976), pp. 87–8, 94–6. Lord Milner was Chairman of the Bank from 1909 to 1916; his successor, Lord Selborne, was a former Under-Secretary of State at the Colonial Office and High Commissioner in South Africa.

20. On the antiquity of the concept see G.V. Mellor, *British Imperial Trusteeship, 1783–1850* (1951); and for assessments Kenneth Robinson, *The Dilemmas of Trusteeship: Aspects of British Colonial Policy Between the Wars* (1965), and Penelope Hetherington, *British Paternalism and Africa, 1920–1940* (1978). Different stages in the evolution of the idea are discussed by Ronald Robinson, 'The Moral Disarmament of African Empire', in Norman Hillmer and Philip Wigley, eds. *The First British Commonwealth* (1980); and J.M. Lee, *Colonial Development and Good Government: A Study of the Ideas Expressed by the British Official Classes in Planning Decolonization, 1939–1964* (Oxford, 1967). The interpretation offered here gives more weight to financial considerations than is customary.

21. Lugard, *Dual Mandate*, pp. 618–19.

22. See, for example, Robert Gregory, *Sidney Webb in East Africa: Labour's Experiment with the Doctrine of Native Paramountcy* (Berkeley, Calif., 1962).

to miss an essential element in the story. Even before 1914, the costs of occupation had caused the Treasury to call a halt to military expeditions, and problems of viability had helped to determine the boundaries of the new states of colonial Africa.[23] Thereafter, the precarious financial base of colonial rule led the authorities to extend the frontiers of their instinctive paternalism from housekeeping to a type of managerial entrepreneurship whose primary purpose was to solve the revenue question. At the same time, financial constraints set limits to action and reinforced the inherent caution of the bureaucracy. The trajectory of progress was not in doubt, but improvements were to be selective and modest in case they threw up forces which damaged the credit and the credibility of the overlords. From the perspective of trusteeship, fiscal discipline was a moral force as well as a material necessity. As taxation fuelled the colonial machine, so it inculcated the work ethic, promoted individual responsibility and symbolised acceptance of the state.[24] Taxpayers, not surprisingly, often took a rather different view.

If the Indian Civil Service was the most impressive illustration of gentlemanly imperialism in its formal guise, the colonial service in Africa represented its highest stage because it was established later and survived in an undiluted form for longer. As recent research has shown, the rulers of British Africa came almost exclusively from the new urban gentry of southern England, and especially from the Home Counties.[25]

23. Ronald Robinson, 'European Imperialism and Indigenous Reactions in British West Africa, 1880–1914', in H.L. Wesseling, ed. *Expansion and Reaction: Essays on European Expansion and Reactions in Asia and Africa* (Leiden, 1978); Colin Newbury, 'The Economics of Conquest in Nigeria, 1900–1920: Amalgamation Reconsidered', in Ecole des hautes études en sciences sociales, ed. *Etudes africaines offertes à Henri Brunschwig* (Paris, 1982).

24. Lugard, *Dual Mandate*, pp. 231–3, has some interesting comments on these relationships.

25. The literature on this subject is now too extensive to cite in full. Among the important contributions, which contain numerous further references, are: L.H. Gann and Peter Duignan, *The Rulers of British Africa, 1870–1914* (1978); idem, eds. *African Proconsuls: European Governors in Africa* (Stanford, Calif., 1978); and I.F. Nicolson and Colin A. Hughes, 'A Provenance of Proconsuls: British Colonial Governors, 1900–1960', *Jour. Imp. and Comm. Hist.*, 4 (1975). Studies of particular territories include: Robert O. Collins and Francis M. Deng, eds. *The British in the Sudan, 1898–1956* (Stanford, Calif., 1984); M.W. Daly, *Empire on the Nile: The Anglo-Egyptian Sudan, 1898–1934* (Cambridge, 1986); Henrika Kuklick, *The Imperial Bureaucrat: The Colonial Administrative Service in the Gold Coast, 1920–1939* (Stanford, Calif., 1979); and T.H.R. Cashmore, 'Studies in District Administration in the East African Protectorate, 1895–1914', (Ph.D. thesis, Cambridge University, 1965). On the spread of gentlemanly values through education in Africa, see, for example, R.J. Challis, 'The European Educational System in Southern Rhodesia, 1890–1930', *Zambezia*, 9 (1982), and J.A. Mangan, 'Gentlemen Galore: Imperial Education for Tropical Africa: Lugard the Ideologist', *Immigrants and Minorities*, 1 (1982).

The service was dominated by recruits from professional families who had been trained, expensively, at public schools and at Oxford and Cambridge to become enlightened guardians of the state, and who had been selected by a procedure which discriminated between members of the elite (largely on grounds of 'character') and effectively excluded competition from non-gentlemen.[26] Colonial service was relatively well paid, especially at the top of the hierarchy, and there were additional rewards of prestige, formalised through the honours system and liberally bestowed, which together compensated for the high entry costs.

Given their background, it is not surprising that Britain's representatives in Africa were champions of the gentlemanly values we described earlier. In its secular dimension, their sense of mission was shaped by Gladstonian orthodoxy and Treasury norms, by a distaste for industry and by a suspicion of commerce. Their closest links with the world of business were with the City and the colonial banks, and they showed little inclination to favour manufacturing interests.[27] Spiritually they were reinforced by the Church militant in Africa: conversion to Christianity implied acceptance of colonial values, even if it did not guarantee submission to colonial rule. The link between the worldly and the spiritual elements of gentlemanly imperialism had many personifications, but few were more memorable than Henry Gwynne, the crusading Bishop of Egypt and the Sudan.[28] Gwynne dedicated his life to the task of persuading the Sudanese to redeem themselves for the fate of General Gordon, whose death, elevated to martyrdom, became a symbol of Christian sacrifice in the

26. The principal selector, Sir Ralph Furse (1887–1973), was educated at Eton and at Balliol College, Oxford. He published a revealing autobiography, *Aucuparius: Recollections of a Recruiting Officer* (1962). For an assessment see Robert Heussler, *Yesterday's Rulers: The Making of the British Colonial Service* (New York, 1963). See also pp. 23–7 above.

27. The sources are given in notes 12, 13, 19 and 25 above. A particularly interesting case study of these values in action is G.N. Sanderson, 'The Ghost of Adam Smith: Ideology, Bureaucracy, and the Frustration of Economic Development in the Sudan, 1934–1940', in M.W. Daly, ed. *Modernization in the Sudan: Essays in Honour of Richard Hill* (New York, 1985), which is complemented by John Tosh, 'The Economy of the Southern Sudan under the British, 1898–1955', *Jour. Imp. and Comm. Hist.*, 9 (1981). Colonial governments began to work more closely with the large commercial firms in the late 1930s, but the alliance was largely a reflection of the conversion of 'big business' to bureaucratic ways of thinking and of the increasing concentration of decision-making in London. An important contribution to this unexplored subject is David Meredith, 'The Colonial Office, British Business Interests and the Reform of Cocoa Marketing in West Africa, 1937–1945', *Jour. African Hist.*, 29 (1988).

28. Collins and Deng, *The British in the Sudan*, Ch. 6. Gwynne (1863–1957) spent the whole of his career in the front line of empire, beginning as a missionary in Khartoum in 1899, and continuing as an itinerant bishop from 1908 to 1946.

performance of military duty and thus a manifestation of the permanent union of Church and state.

By 1914 the framework of colonial rule had been put in place. The first generation of officials assessed their subjects and administered, as new districts and provinces, the spaces allotted to them by partition. In parallel fashion, the expatriate firms established branches inland and divided markets in an unpublicised partition of their own.[29] The abolition of inland tolls created areas of free trade; the spread of colonial currencies aided commercial transactions and tax-gathering; the demand for labour in export-producing regions encouraged migration; railways cut the cost of moving goods and people, and hence hastened the development of the labour market. Buoyant prices for raw materials between 1900 and 1913 provided an incentive to expand exports and helped the new rulers to establish their authority by binding producers to the colonial economy, generating revenues and funding the first clutch of sizeable colonial loans. Underlying these developments were fundamental changes in property rights, especially over land and labour, which in turn were reflected in decisions made about the forms taken by trusteeship, notably the distinction between regions allocated to white settlers and those where indigenous rights were to be preserved. In these ways, the colonial frontier was defined and stabilised, if still not entirely occupied, and the shadowy imperial presence of the nineteenth century acquired substance and, so it seemed, permanence too.

WORLD WAR I IN TROPICAL AFRICA

World War I threatened to bring down the newly built structures of British rule by exposing the African colonies to invasion and by disrupting the export sector.[30] The war itself was carried to sub-Saharan Africa, where hostilities centred on a struggle for control of the German colonies. The campaigns were of varying intensity and duration (being particularly marked and extended in East Africa), but

29. This facet of the history of the expatriate firms has been neglected. For an exploratory account see A.G. Hopkins, 'Imperial Business in Africa. Part II: Interpretations', *Jour. African Hist.*, 18 (1976).

30. A good starting point is Richard Rathbone, ed. 'World War I and Africa', *Jour. African Hist.*, 19 (1978). See also Melvin Page, ed. *Africa and the First World War* (1987). As yet, there is no study of Africa to compare with Bill Albert, *South America and the First World War* (Cambridge, 1988), though Marc Michel, *L'Appel à l'Afrique: contributions et réactions à l'effort de guerre en A.O.F., 1914–18* (Paris, 1982), is important for French West Africa.

by 1918 all of Germany's colonies had been occupied by allied forces.[31] By then, too, Britain's war aims had expanded to match the increasing cost and length of the conflict. As early as 1916, there was a popular argument to the effect that 'the Germans have no genius for the high task of colonisation', and that Britain had a duty as well as a right to take over Germany's African colonies when the war ended.[32] This view was shared by Harcourt, the Secretary of State for the Colonies, and was supported by influential imperialists, such as Curzon and Amery, who were busy redrawing the map of Africa in anticipation of a punitive peace settlement.[33] In 1918 Britain's imperial ambitions spread wider still and included a project for establishing a protectorate over Abyssinia, which was thought to offer scope for commercial concessions and white settlement.[34] The Abyssinian scheme, a piece of fantasy brought on by terminal war fever, was liquidated in 1919. But Britain achieved her other war aims: by adroit use of the mandate system she was able to establish colonies in camouflage, and thus avoided giving open offence to the United States.[35] Togo and Kamerun were divided with France, South-West Africa was managed by the Union of South Africa (as the reward for conquering it), and German East Africa was assigned to Britain, apart from the small region of Ruanda-Urundi, which was allocated to Belgium.

Britain's determination to acquire new colonies was matched by her firmness in holding those she already possessed. Although the demand for essential supplies for the war effort brought windfall gains for a fortunate minority of producers in Africa, the general dislocation of international markets also caused widespread hardship,

31. On East Africa see Geoffrey Hodges, *The Carrier Corps: Military Labor in the East African Campaign, 1914–1918* (New York, 1986), and Gregory Maddox, '"*Mtunya*"': Famine in Central Tanzania, 1917–20', *Jour. African Hist.*, 31 (1990). On the campaign in South-West Africa (and the initial reluctance of Afrikaner officers to move against Germany), see N.G. Garson, 'South Africa and World War I', in Hillmer and Wigley, *The First British Commonwealth* (1980).

32. Albert F. Calvert, *The German African Empire* (1916), pp. xxi, and xxiii–xiv.

33. John S. Galbraith, 'British War Aims in World War I: a Commentary on Statesmanship', *Jour. Imp. and Comm. Hist.*, 13 (1984).

34. This little-known scheme has been disinterred by Peter J. Yearwood, 'Great Britain and the Repartition of Africa, 1914–19', *Jour. Imp. and Comm. Hist.*, 18 (1990).

35. Gaddis Smith, 'The British Government and the Disposition of the German Colonies in Africa, 1914–1918', in Prosser Gifford and William Roger Louis, eds. *Britain and Germany in Africa* (New Haven, Conn., 1967); William Roger Louis, 'The United States and the African Peace Settlement of 1919: the Pilgrimage of George Louis Beer', *Jour. African Hist.* 4 (1963). Italy's claims were largely brushed aside, as Robert L. Hess has shown: 'Italy and Africa: Colonial Ambitions in the First World War', *Jour. African Hist.*, 4 (1963). Benjamin Gerig, *The Open Door and the Mandate System* (1930) is still worth consulting for the legal and constitutional aspects.

discent and, on occasion, open revolt.[36] Under these pressures, the machinery of colonial rule faltered at times but it never stalled. Political control was firmly maintained, taxes were collected and debts continued to be serviced. Indeed, the imperatives of war were used by imperial enthusiasts, like Milner, to expand government power in London and the colonies, initially to supply essential materials and then to establish a form of central direction which aimed at extending state enterprise into areas where private firms were reluctant to venture.[37]

This is not the record of a hesitant imperial power. On the contrary, the war enhanced the importance and popularity of the empire, and the additions made in 1919 provide evidence of Britain's continuing sense of imperial mission and appetite for territory. In the corridors of power, attitudes towards the disposition of other peoples' lands were essentially the same as they had been in the late nineteenth century, when the scramble for Africa began. From this perspective, the peace settlement was the final act in the partition of the continent.[38] Thereafter, policy towards the tropical colonies was enveloped in the broader aim of reconstructing the pre-war international order by trying to restore free trade and the supremacy of sterling. Opportunist schemes, devised under the stress of war, for extracting resources from the colonies were soon discarded as renewed supplies of tropical products quickly outpaced demand.[39] But other legacies of war remained: public awareness of the empire was heightened and greatly extended by novel techniques of publicity and propaganda;[40]

36. For the contrast between winners and losers see J.D. Overton, 'War and Economic Development: Settlers in Kenya, 1914–18', *Jour. African Hist.*, 27 (1986), and Akinjide Osuntokun, *Nigeria in the First World War* (1979). Michael Crowder, *Revolt in Bussa: A Study in 'Native Administration' in Nigerian Borgu, 1902–1935* (1973), shows how wartime difficulties intersected with administrative changes to produce a rebellion in 1915.

37. Hancock, *Survey*, Vol. II, Pt. 1, Ch. 2; Suzanne Buckley, 'The Colonial Office and the Establishment of an Imperial Development Board', *Jour. Imp. and Comm. Hist.*, 3 (1974); David Killingray, 'The Empire Resources Development Committee and West Africa, 1916–20', *Jour. Imp. and Comm. Hist.*, 10 (1982).

38. At least in sub-Saharan Africa. There were worrying developments in Egypt, but these were managed in such a way as to safeguard Britain's essential interests. See John Darwin, *Britain, Egypt and the Middle East: Imperial Policy in the Aftermath of War, 1918–1922* (1981).

39. Hancock, *Survey*, Vol. II, Pt. 1, pp. 106–9, 113, 116, 122; Stephen Constantine, *The Making of British Colonial Development Policy, 1914–1940* (1984), Chs. 2–3.

40. In ways revealed in John M. MacKenzie's notable study, *Propaganda and Empire: The Manipulation of British Public Opinion, 1880–1960* (Manchester, 1984). A particularly relevant case study is Stephen Constantine, '"Bringing the Empire Alive": the Empire Marketing Board and Imperial Propaganda, 1926–33', in Mackenzie, *Imperialism and Popular Culture*.

air power, developed experimentally during the war, provided a new and effective means of colonial control in peacetime;[41] and the 'imperial visionaries', headed by Milner, Amery and Cunliffe-Lister, carried their programme of empire development into the post-war period and ensured that it stayed in the public eye.[42]

DEVELOPMENT AND CONTROL IN THE 1920s

The main issue within policy-making circles in the 1920s was not commitment to the empire, which was generally accepted even by Labour governments, but the extent to which subsidies of various kinds should be given to fund colonial development and to strengthen links between the empire and the mother country.[43] The debates of the period can therefore be seen as episodes in a long-running saga which cast the Treasury and its allies against claimants who were trying to turn special interests into national policy. The imperialist lobby led by Milner and his disciples was especially adept at publicising the case for state-supported development, but it failed to convert colonial policy, and the concessions it won turned out to have more promise than substance. A programme of empire-settlement was widely advertised in the early 1920s, but its effect on the tropical colonies was very limited: increases in the number of white immigrants in Southern Rhodesia and Kenya owed more to perceived opportunities and to existing inducements than to hastily mixed schemes for providing lands fit for heroes.[44] Similarly, efforts to promote commercial ties with the empire by introducing tariff preferences aroused hope among the advocates of closer union and

41. David Killingray, 'A Swift Agent of Government: Air Power in British Colonial Africa, 1916–1939', *Jour. African Hist.*, 25 (1984); Robert L. McCormack, 'Airlines and Empires: Great Britain and the "Scramble for Africa"', *Canadian Journal of African Studies*, 10 (1976); David E. Omissi, *Air Power and Colonial Control: The Royal Air Force, 1919–39* (Manchester, 1990); and, for an illuminating comment by a contemporary, Raymond L. Buell, *The Native Problem in Africa* (New York, 1928), p. 717.

42. See Drummond, *British Economic Policy*, Ch. 2; Constantine, *The Making of British Colonial Development Policy*; and, for a sample of the programme, L.S. Amery, 'Economic Development of the Empire', *United Empire*, 16 (1925).

43. On the Labour Party's voyage towards empire during this period see Gregory, *Sidney Webb in East Africa*.

44. The authoritative treatment is in Drummond, *Imperial Economic Policy*, Chs. 2–3. See also Brett, *Colonialism and Underdevelopment in East Africa*, Ch. 6, and Paul Mosley, *The Settler Economies: Studies in the Economic History of Kenya and Southern Rhodesia, 1900–1963* (Cambridge, 1983), pp. 16–24.

fear among third parties, but made little impression either on tropical Africa or on the direction of imperial trade as a whole.[45] Plans for channelling investment into the colonies through the Trade Facilities Acts (1921 and 1924), the East African Loans Acts (1924 and 1926), and the Colonial Development Act (1929) also produced results which fell far short of the ambitions of the promoters.[46]

A great deal could be said about all of these ventures, but for present purposes comment can be confined to the attempts to draw investment into tropical Africa.[47] Anxiety about unemployment in Britain provided the background to the legislation introduced in the 1920s, and to this extent it can be said that parliament was responsive to the needs of manufacturing interests, especially the older staple industries.[48] As in India, however, manufacturers made headway because their interests were congruent with larger policy aims rather than because they had laid hands on the machinery of state. In the early and mid–1920s, for instance, politicians were preoccupied by the fear that unemployment would lead to civil disorder and might even provoke revolution. In addition, policy throughout the decade was influenced by the prospect that increased colonial trade would help the dependencies to service their debts, assist Britain's balance of payments, and, in particular, reduce her obligations to the United States. The Colonial Development Act (1929), for example, was devised not only to cut unemployment in Britain but also to raise money to cover interest payments on existing debts contracted by the colonies, thus enabling them to float new development loans on the open market. Even so, the concessions made by the Treasury were very limited, and economic orthodoxy, represented by free trade,

45. Meyer, *Britain's Colonies*, pp. 10–11; United States Tariff Commission, *Colonial Tariff Policies* (Washington, DC, 1922).

46. Constantine, *The Making of British Colonial Development Policy*, Chs. 4–6.

47. George C. Abbott, 'British Colonial Aid Policy during the Nineteen Thirties', *Canadian Jour. Hist.*, 5 (1970), and the criticism by Ian M. Drummond, 'More on British Colonial Aid Policy in the Nineteen Thirties', *Canadian Jour. Hist.*, 6 (1971). Thereafter: Brett, *Colonialism and Underdevelopment*, pp. 131–3; and Meredith, 'British Government and Colonial Economic Policy', pp. 487–9. D.J. Morgan, *The Official History of Colonial Development*, Vol. I (1980), Chs. 5–6, says enough to suggest that this subject needs to be looked at afresh.

48. In the early 1920s Manchester was particularly exercised by problems of cotton supply and by the decline of its share of the Indian market. Its renewed interest in Africa, and the foundation of the Empire Cotton Growing Association in 1921, are examined by W.A. Wardle, 'A History of the British Cotton Growing Association, 1902–39, with Special Reference to its Operations in Northern Nigeria', (Ph.D. thesis, University of Birmingham, 1980), pp. 158–68. The most publicised experiment in cotton-growing is dealt with by A. Gaitskell, *Gezira: A Story of Development in the Sudan* (1959).

sound money and self-sufficiency, survived, if not intact, then with only a few dents. Apart from the fact that the sums involved in the various Acts were kept to modest levels, the Treasury succeeded in opposing the idea that the loans should be interest-free and instead offered a guarantee, which provided investors with the incentive they needed. Consequently the burden of repayment fell on African taxpayers, and colonial officials redoubled their tax-gathering efforts in the 1920s to ensure that budgets were balanced and debt service was maintained.[49] Not surprisingly, the anti-colonial protests of the period were often related to grievances about the weight of taxation.[50]

The promotion of the imperial mission after World War I was accompanied by a revitalisation of the principle of trusteeship. Particular prominence was given to the twin doctrines of indirect rule and 'native paramountcy', which affirmed the importance of preserving indigenous interests within the framework of colonialism. The point of reference for both concepts was what Lugard termed the dual mandate, which stressed the mutual interests of rulers and ruled and underlined the need to balance progress, in the form of economic development, against disruption, in the shape of untoward social change and the attendant danger of political instability.[51] This idea, like many other principles of imperial government, can be traced to Britain's experience in India. Lugard's contribution was to apply the notion of indirect rule with great vigour, and to exert his considerable influence to spread it from Nigeria to other parts of colonial Africa. By the close of the 1920s the process of administrative infill was

49. A sad tale, well told, is that by Leroy Vail, 'The Making of an Imperial Slum: Nyasaland and its Railways, 1895–1935', *Jour. African Hist.*, 16 (1975).

50. For example: Philip A. Igbafe, *Benin under British Administration: The Impact of Indirect Rule on an African Kingdom, 1897–1938* (1979), Ch. 9; Diana Ellis, 'The Nandi Protest of 1923 in the Context of African Resistance to Colonial Rule in Kenya', *Jour. African Hist.*, 17 (1976); Susan M. Martin, *Palm Oil and Protest: An Economic History of the Ngwa Region, South-Eastern Nigeria, 1800–1980* (Cambridge, 1988), Ch. 9.

51. Lugard, *The Dual Mandate*. Frederick Dealtry Lugard (1858–1945) was born in India and educated at Rossall School and Sandhurst. He made his career in the army and in the empire, especially in Africa and above all in Nigeria, from where he retired as Governor in 1919. Thereafter, he became an active publicist for empire and for his own ideas about how it should be governed. In action and thought, Lugard's military values marched with a strong sense of Christian ethics, which he derived from his parents, and particularly from his father, a chaplain in the East India Company. The standard biography is Margery Perham, *Lugard*, 2 vols. (1956 and 1960), but more recent work takes the view that Lugard was better as a propagandist than as an administrator. See especially I.N. Nicholson, *The Administration of Nigeria, 1900–1960: Men, Methods, and Myths* (Oxford, 1969), and the valuable overview by John E. Flint, 'Frederick Lugard: the Making of an Autocrat (1858–1945)', in Gann and Duignan, *African Proconsuls*. For a French perspective see Claude Horrut, *Frederick Lugard et la pensée coloniale britannique de son temps* (Paris, 1975).

complete, and indirect rule had been realised or planted in territories as distant and as different as Tanganyika, Uganda and the Sudan, as well as West Africa. As its name implies, indirect rule was based upon the use of indigenous authorities as agents of colonial government. This policy, in turn, involved restrictions on forms of foreign enterprise which might have undermined the social order and discredited chiefly authority by raising potentially explosive issues of land rights and labour use. In West Africa, to take the best known example, expatriate firms were kept out of primary production, with the exception of some mining operations, and confined largely to the import–export trades. On the traders' frontier, as it has been called,[52] there was no place even for a capitalist as powerful as W.H. Lever, whose schemes for palm-oil plantations in British West Africa were repeatedly turned down by the Colonial Office and had to be transferred to the Belgian Congo, where the climate, though still tropical, was also more receptive.[53]

Indirect rule was a construct that diverted the past in the name of tradition.[54] In practice, Lugard's 'traditional' chiefs were not on standby awaiting the call to colonial duty. If the emirates of Northern Nigeria came closest to his ideal of indigenous authority, too many other regions fell far short of it, lacking either centralised states or a

---

52. The distinction between traders' and settlers' frontiers has long been a central theme in the historiography of colonial Africa. The most influential statement, still unsurpassed, is in Hancock, *Survey of British Commonwealth Affairs*, Vol. II, Pt.2, which in turn drew inspiration from the work of Frederick Jackson Turner on the United States.

53. Hancock, *Survey of British Commonwealth Affairs*, Vol. II, Pt. 2, pp. 173–200; and, for the subsequent history of Lever's interests, D.K. Fieldhouse, *Unilever Overseas: The Anatomy of a Multinational* (1978), Chs. 6 and 9.

54. There is now a sizeable revisionist literature on this subject. Illustrations of the comments made here include: A.E. Afigbo, *The Warrant Chiefs: Indirect Rule in Southern Nigeria, 1891–1929*, (1972); Ralph Austen, 'The Official Mind of Indirect Rule: British Policy in Tanganyika, 1916–1939', in Gifford and Louis, *Britain and Germany in Africa*; Martin Chanock, *Law, Custom and Social Order: The Colonial Experience in Malawi and Zambia* (Cambridge, 1985); D.C. Dorward, 'Ethnography and Administration: a Study of Anglo-Tiv "Working Misunderstanding"', *Jour. African Hist.*, 15 (1974); Cyril Ehrlich, 'Some Social and Economic Implications of Paternalism in Uganda', *Jour. African Hist.*, 4 (1963); Beverly Gartell, 'British Administrators, Colonial Chiefs, and the Comfort of Tradition: an Example from Uganda', *African Stud. Rev.*, 26 (1983); Owen J.M. Kalinga, 'Colonial Rule, Missionaries, and Ethnicity in North Nyassa District, 1891–1938', *African Stud. Rev.*, 28 (1985); Peter K. Tibenderana, 'The Irony of Indirect Rule in the Sokoto Caliphate, Nigeria, 1903–1944', *African Stud. Rev.*, 31 (1988); John Tosh, *Clan Leaders and Colonial Chiefs in Lango: The Political History of an East African Stateless Society c.1800–1939* (Oxford, 1978); Landeg White, '"Tribes" and the Aftermath of the Chilembwe Rising', *African Aff.*, 83 (1984). For a comparative approach see E.J. Hobsbawm and T.O. Ranger, eds. *The Invention of Tradition* (Cambridge, 1983).

political hierarchy which fitted readily into the colonial mould. The attempt to identify indigenous forms of authority often resulted in social engineering which invented as much as it codified 'native law and customs', increased an awareness of 'ethnicity' and 'tribalism', and created chiefs whose titles lacked historical legitimacy. These innovations had profound consequences for African societies, but they also had an important influence on colonial governments, making administrators more interventionist than the model of indirect rule envisaged, and encouraging forms of bureaucratic paternalism which survived the demise of colonial rule itself.

In the eyes of its advocates, indirect rule was both a necessity and a virtue. The poverty of most of tropical Africa, combined with the shortage of foreign capital, meant that colonial government had to be economical. Indirect rule recommended itself because it was cheap and, to the extent that it was self-policing, it was also unobtrusive. It was adopted either where settlers failed to materialise in sufficient numbers, as in Uganda and Tanganyika, or where export growth was already being promoted by 'native enterprise', as in Nigeria and the Gold Coast.[55] The distinction between traders' and settlers' Africa was not, therefore, simply a matter of climate: it also rested on judgements about the most cost-effective means of meeting the priorities of imperial policy.[56] However, judgement was a matter of principle as well as of interest. Africa's gentlemanly rulers saw themselves as conservationists – of people as well as of game.[57] They were inclined to idealise rural Africa, to identify with 'natural' pastoralists and cultivators, and to view urbanised and supposedly 'detribalised' Africans with a mixture of disdain and alarm. These perceptions mirrored their reactions to the spread of industrial society in Britain. In searching for 'lost tribes and vanished chiefs',[58] officials were trying to 'strengthen the solid elements in the countryside . . .

55. Thomas Taylor, 'The Establishment of a European Plantation Sector within the Emerging Colonial Economy of Uganda, 1909–1919', *Int. Jour. African Hist. Stud.*, 19 (1986); Jan S. Hogendorn, 'Economic Initiative and African Cash Farming: Pre-Colonial Origins and Early Colonial Developments', in Gann and Duignan, *Colonialism in Africa*, IV, Ch. 8.

56. The main issues are summarised in A.G. Hopkins, *An Economic History of West Africa* (1973), pp. 211–16.

57. On the latter see John M. Mackenzie's fascinating study, *The Empire of Nature: Hunting, Conservation, and British Imperialism* (Manchester, 1988). Conservation measures also enlarged the role of the state, as Ian Phimister, for example, has shown: 'Discourse and the Discipline of Historical Context: Conservationism and Ideas about Development in Southern Rhodesia, 1930–1950', *Jour. Southern African Stud.*, 12 (1986).

58. A phrase used by Sir James Currie (a former Director of Education in the Sudan and a critic of indirect rule) in 1926. Quoted in Daly, *British Administration*, p. 175.

before the irresponsible body of half-educated officials, students and town riff-raff takes control of the public mind'.[59]

Whereas in West Africa colonial policy prevented intrusions into 'native rights', in parts of East and Central Africa it lent support to white settlers. At the time of partition, as we have seen, East and Central Africa were thought to have considerable potential for white settlement, and there was extravagant talk of creating a new Australia in the Dark Continent. However, once the brief 'jungle boom' at the turn of the century had passed, more sober appraisals prevailed, and the City returned to its former caution.[60] Consequently, the number of settlers was limited and they also tended to be self-financing.[61] Kenya, for example, attracted a high proportion of officers and gentlemen from upper- and middle-class families whose backgrounds and values were very similar to those of members of the colonial service. Lord Delamere, the most famous of the founding settlers, acquired 100,000 acres in Kenya in 1903, following a hunting visit a few years earlier. He was joined by Lord Cranworth and his brother-in-law, Mervyn Ridley, who arrived shortly afterwards with £1,500 and a pack of foxhounds.[62] Although Kenya never lost its aristocratic tinge, farming became a serious business with the development of maize, coffee and tea, and it is now clear that, amidst the dilettantes and the inefficient, there were many serious and shrewd entrepreneurs.[63] The gentlemen farmers of Kenya were escaping from the decline of agriculture, the growth of industry and the spread of democracy in Britain, but they were not refugees from all forms of capitalism.

The divergence in policy towards different parts of tropical Africa was largely a reflection of official calculations about the most appropriate means of realising the potential of various regions. In Kenya

59. Minutes of a meeting of Governors of Northern Sudan, 1920. Quoted in Daly, *British Administration*, p. 173.

60. Speculation in gold and rubber in West Africa at this time involved 'the shadier fringes of the Edwardian capital market'. See J. Forbes Munro, 'Monopolists and Speculators: British Investment in West African Rubber, 1905–1914', *Jour. African Hist.*, 22 (1981), p. 277. A similar boom in gold-mining shares in Southern Rhodesia collapsed in 1903.

61. By 1939 there were approximately 21,000 white settlers in Kenya and 63,000 in Southern Rhodesia. See Dane Kennedy, *Islands of White: Settler Society and Culture in Kenya and Southern Rhodesia, 1890–1939* (Durham, NC, 1987). M.P.K. Sorrenson, *Origins of European Settlement in Kenya* (1968), and Richard Hodder-Williams, *White Farmers in Rhodesia, 1890–1965* (1983), are also helpful.

62. Kennedy, *Islands of White*, p. 44.

63. Mosley, *The Settler Economies*, Ch. 2; Lonsdale, 'The Conquest State'. Also C.C. Wrigley, 'Kenya: the Patterns of Economic Life, 1902–1945', in Vincent Harlow and E.M. Chilver, eds. *History of East Africa* (Oxford, 1965).

and Southern Rhodesia, the administration lent its weight to a form of imported agrarian capitalism by helping white farmers to secure access to supplies of land and labour. By controlling the market for the principal factors of production, colonial governments hoped to attract both well-capitalised settlers and those who needed to raise money on the strength of guaranteed land rights. But official support had its limits. The authorities had to balance the demands of settler farmers against those of expatriate commercial interests whose priorities were often different, and to do so without wholly ignoring the claims of indigenous societies.[64] The need to hold the ring against several contestants gave the administration a degree of independence from any one of them, even if this had then to be mortgaged to purchase a series of unequal and temporary compromises. More important still, colonial governments were instruments of imperial policy; as such, their primary task was to ensure that local interests of all kinds were subordinated to priorities laid down by the metropole. This mixture of encouragement and restraint can be seen very clearly in the handling of white nationalism in Kenya and Southern Rhodesia in the aftermath of World War I.

The formation of the colony of Kenya from the East Africa Protectorate in 1920 created important financial and political opportunities. As a colony, Kenya was able to take advantage of the favourable borrowing terms authorised by the Colonial Stock Acts, and immediately did so. The corollary, of course, was that the new colony was subjected to London in financial and monetary matters. The extent of this dependence became apparent in 1921, when the colony was struck by a serious currency crisis.[65] Kenya's currency, the silver rupee, appreciated significantly against sterling after 1918, when the pound was still floating against other currencies. This trend presented problems for sterling-holders in Kenya who had to make payments in rupees. The white settlers, supported by an indulgent governor, tried to introduce unorthodox currency reforms in a bid to

64. There were differences of interest among farmers and also between farmers as a group and expatriate mine-owners (over labour supplies, for example). Commercial interests were represented by the Joint East Africa Board, on which see Stahl, *Metropolitan Organization*, pp. 189–98, and Brett, *Colonialism and Underdevelopment*, pp. 59–65. The juggling act is described in detail by John Lonsdale and Bruce Berman, 'Coping with the Contradictions: the Development of the Colonial State in Kenya, 1895–1914', *Jour. African Hist.*, 20 (1979).

65. Robert M. Maxon, 'The Kenya Currency Crisis, 1919–21 and the Imperial Dilemma', *Jour. Imp. and Comm. Hist.*, 17 (1989). See also R.M.A. van Zwanenberg with Anne King, *An Economic History of Kenya and Uganda, 1800–1970* (1975), pp. 281–7.

cut the cost of their rupee payments. The response of the imperial banks in Kenya was immediate: they stopped the agitation in its tracks by threatening to call in local advances. The Colonial Office and the Treasury, with the support of the banks, then decided to resolve the problem by extending the Currency Board system to East Africa. In the ensuing discussions, the governor tried to fix an exchange rate with sterling which was more favourable to settler interests than that recommended by the banks and supported by the Colonial Office. The banks reacted by proposing to boycott all transactions in Kenya, and Whitehall imposed the rate approved in London.

The settlers also tried to use the new constitution to entrench their power, and in the early 1920s the militants among them began to make plans for self-government.[66] These ambitions ran into the aspirations of Indian settlers, who had been encouraged by recent constitutional concessions in India to claim equal rights in Kenya. The political crisis produced by the meeting of these forces culminated in an extraordinary plot, mounted by a group of white settlers in 1923, to kidnap the governor and install Lord Delamere as head of a provisional government. It is instructive to note that one of the principal instigators, Brigadier General Wheatley, came from a family of landed gentry which had held on to its respectability rather better than to its fortunes. Wheatley himself arrived in Kenya in 1919 under the auspices of the settlement scheme for ex-officers and set about turning his new estate into 'a real gentleman's place'.[67] Given his background, it is not surprising that Wheatley ranked as a die-hard, even by exacting settler standards, and advocated direct action to halt the threat to his plans to secure what he regarded as being his rightful social position.

The values represented by Wheatley and his associates were, broadly speaking, those of Whitehall too, but the planned insurrection broke the rules of the game. In 1923 London imposed a compromise, the celebrated Devonshire Declaration, which formally reserved Kenya for Africans.[68] This was something of a masterstroke in that it

66. Robinson, 'Moral Disarmament'; C.J.D. Duder, 'The Settler Response to the Indian Crisis of 1923 in Kenya: Brigadier General Philip Wheatley and Direct Action', *Jour. Imp. and Comm. Hist.*, 17 (1989).

67. Duder, 'The Settler Response', p. 352.

68. Robinson, 'Moral Disarmament'; Jidlaph G. Kamoche, *Imperial Trusteeship and Political Evolution in Kenya, 1923–1963* (Washington, DC, 1981), Chs. 1–2. The activities of the 'humanitarian' pressure group are discussed by Diana Wylie, 'Confrontation over Kenya: the Colonial Office and its Critics, 1918–1940', *Jour. African Hist.*, 18 (1977).

appeared to neuter both settler and Indian demands without actually giving the indigenous inhabitants anything that they did not have already. The settlers continued to hanker after self-government, and their claims resurfaced in the late 1920s. Again, however, the proponents of white supremacy were defeated, and the principle of native paramountcy was reaffirmed in 1929. The outcome was that the white settlers gained to the extent that their position in the White Highlands was confirmed and their Indian rivals were denied equality; but their wider ambitions were contained. Self-government was ruled out by the Colonial Office with the support of the India Office, the humanitarian lobby, and expatriate commercial interests which had begun to acquire a stake in low-cost production by African exporters. It was also opposed by the Treasury and the City, and by more sober minds among the settlers themselves, who realised that Kenya's credit depended upon imperial guarantees. Although the new constitution widened the scope for political activity, financial realities ensured that the colony remained bound firmly to London.

The settlers in Rhodesia, on the other hand, were granted self-government in 1923.[69] The concession was made partly because their numbers and viability were greater than in Kenya, but also because financial considerations there favoured rather than obstructed a larger degree of 'responsible' government. Down to 1923, the Rhodesias were administered by the British South Africa Company on behalf of the British government. By the early 1920s the Company was anxious to give up its administrative burdens and to be compensated for them, while the settlers were keen to advance their political claims. The Treasury, however, was determined to minimise the cost of devolution, and for this reason supported a scheme for linking the settlers to the Union of South Africa, which had thoughtfully offered to settle the British government's debt with the Company. The plan went awry in 1922, when the settlers voted for self-government with colonial status rather than for joining the Union. Nevertheless, the Treasury still charged a price for self-government, and insisted that Southern Rhodesia should meet half the Company's bill for administrative services. In an associated deal, completed in 1924, the British government confirmed the Company's mineral rights in Northern Rhodesia and transferred the territory to the Colonial Office. In exchange, the Company agreed to cancel its charges for past administrative services there.

69. Robinson, 'Moral Disarmament'; Ian Phimister, *An Economic and Social History of Zimbabwe, 1890–1948* (1988), Chs. 2–3; and, for the longer view, Martin Chanock, *Unconsummated Union: Britain, Rhodesia and South Africa, 1900–45* (Manchester, 1977).

The achievement of self-government in Southern Rhodesia was a success for settler aspirations, but it was not a defeat for British imperialism. The substance of Britain's interests remained untouched, and the new constitution was hedged with qualifications and restrictions. External affairs, including monetary and tariff policy, remained firmly under London's control. The new government continued to protect foreign investment, and showed itself to be a conservative and reliable successor to Company rule. Events in Kenya and Rhodesia made it clear that the major decisions were still being shaped by the metropole, and that the financial status of territories, especially their standing as debtors or creditors, exerted a powerful influence on their political fortunes.

IMPOSING AND REAPPRAISING ORTHODOXY: THE 1930s

In tropical Africa, as elsewhere, the slump put an end to hopes of reconstructing the pre-war international economic order.[70] By damaging the profitability of export production in the colonies, it also squeezed revenues and strained the principles of trusteeship. Moreover, it is now apparent that the downturn in the international economy transmitted by the industrial world coincided with longer-term structural problems in African economies which began to reveal the limits to further export expansion in the absence of an agricultural revolution.[71] This was a broad trend as well as a new one, and there were exceptions to it, both regionally and socially.[72] Nevertheless, the generalisation holds: the agricultural innovations which pulled parts of the African coast out of the crisis of legitimate commerce in the late nineteenth century were not repeated in the 1930s. The most profitable alternative, a 'lucky strike' of valuable minerals, was rarely

70. Starting points for studying this subject include: Hopkins, *Economic History*, Ch. 7; 'L'Afrique et la crise de 1930', *Revue française d'histoire d'Outre-Mer*, 63 (1976); J.M. Lonsdale, 'The Depression and the Second World War in the Transformation of Kenya', in D. Killingray and R. Rathbone, eds. *Africa and the Second World War* (1986); and Ian Brown, ed. *The Economies of Africa and Asia in the Inter-War Depression* (1989).

71. See, for example, David Anderson, 'Depression, Dust Bowl, Demography and Drought: the Colonial State and Soil Conservation in East Africa during the 1930s', *African Affairs*, 83 (1984); and S.M. Martin, 'The Long Depression: West African Export Producers and the World Economy, 1914–45', in Brown, *The Economies of Africa and Asia*.

72. These are explored in Brown, *The Economies of Africa and Asia*.

made, and local manufactures were not a serious prospect in tropical Africa, as they were in the Dominions.[73] In these circumstances, it is understandable that producers responded to falling export prices by increasing output, not by reducing it, except in rare cases where they tried to control supplies through cartels or by exerting political pressure. Colonial governments therefore found themselves coping with the unforeseen consequences of previous developments in the international economy, which had vastly increased supplies of tropical raw materials on world markets, and which, in conditions of static or declining demand, had worrying implications for budgets, debt service and expectations.

The threat to the principle of self-sufficiency needs emphasising because it had an important, if indirect, influence on the approach to trusteeship and, in this way, on the whole imperial enterprise in Africa. As noted earlier, after 1900 the new African colonies con-tracted foreign loans to fund state-building activities, especially railways and administration. The money was raised by colonial governments at fixed rates of interest, and the debt was serviced from revenues which depended heavily on export earnings. In this phase of development debt, dominated by public-sector borrowing, the burden of repayment increased at times of depression, when earnings were reduced.[74] The problem of the rigidity of the debt structure in tropical Africa was compounded by the growth and increased cost (through higher interest rates) of public indebtedness after 1913. According to one estimate, the funded debt of all the British territories in Africa (apart from South Africa) grew by more than one-third in real terms between 1925 and 1935.[75] The link between increased debt and static or falling revenues during the slump is clearly illustrated by the history of public finance in two of the leading colonies in tropical

73. Rich deposits of iron ore were found in Sierra Leone in 1933. Copper was already being produced in Northern Rhodesia, and the price fell in 1929. However, the development of new mines and the discovery of high-grade ore helped to pull the colony out of the slump in the late 1930s. The rise in the price of gold also encouraged new (and often marginal) mines to enter production: see Andrew D. Roberts, 'The Gold Boom of the 1930s in Eastern Africa', *African Affairs*, 85 (1986). Import-substituting manufactures are discussed by Brett, *Colonialism and Underdevelopment*, pp. 278–81, 298–9, and Gervase Clarence Smith, 'The Effect of the Great Depression on Industrialisation in Equatorial and Central Africa', in Brown, *The Economies of Africa and Asia*.

74. In contrast, where capital was provided mainly by private finance in the form of equities, as in the case of the South African gold-mines, reduced earnings were compensated to some extent by reduced dividend payments. See Frankel, *Capital Investment*, p. 179.

75. Frankel, *Capital Investment*, Table 36, p. 178.

Africa, Nigeria and Kenya, where the ratio of debt charges to gross revenue rose from 14 per cent and 18 per cent respectively in 1926 to 33 per cent and 34 per cent in 1934.[76] The financial problems of these important colonies concentrated the official mind to the extent of influencing the reappraisal of colonial rule which began in the late 1930s.

In the short run, however, the challenge to self-sufficiency was met by unwavering orthodoxy. Public expenditure was cut and the efficiency of tax collection was improved. There was neither a hint nor any prospect of devaluation: when the pound left the gold standard in 1931, the colonies automatically joined the sterling bloc at rates of exchange determined by London. Even in the depths of recession, the African colonies serviced their debts promptly and balanced their budgets with little or no assistance. On leaving Tanganyika in 1931, Governor Cameron declared that one of his proudest achievements was that the colony had paid its way since 1926 and had ceased to be a burden on the Treasury.[77] This record was matched by other struggling territories, such as the Sudan and Nyasaland.[78] Debts were not rescheduled, even where it was technically possible to do so. When the idea was mentioned by unofficial members of the Gold Coast Legislative Council in 1933, Governor Slater's response barely contained his apoplexy:

> If the rate of interest were to be compulsorily lowered before the expiry of the specified period, subscribers to the loan would have to accept a reduction in their income. The suggestion implies, therefore, that persons [British investors] who are already making enormous sacrifice in aid of their own country should accept yet another burden for the relief of persons in another country who have enjoyed all the benefits but will not accept their obligations.[79]

The governor concluded: 'I do not believe for one moment that the suggestion finds favour with the general public'.[80] This was an inherently improbable claim, though not one that could be tested directly in an undemocratic system. Nevertheless, there were manifest signs of discontent with low produce prices and of opposition to government exactions in colonial Africa during the 1930s (not least in

76. Ibid. pp. 178, 181–3.
77. Sir Donald Cameron, *My Tanganyika Service and Some Nigeria* (1939), p. 280.
78. Daly, *Empire on the Nile*, pp. 194–5; Vail, 'The Making of an Imperial Slum'. Tanganyika's budget buckled in the early 1930s, but was soon straightened out. See Brett, *Colonialism and Underdevelopment*, pp. 143–5.
79. Quoted in N.A. Cox-George, *Studies in Finance and Development* (1973), p. 110.
80. Ibid.

the Gold Coast), and indications, too, that these were beginning to find a political voice outside the islands of white settlement.[81]

The priority attached to securing British capital and servicing the public debt also influenced international trade policy. Colonial governments became increasingly involved in export-marketing schemes during the 1930s, whether by sponsoring agricultural cooperatives or by approving cartels formed by mining interests, white farmers and the large expatriate trading firms.[82] The purpose in all cases was to raise export prices, either by improving quality or by restricting output, and hence to boost land values, incomes and revenues with the aim of averting the collapse of private credit and of meeting public–sector fiscal targets. Similar motives operated to shape the colonial tariff regime, which remained essentially an instrument of fiscal rather than of commercial policy. When imperial tariffs were renegotiated at Ottawa in 1932, the Colonial Office ensured that exports from the tropical colonies were allowed to enter Britain and the dominions on the most favourable terms. No significant preferences were given in return because most of the African colonies were committed by international agreements (made at the time of partition), to preserve free trade.[83] Sales of cheap goods from Japan and India expanded rapidly in the 1930s, especially in East Africa, and a number of British firms adjusted to commercial realities by becoming agents for Manchester's new competitors.[84]

The most publicised breach of free trade in tropical Africa occurred in 1934, when quotas were imposed on Japanese goods imported into Nigeria and the Gold Coast.[85] This was a clear case of official intervention in favour of British manufactures, and it demonstrates that colonial tariffs could be manipulated to an extent that was

81. J. Ayodele Langley, *Pan-Africanism and Nationalism in West Africa, 1900–1945* (Oxford, 1973).

82. A perceptive introduction is in Ian M. Drummond, *British Economic Policy and the Empire, 1919–1939* (1972), pp. 114–20. See also Meredith, 'The Colonial Office'. Examples of policy in Africa include: J.C. de Graft-Johnson, *African Experiment: Co-operative Agriculture and Banking in British West Africa* (1958); John McCracken, 'Planters, Peasants and the Colonial State: the Impact of the Native Tobacco Board in the Central Province of Malawi', *Jour. Southern African Stud.*, 9 (1983); and Kenneth Vickery, 'Maize Control in Northern Rhodesia', *Jour. Southern African Stud.*, 11 (1985).

83. Meyer, *Britain's Colonies*, pp. 10–11, 32–5; Brett, *Colonialism and Underdevelopment*, pp. 148–56.

84. Stahl, *Metropolitan Organization*, p. 212.

85. Followed by limited discriminatory measures in 1936. See Meyer, *Britain's Colonies*, pp. 64–6, 80–5; Brett, *Colonialism and Underdevelopment*, pp. 156–60; Charlotte Leubuscher, 'The Policy Governing External Trade', in M. Perham, ed. *Mining, Commerce, and Finance in Nigeria* (1948), pp. 158–63; Arthur Redford, *Manchester Merchants and Foreign Trade*, Vol. II, *1850–1939* (Manchester, 1956), pp. 250–9.

impossible in India or China, where Manchester's textile exports had been badly damaged by low-cost competitors in the 1920s. On closer inspection, however, it appears that government intervention was a gesture rather than a substantial measure of support for Britain's ailing staple industry. The quota system affected less than 5 per cent of the import trade of British West Africa, and fell far short of the Manchester lobby's pleas for comprehensive assistance. Japan found compensation elsewhere, and her share of the West African market was quickly filled by suppliers other than Britain. Manchester's cause was weakened partly by its own evident decline and partly by countervailing pressures from other powerful business interests which continued to favour free trade. More important still, however, was the fact that the Colonial Office had decided that existing commercial treaties suited the international trade and payments of both Britain and her colonies. This position was endorsed by the Foreign Office, which was concerned to avoid provoking Germany, Japan or the United States at a time when imperial policy had become entwined with negotiations for preserving world peace.

The international context of Britain's colonial policy can only be touched on here; but it is important to underline the point that the 1930s were a period of renascent imperialism in Africa, as they were in South America and China. The 'imperial problem', as defined by contemporaries,[86] was particularly acute in the case of Africa because the continent had been divided and parts of it reassigned comparatively recently. The 'problem' itself was not, as hindsight might misleadingly suggest, how to deal with nationalism, but how to accommodate the 'have-not' nations without weakening the empire. The 'have-nots', in the terminology of the day, were those deprived, not of food, but of colonies, and referred principally to Germany, Japan and (since demand for other people's territory was readily expandable) to Italy.[87] In dealing with claims from the rich but unsatisfied, Britain had also to fend off the attentions of the United States, which was both wealthy and anti-colonial. Neither group could be ignored: Germany's claims to her former colonies became tied up with wider issues of peace and stability in Europe; the United

86. The fullest statement is Royal Institute of International Affairs, *The Colonial Problem* (1937). See also Norman Angell, *The Defence of the British Empire* (New York, 1937), and idem, *Who Owns the British Empire?* (1942).

87. Norman Angell, *This Have and Have Not Business: Political Fantasy and Economic Fact* (1936); Douglas Rimmer, 'Have-Not Nations: the Prototype', *Economic Development and Cultural Change*, 27 (1979).

States was the British empire's leading foreign trade partner and the creditor of last resort should diplomacy fail and war follow.[88]

The attempted repartition of Africa began in 1935, when Italy invaded Ethiopia.[89] Although Britain did not favour this act of aggression, she was able to accommodate it because her own interests were not directly involved, and in 1938 she gave formal recognition to Italy's acquisition. This event had wider ramifications, stirring black nationalism in tropical Africa, raising questions about the nature of trusteeship and, more immediately, lending impetus to Germany's demands for the restoration of her former colonies. Between 1935 and 1938 the Foreign Office gave serious consideration to plans for making colonial concessions to Germany in the hope of securing a peace settlement in Europe. This policy has been treated as evidence that Britain was losing both the will and the ability to defend the empire. But Chamberlain never offered to transfer territory that was considered, by its constitution and longevity, to be an integral part of the empire. His idea was to give away other people's possessions by carving up portions of Germany's former colonies in tropical Africa and by spicing the offer with concessions in central Africa, which – *perfide Albion* – were to be made at the expense of Belgium and Portugal. Seen in this light, and leaving aside the lack of realism which pervaded the negotiations, Chamberlain's thinking demonstrates a fundamental continuity with the nineteenth century: Africa was still a continent to be divided and apportioned for the sake of greater European interests. While Chamberlain believed that Hitler was a Christian and a gentleman, he dealt with him as Salisbury dealt with Bismarck. After 1938, when it appeared that he was neither, concessions were no longer on the menu.

Further evidence that the British retained a strongly imperial cast of mind can be found in the extensive publicity campaign which accompanied diplomacy but also extended far beyond it.[90] In the

88. The importance of trade between the United States and the empire during this period has not been given its full emphasis. The starting point is Meyer, *Britain's Colonies*, Ch. 10.

89. This paragraph draws on: Wolfe W. Schmokel, *Dream of Empire: German Colonialism, 1919–1945* (1964); idem, 'The Hard Death of Imperialism: German and British Colonial Attitudes, 1919–1939', in Gifford and Louis, *Britain and Germany in Africa*; William Roger Louis, 'Colonial Appeasement, 1936–1938', *Revue belge de philologie et d'histoire*, 49 (1971); S.K.B. Asante, 'The Italo-Ethiopian Conflict: a Case Study in British West African Response to Crisis Diplomacy in the 1930s', *Jour. African Hist.*, 15 (1974); and Andrew J.Crozier, *Appeasement and Germany's Last Bid for Colonies* (Basingstoke, 1988).

90. Philip M Taylor, *The Projection of Britain: British Overseas Publicity and Propaganda, 1919–1939* (Cambridge, 1981); John M. Mackenzie, ed. *Imperialism and Popular*

1930s the media were mobilised, officially and through private enterprise, to counter fascist propaganda and to disarm critics of empire in the United States and the League of Nations. The British Council was founded in 1934 specifically for this purpose; the BBC advanced its own characteristically restrained advertisement for the monarch and his empire; astute use was made of film to portray the white man, especially the white gentleman, in a favourable light; and a stream of publications, from comics and newspapers to histories of the empire written in approving, Whiggish style by high authorities in high places, combined to popularise and endorse the imperial mission. This process of moral rearmament won many converts, not least at home, and helped to prepare the British for a war that would carry forward the imperial enterprise, as well as end the threat of fascism.

The continuing vitality of the imperial mission was associated, as both cause and consequence, with a far-reaching reappraisal of the concept of trusteeship at the close of the 1930s.[91] It was clear by then that indirect rule had failed to deliver economic progress or to contain social change. 'Native paramountcy' sounded well, but was an empty barrel, and its promise had been contradicted by the support given to white settlers and by the cavalier attitude taken towards the repartition of Africa – most glaringly in the case of Ethiopia. Expressions of political and economic unrest in Africa, though not a serious challenge to colonial rule, were bad publicity and caused thoughtful governors to question the assumptions of the Lugardian system.[92] The publication of Hailey's *African Survey* in 1938 revealed how much had still to be learned about the peoples and resources of colonial Africa and initiated a debate in official circles which was to divide policy-makers into preservationists and modernisers. Hailey's signal from Africa joined Macmillan's *Warning from the West Indies* (1936) and accompanied outbreaks of mass discontent in the Caribbean in 1937 and

---

Culture (Manchester, 1986); idem, *Propaganda and Empire*; J. Richards, 'Patriotism with Profit: British Imperial Cinema in the 1930s', in J. Curran and V. Porter, eds. *British Cinema History* (1983); Rosaleen Smyth, 'The Development of British Colonial Film Policy, 1927–1939, with Special Reference to East and Central Africa', *Jour. African Hist.*, 20 (1979); Andrew Roberts, 'Africa on Film to 1940', *History in Africa*, 14 (1987).

91. Lee, *Colonial Development*, Chs.2–3; R.D. Pearce, *The Turning Point in Africa: British Colonial Policy, 1938–1948* (1982), Chs. 2–3; Robinson, *Dilemmas of Trusteeship*.

92. The most influential of the official critics in the late 1930s was Sir Bernard Boudillon (Governor of Uganda, 1932–35 and of Nigeria, 1935–9). See Robert Pearce, 'The Colonial Economy: Nigeria and the Second World War', in Ingham and Simmons, *Development Studies and Colonial Policy*; and idem, *Sir Bernard Bourdillon: The Biography of a Twentieth-Century Colonialist* (Oxford, 1987).

1938.[93] The West Indies, ignored for so long, now commanded immediate attention because they were the 'show window'[94] of the branch of British colonialism closest to the United States, whose support against Hitler was becoming a vital consideration. As the Colonial Office recognised, the disturbances expressed, in acute form, a level of disaffection that was present elsewhere too, and the goverment feared a reaction that would ignite the whole of the colonial empire.

Underlying the unease with the colonial record in official circles was a growing realisation of the limitations of orthodox responses to the world slump and a perception that the tropical colonies had been set on a course of export development which had more of a past than a future. The fiscal rigour which characterised policy in the 1930s was successful in balancing budgets and servicing debts, but it also alienated key groups of producers and wage-earners who were already suffering from persistently low export prices, and it cast more than doubt on the claim that colonial rule was an improving influence. Logically, there were only two solutions to this problem: one was to abandon the colonies; the other was to give up the policies which had failed to fulfil their promise. Since the first possibility was never considered, it was the latter which was chosen. Once again, fiscal imperatives drove policy in novel directions. The search for revenue had first cast trusteeship in the form of indirect rule, and it now helped to bring about its downfall. The answer to the question of poverty in Africa and to the need to find new, secure sources of revenue was to be not less government but more.[95] The covert interventionism which already existed was to be made manifest, building was to replace caretaking, and a new ideology of development, a redefinition of trusteeship, was to be put in place. If these innovations appeared to steal newly fashionable radical clothing, and even to add a touch of what, in the half-light, looked like 'state

---

93. See Mona Macmillan, 'The Making of *Warning from the West Indies*', *Jour. Comm. and Comp. Pol.*, 18 (1980); and Hugh Macmillan and Shula Marks, eds. *Africa and Empire: W.M. Macmillan, Historian and Social Critic* (1989). On the situation in the West Indies see Howard Johnson, 'Oil, Imperial Policy and the Trinidad Disturbances, 1937', *Jour. Imp. and Comm. Hist.*, 4 (1975); and Maurice St Pierre, 'The 1938 Disturbances: a Portrait of Mass Reaction Against Colonialism', *Social and Economic Studies*, 27 (1978).

94. Howard Johnson,'The West Indies and the Conversion of the British Official Classes to the Development Idea', *Jour. Comm. and Comp. Pol.*, 15 (1977), p. 66.

95. These trends in official thinking are discussed by Lee, *Colonial Government*, Chs. 2–3; and Pearce, *Turning Point*, Chs. 2–3.

socialism', so much the better.[96] There were plenty of precedents for laying hands on the untouchable and making it wholesome, and the imperial tradition had long come to terms with the paradox that freeing individuals from their pre-colonial past was a duty that required governments to take special and extensive powers.

Elements of the new thinking were already beginning to influence policy before World War II. In London, the Colonial Office prepared for its new role by becoming a larger and more specialised organisation.[97] On the ground in Africa, officials experimented with alternative ways of funding colonial rule which would also update the notion of trusteeship. In west Africa there was an emerging awareness of the need to promote research into tropical agriculture and of the importance, in the longer term, of encouraging wide-ranging innovations in land-management to raise productivity and taxable incomes.[98] In east Africa, the vulnerability of white farmers during the slump, combined with the costs of protecting settler agriculture thereafter, produced a significant shift in official thinking, especially in Kenya, where openings were created for low-cost African farmers whose taxable earnings were the mainstay of the colonial budget.[99] The significance of fiscal considerations was underlined by Sir Alan Pim, whose roving commissions in the late 1930s produced recommendations which criticised the status quo, pointed towards more active development policies (including more opportunities for Africans), and led to an event that was as notable for its symbolism as for its material impact: the imposition, finally, of income tax on white settlers in Kenya.[100]

These intimations of change were brought together in the Colonial Development and Welfare Act, which was passed in 1940 (but

96. On the 'state socialism' of a government formally dedicated to what it thought were the economics of Adam Smith, see the excellent discussion of policy-making in the Sudan in Sanderson, 'The Ghost of Adam Smith', pp. 101–11.

97. Lee, *Colonial Development*, Ch. 2; Robinson, *Dilemmas of Trusteeship*, p. 36. See also Charles Jeffries, *Whitehall and the Colonial Service: An Administrative Memoir, 1939–1956* (1972).

98. David Meredith, 'Government and the Decline of the Nigerian Oil-Palm Export Industry, 1919–1939', *Jour. African Hist.*, 25 (1984).

99. David Anderson and David Throup, 'Africans and Agricultural Production in Colonial Kenya: the Myth of the War as a Watershed', *Jour. African Hist.*, 26 (1985); idem, 'The Agrarian Economy of Central Province, Kenya, 1918–1939', in Brown, *The Economies of Africa and Asia*; Wolfgang Dopcke, '"Magomo's Maize": State and Peasants during the Depression in Colonial Zimbabwe', in Brown, *The Economies of Africa and Asia*; Lonsdale, 'The Depression and the Second World War', pp. 105–19.

100. Pim entered the Indian Civil Service in 1894 and turned his attention to Africa after taking formal retirement in 1930. His influence, like his reports, merits further study. His book, *An Economic History of Tropical Africa* (1940), is also unread today.

formulated before the outbreak of war).[101] The new Act differed in conception from the Act of 1929. It breached the principle of self-sufficiency, promoted the idea of social welfare, recognised the need for central initiatives, and made provision for expenditure on research. The Treasury resisted the measure, believing that the end of Gladstonian finance was at hand and fearing that the proposal would put the colonies 'on the dole from henceforth and forever'.[102] But Mac-Donald, the Colonial Secretary, argued that unless the Act was passed Britain might lose her colonies, and would certainly deserve to do so. Without new investment, the colonial economies would founder; without welfare measures to improve health and education, there was little prospect of renewing the loyalty of colonial subjects or of tempering criticism from the United States; and without a secure empire, Britain's global defence strategy was at risk. These arguments succeeded. By associating the colonial issue with the fundamental question of national survival at a time of acute international tension, the Colonial Office appeared to have cracked the Treasury safe and found a means, finally, of overcoming the shortage of capital that had confined colonial policy for so long.

COLONIAL RULE WITH LIMITED SUPPLIES OF CAPITAL

It is plain that the vitality of British imperialism remained undiminished in Africa during the period under review. Anti-colonial protests undoubtedly gathered pace in the 1930s, but black nationalism was not yet a force to be reckoned with and white nationalism was managed in ways that left Britain's essential interests untouched, as the examples of Southern Rhodesia and Kenya have shown. Moreover, estimates of the importance of the nationalist movements, which have been exhaustively studied, have to be set against countervailing forces, still to be fully investigated, such as air power and radio communication, which did much to enable colonial governments to strengthen their grip after

---

101. J.M. Lee and Martin Petter, *The Colonial Office, War and Development Policy* (1982), Ch. 1; Lee, *Colonial Development*, Chs. 2–3; Pearce, *Turning Point*, Chs. 2–3; Jane H. Bowden, 'Development and Control in British Colonial Policy with Reference to Nigeria and the Gold Coast' (Ph.D. thesis, University of Birmingham, 1981).

102. Quoted in Bowden, 'Development and Control', p. 103. On the bureaucratic fixing involved see Howard Johnson, 'The Political Uses of Commissions of Enquiry: the Imperial-Colonial West Indies Context', *Soc. and Econ. Stud.*, 27 (1978).

1914. While dealing successfully with claims from within the empire, Britain also fought off challenges from rival 'have-not' powers and applied a policy of manipulative intent towards the United States with the aim of softening her anti-colonial stance. It has not been our purpose to discuss these international rivalries in any detail, but just enough has been said, it is hoped, to make the point that the 'age of imperialism' did not come to an end in 1914, and that the 1930s, in particular, witnessed a renewal of imperialist competition which needs emphasising both for its intensity and for the novelty of the techniques used, especially in the developing service industries, such as communications.

As to the purpose of the enterprise, the reason for 'staying on', we have suggested that this can best be viewed through the prism of trusteeship, a concept that was solid with respect to principle but flexible with regard to circumstance. The principles, material and moral, were those we have associated with the gentlemanly order in Britain, and, as we have now tried to indicate, with its extensions in tropical Africa. In escaping from industry and democracy, and in promoting a squirearchy in a tropical arcadia, the rulers of Africa were seeking to perpetuate 'traditional' British values and authority structures. But, with some notable exceptions, the white chiefs of Africa did not represent atavistic forces which were hostile to all forms of capitalism, despite their antipathy towards manufacturing industry. They were well aware that they lived in a material world of revenues, expenditures, salaries and pensions; they accepted liberal ideals of progress; and they acted in the belief that economic orthodoxies centred on Gladstonian finance and free trade would generate economic development and moral improvement. Their preference was for rural-based forms of capitalism which would make haste slowly without provoking social dislocation and civil disorder. This inclination, as we have argued, was powerfully reinforced by the shortage of capital needed to fund an alternative programme. This deficiency was turned to advantage: by claiming to promote both progress and conservation, Britain's version of trusteeship offered a vision of an international system which could compete with the appeal of Bolshevism and fascism. Although the world order envisaged by the British was neither democratic nor populist, the script for the civilising mission emphasised the merits of a multi-ethnic enterprise united in its diversity by long chains of loyalty which led ultimately to the imperial monarch.[103]

103. The creation of an 'ideology of loyalty' is discussed by Terence Ranger, 'Making Northern Rhodesia Imperial: Variations on a Royal Theme, 1924–1938', *African Aff.*, 79 (1980).

Flexibility in applying these principles can be seen by looking along the axes of space and time. The spatial axis shows that trusteeship could be invoked to defend both 'native paramountcy' and settler dominance. Each was viewed, in different regions, as being the most promising agent of conservative progress, including (by definition) the capacity to raise taxable incomes to meet administrative services and debt payments. The chronological dimension illustrates how the means of fulfilling the principles of trusteeship, including of course the maintenance of colonial control, shifted between 1914 and 1940 from indirect rule, with its assumption of gradual change, to direct government action to achieve rapid economic development. Once again, fiscal considerations were important in explaining this evolution: by the late 1930s indirect rule was bankrupt, and the treasuries of the colonies nearly so following their strenuous efforts to pay their way during the world slump. It was then that a radical change in policy presented itself as the only alternative to the loss, by subsidence, of the colonial empire, and the civilising mission was galvanised by becoming committed to an ambitious programme of state-led development.

The next chapter in this story cannot be written here. But it is worth noting that the interpretation we have advanced could be developed further for the period after 1940, for it is now known that World War II was fought to defend the empire as well as to defeat fascism, that the battle over the shape of post-war colonial policy was continued even as bombs fell on London, and that new development plans, controlled by enlarged bureaucracies, were set in motion as soon as peace returned.[104] In 1945, amidst a war-shattered Europe that had ceased to pose a threat but also appeared to offer little promise, Britain still saw her future as being at the centre of a revitalised empire. The African colonies, in particular, had proved their value during hostilities, and their resources (including their enlarged sterling balances) were regarded as being vital to Britain's post-war recovery. The new deal for the colonies offered them development funds, but it also bound them more closely to the sterling area and to directives from London. Treasury control, at risk in 1940, had been revised rather than abandoned.

104. Starting points for what is now a sizeable literature include: William Roger Louis, *Imperialism at Bay: The United States and the Decolonization of the British Empire, 1941–1945* (Oxford, 1977); Michael Cowen and Nicholas Westcott, 'British Imperial Economic Policy during the War', in Killingray and Rathbone, eds. *Africa and the Second World War*; Herward Sieberg, *Colonial Development: Die Grundlegung moderner Entwicklungspolitik durch Großbritannien, 1919–1949* (Wiesbaden, 1985); Lee and Petter, *The Colonial Office*; and Pearce, *Turning Point*.

CHAPTER TEN

'The Only Great Undeveloped Market in the World': China, 1911–49[1]

With the fall of the Ch'ing dynasty in 1911, China ceases to feature in studies of British imperialism, as does South America after 1914. Neither region was incorporated into the formal empire, and it is generally assumed in both cases that Britain's invisible influence was irreparably damaged by World War I and by the quickening pace of her industrial decline thereafter. There is, of course, a substantial and valuable literature on diplomatic relations among the great powers, especially in the 1930s, when the Great Game in the Far East became one of the antecedents of World War II, but this rarely taps the domestic roots of policy-making in Britain, and only exceptionally does it set the problems of the Far East in the wider context of the history of imperialism.[2] Consequently, there is room for an account which shows how the evolution of Britain's continuing imperialist ambitions intersected with events in the Far East, and how this junction prompted significant changes in policy towards China during a turbulent period which began with one revolution and ended with another.

At the outset of the period under review, the central problem facing British policy-makers was the need to safeguard Britain's substantial investments in China without antagonising a queue of powerful and suspicious rivals. The rapid growth of foreign lending

1. The quotation is from a comment made by D.G.M. Barnard of Jardine, Matheson & Co in 1936 and cited in Jürgen Osterhammel, 'Imperialism in Transition: British Business and the Chinese Authorities, 1931–37', *China Quarterly*, 98 (1984), p. 260.
2. Studies which we have found particularly helpful are listed in n.71. In addition, and from a different perspective, guidance is now available from *The Cambridge History of China: Republican China, 1912–1949*, Vol. 12, ed. John K. Fairbank (Cambridge, 1983), and Vol. 13, ed. John K. Fairbank and Albert Feuerwerker (Cambridge, 1986).

between 1895 and 1911 had concentrated China's fiscal system on Peking and given the major powers, especially Britain, a vested interest in upholding central authority there. However, the centralisation of financial and political power fed discontent in the provinces and stoked the opposition which led to the upheaval of 1911. The foreign powers, coordinated by Britain, responded by taking a tighter grip on government finance and by redoubling their efforts to hold China together. There was no withdrawal after the revolution; there was even room for a degree of optimism, despite the weighty uncertainties surrounding China's future in 1911, for the new regime was thought in some quarters to be more cooperative and more 'progressive' than its predecessor.[3] Seen from this perspective, the revolution of 1911 marked the end of one phase of imperialism, but not the end of imperialist ambitions.

World War I undoubtedly made heavy calls on Britain's resources of capital and manpower, but the evidence now available no longer supports the view that Britain had already begun a 'long retreat' from China,[4] or that she suffered a progressive 'diminution of will' during the inter-war period.[5] The myth of the China market continued to exert a powerful and unique influence on policy-makers and public opinion.[6] Experienced China-watchers had no illusions about the ease of 'opening up' the interior, but they could not afford to be caught looking the wrong way in case the long-predicted, if also unexpected, event finally happened. Meanwhile, the reality of China's indebtedness and the need to secure repayment implied more foreign intervention, not less. Consequently, Britain made strenuous efforts to retain the dominant position she had held in China's affairs before 1911, first by trying to restore pre-war methods of control and then by adapting to the nationalist movement and to new economic opportunities, as she did in South America and India. During the 1930s this evolution became caught up, as in South America too, with renewed international competition between the 'have' and the 'have not' nations. In the case of China, however, international rivalries proved to be uncontrollable. Japan's invasion of China in 1937 marked the

3. See, for example, Marius Jansen, 'The 1911 Revolution and United States East Asian Policy', in Eto Shinkichi and Harold Z. Shiffrin, eds. *The 1911 Revolution in China* (Tokyo, 1983).

4. Nicholas R. Clifford, *Retreat from China: British Policy in the Far East, 1937–1941* (1967) traces this to the Anglo-Japanese alliance of 1902.

5. Christopher Thorne, *The Limits of Foreign Policy: The West, the League and the Far Eastern Crisis of 1931–1933* (1972), pp. 46–7.

6. For this perception (and others) see William Roger Louis, *British Strategy in the Far East, 1919–1939* (Oxford, 1971).

final breakdown of policies of cooperative imperialism and signalled the onset of a bid for territory which was the high point of aggressive imperialism in the Far East, the beginning of World War II, and the prelude to the revolution of 1949.

TRADE AND FINANCE: AN OVERVIEW

Quantitative measures of Britain's economic stake in China are fragile and can easily deceive; consequently the data are better treated as orders of magnitude than as precise indices.[7] Contrary to received opinion, it is now becoming clear that the Chinese economy experienced both growth and structural change during this period, but that these developments were not fully reflected in China's overseas trade.[8] This was not only because the outside world accounted for only a very small part of China's total economic activity, but also because the domestic economy appears to have grown faster than the overseas sector, which remained sluggish for the greater part of the period under review. China's staple exports of tea and silk declined, and were replaced by a miscellany of agricultural exports; but none of these functioned as a leading sector in the process of development, even though they enabled the export economy to avoid the worst features of monoculture. From the standpoint of British manufacturers, China remained a land of unrealised potential which absorbed, almost without trace, a mere 2 or 3 per cent of Britain's total exports between 1911 and 1937. This was much the same as in 1889–93, on

7. The quantitative evidence summarised here is derived mainly from: *Statistical Abstract for the United Kingdom, 1913 and 1924–1937* (1939); Hsiao Liang-lin, *China's Foreign Trade Statistics, 1864–1949* (Cambridge, Mass. 1974); Cheng Yu-Kwei, *Foreign Trade and Industrial Development of China* (Washington, DC, 1956); Hou Chi-ming, *Foreign Investment and Economic Development in China, 1840–1937* (Cambridge, Mass., 1965). Mention should also be made of the pioneering work of Carl Remer, *Foreign Investments in China* (New York, 1933). The *Statistical Abstract* gives f.o.b. values for British exports and c.i.f. values for imports. On the difficulties of interpreting the data see Rhoads Murphey, 'The Treaty Ports and China's Modernization', in Mark Elvin and G. William Skinner, eds. *The Chinese City Between Two Worlds* (Stanford, Calif., 1974), and Ramon H. Myers, 'The World Depression and the Chinese Economy, 1930–36', in Ian Brown, ed. *The Economies of Africa and Asia in the Inter-War Depression* (1989).

8. Important revisionist research is contained in Loren Brandt, 'Chinese Agriculture and the International Economy, 1870–1930s: a Reassessment', *Explorations in Economic History*, 22 (1985); idem, *Commercialization and Agricultural Development: Central and Eastern China, 1870–1937* (Cambridge, 1990); and Thomas G. Rawski, *Economic Growth in Prewar China* (Berkeley and Los Angeles, Calif., 1989).

the eve of the scramble to open the interior. Moreover, Britain's share of China's imports continued to fall – from 17 per cent in 1913 to 8 per cent in 1931 – before recovering to 12 per cent in 1936.[9] The larger 'imperial unit' of Britain, Hong Kong and India performed more impressively, and accounted for about 31 per cent of China's imports in 1928–9. But this figure was also well down from the pre-war total of 54 per cent in 1913, and it fell further – to about 16 per cent – in 1936. As far as commodity trade was concerned, the most striking feature of the early 1930s was the elimination of British cotton goods from the Chinese market, an event which put an end to a century of wishful thinking about clothing 400 million Chinese in textiles manufactured in Manchester.

Earnings from foreign investment and other invisibles also suffered after 1911, and even more so after 1914. Political instability made China less attractive to foreign investors, and World War I reduced Britain's ability to supply new capital for investment overseas. Nevertheless, China still received about 6 per cent of Britain's overseas investment in 1933,[10] and Britain's share of all foreign investment in China was little changed, amounting to 38 per cent in 1914, 37 per cent in 1931 and 35 per cent in 1936.[11] These figures mask an important and continuing shift away from government loans and towards direct private investment, which rose from 66 per cent of the total in 1913 to 81 per cent in 1930, and grew further, especially in the mid-1930s, when conditions at last began to favour new investment in China.[12] The main attractions, as in the past, lay in banking, commerce, property and, increasingly, local industry in and around the Treaty Ports, above all Shanghai. In the early 1930s foreign banks, headed by British firms and by the Hongkong and Shanghai Bank in particular, still financed over 90 per cent of the foreign trade of Shanghai, the greatest of China's ports.[13] But it is

9. Japan's occupation of Manchuria in 1931 appears to have had little effect on this trend since Britain's trade was concentrated on south and central China. On Manchuria see Ramon H. Myers, *The Japanese Economic Development of Manchuria, 1932–1945* (New York, 1982).

10. Stephen L. Endicott, *Diplomacy and Enterprise: British China Policy, 1933–1937* (Manchester, 1975), p. 22.

11. Hou, *Foreign Investment*, p. 17.

12. Hou, *Foreign Investment*, p. 17, though Britain still dominated the government loans business: ibid. p. 229. See also Arthur N. Young, *China's Nation-Building Effort, 1927–1937: The Financial and Economic Record* (Stanford, Calif., 1971), pp. 365–6, 372–6, and Jürgen Osterhammel, 'British Business in China, 1860s–1950s', in R.P.T. Davenport-Hines and Geoffrey Jones, eds. *British Business in Asia Since 1860* (Cambridge, 1989), pp. 201–2.

13. Hou, *Foreign Investment*, pp. 54, 226.

interesting to note that in 1936 Britain's investments in local manufacturing were also a long way ahead of those made by rival foreign powers, including Japan.[14] British-registered vessels, too, held on to the greater part of their share of the China market, and were responsible for about half the foreign shipping entering and clearing Chinese ports during the period under review, though they carried a decreasing proportion of British goods.[15]

STRATEGY AND STRATEGISTS

China was (with South America) the most tempting of the unclaimed regions of the world after 1914 – unclaimed, that is, except by the indigenous peoples, and in the Chinese case that did not carry much weight. China being the more vulnerable, it was there that imperialist rivalries became rampant both during the two world wars and in the inter-war years. From the British perspective, the main problem was to contain two major competitors, Japan and the United States, while pushing ahead, cautiously, with her own plans for controlling China's finances and development prospects. Japan posed the more serious problem because China was far more important to her than to the United States and because her expansionist ambitions on the mainland were readily transformed into aggressive imperialism.[16] The comparison made with Britain, the other island empire, suggested a measure of parity which was acceptable while the Anglo-Japanese alliance lasted, but later served to legitimize a degree of assertiveness which was eventually directed at Britain as well as at China. The United States, though beguiled by the myth of the China market, was less involved in the penetration of the interior and had limited political objectives.[17] She was concerned, nevertheless, to defend her interests in China and to frustrate Japan's ambitions once it became clear that

14. Ibid. pp. 80–1.
15. Ibid. pp. 60–1; Peter Duus, Ramon H. Myers and Mark R. Peattie, eds. *The Japanese Informal Empire in China, 1895–1937* (Princeton, NJ, 1989), pp. 3, 28–9.
16. The best entry into this subject is now via W.G. Beasley, *Japanese Imperialism, 1894–1945* (Oxford, 1987), and Duus, Myers and Peattie, *Japanese Informal Empire*. On the broader setting, see Akira Iriye, *Pacific Estrangement: Japanese and American Expansion, 1897–1911* (Cambridge, Mass., 1972), and idem, *After Imperialism: The Search for a New Order in the Far East, 1921–1931* (Cambridge, Mass., 1965).
17. James J. Lawrence, *Organized Business and the Myth of the China Market: The American Asiatic Association, 1897–1937* (Philadelphia, Pa, 1981); Ernest R. May and John K. Fairbank, eds. *America's China Trade in Historical Perspective* (Cambridge, Mass., 1986).

they would jeopardise the principle of the open door. Russia offered less of a direct threat after 1917, though this did not prevent the capitalist states from frightening themselves with fears, imagined as well as real, about the spread of Bolshevism.[18] The German challenge lost momentum after 1918, but revived in the 1930s, when China became, briefly, part of Nazi plans for rearmament.[19]

British strategy centred upon ways of continuing her financial control, both to bind the Chinese government and to fetter rival powers. This priority explains the importance attached in the 1920s to the Second Consortium, which Britain saw as a device for restraining competitors by controlling political loans to China. When this strategy broke down in the 1930s, Britain used her leverage to secure financial reforms in China, made a bid to tie China to sterling, and adopted a more assertive policy in defence of her interests in central and southern China, while trying to divert Japan to marginal areas, such as Manchuria. As is well known, the failure to buy off Japan brought war nearer and drove Britain further towards a subordinate relationship with the United States. What is less well appreciated is the extent to which, on the eve of Japanese aggression in 1937, British policy had achieved a transformation which held out the prospect of continuing influence at a moment when China appeared, at last, to be entering a process of successful economic development.

The men charged with managing Britain's interests in China during this period of extreme turbulence and uncertainty, though far fewer in number than those involved with India and Africa, came from much the same stock and viewed the world from broadly similar perspectives. Victor Wellesley, who presided over the Far Eastern desk at the Foreign Office between 1925 and 1936, approached Chinese affairs with a degree of patrician detachment inherited from calmer times, when alien societies could be dealt with without being fully understood.[20] His inactivity in the face of China's political turmoil was less than masterly; but he was reinforced at a crucial

18. It is easy today to underestimate the extent of the alarm felt in Britain during the 1920s. As with the fear of Jacobinism in the 1790s, there was acute anxiety about the spread of an alien ideology which was not only anti-monarchical and anti-Christ but which also travelled 'on the wind' and so could cross the Channel. The need to produce an antidote to Bolshevism added to the determination to restore capitalism to health after World War I.

19. This theme is noted below and references given in n. 88. The French attempt to match British finance was belated and unsuccessful. See Nobutaka Shinonaga, 'La formation de la Banque Industrielle de Chine', *Le mouvement social*, 155 (1991).

20. Victor Wellesley (1876–1954) was a godson of Queen Victoria and a descendant of the first Duke of Wellington.

moment by Sir John Pratt, whose determination to uphold British interests was informed by an unrivalled knowledge of Asian affairs.[21] Pratt's expertise, which was quite exceptional in the higher reaches of the Foreign Office during this period, did much to transform British policy towards China in the late 1920s. The British Legation continued to be stocked by career diplomats who viewed China from Peking as their colleagues at home viewed England from London, and who resisted Pratt's ultimately successful bid to alter traditional priorities. Lower down the hierarchy, the consular officials came mostly from professional, service and other gentlemanly families, though the unattractive salaries which resulted from rigorous Treasury control meant that recruits had to be drawn from the lower ranks of society too.[22]

The most influential of Britain's unofficial representatives were bankers, above all Sir Charles Addis, the London Manager of the Hongkong and Shanghai Bank.[23] The continuing importance of banking interests is not surprising, given the long-standing connection between finance and strategy in China; but after 1911 the problems thrown up first by World War I and then by the world slump encouraged leading bankers to aspire to an even more prominent role in international affairs. At such times, bankers tend to lose confidence in politicians and begin to imagine that international affairs can be managed by a small committee of businessmen led by themselves and guided by a set of universal principles based on free markets, sound money and solid security.[24] After Addis retired from the Bank in 1921, he continued his advocacy of these principles in his capacity as Britain's chief representative of the Second China Consortium and as an Adviser to the Governor of the Bank of England (of which he was also a Director). As an internationalist, Addis tried to draw Japan and the United States into a global fraternity of bankers;

21. Sir John Pratt (1876–1970) was educated at Dulwich and Middle Temple, and spent his early career in the Consular Service in China before being transferred to the Foreign Office in 1925. He retired in 1938 but was active thereafter as an expert on the Far East. He published a number of books, the most interesting of which in the present context is *War and Politics in China* (1943).

22. P.D.Coates, *The China Consuls: British Consular Officers, 1843–1943* (Oxford, 1988). On the expatriate communities generally, see Albert Feuerwerker, *The Foreign Establishment in China in the Early Twentieth Century* (Ann Arbor, Mich., 1976).

23. There is now a valuable biography by Roberta Allbert Dayer, *Finance and Empire: Sir Charles Addis, 1861–1945* (1988).

24. This political aspiration reflects the fact that capital flows over boundaries as well as being generated within them. To say that capital 'knows no frontiers' makes a point; but it also underplays the extent to which overseas investment was nourished by the nation state in the period under review.

as an imperialist, he did his best to ensure that joint action served Britain's interests. The Hongkong and Shanghai Bank itself remained the most prominent foreign bank in China, notwithstanding Addis's departure, and it also retained close connections with leading firms in the City. After World War I, as before, the Bank provided a 'field of employment' for the products of public schools in England and Scotland, applying selection procedures which mirrored the principle of preferment by connection adopted by Sir Ralph Furse for the Colonial Service.[25]

REVOLUTION, WAR AND WAR-LORDS, 1911–18

The political uncertainty which followed the revolution of 1911 drew the foreign powers further into China's internal affairs. Central government had to be upheld to ensure that revenues continued to flow to Peking and that the external debt was serviced. This aim called for some astute diplomatic juggling: provincial aspirations had to be defused without being detonated, and central authority had to be warmed up without being allowed to escape from the bottle. Since stability took priority over schemes for democratic reform and economic development, the powers gave their backing to Yuan, the former Ch'ing general, rather than Sun Yat-sen, the liberal nationalist, whose idealism was thought to point too clearly in the direction of greater independence.[26] In this matter, as in so many others, the Hongkong and Shanghai Bank and the Foreign Office thought as one. Addis had already identified Yuan as the man for the job on the eve of the revolution, and the Foreign Office, in turn, had given the Bank virtually exclusive backing in negotiating a Reorganisation Loan in 1912.[27] These manipulations provoked a nationalist reaction which caused the loan to be postponed, but it was finally issued in 1913,

25. Frank H.H. King, *The Hongkong Bank Between the Wars and the Bank Interned, 1919–1945: Return to Grandeur* (Cambridge, 1988), pp. 5, 263–4, 318–24; Sir Ralph Furse, *Aucuparius: Recollections of a Recruiting Officer* (1962). Also above, pp. 23–7 and 210.

26. Roberta Allbert Dayer, *Bankers and Diplomats in China, 1917–1925: The Anglo-American Relationship* (1981), pp. 161–3. Washington shared London's doubts: Brian T. George, 'The State Department and Sun Yat-sen: American Policy and the Revolutionary Disintegration of China, 1920–1924', *Pacific Hist. Rev.*, 46 (1977). Sun's view of imperialism and development seems unexceptional today: indeed, his programme had much in common with the policies adopted by Chiang in the 1930s. See A. James Gregor and Maria Hsia Chang, 'Marxism, Sun Yat-sen and the Concept of Imperialism', *Pacific Affairs*, 55 (1982).

27. Dayer, *Addis*, pp. 64–5; King, *Hongkong Bank*, pp. 453, 464, 482–96, 506–7.

when Yuan had subdued his opponents.[28] His political success, however, was bought at the cost of greater external financial dependence: the loan funded his regime, but was secured only by allowing the International Consortium of bankers to control the salt tax and to receive payments from customs duties directly from the revenue commissioners.[29] In these circumstances, the loan was viewed favourably by the City; coincidentally, Addis was given a knighthood in recognition of his sterling service in championing British interests in the Far East.[30]

World War I posed an obvious threat to Britain's leadership of the foreign powers in the Far East. The outbreak of war directed her attention and resources towards Europe, unsettled the collective imperialism represented by the Consortium, and provided an opportunity for ambitious rivals, such as Japan and the United States, to promote their own interests. Britain's 'one China' policy was also jeopardised by President Yuan's death in 1916, which was followed by a period of internal instability that led, in turn, to the era of war-lord politics.[31] Following the outbreak of war, Japan occupied Shantung, Germany's sphere of influence in China, and in 1915 announced the 21 demands, whose length and lack of guile left no doubt about her acquisitive intentions.[32] These actions were accompanied by a significant degree of commercial and financial penetration, including the secret Nishihara loans of 1917–18, which gave Tokyo considerable influence in Peking. The advance of the United States was pacific and more restrained, but was seen in London as a symptom of a wider and potentially greater threat to Britain's position as a world power.[33] No one in London (or perhaps even in Washington) knew exactly where the formula 'for God, for China and for Yale'[34] might

---

28. Anthony B. Chan, 'The Consortium System in Republican China, 1912–1913', *Jour. Eur. Econ. Hist.*, 6 (1977), pp. 597–640.

29. Dayer, *Addis*, pp. 69–70; King, *Hongkong Bank*, p. 471. Until then, the Inspector General (Hart), though an expatriate, had managed the Imperial Maritime Customs as an employee of the Chinese government.

30. Dayer, *Addis*, pp. 70–1.

31. The traditional view of the war-lord era has been reappraised in recent years. See, for example, Jerome Ch'en, *The Military-Gentry Coalition: China under the Warlords* (Toronto, 1979); C. Martin Wilbur, *The Nationalist Revolution in China, 1923–1928* (Cambridge, 1983); and Marie-Claire Bergère, *L'Age d'or de la bourgeoisie chinoise, 1911–1937* (Paris, 1986).

32. Dayer, *Bankers and Diplomats*, pp. 39–42. See also Albert A. Altman and Harold Z. Shriffrin, 'Sun Yat-sen and the Japanese, 1914–16', *Mod. Asian Stud.*, 6 (1972).

33. Dayer, *Bankers and Diplomats*, pp. 44–8. On the general theme see Carl Parrini, *Heir to Empire: United States Economic Diplomacy, 1916–23* (Pittsburgh, Pa, 1969).

34. Quoted in Jerome Michael Israel, *Progressivism and the Open Door: America and China, 1905–1921* (Pittsburgh, Pa, 1971), p. 19.

eventually lead; but in China, as in South America, the first signs were of schemes to expand trade, establish banks and buy into British firms.[35]

MAINTAINING BRITISH INFLUENCE: THE 1920s

These developments raised the diplomatic stakes in the Far East and forced Britain's mandarins to join a risky game, which they played with habitual skill and considerable success until Japan broke the rules in the 1930s. Japan had to be controlled but not antagonised because the Anglo-Japanese alliance was vital to Britain's strategy of low-cost defence in the Far East. The cheapest and most effective way of restraining Japan was by drawing the United States into the imperialist club (under the guise of partnership in development) and using her financial power to buttress the one-China policy. The dangers were evident: an appeal to the United States might give offence to Japan; if successful, it might also end in subordinating Britain.

Initially, the Foreign Office mounted a holding operation, urging restraint on Japan while seeking, surreptitiously, to prevent the United States from developing a banking infrastructure in China.[36] However, the protraction of the war and Britain's growing financial dependence on the United States encouraged the Foreign Office to cast about for a more systematic solution, while continuing to work with the Hongkong and Shanghai Bank to maintain China's solvency.[37] The outcome was the Second China Consortium, which took embryonic shape in the closing stages of the war and was formally constituted in 1920, essentially to coordinate the financial dealings of the foreign powers with the Chinese government.[38] The Second Consortium, like the first, was the product of close cooperation between the Foreign Office and the Hongkong and Shanghai Bank. Addis, the manager of the British group in the Consortium, insisted on exclusive government support for his members, who

35. Dayer, *Bankers and Diplomats*, pp. 43–9; Noel H. Pugach, 'Keeping an Idea Alive: the Establishment of a Sino-American Bank, 1910–1920', *Bus. Hist. Rev.*, 56 (1982); Joan Hoff Wilson, *American Business and Foreign Policy, 1920–1933* (1971), p. 201.
36. Clarence B. Davis, 'Limits of Effacement: Britain and the Problem of American Co-operation and Competition in China, 1915–1917', *Pacific. Hist. Rev.*, 48 (1979).
37. Dayer, *Banker and Diplomats*, Ch. 3; King, *Hongkong Bank*, Ch. 10.
38. Dayer, *Finance and Empire*, pp. 85, 98–9, 115.

represented 'the elite of City finance'.[39] The demand embarrassed the Foreign Office, which was supposed to remain impartial in matters of private business, but the price had to be paid, in 1920 as in 1911: financial power could not be commanded or directed from Whitehall, and without it Britain's influence in China would rapidly disappear.

The Second Consortium was Britain's chosen vehicle for the return to normality after World War I. In the case of China, the definition of normality was itself problematic; but in British eyes it meant maintaining a stable government which continued to honour its debts, and this implied continuing international supervision. Managing rival powers, however, became more difficult in the post-war years. Britain's own indebtedness to the United States made her vulnerable to pressure from Washington, and caused her to abandon the Anglo-Japanese Alliance when it came up for renewal in 1921.[40] This decision had far-reaching consequences: it knocked a hole in Britain's defence policy and did much to alienate Japan.[41] The Foreign Office hoped that, in return for calming anxieties in the United States about the growing power of Japan, Washington would take a lenient view of Britain's war debts. The prime consideration here was the need to restore Britain's credit-worthiness at a time when London was trying to regain its position as the financial centre of the world. The hope was misplaced. What Washington grasped with one hand it also took with the other: the alliance was ended but Britain's war debts were not rescheduled.

Nevertheless, as Lloyd George told the Cabinet in 1921, the British had no intention of letting the Americans 'walk all over them in China',[42] and in the same year the morale of China hands was boosted by a diplomatic initiative that prevented a group of United States' firms from developing Canton as an alternative to Hong Kong.[43]

39. Addis, quoted in Dayer, *Finance and Empire*, p. 123.

40. Roberta Allbert Dayer, 'British War Debts to the United States and the Anglo-Japanese Alliance, 1920–1923', *Pacific Hist. Rev.*, 45 (1976); John Milton Cooper, 'The Command of Gold Reversed: American Loans to Britain, 1915–1917', *Pacific Hist. Rev.*, 45 (1976). As President Wilson observed in 1917: 'When the war is over we will be able to force them [Britain and France] to our way of thinking, because by that time they will, among other things, be financially in our hands'. Quoted in A.J. Mayer, *Political Origins of the New Diplomacy* (New Haven, Conn., 1958), p. 332.

41. The implications have been considered at length by diplomatic historians. On the strategic aspects see Paul Haggie, *Britannia at Bay: The Defence of the British Empire Against Japan, 1931–1941* (Oxford, 1981), and the saga of the Singapore base recounted by James Neidpath, *The Singapore Naval Base and the Defence of Britain's Eastern Empire, 1919–1941* (Oxford, 1981).

42. Quoted in Dayer, *Bankers and Diplomats*, p. 74.

43. Ibid. pp. 89–92, 240.

Moreover, by drawing the United States into the Second Consortium, the Foreign Office had made her an honorary member of the imperial club, and in this way reduced the risk of an attack on Britain's overall strategy towards China as well as on important specific issues, such as extraterritorial rights. Addis, the manager of the Consortium, regarded it as a fraternity of 'responsible' lenders whose adherence to the universal principles of international finance enabled them to view the world from a perspective other than that provided by the projection of the nation state. This vision was turned to Britain's advantage: J.P. Morgan, the most important United States' bank in the Far East, had strong ties with the City and saw its business in China as complementing that of the Hongkong and Shanghai Bank.[44] The result was that plans devised in Washington for using the Consortium to advance the national interest were modified in New York by the bankers who were supposed to implement them. Washington was no more successful than Whitehall in directing the banking estate, and US finance flowed to Japan rather than to China.[45] Despite fears to the contrary, diplomatic management and market forces combined to ensure that the Americans did not 'walk all over' British interests in China after World War I.

The Consortium was more successful in perpetuating joint financial control than in promoting economic development. China continued to service her foreign debts after the revolution of 1911 and throughout World War I, but difficulties began to appear early in the 1920s. The solvency of the state depended on the health of revenues already assigned to foreign creditors, and government revenues were adversely affected by the post-war slump, by the limited growth of the export sector thereafter, and by the declining value of China's silver currency in terms of gold, all of which discouraged new lending and placed a question mark over China's ability to repay her existing debts.[46] The Consortium was also unable to control the centrifugal forces of Chinese politics. Continuing political instability damaged government finances and lowered China's credit-worthiness in the eyes of potential foreign investors. Provincial war-lords, freshly armed with surplus

44. Roberta Allbert Dayer, 'Strange Bedfellows: J.P. Morgan & Co., Whitehall and the Wilson Administration During World War I', *Bus. Hist.*, 18 (1976).

45. Wilson, *American Business*, pp. 201–3, 209–14, 222–3, 230–1. On the reorientation of US banks towards Japan after 1926 see Dayer, *Bankers and Diplomats*, pp. 123, 173–4, 178–9, 238.

46. Marie-Claire Bergère, 'The Consequences of the Post First World War Depression for the China Treaty Port Economy, 1921–3', in Ian Brown, ed. *The Economies of Africa and Asia in the Inter-War Depression* (1989); King, *Hongkong Bank*, pp. 69, 98.

equipment from World War I, were not the first choice of foreign capitalists seeking partners for a peaceful development programme.[47] An alliance with westernised elements presented problems too: liberal reformers were preferred, but they were few in number and without a constituency;[48] nationalists had a larger following but their hostility to foreign control, and the fear that they were in league with Bolshevism (and even with Indian 'sedition'), made them deeply unattractive.[49] This appraisal flattered the organising skill, if not the vision, of the nationalist leaders; but it is true, nevertheless, that popular expressions of nationalist sentiment increased in China at this time, as they did elsewhere, in reaction to the growth of foreign influence during the war and to the imposition of foreign priorities on the peace settlement.[50] Sun Yat-sen revived the moribund Kuomintang in 1919, the Chinese Communist Party was founded in 1921, and there were serious protests at key points on the coast – a major strike in Hong Kong in 1922, persistent attempts to repossess the customs revenues of Canton between 1918 and 1924, and widespread riots in Shanghai in 1925 – which damaged Britain's trade and dented her image.[51]

By the mid–1920s it was clear that the means of restoring normality in China required review. The Consortium had kept the major powers in line, but it had been unable to mobilise new funds for China. Meanwhile, the continuing weakness of the central government shifted attention to provincial spheres of influence, compelled foreign interests to take nationalist demands seriously and cast doubt on the realism of the one-China policy. These problems prompted a fundamental reappraisal of British policy with the result that in 1926 the Foreign Office adopted a new strategy which set the course of British policy until Japan invaded China in 1937.[52] The new strategy had two elements: the first

47. Anthony B. Chan, *Arming the Chinese: The Western Armament Trade in Warlord China, 1920–1928* (Vancouver, 1982).

48. Eugene Lubot, *Liberalism in an Illiberal Age: New Cultural Liberals in Republican China, 1919–1937* (Westport, Conn., 1982).

49. Dayer, *Bankers and Diplomats*, pp. 125, 188.

50. China had declared war on Germany in 1917 largely in the hope of regaining Shantung, which in the event was transferred to Japan. On the intellectual ferment of the time see Robert A. Scalapino, 'The Evolution of a Young Revolutionary – Mao Zedong in 1919–1921', *Jour. Asian Stud.*, 42 (1982).

51. Dayer, *Bankers and Diplomats*, pp. 163–5, 217. See also Jessie G. Lutz, *Chinese Politics and Christian Missions: The Anti-Christian Movements of 1920–28* (Notre Dame, N.H., 1988).

52. The most important sources analysing this decision are two unpublished, underused and hence underestimated doctoral theses: Peter G. Clark, 'Britain and the Chinese Revolution, 1925–1927', (Ph.D. thesis, University of California at Berkeley, 1973), and William James Megginson, 'Britain's Response to Chinese Nationalism, 1925–1927: the Foreign Office's Search for a New Policy' (Ph.D thesis, George Washington University, 1973).

reordered Britain's international priorities in the Far East by favouring Japan rather than the United States; the second altered policy towards China by supporting the nationalist movement instead of trying to suppress it. This was not only a remarkable reversal but also a striking initiative for a power whose arteries had supposedly hardened.

The attempt to revive the alliance with Japan, albeit informally, recognised that she had become a far more powerful force in China than had the United States. This fact was brought home to China-watchers in 1924, when a new regime was installed in Peking with financial backing from Japan.[53] By that time, too, it had become apparent that Britain had achieved only limited success in persuading the United States to contribute either to the cost of China's development or to the defence of foreign interests there.[54] The deal envisaged with Japan aimed to divert her to northern China and Manchuria, leaving Britain free to consolidate her position in south and central China by controlling Canton and Shanghai. Thus, the traditional policy of supporting a united China under the authority of Peking was abandoned. Instead, the two 'island empires' would manage China from different points of influence as, in the Locarno formula, Britain and France planned to manage Germany.

The decision to cooperate with nationalist elements was even more radical, despite the precedents set in India.[55] To hold hands with Japan was to revive an old relationship; but courting Chinese nationalists was a departure from a tradition of gunboat diplomacy which went back to the 1840s. The fact that the nationalists could not be bombarded into submission was evidently one consideration; another was growing evidence that the anti-foreign movement was falling under Bolshevik influence.[56] From 1923 Sun Yat-sen began to expand his power base in Canton with help from Moscow, and in the following year the Soviet Union presented the acceptable face of international socialism by giving up Tsarist extraterritorial rights in China. Sun's death in 1925 offered an opportunity rather than removed a problem: his successor, Chiang Kai-shek, transformed the

53. Dayer, *Finance and Empire*, pp. 257–9.

54. Ibid. pp. 116, 144–5, 205, 210, 234, 254.

55. See, in addition to Clarke, 'Britain and the Chinese Revolution', and Megginson, 'Britain's Response', Edmund S.K. Fung, 'The Sino-British Rapprochement, 1927–1931', *Mod. Asian Stud.*, 17 (1983), and idem, 'The Chinese Nationalists and the Unequal Treaties, 1924–1931', *Mod. Asian Stud.*, 21 (1987).

56. The last gunboat action on the China coast mounted by the British navy was in September 1926 – just three months before the Foreign Office decided to co-operate with the nationalist movement. See Clark, 'Britain and the Chinese Revolution', pp. 250–61.

Kuomintang into the Nationalist Government of China in 1926 and extended its reach from Canton to the Yangtse; at the same time, the fall of the regime in Peking cast further doubt on the likelihood that Britain's aims would be realised by continuing support for a unitary state. These developments compelled the Foreign Office to rethink its established views about managing China.

It is now clear that the shift in British policy was initiated in London.[57] The 'men on the spot' in Hong Kong and Peking opposed the change, and urged that more effort should be made to hold China together and to put down the anti-imperialist movement. In Britain the election of a Conservative government in 1925 signalled a greater determination to restore Britain's pre-war dominance: hence the return to gold at pre-war parity, the conscious attempt to cut free from the influence of the United States and the priority given to defeating Bolshevism.[58] In Whitehall, Pratt's arrival at the Foreign Office, also in 1925, provided the expertise which enabled Britain's aspirations to be fitted to the evolution of events in China.[59] Towards the close of 1926, following Pratt's advice, the Foreign Office concluded that 'it ought to be a principle of our policy to sympathise with the best elements of the Kuomintang and try to get them on proper lines', and by doing so 'free ourselves from the shackles of Washington and recover our liberty of action'.[60]

The new policy, like the old, was closely bound up with financial considerations. Firms such as the Hongkong and Shanghai Bank, British and American Tobacco, Jardine Matheson, and Swires, which had substantial long-term investments in China, not only backed the new policy but also were independent advocates of it.[61] Following a visit to China in 1921–2, Addis himself had begun to question the wisdom of continuing to support Peking; by 1925 he was recommending a conciliatory policy towards the nationalists; in 1926 he advised the Foreign Office to recognise the government in Canton.[62] Thus, the new policy was not imposed by the Foreign Office but devised in consultation with firms whose importance it had long recognised. Pratt was quite clear which of these made the running:

57. Clark, 'Britain and the Chinese Revolution', pp. 136–7, 149–65, 183–9, 205, 305, 399–405, 490–1.

58. Dayer, *Bankers and Diplomats*, Ch. 7.

59. Clark, 'Britain and the Chinese Revolution', pp. 136–7, 183.

60. FO minute by Wellesley, 1 October 1926. Quoted in Megginson, 'Britain's Response', p. 402.

61. Dayer, *Finance and Empire*, pp. 138–9, 260–4; King, *Hongkong Bank*, pp. 94–5; Clark, 'Britain and the Chinese Revolution', pp. 403–4.

62. Dayer, *Finance and Empire*, pp. 138–9, 234, 260–4.

'whereas financial interests have men of great influence, ability and fluency to speak for them, trade interests are for the most part struck dumb'.[63] Moreover, as Pratt's colleague, Strang, observed: 'the financial interests' did not have to rely on formal delegations because they had 'their own method of keeping in touch with us', and they also carried more weight in official circles than did representatives of other types of business activity.[64]

Why, then, should the banks and their associates press for a change of policy when, for the previous 30 years, their interests had been closely identified with the maintenance of one central authority in China? The answer to this question lies in alterations to the tactics required to defend Britain's investments in China.[65] In the 1920s Japan and the United States wanted to consolidate China's external debts so that the unsecured loans, which they had advanced during and after World War I, would be included in a comprehensive settlement. This scheme implied greater foreign control of Peking and of China's fiscal system. British banks and bond-holders had nothing to gain from consolidation because most of the money they had loaned to the Chinese government was secured on customs and other revenues, and these were now under direct foreign control. On the contrary, consolidation threatened to dilute their own share of China's repayments, while further interference with the fiscal system seemed likely to accelerate the anti-foreign movement and hence to place all debt service at risk. Consequently, Britain began to distance herself from Peking and to devise an alternative, provincial policy.

However, this decision was much more than a reaction to the consolidation plan and its ramifications. The centre-piece of the new strategy was a bold decision to concede tariff autonomy and to give the provinces a share of the revenues which, traditionally, had been paid to Peking.[66] The Foreign Office (or, to be exact, Pratt and Addis) calculated that this concession would help to win the southern

---

63. FO minute by Pratt, 13 July 1926. Quoted in Clark, 'Britain and the Chinese Revolution', p. 188.

64. FO minute by Strang, 16 November 1925. Quoted in Clark, 'Britain and the Chinese Revolution', p. 188. On the trading community see ibid. p. 60.

65. The summary which follows is a reconstruction of an extraordinarily complex and obscure episode in the financial diplomacy of the period. In addition to Clark, 'Britain and the Chinese Revolution', Dayer, *Finance and Empire*, and King, *Hongkong Bank*, there is a great deal of valuable information in Young, *China's Nation-Building*. Arthur Young visited China as a member of Kemmerer's team in 1929 and stayed on as an adviser to the government. He subsequently produced a number of valuable accounts of the period, which he looked back on as a scholar and as a participant.

66. The question of tariff revision had been placed on the agenda at the Washington Conference in 1922.

nationalists from their Bolshevik allies, ward off the possible expropriation of Britain's sizeable private investments in Canton and Shanghai, and create the security on which new loans could be raised.[67] But Britain's conception of tariff autonomy did not include yielding administrative control of the pledged revenues or giving up extraterritorial rights. These were still seen to be crucial to servicing the foreign debt and to maintaining the confidence of overseas investors. The chief losers were British exporters, notably Manchester manufacturers, who opposed tariff autonomy because they foresaw, correctly, that import duties would be raised to ensure that debts could be serviced.[68]

Admittedly, the new policy was a leap in the dark, but Britain had been in the dark as far as China's politics were concerned since at least 1911. Moreover, in this case the Foreign Office landed on its feet: Chiang's forces took control of Nanking in 1927 and captured Peking in the following year. Equally significant, Chiang split from Moscow, conducted a savage purge of his communist supporters, and announced his commitment to honouring China's external debts.[69] The Foreign Office, reassured that 'the best elements' of the Kuomintang were now 'on proper lines', gave official recognition to Chiang's National Government in 1928 and lent substance to diplomacy by handing over control of tariff policy.[70] Far from being a step in a long retreat, the new strategy was a way of giving the nationalists a stake in the welfare of British investments in China; and by the close of the 1920s it had achieved a striking success.

FORGING A NEW PARTNERSHIP: THE 1930s

This vantage point also offers a different perspective on British policy in the 1930s, and in particular on the weighty decision made in 1937 to

67. Dayer, *Finance and Empire*, pp. 264–5; Young, *China's Nation-Building*, pp. 19–20, 48–54, 72–3, 92–3, 110, 116–1; Fung, 'The Sino-British Rapprochement', pp. 95–6.

68. Arthur Redford, *Manchester Merchants and Foreign Trade*, Vol. II, *1850–1939* (Manchester, 1956), pp. 229–31. There was absolutely no wavering on this point: customs duties had to be used to secure loans and the tariff had to be raised to ensure that repayments were made. See Megginson, 'Britain's Response to Chinese Nationalism', Ch. 18.

69. Clark, 'Britain and the Chinese Revolution', Ch. 7; Megginson, 'Britain's Response to Chinese Nationalism', Ch. 22; Dayer, *Finance and Empire*, pp. 269–72; Young, *China's Nation-Building*, p. 154; Osterhammel, 'Imperialism in Transition', p. 263.

70. The phrases are those of Victor Wellesley: see above, n. 59.

support China against Japan. On the assumptions that Britain's economic interests in China were waning and that her diplomacy generally lacked resolution, this decision has to be explained by a combination of special factors operating at the time.[71] However, if the assumptions are altered to take account of the strategy adopted by the Foreign Office in 1926 and its development in the 1930s, it becomes possible to put forward an additional argument which emphasises the continuity of Britain's priorities in China. The main issues, as in the 1920s, were financial, and centred on securing payments on existing debts and creating the conditions for new investment.

Deteriorating economic and political conditions meant that a number of China's external debts had fallen into temporary default by the late 1920s. As in India, tariff autonomy was conceded not only to mollify nationalists but also to provide the means of meeting foreign financial obligations. This step was necessary but not, by itself, sufficient, and additional fiscal and monetary measures were required to ensure that debt service was resumed.[72] Progress was made in bringing local banks into line with western practice after 1928; import duties were denominated in gold rather than in silver from 1930 to preserve the real value of government revenues; serious consideration was given to moving the currency on to a gold standard between 1928 and 1931. These reforms were a cooperative effort: foreign experts, such as Kemmerer, the flying 'money doctor', Salter, the former adviser to the League of Nations, and Addis, the ubiquitous banker, made important contributions; T.V. Soong, the Minister of Finance in the National Government between 1928 and 1933, was a westernised liberal who had studied economics at Harvard and was keen to attract outside expertise and funds for China's development.[73] Minds on both

71. The considerable literature on the diplomatic history of this period can be approached through: Bradford A. Lee, *Britain and the Sino-Japanese War, 1937–1939* (1973); Peter Lowe, *Great Britain and the Origins of the Pacific War: A Study of British Policy in East Asia, 1937–1941* (Oxford, 1977); Aron Shai, *Origins of the War in the East: Britain, China, and Japan, 1937–39* (1976); Christopher Thorne, *The Limits of Foreign Policy: The West, the League and the Far Eastern Crisis of 1931–1933* (1972); and Ann Trotter, *Britain and East Asia, 1933–1937* (Cambridge, 1975).

72. Young, *China's Nation-Building*, pp. 142–6, 177–83; Loren Brandt and Thomas J. Sargent, 'Interpreting New Evidence about China and U.S. Silver Purchases', *Hoover Institute Working Papers*, No. E–87–3 (Stanford, Calif., 1987), p. 23.

73. Kemmerer and Addis have been referred to earlier: see Drake, *Money Doctor in the Andes*, and Dayer, *Finance and Empire*. Arthur Salter (1881–1975) had been Director of the Economic and Finance Section of the League of Nations in the 1920s. His *Memoirs of a Public Servant* (1961) contain a chapter on his mission to China from 1931 to 1933. T.V. Soong (1894–1971) played a key role in linking the Shanghai business world to the Nationalist Government and in introducing Chinese banks to modern banking practices. Soong came from a wealthy Christian family, and his own talents

sides were concentrated by the knowledge that new loans would not be forthcoming until agreement on existing debts had been reached. Addis did his best to ensure that this sequence was followed by using the Consortium to control potentially 'irresponsible' lenders such as Japan (which had funds to lend) from stealing a march on Britain (which did not).[74] Amidst this considerable activity, Britain's old staple manufactures were quietly jettisoned. The leading export, cotton textiles, suffered a dramatic reverse: import duties rose sharply from 1929, and by the early 1930s sales of Manchester goods had been cut to insignificance, thus finally ending the hope that China would provide compensation for the loss of the Indian market.[75]

The most ambitious reform was the attempt to draw China into the emerging Sterling Area after Britain left the gold standard in 1931.[76] This plan was lent urgency by changing monetary conditions in China, which were themselves affected by the global financial crisis. The long decline in silver prices was reversed in 1931, when a rise in world demand began to draw silver out of China. The outflow threatened to deflate the economy and consequently to damage both the recovery of public finances, which had been in train since 1928, and the profitability of British investments.[77] Britain responded by dispatching a senior Treasury adviser, Frederick Leith-Ross, to China to devise a solution which would take the monetary system off the silver standard and also secure British interests.[78] The report drawn up by Leith-Ross and his team in 1935 recommended that China's currency should be linked to sterling, that a Central Reserve Bank should be established, and that the National Government should undertake to balance its budget.

were complemented by those of his sisters: one married Sun Yat-sen; the other Chiang Kai-shek. These advantages became handicaps in 1949, and Soong took refuge in the United States after the revolution.

74. Dayer, *Finance and Empire*, pp. 284–7, 292–5; King, *Hongkong Bank*, pp. 385–6.

75. Stephen L. Endicott, *Diplomacy and Enterprise*, pp. 42–3; Cheng, *Foreign Trade*, pp. 54, 59, 67; Osterhammel, 'British Business', p. 203. On metal goods see R.P.T. Davenport-Hines, 'The British Engineers' Association and Markets in China, 1900–1930', in idem, *Markets and Bagmen: Studies in the History of Marketing and British Industrial Performance, 1830–1939* (1986).

76. See, on this subject, Dayer, *Finance and Empire*, Ch. 11; Endicott, *Diplomacy and Enterprise*, Chs. 4–6; King, *Hongkong Bank*, Ch. 8; Young, *China's Nation-Building*, Chs. 9–10.

77. The established view of the causes of the silver crisis has been challenged by Brandt and Sargent, 'Interpreting New Evidence'.

78. Stephen L. Endicott, 'British Financial Diplomacy in China: the Leith-Ross Mission, 1935–1937', *Pac. Aff.*, 46 (1973/4). Leith-Ross (1887–1968) was Chief Economic Adviser to the British Government, 1932–46. His own account of the mission appears in Ch. 15 of his memoirs: *Money Talks: 50 Years of International Finance* (1968).

Given that this was a composite package, taken from the shelf of universal banking verities, Leith-Ross had more success than local conditions might have allowed. China left the silver standard in 1935, and the new Chinese dollar (which had replaced the tael in 1933) was linked to sterling, as the Treasury, the Bank of England and Addis had hoped.[79] But the link was not exclusive; China wished to preserve her options, particularly the possibility of financial support from the United States, and so adopted a managed exchange standard, which in effect tied her currency to the dollar as well as to sterling. This decision required the cooperation of the foreign exchange banks and particularly of the Hongkong and Shanghai Bank, which played a vital part in helping to maintain the stability of the new system.[80] The Central Reserve Bank was created in 1936, and a member of the advisory team, Cyril Ross, remained in China to ensure that policy ran on lines laid down by the Bank of England. The National Government made considerable progress in balancing the budget, and a settlement of defaulted debts was reached in 1936. This cleared the way for new lending, and in 1937 Addis persuaded members of the Consortium to allow a substantial new railway loan to be issued in London. The decision drew China closer to Britain and, as Addis saw it, made her effectively 'a member of the sterling area'.[81]

The silver crisis and the ensuing monetary reforms also provide the key to understanding the wider relationship between the world slump and Britain's expanding stake in China in the 1930s. Recent research has made it clear that the Chinese economy as a whole was not seriously damaged by the severe depression in world trade after 1929, even though there was a fall in the value and profitability of overseas commerce between 1930 and 1936.[82] The explanation is not that China was isolated from the world economy, but that significant growth took place outside the 'traditional' export sector. Initially, the declining price of silver boosted China's exports and increased the cost of imports, thus reinforcing the protective effect of the new tariff regime and stimulating import-substituting activities. The rise in the price of silver after 1931 threatened to reverse these trends, and it was at this point that the monetary reforms acted to stabilise the economy as a whole. The success of the reforms limited the damage: China's money supply increased during the early 1930s, and the 'modern' sector (especially coal, textiles,

79. Dayer, *Finance and Empire*, pp. 278, 282–93; King, *Hongkong Bank*, p. 399.
80. King, *Hongkong Bank*, pp. 412–17, 442.
81. Addis, diary entry, 14 January 1937. Quoted in Dayer, *Finance and Empire*, p. 301.
82. Rawski, *Economic Growth*, pp. 171–8; Brandt and Sargent, 'Interpreting New Evidence'; Myers, 'The World Depression'.

electrical goods, utilities and banking) experienced significant growth as a result of the continuing buoyancy of the domestic economy.

These developments gave further impetus to Britain's new policy of cooperating with the Nationalist Government. In this case, as in others we have discussed, the implementation of official policy depended heavily on actions taken in the private sector, since the Foreign Office could neither coerce the Chinese government nor direct British business. Fortunately (and exceptionally) the strategy adopted by the expatriate firms operating in China in the 1930s is now known in some detail.[83] By that time, the China lobby was centred on a handful of large firms consisting of trans-national corporations, such as ICI, Unilever, British & American Tobacco, and Shell-BP, Far Eastern conglomerates, such as Jardine, Matheson, and the hardy perennial, the Hongkong and Shanghai Bank. These firms were fitted by their size and structure to meet the capital requirements and the risks of operating in the underdeveloped world; they also reflected impulses transmitted from Britain, where large firms and new industries were finally making their appearance. In essence, what happened in the 1930s was that the large expatriate firms began to move into the interior (especially the hinterlands of Shanghai and Canton), where new economic opportunities were associated with an acceptable level of political stability. There, they took advantage of the tariff protection which had eliminated imported Manchester goods and invested in the modern sector, often through joint ventures with Chinese entrepreneurs.

On the British side, these innovations signalled the end of the gunboat era and cleared the way for the surrender of extraterritorial rights, which had little relevance to activities outside the Treaty Ports; as far as China was concerned, they opened a new phase of co-operative enterprise with western firms.[84] China's entrepreneurs became incorporated by association into Chiang's bureaucratic and military regime, but they also won political protection and this lent

---

83. Thanks largely to the authoritative work of Jürgen Osterhammel, *Britischer Imperialismus in Fernen Osten: Strukturen der Durchdringung und einheimischer Widerstand auf dem chinesischen Markt, 1932–1937* (Bochum, 1982). See also Osterhammel's important general studies, 'Imperialism in Transition' and 'British Business in China'. Osterhammel's work complements that of Endicott, *Diplomacy and Enterprise*, which is concerned more with the policy implications of economic change.

84. Extraterritorial rights were not to be given up lightly, but they had become a card to be played at the appropriate moment rather than a privilege to be defended at all costs. On their final surrender in 1943 see K.C. Chan, 'The Abrogation of British Extraterritorial Rights in China, 1942–43: a Study of Anglo-American-Chinese Relations', *Mod. Asian. Stud.*, 11 (1977).

support to their alliance with foreign business.[85] These developments began to realise the promise of a new deal for China and they go far towards explaining the optimism expressed by well-informed contemporaries in the mid–1930s. As Sir Louis Beale, Britain's Commercial Counsellor in Shanghai, observed in 1936:

> There has never been a time when we were so pre-eminent in prestige in China as we are today, and, if we adopt an enterprising policy of cooperation with China in the development of her vast potential resources, there is no reason why we should not stay permanently in the lead.'[86]

This judgement was echoed in the following year by the captain of Britain's official team in China: 'we are on a very good wicket here and we ought to take full advantage of it'.[87]

The process of reconstruction was both hurried on and ultimately brought down by foreign rivalries, especially with Germany and, above all, with Japan. Germany's revived presence began to make itself felt from the late 1920s, first through military links with the Kuomintang, and then through bilateral trade agreements, which played an important part in supplying raw materials for German rearmament in the 1930s.[88] Japan's interests in China were larger and more forcefully expressed. The end of the Anglo-Japanese alliance in 1921 had left Japan with a grievance and with more scope for remedying it; the world slump helped to convert her long-standing ambitions on the mainland into imperialist aggression.[89] The liberal policies of the civilian government were discredited, the search for markets became more urgent and power shifted towards the army.[90]

85. The relationship between Chiang and China's modernising capitalists is a complex issue which in turn opens up the wider question of the connection between economic development and political representation. See Bergère, *L'Age d'or de la bourgeoisie chinoise*; Parks M. Coble, *The Shanghai Capitalists and the Nationalist Government, 1927–1937* (Cambridge, Mass., 1980); and Richard C. Bush, *The Politics of Cotton Textiles in Kuomintang China, 1927–1937* (New York, 1982).

86. Quoted in Osterhammel, 'Imperialism in Transition', pp. 260–1.

87. Knatchbull-Hugessen, the British Ambassador, to Cadogan, 3 March 1937. Quoted in Dayer, *Finance and Empire*, p. 301.

88. See Bernd Martin, ed. *Die deutsch Beraterschaft in China, 1927–1938* (Düsseldorf, 1981); John P. Fox, *Germany and the Far Eastern Crisis, 1931–1938* (Oxford, 1982); and William C. Kirby, *Germany and Republican China* (Stanford, Calif., 1984). These developments paralleled those in South America. See above, pp. 151–2.

89. Beasley, *Japanese Imperialism*, Ch. 10; Duus, Myers and Peattie, *Japanese Informal Empire*; Akira Iriye, *The Origins of the Second World War in Asia and the Pacific* (1987).

90. The shifts in political power in Japan at this time are dealt with by Kyozo Sato, 'Japan's Position Before the Outbreak of the European War in September 1939', *Mod. Asian Stud.*, 14 (1980). On the limited political infuence of Japanese business see William Miles Fletcher, *The Japanese Business Community and National Trade Policy, 1920–1942* (Chapel Hill, N.C., 1989).

Japan's invasion of Manchuria in 1931 signalled the transition from informal expansion to a form of militarist imperialism. Her withdrawal from the League of Nations in 1933 and the publication of the menacing Amau Statement in the following year were further signposts on the road to war. In 1936 the Anti-Comintern Pact brought Germany and Japan closer together, and gave Japan a freer hand in the Far East.[91] When Japan invaded China in 1937, all hopes for pacific development were sunk.

Despite the ending of the Anglo-Japanese alliance, the Foreign Office continued to base its policy towards the Far East on the assumption that Japan would not act aggressively, or at least not in a way that would damage Britain's interests. If this view seemed justified by events during the 1920s, it became instantly unrealistic after the invasion of Manchuria in 1931. From then on, Britain's mandarins struggled to reconcile the irreconcilable. The success of Britain's new policy towards China strengthened the Nationalist Government and hence checked Japan's influence. Britain was therefore seen in Tokyo to be taking an unfriendly attitude which helped, in turn, to legitimise an assertive response. The only sure way of restraining Japan was for Britain to step up her naval presence in the Far East, but the cost was daunting, if not prohibitive.[92]

This dilemma explains the increasingly intricate acts of contortion performed by the *artistes* of the Foreign Office as they tried to extend a hand to Japan without losing a grip on China. One idea, canvassed by the pro-Japanese lobby, was that Britain should fall in behind Japan's advance and collect some of the gains which would materialise once China had been reorganised and disciplined by an efficient, forward-looking regime.[93] This approach ran parallel to the Treasury's view that the stability of sterling required a low-cost defence policy, which meant, in effect, making concessions to Japan in the Far East.[94] The link between budgetary control, sterling and strategy gave the Treasury considerable prominence in foreign policy in the mid–1930s – much to the displeasure of the Foreign Office. Leith-Ross, for

91. As Fox has shown, the Pact subordinated Germany's economic interests in China to Nazi ideological priorities favouring Japan: see Fox, *Germany and the Far Eastern Crisis*.
92. This dilemma has been thoroughly explored by Lowe, *Great Britain and the Origins of the Pacific War*; Trotter, *Britain and East Asia*; and Shai, *Origins of the War in the East*.
93. Endicott, *Diplomacy and Enterprise*, pp. 28–9; Trotter, *Britain and East Asia*, pp. 27–8, 115, 125–6, 129.
94. Endicott, *Diplomacy and Enterprise*, pp. 28–34; Trotter, *Britain and East Asia*, pp. 6–10;

example, devised a banker's solution to the problem of containing Japan which involved giving her Manchuria and compensating China by offering her a loan on favourable terms. Moreover, the Treasury's view carried weight with Neville Chamberlain, who believed that the cost of rearmament was also unacceptable to the electorate and that, in consequence, Britain ought to adopt a low-cost defence strategy centred on Europe and based on the Air Force.[95]

Nevertheless, an alternative policy prevailed. As the 1930s advanced, it became clear that Japan wanted capitulation rather than concessions. When the scheme for recognising Japan's position in Manchuria failed in 1935, Britain began to adopt a firmer line.[96] The outbreak of the Sino-Japanese war in 1937 confirmed Britain's attitude and stiffened her resolve.[97] Yet the explanation of why Britain decided to support China against Japan ought not to be couched solely in terms of the way in which diplomatic realities gradually imprinted themselves on the official mind. The growing success of Britain's new policy towards China was a powerful consideration in the decision to confront Japan. It is now clear that the Hongkong and Shanghai Bank and the conglomerates which were investing heavily in China in the 1930s exerted strong pressure on the Foreign Office and on Chamberlain, and that their representations strengthened the government's determination to defend Britain's stake in China.[98] In the final analysis, Britain's interests in China were larger than those in Japan, and the Foreign Office also believed (albeit mistakenly) that, in the event of war between the two countries, China would win.[99] Wider considerations played their part, too, as friction between Britain and Japan spread beyond the Far East in the 1930s: faced with rising unemployment and a developing balance of payments problem, Britain could no longer watch benignly as Japan's manufactures penetrated imperial markets; Japan, on the other hand, resented the restrictions placed on her exports following the Ottawa Conference in 1932.[100] By the close of the 1930s, the 'two island empires' had not

95. Endicott, *Diplomacy and Enterprise*, p. 73; Trotter, *Britain and East Asia*, pp. 40–2, 88–92, 212–3.

96. Endicott, *Diplomacy and Enterprise*, 98–9, 150; Trotter, *Britain and East Asia*, pp. 115, 125–6, 131, 142–60. See also S. Olu Agbi, 'The Foreign Office and Yoshida's Bid for Rapprochement with Britain in 1936–1937', *Hist. Jour.* 21 (1978).

97. As did the Tientsin crisis in 1939. See Aron Shai, 'Le conflit Anglo-Japonais de Tientsin en 1939', *Revue d'histoire moderne et contemporaine*, 22 (1975).

98. Endicott, *Diplomacy and Enterprise*, pp. 30–4, 87–97, 173–85.

99. Trotter, *Britain and East Asia*, pp. 204, 217.

100. Ian M. Drummond, *British Economic Policy and the Empire, 1919–1939* (1972), pp. 27–40.

only ceased to be allies but had also embarked on a trade war which spread beyond Asia to Australia, the Middle East, and Africa.[101]

Britain's renewed support for the Chinese government took the traditional form of financial assistance. In 1935 Chamberlain was prepared to give official backing to Leith-Ross's scheme for raising a loan in the City to assist China. Two years later, Britain side-stepped the Second Consortium and supported an advance made by the Hongkong and Shanghai Bank to the Nationalist Government.[102] Export credits were granted to China in 1938, and a guaranteed currency stabilisation loan was issued in 1939.[103] These measures were firm evidence of Britain's intent, but they were limited in substance by the cost of the rearmament programme and by the sterling crisis of 1937–8. In 1938 the United States began to step up its support for the Chinese government at a rate that Britain could not match; and from 1941, when both powers declared war on Japan, US aid to China was increased still further.[104] As the stakes rose, Britain was left behind. To maintain her presence in China during World War II she had to fall back on what the Foreign Office termed 'unlimited flattery' (which included an Oxford doctorate for Chiang Kai-shek) as a substitute for material aid.[105]

TOWARDS 1949

By 1945, China's foreign trade and finance, like Chiang himself, were firmly in the hands of the United States.[106] Even at this late stage, however, it is mistaken to suppose that Britain's ambitions in China had been extinguished or even that they were unrealistic. Britain

---

101. Trotter, *Britain and East Asia*, pp. 16–17, 29–32. Case studies include: D.C.S. Sissons, 'Manchester v Japan: the Imperial Background to the Australian Trade Diversion Dispute with Japan, 1936', *Australian Outlook*, 30 (1976); Yuen Choy Leng, 'Japanese Rubber and Iron Investments in Malaya, 1900–41', *Jour. South-East Asian Stud.*, 5 (1974); and Nicholas Tarling, '"A Vital British Interest": Britain, Japan, and the Security of the Netherlands Indies during the Inter-War Period', *Jour. South-East Asian Stud.*, 9 (1978).

102. Dayer, *Finance and Empire*, pp. 239–40.

103. Ibid, p. 305; King, *Hongkong Bank*, pp. 423–4; Lee, *Britain and the Sino-Japanese War*, p. 211.

104. Dayer, *Finance and Empire*, pp. 303–5; Chan, 'Abrogation of British Extraterritoriality', pp. 262–3; Michael Schaller, *The United States and China in the Twentieth Century* (Oxford, 1980), pp. 48–53.

105. Chan, 'Abrogation of British Extraterritoriality', pp. 263–5.

106. Cheng, *Foreign Trade*, p. 180.

fought World War II to retain her overseas possessions as well as to defeat Germany and Japan, and she made plans to re-establish her presence in the Far East as soon as peace returned. British firms were keen to secure their investments and to resume business, and the British government looked to China, as to other parts of the world beyond Europe, to assist in reconstructing the home economy.[107] By playing on fears in the United States about the spread of communism, the Foreign Office also persuaded Washington to allow Britain to re-enter Hong Kong. Britain's plans were frustrated initially not by a loss of will, but by a deliberate policy decision which reflected the reordered priorities of international trade in the post-war years. In 1947 the Treasury ruled that trade with China could not be developed until Britain's position with respect to hard currency areas had improved and until the dollar gap in particular had been closed.[108] Since China's brief connection with the Sterling Area had been severed during the war, she was relegated to the basement of British commercial policy. After 1949, of course, events in China became the principal influence on Britain's presence there: the communist government nationalised foreign holdings, British business suffered the fate, which was rarer than might be thought, of being taken over without compensation, and investors learned the hard lesson that the value of portfolios not only can go down as well as up, but also can be eliminated.[109]

SAFEGUARDING BRITISH INTERESTS IN AN AGE OF REVOLUTION

The evidence presented above suggests that China ought to have a prominent place in the study of British imperialism in the period following the revolution of 1911. Its disappearance from the literature on this subject, though not justified explicitly, appears to derive from

107. On these issues see: Christopher Thorne, *Allies of a Kind: The United States, Britain and the War Against Japan, 1941–1945* (Oxford, 1978); Shai, *Britain and China*; and Osterhammel, 'British Business', pp. 212–13.

108. Shai, *Britain and China*, pp. 151–2.

109. T.N. Thompson, *China's Nationalisation of Foreign Firms: The Politics of Hostage Capitalism, 1949–1957* (Baltimore, Md, 1979); B. Hooper, *China Stands Up: Ending the Western Presence, 1948–1950* (Sydney, 1986); Aron Shai, 'Britain, China and the End of Empire', *Jour. Contemp. Hist.*, 15 (1980), pp. 287–97; and idem, 'Imperialism Imprisoned: the Closure of British Firms in the People's Republic of China', *Eng. Hist. Rev.*, 104 (1989).

broad assumptions about the decline of British power, whether this is dated from the 1870s or after 1914. Yet, as we showed earlier, Britain's informal influence in China was limited in the middle of the nineteenth century and did not expand until after 1895, when new financial opportunities finally opened up. This influence was maintained and in some respects increased in the years between 1911 and 1937. Subsequent events, even those as momentous as World War II and the revolution of 1949, were treated in London as interruptions rather than as turning points. Imperialist powers are not easily deflected from their historic mission, and in the case of China there were precedents to suggest that Britain could survive war and revolution, and perhaps even gain from them. Of course, if exports of staple manufactures are treated as proxies of British power, then relative decline can indeed be traced to the late nineteenth century and absolute decline to the 1930s. But, as we have argued throughout the present study, this is in general a misleading indicator: in the case of China Britain's strength lay in her finance and commercial services rather than in her manufactured exports.

As we have seen in other contexts, financial leverage was also the more powerful weapon of policy. The ties which joined Whitehall to the City were much closer than those which ran to Manchester, as the example of Sir Charles Addis has shown. The claim that 'in democratic countries the real political power lies with big money and with a comparatively small circle of political wire-pullers' is perhaps too jaundiced and conspiratorial in tone to win acceptance; but, since it was the judgement of the former Deputy Under-Secretary of State at the Foreign Office in charge of Far Eastern affairs, it ought not to be discounted either.[110] The evidence now available confirms that finance had a central part to play in British policy towards China after 1911, as indeed before. As policy-makers relied heavily on financial power to influence the Chinese government, so bankers called upon political support for their own purposes. The two were fused in a particular conception of public interest which, by amalgamating national and imperial values, was able to rise above the level of mere sectional concerns.

The main aim of policy in the aftermath of revolution and world war was to safeguard Britain's investments by tightening her grip on Peking. This policy was successful but also limited, and in 1926 it was replaced by a 'new deal' which guided British policy towards China until 1937 and was not abandoned until the 1950s. The new

110. Wellesley, *Diplomacy in Fetters*, p. 119.

policy established an alliance with suitably cooperative nationalists in the late 1920s, conceded tariff autonomy to the Nationalist Government, and expanded in the 1930s to encompass monetary reform, links with the sterling bloc and joint ventures with Chinese entrepreneurs. The purpose of these innovations was first to ensure that China could service her existing foreign debts and then to create conditions which would encourage a flow of new finance. The result enhanced Britain's presence and influence in China, even though it also damaged her traditional staple exports, especially cotton goods. The success of the alliance with the Nationalist Government gave experienced observers considerable optimism about Britain's future in China. Confidence was undoubtedly shattered by the outbreak of war in 1937, but until then it was not, for once, misplaced. The conventional view that Britain was a declining power expending its remaining energies on managing a 'long retreat' is not one that now draws persuasive support from the historical record.

The story of Britain's continuing and reinvigorated ambitions in China also fits into the wider argument of this study, which suggests that imperialist rivalries extended beyond 1914 and assumed new forms, especially in the 1930s, when there was a struggle for the airwaves and airways of the world. Even before Japan's invasion of Manchuria, foreign competition in China had long been imperialist in the sense of seeking domination rather than parity and in justifying the claim by referring to the duties and burdens of the civilising mission, whether in the guise of the western skills needed to impart the gift of progress or in the shape of the untried benefits of Japan's new Asian order. Each foreign state claimed to be more advanced than its rivals; all agreed that they were superior to China. It was this conviction which justified, in the minds of the outside powers, their right to impose and dispose. In this respect, the language and the mentality of diplomacy were much the same in the 1930s as they had been in the 1890s. What was missing from these calculations was the Chinese perspective; and in China the guardians of the Confucian tradition, even in retreat, looked upon the barbarians with a certainty, unremarked in London or Tokyo, that they, like their predecessors, would be eventually be absorbed and in due course civilised.

PART FOUR

Aftermath – Losing an Empire and Finding a Role

CHAPTER ELEVEN

The City, the Sterling Area and Decolonisation

The last fifty years have seen profound changes in Britain's economy and society as well as her role in the world. Winning the war and losing the empire are the most immediately striking developments in the period; but adjusting to peacetime conditions and recoupling Britain with continental Europe are themes which are no less significant for being protracted and, in some respects, still incomplete. The mountain of commentary produced by these events ideally requires an evaluation of matching size. However, the main purpose of the present study is to explain the expansion of empire not its demise; consequently, the events of the post-war era, though a fascinating and important extension of our story, are not central to its main argument. At the same time, we recognise that the interpretation we have put forward carries implications for understanding the course of recent British history, and hence has a direct bearing on the analysis of contemporary issues. To avoid these matters entirely would be an unnecessary and perhaps a misleading act of discretion because, as we shall suggest, the gentlemanly interests which sustained the empire down to World War II also managed and to some extent planned its demise thereafter. Exactly why the relationship changed is a complex matter which we shall approach from the particular standpoint adopted in this study, though in summary fashion. As with the historical prologue surveying the eighteenth century, our object at this point is less to prove a thesis than to suggest how it might be constructed.

The essence of our argument is that a central preoccupation of British policy, even during the war and still more prominently thereafter, was the preservation of sterling's role in financing international trade and investment, and with it the maintenance of the earning power of the City of London. Between 1940, when the Sterling Area acquired formal status, and 1958, when full convertibility was restored, the pound was nursed within a framework of controls in which the empire, especially its dependent, colonial segment, had a starring if also involuntary role. The restoration of convertibility in the late 1950s then opened a second phase which relaunched sterling on what, in the event, turned out to be the final episode in its long career as an international currency of note. By the late 1950s policy-makers calculated that the City, and invisible earnings generally, had more to gain from emerging opportunities in the wider world than from remaining penned in the Sterling Area. As the value of the imperial component of the Sterling Area diminished, so did the economic obstacles to decolonisation. Indeed, by moving with the nationalist tide, Britain hoped to benefit from informal ties with the Commonwealth while simultaneously promoting sterling's wider, cosmopolitan role. This long-planned but short-lived venture ended with a series of sterling crises which culminated in the devaluation of 1967. By then, decolonisation was virtually complete and informal influence had faded.

THE SURVIVAL OF THE GENTLEMANLY ORDER

One of the fruits of victory in 1945 was the survival of Britain's cultural and institutional heritage. Heading the list of survivors were gentlemanly capitalists who, like the empire they controlled, were saved from liquidation in 1940 by American aid and then given a new role as junior partners in the American-dominated world after 1945. The complex of economic and social institutions and mores which supported the gentlemanly order also emerged intact from the conflict. The pace of economic change in Britain after 1945 was more rapid than hitherto but it often ran along familiar grooves, as the continued predominance of the service sector and of the south-east region indicates.[1] In these circumstances it is not surprising to find that changes in the structure of the British elite were evolutionary

1. The best introductions to the subject of economic growth and structure after 1945 are C.H. Lee, *The British Economy after 1700: A Macro-Economic Study* (Cambridge, 1986), Pt. III; and Sidney Pollard, *The Development of the British Economy, 1914–80* (1983), Chs. 6–8. For a brief but emphatic insight into the dominance of the south-east, see Michael Moran, *Politics and Society in Britain: An Introduction* (2nd edn, 1989), p. 9.

rather than dramatic. Corporations became more important than individuals in the processes of wealth-creation after 1945 and economic growth introduced many new ways of accumulating riches; but it is remarkable how much wealth was still concentrated in traditional areas, such as landownership and commercial and financial businesses, and also how dominant London, and in particular the City, remained in terms of economic power.[2] Continuities among service elites were equally marked: as the public sector grew and educational opportunities were widened, recruitment into the professions increased dramatically and selection became more a matter of merit and expert training; but it was still the case that 'top people' continued to come mainly from the service sector itself, particularly in the south-east of England, and were processed by the public schools and Oxbridge.[3] The dominance of Eton might not have been quite so obvious as before the war, but even as late as 1983 70 per cent of Conservative Members of Parliament were former public schoolboys.[4] The administrative arm of government remained similarly in the grip of tradition. The observation, made in 1926, that 'the English gentleman represents a specific and clearly marked type of humanity', could still be made of the generation which survived the war and managed the peace; while the claim that the gentleman was also 'an unrivalled primary teacher of peoples' remained plausible, too, as a self-description of those who set the timetable for decolonisation after the war.[5]

In the 1950s the City's place within these structures was little different from what it had been in the 1930s. The ties between City elites, the Bank of England, the political world and the wider 'establishment' were extremely close, as the Bank Rate tribunal of 1957 plainly revealed.[6] In the 1960s and 1970s, however, there arose a

2. W.D. Rubinstein, *Men of Property: The Very Wealthy since the Industrial Revolution*, (1981), Ch. 8. In the list of the 200 wealthiest individuals printed in the *Daily Telegraph*, 25 February 1988, the number of aristocratic names is still remarkably large. Famous City names also proliferate and much of the 'new money' in evidence is City-based.

3. Rubinstein, 'Social Origins of British Elites'; François Béderida, *A Social History of England, 1851–75* (1979), pp. 281–7. See also Hugh Thomas, ed. *The Establishment* (1959) for a contemporary critique of the venerability of the nation's ruling elites.

4. John Ramsden, 'Conservatives since 1945', *Contemporary Record* (Spring, 1988), p. 18.

5. These judgements came from the authoritative voice of the professor of international relations at Oxford: Alfred Zimmern, *The Third British Empire* (1926), pp. 102–3.

6. C.S. Wilson and T. Lupton, 'The Social Background and Connections of "Top Decision Makers"', *Manchester School*, 27 (1959); For an entertaining and penetrating description of the scandal see Paul Ferris, *The City* (1960), Ch. 7, a book which has many insights into the gentlemanly nature of the City in the 1950s. See, for example, his account of the relations between the bill-brokers and the Bank of England in Ch. 3. These characteristics of the City were also noticed by Richard Spiegelberg, *The City:*

much more unified business elite than had existed before, and it has been argued that the dominance of finance in the old sense could no longer be expected in Britain since the fraction of capital represented by the City was merged with industry to the extent that the City became only one among a complex set of forces which determined the configuration of the economy and the outcome of policy. This conclusion may be misleading, even though the evidence does suggest that the economic elite became increasingly integrated after 1945.

Our own interpretation of the City's evolution is that financial markets fell steadily under the influence of big institutional investors such as insurance companies, pension funds and unit trusts. At the same time, these institutions became much more involved in raising finance for large-scale industry than was the case before the war, and in the processes of take-over and merger which became a far more important element in City life than hitherto. In practice, business as a whole, including manufacturing, came under the control of a relatively small group of financial managers who formed, via an intricate web of interlocking directorships, the chief decision-making body in the private economy by the 1970s. At the heart of this group were the gentlemanly directors of the clearing banks and merchant banks who were key intermediaries in the system because of the wide range of important directorships they held.[7] This commanding group was closely tied, through kinship and social connection, with the service-elites and the wider gentlemanly establishment; these links were reinforced over the years by the tendency of finance to call upon other professional skills such as law and accountancy, as business became a more bureaucratic and specialised matter.[8] So, although the channels of recruitment to top business positions, including those in the City, widened considerably and finance became steadily more profession-alised,[9] the high-status connections of the principal participants in the world of British big business remained strong.

Power without Accountability (1973), pp. 7, 19, and pp. 125–6 in relation to the clearing-bank directors. It is worth quoting the comment of one young City executive that the top brass of the Square Mile 'are not so much members of the Establishment because they have succeeded in the City; they have succeeded in the City because they are members of the Establishment'. Victor Sandelson, 'The Confidence Trick', in Thomas, *The Establishment*, p. 139.

7. Spiegelberg, *The City*, pp. 65–6.

8. John Scott, *The Upper Classes*, pp. 139ff. Much of Scott's analysis is confirmed in detail in Spiegelberg, *The City*, Chs. 1 and 2. See also the views of Geoffrey Ingham, *Capitalism Divided? The City and Industry in British Social Development* (1984), Ch. 3.

9. Kathleen Burk, *Morgan Grenfell, 1838–1988: The Biography of a Merchant Bank* (Cambridge, 1989), pp. 191–2; Spiegelberg, *The City*, p. 19.

There is a very real sense in which the industrial sector in Britain was incorporated after 1945 into a structure dominated by traditional financial institutions and forced into conformity to their practices. One instance of this was the extent to which the emergence of the large firm through mergers and take-overs was shaped by the attractions of short-term financial gain rather than by a felt need for greater efficiency and more assured long-term profitability.[10] Another example was the reluctance of the major banks to follow the path taken by their counterparts in Germany and Japan and to lend to industry on a long-term basis, a reluctance which stemmed from the almost obsessive desire of the banks to stay liquid in the face of exacting demands from the Bank of England and the financial markets, set with international financial criteria in mind.[11] It is also worth noting in this context that banking profits were much higher in Britain than in countries where finance and industry were more closely allied.[12]

INTERNATIONAL ECONOMIC POLICY, 1939–55

These continuities in elite formation and practice in the private sector were paralleled in the sphere of public policy although, as we have seen, the outbreak of war appeared to threaten the continuance of gentlemanly wealth and life-styles. After the fall of France it became obvious that the national interest now had to be defined in terms of the full employment of all available productive resources and that traditional financial orthodoxy would have to be set aside, at least for the duration of the war. Keynesian budgetary techniques were in use as early as 1940 and the shift in priorities encouraged an alliance between government, industry and trades unions and depressed the influence of the financial authorities in the domestic arena. The creation, over the next few years, of a war economy also helped to convince the electorate that, when peace arrived, governments could act as a positive force in the economy and that profits for private

10. Spiegelberg, *The City*, Ch. 7.
11. Grahame Thompson, 'The Relationship between the Financial and Industrial Sector in the United Kingdom Economy', *Economy and Society*, VI (1977); John Carrington and George T. Edwards, *Financing Industrial Investment* (1979); Richard Minns, *Take Over the City: The Case for Public Ownership of Financial Institutions* (1982), pp. 21–6.
12. Minns, *Take Over the City*, p. 23.

industry were compatible with commitments to full employment and a welfare state. The Labour government of 1945 was the fruit of this conviction.[13] Nonetheless, despite the high profile of the producers in wartime and during the period of reconstruction which followed, the conduct of international economic policy remained the preserve of the gentlemanly elite. They were only reluctant converts to the Keynes–Beveridge policy consensus which began to emerge in these years. Although the crises of the time often revealed strong differences of opinion among the traditional authorities over tactics, there was little dispute over the main post-war objective of policy in this arena – a continued world role for sterling and for the City.

It was the gentlemen in Whitehall who were left to deal with the distasteful consequences of burgeoning American financial supremacy after 1940.[14] American aid was given on onerous terms. In 1942 Britain reluctantly agreed to consider abandoning trade discrimination after the war, though this would jeopardise the Ottawa system; British capital assets abroad often had to be sold, sometimes at ruinous prices, before aid was given and export capacity had to be run down, preventing the accumulation of reserves and forcing Britain to incur huge debts with Sterling Area countries. These sterling balances were, by 1945, equivalent to seven times the value of Britain's gold and dollar reserves.[15] Sterling had to be made inconvertible in 1939, when the loosely structured sterling bloc of the 1930s became the rigorously controlled Sterling Area of wartime emergency in which all dollar and gold earnings were pooled and rationed.[16] Convertibility had been vital to sterling's international position in its heyday and was maintained even in the crisis of the

13. Scott Newton and Dilwyn Porter, *Modernization Frustrated: The Politics of Industrial Decline in Britain since 1900* (1988), Ch. 4; Paul Addison, *The Road to 1945* (1975); Keith Middlemass, *Politics in Industrial Society: The British Experience since 1911* (1979), Ch. 10.

14. The most authoritative account of Anglo-American financial diplomacy is now L.S. Pressnell, *External Economic Policy since the War*, Vol. 1: *The Post-war Financial Settlement* (1986). For a shorter account see Alan P. Dobson, *The Politics of the Anglo-American Economic Special Relationship, 1940–1987* (Brighton, 1988). There is also some fascinating detail in Sir Richard Clarke, *Anglo-American Economic Collaboration in War and Peace* (Oxford, 1982). However, the earlier study by Richard N. Gardner, *Sterling-Dollar Diplomacy: The Origin and Prospects of our International Economic Order* (1980 edn.), is still well worth using, as is R.S Sayers, *Financial Policy, 1939–45* (1956).

15. On Lend-Lease (as American aid was known) the authoritative account is now A.P. Dobson, *U.S. Wartime Aid to Britain* (1986).

16. Michael Cowen and Nicholas Westcott, 'British Imperial Policy during the War', in David Killingray and Richard Rathbone, eds. *Africa and the Second World War* (1986); K.M. Wright, 'Dollar Pooling in the Sterling Area, 1939–52', *American Economic Review*, 44 (1954).

1930s; but the huge overhang of sterling indebtedness meant that any return to convertibility in the immediate post-war period without American assistance would have led to an unsustainable drain on the gold and dollar reserves. American aid ceased abruptly at the end of the war;[17] the Bank of England felt that the best strategy for the immediate future was to reinforce the Sterling Area by attracting European adherents who might be tempted to join a defensive financial and trading alliance against the dollar.[18] For, although the sterling balances were burdensome liabilities, they also served, as we shall see, to emphasise the importance of both formal and informal overseas connections and of the need to maintain them in peacetime.

The principal opponent of this approach was Keynes, who had the tentative support of the Treasury. Keynes was well aware of the importance of both the empire and the Sterling Area, but believed that it was in Britain's interest to go along with American demands for rapid progress towards multilateralism at the end of hostilities. He did not expect that a tightly enclosed Sterling Area would be capable of maintaining Britain's income at levels compatible, in the long term, with the ambitious full employment and welfare schemes all British governments were now committed to introduce. Keynes also feared that, faced with a protective bloc organised around an inconvertible currency, the United States would use its trading power and 'dollar diplomacy' to lure away some of the Sterling Area's leading members. More positively, Keynes shared the gentlemanly assumption that the recovery of the City was of the 'greatest possible importance' to the nation and he was convinced that Britain's invisible trade would recover former glories only in a multilateral environment.[19]

His proposals for a new world monetary order, presented at the Bretton Woods conference in 1942,[20] were a daring attempt both to solve Britain's impending exchange crisis without disastrous deflation

17. George C. Herring, 'The United States and British Bankruptcy, 1944–5: Responsibilities Deferred', *Political Science Quarterly*, LXXXVI (1971).

18. The Bank's arguments are laid out in Pressnell, *External Economic Policy*, pp. 137–43, 232–4.

19. *The Collected Writings of John Maynard Keynes*, XXV (Cambridge, 1980), pp. 410–17.

20. On the emergence of the Clearing Union proposals in the context of policy as a whole see Pressnell, *External Economic Policy*, Chs. 1–4. Bretton Woods is also discussed in great detail in Armand Van Dormael, *Bretton Woods: Birth of a Monetary System* (1978); and Dobson, *The Politics of the Anglo-American Economic Special Relationship*, pp. 48ff. For a recent study of Keynes's contribution to wartime and post-war economic policy in general see Alan Booth, *British Economic Policy, 1931–49: Was there a Keynesian Revolution?* (1989)

and to maintain an international role for sterling. A new currency, bancor, was to be created to replace gold as the basis of the world monetary system and to allow an extension of credit which would ensure a rapid revival of international trade financed, it was hoped, by the City after the war.[21] But even when the Americans killed the Keynes Plan and substituted a modified gold standard with only meagre credits available for a dollar-starved world, Keynes still argued that it was important to follow where the United States led. He expected that the post-war dollar crisis would be short lived as Europe quickly recovered its export capacity, and that the Sterling Area would soon be able to return to convertibility.[22] The upshot was the Anglo-American agreement of 1945, which traded a British promise of a return to convertibility in 1947 against a substantial dollar loan.[23] However, exports to the United States recovered only slowly, while reconstruction needs pushed up the demand for dollar imports substantially in 1947 with the result that the convertibility experiment lasted a mere three weeks.[24]

Britain's dependence on her empire had increased markedly in wartime and, as we shall see, the empire had an important part to play in plans for post-war reconstruction and in providing Britain with dollars. But the drive towards empire development could not, at first, be squared easily with support for the new world order promoted by the United States. Although American hostility to the preferential system and the Sterling Area began to diminish at the end of the war, in the immediate post-war period British advocates of a rapid return to multilateralism and convertibility were often seen as the enemies of empire or as unwitting collaborators in an American drive for world economic domination.[25] However, with the onset of the Cold War, American attitudes to colonialism softened. The British empire finally ceased to be an obstacle on the road to progress and

21. Keynes, *Collected Writings*, pp. 4–7, 82–4, 93–4, 100, 123–5, 181–3.
22. There is an exhaustive discussion of Keynes's views on the 1945 loan in Pressnell, *External Economic Policy*, Chs. 5–9. Gardner, *Sterling-Dollar Diplomacy*, pp. 121–43, is also useful here.
23. Pressnell, *External Economic Policy*, Ch. 10; Alec Cairncross, *Years of Recovery: British Economic Policy, 1945–51* (1985), Ch. 5.
24. Cairncross, *Years of Recovery*, Ch. 6, has the details on the 1947 crisis. The enthusiasm for convertibility in the City during 1947 was closely related to anxieties about the future world status of the currency. D.R. Wightman, 'The Sterling Area, Part II: World War II Regulations and Convertibility Crisis', *Banco Nazionale Del Lavoro Quarterly Review*, 4 (1951), pp. 153–4.
25. The anti-American, pro-empire faction is dealt with by Van Dormael, *Bretton Woods*, pp. 131ff. For a vigorous contemporary statement see L.S. Amery, *The Washington Loan Agreements* (1946).

became instead a bulwark against the Communist menace. Multilateralism remained the primary goal, but it was now recognised in Washington that reaching it would be a slow process that required massive American aid to Europe. As a result of this shift in priorities during 1947, it became easier for Britain to pursue an imperial policy in the style of Joseph Chamberlain,[26] while at the same time accepting that a return to convertibility was a desirable aim in the longer term.

Convertibility proved difficult to achieve. Despite Marshall Aid, which paid for a considerable portion of Britain's dollar imports between 1948 and 1952,[27] there were further balance of payments crises in 1949, which precipitated a large devaluation of sterling,[28] and in 1951–2, when the Korean War led to a sharp rise in import prices. The Korean crisis led to a significant change in the emphasis of policy. In 1951, with Marshall Aid nearing its end, both the Treasury and the Bank of England came to the conclusion that the dollar shortage would soon reappear; taking advantage of the arrival of a Conservative government pledged to restore greater market freedoms and ideologically more amenable to gentlemanly persuasion than its predecessors, they argued that the problem should now be approached by moving quickly towards convertibility rather than by relying on a restrictive form of imperialism. In the ROBOT scheme of 1951–2 the Treasury, with the support of the Bank, proposed a 1930s-style floating, convertible pound with the proviso that sterling balances would have to be blocked to avoid a repetition of the 1947 crisis.[29]

26. Allister Hinds, 'Sterling and Imperial Policy, 1945–51', *Jour. Imp. and Comm. Hist.*, XV (1987). One of the ironies of the time was that trade with Canada, a dollar-based country within the empire, was seriously affected by the restrictions imposed by an imperial policy which was intended to economise on foreign exchange. See Tim Rooth, 'Debts, Deficits and Disenchantment: Anglo-Canadian Economic Relations, 1945–50,' (Discussion Paper No. 19, Department of Economics, Portsmouth Polytechnic, May 1991.)

27. Michael J. Hogan, *The Marshall Plan: America, Britain and the Reconstruction of Western Europe, 1947–52* (Cambridge, 1987); Henry Pelling, *Britain and the Marshall Plan* (1988). It should be noted that, in distributing aid, the Americans did not follow British advice, which was to give substantial direct grants to the Third World – much of which was, of course, within the British empire. The British argument was that the best way to cure the dollar shortage was to revive the export capacity of those primary producing countries which had traditionally been large dollar earners and which had played such an important role in the multilateral settlements pattern centred on Britain before 1939. This question is discussed in C.C.S. Newton, 'The Sterling Crisis of 1947 and the British Response to the Marshall Plan', *Econ. Hist. Rev.*, 2nd ser. XXXVII (1984).

28. Alec Cairncross and Barrie Eichengreen, *Sterling in Decline: The Devaluations of 1931, 1949 and 1967* (1983), Ch. 4.

29. Cairncross, *Years of Recovery*, Ch. 9; C.C.S. Newton, 'Operation "ROBOT" and the Political Economy of Sterling Convertibility, 1951–1952', *European University Institute Working Paper*, No. 86/256 (Florence, 1986).

The plan was scuppered eventually because it might have threatened the full employment policy to which the government was committed for good electoral reasons, but it was only the first of a number of schemes in the early 1950s designed to speed Britain's return to convertibility. All of them would have involved raising trade barriers against other European states since countries with non-convertible currencies would otherwise have directed their exports to Britain in order to gain dollars. This would have had severe repercussions upon the growth of world trade and harmed British commodity exports. But the authorities, with their eyes on the invisible account and intent upon restoring sterling to its rightful position in the world, apparently felt that the price was worth paying. Without convertibility, it was feared that sterling would soon fall irretrievably behind the dollar as an international currency; with it, there was a good chance that London would at least become the world centre for non-dollar trade, with large parts of Europe included in an expanded Sterling Area.[30]

The Korean War crisis soon evaporated. Balance of payments surpluses reappeared from 1952 and, despite the ending of Marshall Aid, the European dollar problem was eased by rising exports in a growing world economy and by the flow of American private investment. By the middle of the decade it was possible to convince wary politicians that convertibility was compatible with commitments to welfare and full employment; it was gradually introduced, at fixed rates, between 1955 and 1958.[31]

As in 1918–25, international economic policy was largely decided by gentlemen who clearly believed that re-establishing sterling internationally was more important than worrying about the fate of commodity exports or even the future of the empire both of which, it was assumed, would fall into place if the prior financial problem was solved. Indeed, there was even less opposition to the policy in the 1950s than there was to the return to gold in 1925, principally because, in marked contrast to the 1920s, rapid growth after World War II applied a powerful anaesthetic to criticism.

30. Alan S. Milward, 'Motives for Currency Convertibility: the Pound and the Deutschmark, 1950–5', in Carl-Ludwig Holtfrerich, ed. *Interactions in the World Economy: Perspectives from International Economic History* (1989). According to Milward, Bank of England officials even speculated that 'eventually the Soviet Union and its satellites would enter the London non-dollar world' (p. 268). He also points out that the German government resisted an early return to convertibility precisely because of fears about its effects on commodity exports (pp. 268–71).

31. Dobson, *The Anglo-American Economic Special Relationship*, Ch. 5, charts the progress towards the final objective. In the end, fixed rates were adopted to please the Americans.

THE EMPIRE IN WAR AND RECONSTRUCTION

The war to defeat the Axis powers was also fought to defend, and even to extend, the British empire. As far as imperial policy was concerned, the immediate effect of hostilities was to strengthen links between Britain and the empire and to centralise decisions upon London, both to coordinate defence and to mobilise strategic resources. As the sterling bloc took formal shape as the Sterling Area in 1940, colonial trade was brought under the control of new government organisations and tightly regulated. Vital imports from the colonies were subjected to compulsory purchase; manufactured exports were strictly rationed.[32] Since Britain was unable to meet the cost of essential imports and overseas defence expenditures, suppliers in the Sterling Area (and certain associated countries) accumulated credits, or sterling balances, which were held in London.[33] These balances, which were essentially loans to Britain volunteered by creditors who had virtually no choice in the matter, were crucial to the war effort.

It is now clear that the cost of the war, mountainous though it was, did not crush Britain's belief in her role as a world power at the head of a great empire.[34] It is true, of course, that some parts of the empire had been overrun, and that others, notably India, had experienced widespread civil unrest. But, as recent research has shown, even at the darkest moment – after the fall of Singapore in 1942 – plans were being laid to recapture the occupied parts of the empire and to rejuvenate the imperial mission.[35] As seen from Whitehall, the question was not whether the British empire had a future but how

32. Cowen and Westcott, 'British Imperial Policy', pp. 40–9; David Meredith, 'State Controlled Marketing and Economic Development: the Case of West African Produce During the Second World War', *Econ. Hist. Rev.*, 2nd ser. XXXIX. (1986). Older studies by W.K. Hancock and M.M. Gowing, *British War Economy* (1949), H.D. Hall and C.C. Wrigley, *Studies in Overseas Supply* (1956), and Charlotte Leubuscher, *Bulk-Buying from the Colonies* (1956) are of continuing value for students of the war years.

33. Allister Hinds, 'Imperial Policy and the Colonial Sterling Balances', *Jour. Imp. and Comm. Hist.*, 19 (1991), and the further references given there.

34. William Roger Louis, *Imperialism at Bay: The United States and the Decolonisation of the British Empire, 1941–45* (Oxford, 1977).

35. J.M. Lee and Martin Petter, *The Colonial Office, War and Development Policy* (1982); and the case studies by A.J. Stockwell, *British Policy and Malay Politics During the Malayan Union Experiments, 1945–48* (Kuala Lumpur, 1979); Nicholas Tarling, '"A New and Better Cunning": British Wartime Planning for Post-War Burma, 1942–43', *Jour. South-East Asian Stud.*, 13 (1982), (and the sequel in ibid.); and Robert Pearce, 'The Colonial Economy: Nigeria and the Second World War', in Barbara Ingham and Colin Simmons, eds. *Development Studies and Colonial Policy* (1987).

and when it was to be realised. By 1945 Britain had regained Burma, had argued her way back into Hong Kong, Singapore and Malaya, had taken control of Italy's colonies in Africa and had extended her grip on Egypt.[36] Even the occupation of Germany was viewed from London as being an exercise in colonial administration that required expertise from India. Nor were areas of informal influence written off, despite experiencing a sharp fall in British trade and investment during the war. Britain still aimed to develop the promising position she had held in China before the Japanese invasion in 1937, to keep her special place in Argentina (despite hostility from the United States), and to enlarge her influence in key areas in the Middle East.[37]

The fact that the empire had proved its value during the war undoubtedly lent weight to traditionalists, such as Churchill, whose instruction to Eden at the close of 1944 left no room for misunderstanding: 'hands off the British empire is our maxim and it must not be weakened or smirched to please sob-stuff merchants at home or foreigners of any hue'.[38] But the renewed commitment to empire was as much a matter of calculation as it was of sentiment. Quite simply, the imperial option appeared to be far more promising than the alternatives, especially in war-torn Europe. Among those who looked forward, rather than back, it was agreed that reform was essential if the empire was to be retained. By the close of the war, the Colonial Office had devised a development programme for the dependent empire: the Colonial Development and Welfare Act was renewed and enlarged, and agreement reached on replacing the hallowed but also creaking Lugardian system of indirect rule by an administrative structure staffed by a new generation of educated colonial subjects.[39]

36. Louis, *Imperialism at Bay*, pp. 555–62; Thorne, *Allies of a Kind*, pp. 311, 444, 558. Churchill also had a scheme, which the Americans vetoed, for taking over Thailand.

37. See pp. 259–60 . Also William Roger Louis, *The British Empire in the Middle East, 1945–1951* (Oxford, 1984); C.A. MacDonald, 'The Politics of Intervention: the United States, Britain and Argentina, 1941–46', *Jour. Latin Am. Stud.*, 12 (1980); idem, 'The United States, Britain and Argentina in the Years Immediately after the Second World War', in Guido Di Tella and D.C.M. Platt, eds. *The Political Economy of Argentina, 1880–1946* (1986); and Guido Di Tella and D.C. Watt, eds. *Argentina between the Great Powers, 1939–46* (1989), to which MacDonald makes a further important contribution.

38. Quoted in Jane Bowden, 'Development and Control in British Colonial Policy, with Reference to Nigeria and the Gold Coast, 1935–48'(Ph.D. thesis, University of Birmingham, 1981), p. 246.

39. Ronald Robinson, 'Andrew Cohen and the Transfer of Power in Tropical Africa, 1940–51', in W.H. Morris-Jones and Georges Fischer, eds. *Decolonisation and After: The British and French Experience* (1980); Robert A. Pearce, *Turning Point in Africa: British Colonial Policy 1938–48* (1982), Chs 5–8.

Moreover, this programme commanded bipartisan agreement. Once elected, the Labour Party hoisted the burdens of empire with all the enthusiasm of the converted, despite its long-proclaimed opposition to imperialism.[40] In seeing the light, Bevin, the Foreign Secretary, also saw the way: 'our crime', he observed of the empire, 'is not exploitation; it's neglect'.[41] There followed what has been termed the 'second colonial occupation', which was characterised by an intensive effort to press ahead with development and reform.[42] The array of wartime controls was adapted to the needs of peace, instead of being scrapped, the direction of imperial economic policy remained firmly in London, and the Colonial Office duly increased its size and strengthened its links with other ministries in Whitehall.[43] The result, in the most general terms, was to revitalise the imperial mission by giving it a new sense of purpose.[44]

The explanation of this transformation in colonial policy is both complex and, as yet, incomplete. The momentum for change had already begun to build up during the 1930s, as we have seen,[45] but the need to conciliate the United States caused the pace to quicken during the war. The story of how the United States shifted from overt anti-colonialism to tacit support for the more viable of the European empires has now been told in some detail.[46] In essence, the turning point came towards the close of the war, when fear of communism replaced fear of fascism and Washington was persuaded, by a mixture of self-induced anxiety and skilful British diplomacy, that a friendly empire spanning the globe would be a useful ally in

40. D.K. Fieldhouse, 'The Labour Governments and the Empire-Commonwealth, 1945–51', in R. Ovendale, ed. *The Foreign Policy of the British Labour Government, 1945–51* (Leicester, 1984).

41. Quoted in Pearce, *Turning Point*, p. 95.

42. D.A. Low and J.M. Lonsdale, 'Towards the New Order, 1945–63', in D.A. Low and Alison Smith, eds. *The Oxford History of East Africa*, Vol. 3 (1976), pp. 12–16, and the comment by John. D. Hargreaves, *The End of Colonial Rule in West Africa* (1979), pp. 41–2.

43. J.M. Lee, 'Forward Thinking and the War: the Colonial Office during the 1940s', *Jour. Imp. and Comm. Hist.* 6 (1977). Labour turned towards the empire in search of salvation rather than take up the challenge of leadership of the European group that formed the nucleus of what later became the EEC. See Scott Newton, 'Britain, the Sterling Area and European Integration, 1945–50', *Jour. Imp. and Comm. Hist.*, 13 (1985).

44. R.D. Pearce, 'Morale in the Colonial Service in Nigeria During the Second World War', *Jour. Imp. and Comm. Hist.*, 11 (1983); John W. Cell, 'On the Eve of Decolonisation: the Colonial Office's Plans for the Transfer of Power in Africa', *Jour. Imp. and Comm. Hist.*, 8 (1980); Charles Armour, 'The BBC and the Development of Broadcasting in British Colonial Africa, 1946–56', *African Affairs*, 83 (1984).

45. See pp. 229–30.

46. Louis, *Imperialism at Bay*; Thorne, *Allies of a Kind*.

containing the threat to what was becoming known as the Free World. Effectively, a compromise was reached: the United States agreed not to press for immediate decolonisation; in return, Britain undertook to modernise her empire.[47]

The onset of the Cold War confirmed this understanding. Following the acute sterling crisis in 1947, the United States realised that Britain needed to be buttressed if she was to stand firm as an ally in Western Europe. This perception implied that the Sterling Area had to be maintained and that the empire had to be encouraged to play its part in the recovery of the British economy by supplying essential raw materials and by earning much-needed dollars. This meant, in turn, that imperial preference, long an irritant in Washington, had to be left in place, at least in the short term.[48] Stafford Cripps, speaking for the Treasury in 1947, was therefore able to proclaim a doctrine of imperial complementarity which appeared to meet the needs of wider interests: 'the further development of African resources', he declared, 'is of the same crucial importance to the mobilisation and strengthening of Western Europe as the restoration of European productive powers is to the future progress and prosperity of Africa'.[49] President Truman nodded, and so too, one imagines, did Joseph Chamberlain. Suitably framed and implemented, Labour's new deal for the colonies also held out the prospect of satisfying the reformist, Fabian element in the party (and in Whitehall) and, with luck, of enabling Britain to keep pace with growing nationalist demands in the colonies.[50] Liquidation was not on the agenda: the empire was to be given a shot in the arm rather than in the head.

Calculations of advantage were based primarily upon a heightened awareness of the economic worth of empire during the period of post-war reconstruction. Of course, the empire itself was far from uniform, and the value attached to the component parts varied according to their ability to meet the needs of the metropole. The dominions could not be organised for peace as, by negotiation, they

47. William Roger Louis, 'American Anti-Colonialism and the Dissolution of the British Empire', *International Affairs*, 61 (1985); and, for a case study, Hoosain S. Faroqui, 'In the Shadow of Globalism: The United States, South Asia and the Cold War, 1939–53' (Ph.D. thesis, Cornell University, 1986, Ch. 4).

48. The terms of the Lend-Lease Agreement of 1942 bound Britain to restore non-discriminatory trading practices, and the General Agreement of Trade and Tariffs prohibited new preferences in the Commonwealth in 1947. Nevertheless, existing preferences remained in place and were not phased out until after 1973, when Britain joined the EEC.

49. Quoted in Bowden, 'Development and Control', p. 361.

50. Robinson, 'Andrew Cohen'; and the commentary by Hargreaves, *The End of Colonial Rule*, Ch. 2.

had been mobilised for war, though self-interest kept them within the Sterling Area.[51] India could no longer be controlled, despite Churchill's endeavours, and was granted independence in 1947 with a degree of haste which Mountbatten was charged to disguise as forethought. But this event, for all its significance in the history of Anglo-Indian relations, did not bring down the rest of the British empire; and its economic implications, as we have seen, were less important than might be supposed.[52] After 1945, India ceased to be vital to Britain's pressing needs, being neither a source of essential supplies nor a net contributor to the dollar pool.[53]

The displacement of India gave prominence to other, formerly less significant parts of the empire. Far from being abandoned after 1947, the empire was repositioned in Africa, Malaya, and, informally, in the Middle East.[54] These regions were sources of vital supplies; they contributed to the hard currency pool through their dollar earnings; and they were all directly or indirectly under British control. They also held sizeable sterling balances which could be manipulated more freely than was possible elsewhere. Britain's new colonial policy needs to be interpreted with these priorities in mind. The Colonial Development and Welfare Act of 1945, like the Colombo Plan of 1951, served not only to fund overseas development projects but also to manage expenditures drawn from the balances.[55] By retaining the balances of dependent territories at high levels, Britain controlled the amount available for their development plans while ensuring that they contributed to the reserves held in London and hence to support for the pound. By forming the Colonial Development Corporation in 1947, Britain hoped to promote the production of food and other raw

51. John Darwin, *Britain and Decolonisation* (1988), pp. 135–6. Canada, of course, was already linked to the US dollar.

52. See pp. 196–7.

53. B.R. Tomlinson, 'Indo-British Relations in the Post-Colonial Era: the Sterling Balances Negotiations, 1947–49', *Jour. Imp. and Comm. Hist.*, 13 (1985).

54. Louis, *The British Empire in the Middle East*; Martin Rudner, 'Financial Policies in Post-War Malaya: the Fiscal and Monetary Measures of Liberation and Reconstruction', *Jour. Imp. and Comm. Hist.*, 3 (1975); A.J. Stockwell, 'British Imperial Policy and Decolonisation in Malaya, 1942–52', *Jour. Imp. and Comm. Hist.*, 13 (1984). We are indebted, too, to Gerold Krozewski, 'Sterling, the Minor Territories and the End of Formal Empire, 1939–58', *Econ. Hist. Rev.* (forthcoming). Apart from the Middle East, Britain's remaining areas of informal influence are rarely discussed in studies of 'late colonialism', and there is no space to do so here. However, it is worth noting that they were pressed into service where it was possible to do so. Plans to harness China had to be abandoned, but Britain struck hard bargains with Argentina and Brazil (see pp. 161, 167).

55. D.J. Morgan, *The Official History of Colonial Development*, Vol. 3 (1980), pp. 29–33; Krozewski, 'Sterling'.

materials urgently needed at home.[56] By then purchasing colonial exports through official marketing boards, Britain shifted part of her burdens as a debtor to satellites that were her creditors, and hence made the austerity suffered at home somewhat less severe than it would otherwise have been.[57]

None of these measures could have been imposed without London's political authority; it is no coincidence that the regions of greatest economic value in the period of reconstruction were also those where Britain's determination to perpetuate her control was particularily marked.[58] This was especially the case where Britain's presence was associated with white enterprise and capital, typically in mines and estates. In Malaya and Kenya, coercion tended to be the first resort of policy. The bogey of communism was invoked, where it was not already present, and this sufficed in the early stages of the Cold War to legitimise the use of force. Confrontation also occurred in colonies where production depended directly on the cooperation of a multiplicity of indigenous entrepreneurs, as in the Gold Coast in 1948. But in these areas confrontation was followed more readily by accommodation. Nationalists were designated 'agitators' rather than 'terrorists', and constitutional reforms were set in train with the aim of turning opponents into partners.[59] In the Middle East, which lay outside the empire, a combination of techniques was used: the region was strongly fortified, but the aim was to economise on defence costs by raising up a generation of like-minded leaders who would maintain political stability and keep the oil wells flowing.[60]

This neo-mercantilist system served its short-term purpose. Britain's ties with the overseas Sterling Area were greatly strengthened in the decade after 1945, and sterling itself remained a formidable force in world trade, accounting for about half of all international transactions at the close of the 1940s.[61] Devaluation in 1949, though not the first choice of policy, gave a fillip to exports. By then, too, the commodity boom was under way, propelled first by Europe's

---

56. M. Cowen, 'Early Years of the Colonial Development Corporation: British State Enterprise Overseas During Late Colonialism', *African Affairs*, 83 (1984).

57. Meredith, 'State Controlled Marketing', and the further references given there.

58. Krozewski, 'Sterling'. Military bases were defended with equal firmness at least until the late 1950s, when defence cuts and the adoption of the nuclear deterrent shifted priorities.

59. Robinson, 'Andrew Cohen'; John Flint, 'Planned Decolonisation and its Failure in Africa', *African Affairs*, 82 (1983); Robert Pearce, 'The Colonial Office and Planned Decolonisation in Africa', *African Affairs*, 83 (1984).

60. Louis, *The British Empire in the Middle East*.

61. Judd Polk, *Sterling: Its meaning in World Finance* (1956), p. 3.

reconstruction needs, next by Marshall Aid, and finally by the Korean War. These developments eventually boosted the earnings of the Sterling Area and helped to close the dollar gap.[62] Britain's balance of payments remained fragile rather than robust, but by the mid–1950s policy-makers were ready to move towards convertibility on the assumption that sterling could extend its operations beyond its immediate post-war confines in competition with the dollar. As we shall see, this step entailed a reappraisal of the role of the empire and ultimately of the Sterling Area in the international order.

THE STERLING AREA: THE FINAL PHASE, 1955–72

When Britain decided to return to convertibility in the late 1950s it was assumed that the Sterling Area would provide the solid base from which the pound could launch itself into the wider world. But the decisions were also taken in the light of the fact that the Sterling Area was now shrinking in relative importance and that Britain's links with many of its members were weakening.[63] By the mid-1950s it was becoming evident that the most dynamic centres of growth were Western Europe and Japan and that trade between the great industrial powers themselves was now the crucial element driving world trade forwards. In the late 1940s Britain conducted about half of her foreign trade with the Commonwealth and with other members of the Sterling Area, and about one-quarter with Western Europe; by the early 1970s this position had been reversed.[64] This trend was already apparent in the 1950s, though it accelerated in the following decade. In fact, Britain's own trade with Western Europe increased so rapidly that by 1961 she felt obliged to apply for membership of the EEC, though she was not accepted into the fold until twelve years later. Moreover, despite the fact that the rate of growth of Britain's economy was high when judged by her own past record, it was low in comparison with that achieved in most other advanced countries,[65]

62. Newton, 'Britain, the Sterling Area', pp. 168–80.
63. An excellent account of the Sterling Area in the 1950s and 1960s can be found in J.D.B. Miller, *Survey of Commonwealth Affairs: Problems of Expansion and Attrition, 1953–1969* (1974), Ch. 12.
64. For an outline of the major changes in the structure and direction of foreign trade as a whole, see Pollard, *The Development of the British Economy*, pp. 352–65; M.J. Artis, ed. *Prest and Coppock's The U.K. Economy* (1986), pp. 130–53.
65. To put British growth in context, see Angus Maddison, *Phases of Capitalist Development* (Oxford, 1982), Chs. 3, 5 and 6.

with the result that countries once dependent on Britain in trade were pulled into the orbit of more dynamic economies. One typical outcome of these sea-changes in the world economy and Britain's relations with it was the rapid erosion of her trading links with the white Dominions. In 1948 the four Dominions accounted for 25 per cent of British trade; by 1963 this had declined to 17 per cent. The process was particularly marked in the case of Australia. She had taken half her imports from the mother country in 1948–9 and exported 40 per cent of her own produce to Britain; by 1963–4 the figures were 28 per cent and 18 per cent respectively and Japan was on the brink of becoming Australia's chief trading partner.[66] If sterling was to have a secure future, it had to be found outside the traditional area of sterling dominance.

But, while the base was crumbling, Britain also found it difficult to establish sterling's credibility elsewhere. Widespread use of sterling depended on international confidence, which was constantly being undermined by balance of payments crises caused ultimately by Britain's relatively slow growth, poor export performance and increasing vulnerability to the penetration of manufactured imports. Governments found it impossible to maintain policies of full employment without inducing a level of imports which deranged the balance of payments; once a deficit showed itself, holders of sterling would precipitate a crisis by selling pounds for fear that the authorities would try to solve the problem by devaluation, as they had done in 1949.[67] Balance of payments difficulties were accentuated by policy. In the 1950s and early 1960s governments spent large amounts – equivalent at their peak to about 10 per cent of the value of exports – on defence abroad. Some of this expenditure was caused by lingering imperial obligations and emergencies, but it also reflected continuing gentlemanly fantasies about great-power status.[68] Ironically, sterling's problems were compounded by the resumption of the City's role as provider of investment funds for the empire. This was sometimes necessary to ensure that the more independent members remained loyal to sterling, but if heavy foreign investment brought in a useful income from abroad it also led to a sizeable outflow of funds at times

---

66. J.D.B. Miller, *Britain and the Old Dominions* (1966), Ch. 8.

67. Phillip W. Bell, *The Sterling Area in the Post-War World: Internal Mechanism and Cohesion, 1946–52* (Oxford, 1956), offers a good, early analysis of incipient problems.

68. The extent to which this followed naturally from Britain's acceptance of American aid in the 1940s is discussed in T. Brett, S. Gilliat and A. Pople, 'Planned Trade, Labour Party Policy and U.S. Intervention: the Success and Failure of Post-war Reconstruction', *History Workshop*, 13 (1982). See also Arthur Robert Conan, *The Problem of Sterling* (1966), pp. 24–5.

when sterling was weak and aggravated crises by adding to drains on Britain's reserves of gold and dollars.[69]

When faced with a severe fall in the reserves, the almost invariable reaction of governments of whatever political colour was to defend the value of the pound by deflation, which reduced the rate of growth and curbed imports, and by high interest rates, which were designed to attract short-term capital to London and to repel speculative attacks on sterling. This policy has frequently been condemned as short-sighted and self-destructive because it lowered the rate of industrial investment and thus ensured that the industrial capacity of the nation was inadequate for its needs when boom conditions returned, the inevitable result being, it is alleged, that a further surge of industrial imports soon produced another trade deficit and a renewed crisis of confidence in sterling.[70] It has also been claimed that the stifling of home demand under the 'stop-go' regime gave the larger firms an incentive to invest abroad, turning Britain into a leading centre of multinational business, a process fostered by the vast network of overseas connections built up through the City in the past.[71]

Policy in times of crisis was certainly reminiscent of that adopted in defence of the gold standard in the 1920s; but it would be mistaken to assume that it was dictated by the 'City–Bank–Treasury nexus'[72] on entirely traditional lines. Government was now too big and complex, and all parties were too committed to welfare and to raising living standards, for it to be possible to invoke the simple balanced-budget verities of the pre-1939 era. The Labour government of the 1960s resisted devaluation not just on the City's behalf but because of

69. For an excellent analysis of the impact of the imperial and other burdens which aggravated Britain's external payments problem, see Susan Strange, *Sterling and British Policy: A Political Study of a Currency in Decline* (Oxford, 1971), Chs. 5 and 6. Strange emphasises the fact that allowing heavy overseas flows of capital to the Sterling Area was essential to retain the allegiance of sterling-holders and sterling's position as a world currency. The British banks operating within the area also encouraged British investment in former colonies in order to gain favour with new political masters. Cf. Ingham, *Capitalism Divided*, pp. 202–12.

70. For powerful arguments in support of this view, see Andrew Shonfield, *British Economic Policy since the War* (1958); Sidney Pollard, *The Wasting of the British Economy* (1982); Newton and Porter, *Modernisation Frustrated*, Chs. 5–7. To put this subject in context see Keith Smith, *The British Economic Crisis: Its Past and Future* (1986). For overall analyses of policy see Pollard, *The Development of the British Economy*, pp. 409–30; F.T. Blackaby, ed. *British Economic Policy, 1960–74* (Cambridge, 1978); Fred Hirsch, *The Pound Sterling: A Polemic* (1965); and Douglas Jay, *Sterling* (Oxford, 1986), Chs. 16 and 17.

71. Andrew Gamble, *Britain in Decline: Political Strategy and the British State* (2nd edn. 1985), pp. 109–112.

72. The phrase appears in Colin Leys, 'The Formation of British Capital', *New Left Review*, 160 (1986).

fears that it might trigger a world economic crisis. In addition, although willing to deflate to prevent devaluation, Labour did so by curbing private rather than public spending, much to the annoyance of the Bank of England and the City. Moreover, given the electoral imperatives of the day, all governments were quick to ease credit and boost spending once a crisis had passed, despite Cassandra-like objections from the financial authorities.[73] Nonetheless, Labour no less than the Conservatives saw the defence of sterling as being a fundamental priority of economic policy; it was almost inconceivable that any strategy which challenged this or the position of traditional authority, such as the Treasury, could have been adopted. When industry, in the shape of the CBI and the trade unions, became dissatisfied with the failure to arrest relative decline and the Labour government adopted a modernising strategy, the plans failed because of resolute hostility from the Treasury.[74] Attempts by the Conservatives to break out of the weary round of currency crises in 1963–4 and 1972–3 also came to grief when they posed a threat to sterling. They decided to allow the economy to run at a level high enough to induce a surge in industrial investment in the hope that, by permanently enlarging capacity, exports would grow more quickly and the economy's appetite for imported manufactures would be blunted. This tactic failed, partly because in both cases balance of payments problems led to runs on the reserves which panicked the authorities into deflation before the medicine had had time to prove its worth.[75]

A succession of financial crises from the mid–1950s onwards culminated in the forced devaluation of 1967, an event which marked the beginning of the end of the Sterling Area.[76] Many countries that had dutifully followed Britain's lead in 1949 now failed to do so, and the Bank of England was driven to the undignified expedient of promising to indemnify sterling holders against the effects of further devaluations in the hope of rallying them to the cause. This tactic was not a great success; Australia, for example, contemplating shrinking trade links, Britain's courtship of the EEC and increasing dependence

73. Rob Stones, 'Government-Finance Relations in Britain, 1964–7: a Tale of Three Cities', *Economy and Society*, 19 (1990).

74. Newton and Porter, *Modernisation Frustrated*, Ch. 5; Stephen Blank, 'Britain: the Politics of Foreign Economic Policy, the Domestic Economy, and the Problem of Pluralistic Stagnation', *International Organization*, 31 (1977); Ingham, *Capitalism Divided*, pp. 212–18.

75. John Cooper, *A Suitable Case for Treatment: What to Do about the Balance of Payments* (1968), has an excellent section dealing with the so-called Maudling Experiment of 1963–4.

76. Cairncross and Eichengreen, *Sterling in Decline*, Ch. 5.

on American investment, resolutely refused to hold more than 40 per cent of her reserves in sterling after 1967.[77] The end of the Sterling Area finally came in 1972 when, in the wake of the collapse of the Bretton Woods fixed exchange-rate regime and the devaluation of the dollar, the pound was allowed to float.[78]

GLOBAL ECONOMIC CHANGE AND THE END OF EMPIRE

The empire which had been reconstructed with such determination after World War II began to fall apart in the mid–1950s. Within ten years the most important constituents had voted for independence, sometimes with their hands but more often with their feet; thereafter, Britain was concerned to hurry on the process of decolonisation with as much dignity as the pressures of nationalism and the need for economy would allow. The Sudan became independent in 1956, Malaya and the Gold Coast in 1957, Nigeria in 1960 and Kenya in 1963. The West Indies were bundled briefly into a federation in 1957 before Jamaica broke free in 1962. Long-held strategic bases were discarded: Cyprus in 1960, Malta in 1964 and Aden in 1967. Outside the empire, Britain lost ground in her most important remaining sphere of informal influence, the Middle East, a process which began in Egypt and Iran in 1951 and culminated in the Suez crisis five years later. As these events queued for attention, Whitehall's busiest department was stamping out new constitutions from the old Westminster model, and recently jailed 'agitators' were being released and turned into 'responsible leaders' with unprecedented speed. Some awkward and often sizeable issues had still to be resolved, notably in central Africa, but by the mid–1960s the outcome was not in doubt; shortly afterwards the empire sank, leaving only the ripples of the Commonwealth behind.

The question of why the empire became unstuck so soon after it had been reglued has engaged many minds and stimulated much excellent research.[79] It is probably fair to say, in the briefest summary

---

77. Miller, *Survey of Commonwealth Affairs*, p. 295. See also Strange, *Sterling and British Policy*, pp. 90–5.

78. Andrew Shonfield, 'The World Economy, 1979', *Foreign Affairs*, 58 (1979).

79. The best entry is through the following: Darwin, *Britain and Decolonisation*; R.F. Holland, *European Decolonisation, 1918–81* (1985); Prosser Gifford and William Roger Louis, eds. *The Transfers of Power in Africa: Decolonization, 1940–60* (New Haven,

possible, that most historians of decolonisation favour a multicausal explanation which features, with varying emphases, the decline of British power, the rising costs of empire, the loss of imperial will, the irresistible force of colonial nationalism and the pressures of international opinion, including of course the attitude of the United States. Our purpose here is not to attack or choose between existing approaches but rather to link them together by suggesting how our particular interpretation of imperial expansion bears upon the problem of imperial decline.

By the mid-1950s, as we have seen, there were grounds for thinking that the post-war crisis had been overcome and that Britain could create a wider role for sterling by moving towards convertibility, as indeed happened between 1955 and 1958. Fundamentally, this change of direction was the product of hard-headed, if narrow calculations about shifting opportunities in the international economy, though it also appealed to ritualistic assumptions which connected the strength of the pound to the virility of the nation. The perception was that convertibility would offer more opportunities for the City and for Britain's trade generally, and that the move would have to be made before the dollar, already powerful, became almighty. Two developments in particular pointed towards this conclusion: the declining value of the colonies and the rising importance of the industrial economies in Europe and elsewhere.

The end of the Korean War in 1953 brought the long boom in commodity prices to a close. Thereafter, the export earnings of countries producing raw materials were less buoyant and their import-purchasing power grew more slowly. As a result of these trends, an increasing number of Britain's colonies began to run deficits with the United States in place of the surpluses which had made them such a vital part of the Sterling Area in the crucial period of reconstruction after World War II.[80] These were not markets to be given up lightly, but their growth potential now appeared to be limited and they had ceased to provide a refuge for Britain's older

---

Conn., 1982); idem, *Decolonization and African Independence: The Transfers of Power, 1960–80* (New Haven, Conn., 1988); J.D. Hargreaves, *Decolonization in Africa* (1988); and Michael Twaddle, 'Decolonisation in Africa: a New British Historiographical Debate', in B. Jewsiewicki and D. Newbury, eds. *African Historiographies* (Beverly Hills, Calif., 1986). A.N. Porter and A.J. Stockwell have edited a useful selection of relevant official documents: *British Imperial Policy and Decolonisation, 1938–64* (2 Vols., 1987 and 1989).

80. Conan, *The Sterling Area*, Ch. 3; David Fieldhouse, *Black Africa, 1945–1980: Economic Decolonization and Arrested Development* (1986), pp. 6–7.

staples.[81] Moreover, by the close of 1952 the Conservative government also recognised that imperial preference no longer had a part to play in extending the trade of the Sterling Area and had ceased to be an effective instrument of economic policy, even within the Commonwealth.[82]

The counterpart of these developments was the revival of the economies of continental Europe and Japan. This was not just a matter of renewed growth but involved structural change, promoted by the United States, which gave rise to a new set of complementarities linking the advanced, highly specialised economies of the world.[83] As we have seen, the trade of the Sterling Area shrank in importance and overseas investment flows shifted accordingly. Beginning in the 1950s, and with increasing rapidity thereafter, British capital was directed away from India, South America, China and the tropics, and towards Europe and the United States. Canada, Australia and South Africa remained attractive to British investors, but this was the result of economic incentives which were largely independent of Commonwealth membership.[84] By the close of the 1950s, it was apparent that Britain's future international economic policy could no longer be based on the Commonwealth, still less on its colonial component. That sterling had a future as an international currency was not doubted by policy-makers in London, but the value of the Sterling Area, as then constituted, was less certain.[85] If Britain was to take advantage of the new opportunities opening in Europe, and in doing so avoid falling further under the influence of the United States, she had to begin marching in step with her continental neighbours. In 1956 these considerations led to the formulation of Plan G, which became the basis of the European Free Trade Association in 1959, and in turn the prelude to Britain's application to join the European Economic Community in 1961.[86]

If sterling was to resume its historic role as a major international currency, action had to be taken to secure the reserves held in London.

---

81. The final episode of a long story is told by John Singleton, 'Lancashire's Last Stand: Declining Employment in the British Cotton Industry, 1950–70', *Econ. Hist. Rev.*, 2nd ser. XXXIX (1986), pp. 95, 98–9, 105–6. See also the fuller account in idem, *Lancashire on the Scrapheap: The Cotton Industry, 1945–1970* (1991).

82. D.J. Morgan, *The Official History of Colonial Development*, Vol. III (1980), pp. 5–6.

83. This theme is developed by F.V. Meyer, *International Trade Policy* (1978).

84. Pollard, *The Development of the British Economy*, pp. 358–61.

85. These issues provoked considerable public, as well as academic and official, discussion in the late 1950s. See, for example, Shonfield, *British Economic Policy Since the War*.

86. On Plan G, see Morgan, *Official History*, III, pp. 9–13.

As far as colonial policy was concerned, this meant scrutinising overseas expenditure and controlling the rate at which the sterling balances were used. The need for economy, combined with the declining value of parts of the empire, encouraged the Treasury (in alliance with Conservative Chancellors of the Exchequer) to question the wisdom of investing in the colonies from the mid–1950s and to readvertise the merits of the traditional doctrine of self-sufficiency.[87] For the same reasons, moves were made to curb defence costs, with the result that coercion began to give way to persuasion, where circumstances allowed, in dissident parts of the empire and the semi-colonies. This shift of emphasis also fitted with the changing mood of the United States: as the Cold War entered a phase of 'competitive coexistence', it was all the more necessary to offer the subject peoples of the world something other than repression. If the promise of economic development was not now to be swiftly executed, then constitutional concessions offered a cheap and ideologically congenial alternative, as well as being an increasingly necessary response to nationalist pressures. This adjustment recommended itself, too, as a means of dealing with the outstanding sterling balances, which had now become a problem instead of an asset.[88] Once sterling became fully convertible, the balances could be drawn on more freely, if not at will. Given that the most important colonies were on course for increasing degrees of self-government, convertibility raised the prospect of a raid on the reserves which would provoke a run on the pound.

Taken together, these considerations pointed in one direction: the route to be followed was that marked by negotiation, and the purpose of the exercise was to transfer power to friendly rather than to hostile nationalists. In this way, Britain hoped to keep the Commonwealth 'sterling-minded', and if possible to persuade other countries to join the club. By the close of the 1950s the new strategy for dealing with the all-important sterling balances was well under way. Not for the first time, Britain pressed home the argument that it was scarcely in the interests of newly independent states to take action which might jeopardise London's ability or willingness to fund their development programmes.[89] Simultaneously, and with practised diplomacy, Brit-

87. Morgan, *Official History*, III, pp. 32–9; David Goldsworthy, 'Keeping Change within Bounds: Aspects of Colonial Policy during the Churchill and Eden Governments, 1951–57', *Jour. Imp. and Comm. Hist.*, 18 (1990), p. 87.

88. Morgan, *Official History*, III, Chs. 4–5. On this question, and related issues, we are indebted to Krozewski, 'Sterling'.

89. Yusuf Bangura, *Britain and Commonwealth Africa: The Politics of Economic Relations, 1951–75* (Manchester, 1983), pp. 30–4; Hinds, 'Imperial Policy', pp. 37–41.

ain made plans to reduce official investment in the new Commonwealth and prompted members to seek other sources of long-term capital.[90] Piece by piece, agreement was reached on a phased rundown of the outstanding balances (as had happened in the case of India). At the close of 1954, Britain allowed the colonies to issue currencies on a fiduciary basis, thus freeing balances held in London for approved development purposes.[91] The colonies were also encouraged to establish central banks in the hope that they would serve as agents of 'responsible' management and check the ambitions of politicians whose promises could not be funded by orthodox means.[92] Finally, the Colonial Development and Welfare Act of 1959 was designed, among other purposes, to tie withdrawals from London to agreed projects. If one example has to be selected to summarise the remarkable transition of the 1950s then it must be that of Kwame Nkrumah and the Gold Coast. Nkrumah was first jailed in 1950 and then released in 1951 to become chief minister of a newly elected assembly. Thereafter, the mood was one of cooperation: Nkrumah agreed to respect the rules governing the Sterling Area in 1956, and he led his country to independence in the following year.[93]

None of these decisions was made in a mechanical fashion, and the trend is doubtless clearer in retrospect than it was at the time. The Conservatives, for example, were caught in a particularly painful dilemma because they championed the pound and the empire with equal fervour. When the interests of the two began to diverge, there was uncertainty over which way to jump. The significance of the Suez crisis, from the British perspective, was precisely in highlighting the contradiction between upholding sterling and funding the military operations needed at times to defend Britain's world role.[94] The Treasury's early warning about the effect of military action on sterling was ignored; the war led to an immediate run on the pound; and the United States refused financial help until Britain agreed to withdraw

90. Morgan, *Official History*, III, pp. 13–17, 189, 237.

91. Hinds, 'Imperial Policy', p. 39.

92. For a contemporary discussion of the main issues, see W.T. Newlyn and D.C.Rowan, *Money and Banking in British Colonial Africa* (Oxford, 1954), Chs. 10–13.

93. Darwin, *Britain and Decolonisation*, p. 178; Goldsworthy, 'Keeping Change Within Bounds', p. 91.

94. See, in this context, Diane B. Kunz, 'The Importance of Having Money: the Economic Diplomacy of the Suez Crisis', in William Roger Louis and Roger Owen, eds. *Suez 1956: The Crisis and its Consequences* (Oxford, 1989); and Howard J. Dooley, 'Great Britain's "Last Battle" in the Middle East: Notes on Cabinet Planning during the Suez Crisis of 1956', *International History Review*, XI (1989). As specialists will infer, neither this evidence nor our argument lends weight to recent suggestions that the significance of the Suez crisis has been overestimated.

her troops. Faced with bankruptcy, Britain complied. This searing experience caused Macmillan to undergo spontaneous conversion: after 1956, the advocate of empire and coercion stood four-square for sterling and peace. One of his first actions as Prime Minister in 1957 was to order a round of defence cuts specifically to help the pound. This was followed between 1957 and 1960 by a series of high-level reviews of Britain's current position and future options as a world power.[95] The results, in general terms, confirmed the declining economic and military value of the Commonwealth. In 1959 Macleod was appointed Colonial Secretary to speed decolonisation, while Macmillan set about persuading his uncertain Cabinet to support Britain's application to join the European Economic Community. The wind of change was already blowing long before Macmillan named it, and if events in the 1960s formed less of a pattern than hindsight suggests, they nevertheless followed trends which had already emerged in the mid-1950s.

Far from being in decline, imperialism and empire were revitalised during the war and in the period of reconstruction which followed. The basic aim of policy was to harness the resources of the empire to metropolitan needs, and then to buy off colonial discontent with a programme of economic development. Since the first aim took precedence over the second, the original strategy had eventually to be revised. The result was that political advance, which was cheap, was offered as a substitute for rapid economic progress, though in stages which the Colonial Office still hoped to control. At the same time, the empire became progressively less important to Britain's needs and it became easier, even for Conservative policy-makers, to envisage and then to speed the process of decolonisation. This sequence suggests that some revision to the orthodox chronology of imperial decline is required, and also that the underlying causation needs to be reviewed.[96] Our argument holds that calculations about the means of maintaining Britain's position as a major financial centre are a vital

---

95. Morgan, *Official History*, V, pp. 88–93, 96–102. Also Peter Hennessy reporting on newly released documents in *The Independent*; 7 January 1991, and *The Economist*, 20 April 1991.

96. The case for revising the chronology of decline has been put by J. Gallagher, *The Decline, Revival and Fall of the British Empire* (Cambridge, 1982), and John Darwin, 'Imperialism in Decline? Tendencies in British Policy between the Wars', *Hist. Jour.*, 23 (1980). For a related commentary on causation see B.R. Tomlinson, 'The Contraction of England: National Decline and the Loss of Empire', *Jour. Imp. and Comm. Hist.*, 11 (1982). For a view of the post-war period which is close to the one put here see R.F. Holland, 'The Imperial Factor in British Strategies from Attlee to Macmillan, 1945–63', *Jour. Imp. and Comm. Hist.*, 13 (1984).

and underestimated part of the explanation of rebuilding the empire and then of transferring power.[97] We are not claiming that they were the sole cause; only that existing interpretations ought to give more weight to this consideration, and that accounts which rely on broadly phrased formulations about the rising costs and diminishing returns of empire could gain from being specified in the way we have suggested.[98] This perspective helps to explain the 'paradox', noted by specialists, that the empire became more important shortly before the process of transferring power gathered pace. It also throws light on the argument that decolonisation was merely a smokescreen to cover neo-colonialism. From the standpoint adopted here, neo-colonialism could not have been planned in 1945 for the simple reason that decolonisation was not then envisaged. It was only later, in the 1950s, that serious thought was given to ways of perpetuating British influence in the post-imperial world, but by then Britain's aims were limited by her changing interests and not simply by the resources at her disposal.

Unfortunately for those who had so carefully planned to extend the global role of sterling by dissolving the connection between formal empire and the Sterling Area, the strategy did not work. All the elaborate attempts to persuade ex-colonies to contribute to the strength of the area came to nothing because, as we have seen, the pound rapidly ceased to be a currency of major international importance. The City had to face a new struggle for survival.

EPILOGUE: THE CITY IN THE POST-IMPERIAL WORLD

By the early 1970s, then, Britain had finally lost the imperial power base which had sustained her position in the world for so long and was faced with the prospect of becoming 'once more nothing but an

---

97. The corollary, which cannot be explored here, is that manufacturing interests were no more successful in steering policy after 1945 than they were before. Although this proposition has yet to be fully tested (and is blurred by the growth of 'corporatism'), it finds support in Kathleen M. Stahl, *The Metropolitan Organisation of British Colonial Trade: Four Regional Studies* (1951), p. 297; Lee, *Colonial Development*, pp. 31, 73–7; Fieldhouse, *Black Africa*, pp. 9–12.

98. The idea that decolonisation was related to changing interests in the metropole and not simply derived from a generalised law of the inevitability of imperial decline has been worked out in some detail in Jacques Marseille's important study, *Empire colonial et capitalisme français: histoire d'un divorce* (Paris, 1984).

insignificant island in the North Sea'.[99] The only viable alternative was membership of the EEC, which threatened to intensify competition in the domestic market. At the same time, Britain's troubles were aggravated by the ending of the post-war boom and by the rapid inflation associated with the OPEC price rise.

This 'post-imperial crisis' eventually provided the opening for the success of the Thatcherite Conservatives with their potent combination of emotive nationalism (most evident during the Falklands War in 1982) and free market economics. They claimed that Britain's economic problems could be solved by reducing the role of the state and allowing market forces to work unhindered. Thatcher's first government came into office in 1979 convinced that excessive public expenditure had 'crowded out' private investment and that rigorous control of the money supply would remove inflation and encourage industrial revival.[100] Keynes and Beveridge were abandoned and public expenditure attacked with a fervour which would have enthused Gladstone. The regime of high interest rates, deflation and rising exchange rates adopted in 1979–81 was designed to separate sound businesses from those sickly creatures which depended for survival on the unnaturally high level of demand sustained by extravagant governments during the previous 30 years. The chief result of these policies was the destruction of a large slice of an already ailing manufacturing sector. Services, boosted by the income from North Sea oil, responded much better to Thatcherism, and the long-standing 'North–South divide' became more pronounced. Given the government's ideological assumptions and the fact that the south-east remained the chief area of Conservative electoral support, it was not difficult for Thatcherites to believe that the outcome, though unexpected, was for the best.[101]

The most successful adaptation to the new regime took place in the money market. By the early 1970s City gentlemen could no longer rely on either the empire or the Sterling Area to provide them

99. This vision of the future haunted several generations of British statesmen and officials. The example cited is taken from an earlier moment when the world seemed to be closing in on Britain: Chatfield to Fisher, 16 July 1934, quoted in S.L. Endicott, *Diplomacy and Enterprise: British China Policy, 1933–1937* (Manchester, 1975), p. 69.

100. The intellectual inspiration behind this can be found in Roger Bacon and Walter Eltis, *Britain's Economic Problem: Too Few Producers* (1977).

101. On the economic policy of the Thatcher years see Paul Whiteley, 'Economic Policy', in Patrick Dunleavy, Andrew Gamble and Gillian Peele, eds. *Developments in British Politics*, 3 (1990); Jay, *Sterling*, Ch. 19; Geoffrey W. Maynard, *The Economy under Mrs Thatcher* (1988); J. McInnes, *Thatcherism at Work* (1987), Ch. 5. See also James Douglas, 'The Changing Tide – Some Recent Studies of Thatcherism', *British Journal of Political Science*, 19 (1989).

with a world role. Yet the City survived as a global financial centre. As the good ship sterling sank, the City was able to scramble aboard a much more seaworthy young vessel, the Eurodollar.[102] From small beginnings in the late 1950s, the Eurodollar market expanded very quickly in the following decades, principally because it proved useful to the vast multinational companies which had become the main players in world trade and investment. City elites were quick to recognise the potential of this market and London was able to attract the bulk of the Eurodollar and Eurobond business mainly because it was, at the time, by far the most open money market in the world.[103] Competition for financial business became much fiercer from the late 1970s as the computer revolution began to make security markets truly international for the first time, and Tokyo and New York became more serious rivals. When, as a part of the Thatcherite programme, exchange controls were abolished in 1979, the Bank of England was shocked by the amount of business transferred to other centres. The City responded in 1986 by embracing 'Big Bang', a series of reforms which removed restraints on Stock Exchange membership and abolished many restrictive practices. Once again, gentlemanly capitalists demonstrated a remarkable ability to adapt to changing times. But there was a high price to be paid: the reforms encouraged a large number of foreign firms to establish themselves in London, and they rapidly became the dominant force in the market.[104]

As the imperial basis of its strength disappeared, the City survived by transforming itself into an 'offshore island' servicing the business created by the industrial and commercial growth of much more dynamic partners. And, as the already established dominance of the south-east and of services became yet more pronounced, the role of the City within the complex of service activities reached an unprecedented level of importance. Thatcherites had no natural affinity

---

102. These were US dollars which, for a variety of reasons, could not find a profitable niche in the United States.

103. The best detailed study of this is Jerry Coakley and Laurence Harris, *The City of Capital: London's Role as a Financial Centre* (Oxford, 1983). See also Strange, *Sterling and British Policy*, pp. 237–56; Philip Coggan, *The Money Machine: How the City Works* (1986), Ch. 11. We have also greatly benefited from Kathleen Burk, 'Eurodollars and Eurobonds', *Journal of Contemporary European History*, 1 (1992), which Dr Burk was kind enough to allow us to see before publication. It is worth noting that some countries, such as Germany, were keen to discourage the Eurodollar market from settling in their territories because they feared that the price of according it houseroom would be diminished control over the domestic money supply. See Strange, *Sterling and British Policy*, p. 213.

104. On the transformation of the City in the 1980s see Coggan, *The Money Machine*, Chs. 1 and 2; Adrian Hamilton, *The Financial Revolution* (1986), Pt. 1.

with the City and, indeed, were known to have an instinctive preference for 'enterprise which manufactures things to those which make money from money';[105] but, when the free market philosophy was applied to industry and finance, the former wilted under the strain while the latter embraced it with enthusiasm. Ironically, the pace of change in the international monetary sphere was so rapid that it exposed the contradictions within Thatcherite ideology and eventually precipitated a political crisis. The relentless pressure for greater European economic unity, for financial integration and for the creation of a single currency offended the nationalists among the Thatcherites and cost Mrs Thatcher the leadership of the Conservative Party in 1990.

Thatcher governments were not friendly to the gentlemanly element in British capitalism, especially since gentlemanly power after 1945 had often become closely associated with the extension of the role of the state. Ideologically, they had more in common with Cobdenite liberalism, and with the world of the small producer which inspired that brand of liberalism, than they had with the paternalist Tory tradition stretching from Disraeli to Macmillan. The gentlemanly element within the party was progressively ousted from power, and professional monopolies and privileges came under attack. In the longer term, however, the withdrawal of the state, not only from direct influence upon the market but also to some degree from welfare and education, may mean that the gentlemanly networks of power associated with concentrated wealth and its inheritance, and with the institutions which wealth to a large extent controls, will actually be reinforced in the future. If so, the Thatcherite forces could be absorbed eventually by the gentlemanly culture which has shown such great powers of adaptation and assimilation in the past. Whether Mrs Thatcher's replacement by John Major in 1990 is a sign of the irresistible rise of the new, self-made Conservative man or of a return to a less confrontational form of Conservative politics, in which a modified gentlemanly element can reassert itself, cannot yet be determined.

The greatest danger to the survival of the gentlemanly element in British economic life at present stems from the massive inflow of foreign capital into the City following Big Bang. The City has become much more of a centre for multinational business and finance than a British financial market, and the most powerful institutions are

---

105. M. Reid, 'Mrs. Thatcher and the City', in Dennis Kavanagh and Antony Seldon, eds. *The Thatcher Effect: A Decade of Change* (Oxford, 1989), p. 49.

now based on American, Japanese or German capital, even if they still rely on the expertise of British managers recruited in the time-honoured manner. Consequently, the present generation of City people must act increasingly on behalf of interests whose central decision-making processes lie outside Britain.[106] Gentlemen still exist in some numbers in the money market, and famous firms can still find a niche for themselves as providers of specialist services based on local 'know how' and connections which the giant American and Japanese firms cannot supply.[107] However, most of them are now beholden to far less gentlemanly capitalists whose ultimate loyalties lie outside Britain.[108] Whether the ever-increasing demands of cosmopolitan finance will make it impossible for gentlemanly capitalists to appear plausible as defenders of the 'national interest' in the future remains to be seen.

The decline in gentlemanly capitalist influence under the Thatcherite regime was particularly evident in the reduced condition of the Bank of England. In the 1960s the Bank was still the crucial intermediary between a socially cohesive City, whose power was based on Britain's position in the world, and governments which readily recognised the Bank's authority in money matters. Thatcherite administrations in particular have diminished the Bank's authority by taking more direct control of money supply and interest rates and by breaking down the cartelisation of financial markets through which the Bank exercised some of its power. The flood of foreign capital into the City in recent years has also undermined the Bank's moral authority in the market. Yet the Bank is still recognisably a gentlemanly institution with considerable weight in the City, and the collapse of Thatcherism may mean that it will recover some of the influence with government which it surrendered in the 1970s and 1980s.[109]

---

106. On this theme see the collection of papers on the modern City in Laurence Harris, Jerry Coakley, Martin Croasdale and Trevor Evans, eds. *New Perspectives on the Financial System* (1988).

107. See, for example, *Financial Times*, 17 March 1990, and the *Sunday Times*, 17 February 1991, on Robert Fleming and Barings respectively.

108. A good example of a gentleman making an honest penny (and rather more) for a foreign firm in the City is provided by the Hon. Peregrine Moncrieffe who, in 1988, earned £1m. working for the American bankers E.F.Hutton. See *Sunday Times*, 9 November 1988.

109. In trying to understand the evolution of the modern Bank we have found the following particularly useful: M.J. Artis, *Foundations of British Monetary Policy* (Oxford, 1965); Michael Moran, 'Finance-Capital and Pressure Group Politics in Britain', *Brit. Jour. Pol. Sci.*, II (1981); Stephen Fay, *Portrait of an Old Lady: Turmoil at the Bank of England* (1988).

Britain's power has declined, and it is no longer possible to provide the City with a British-dominated, world-wide arena based on formal and informal imperialism: the City can now function successfully only by acting as an intermediary for powers whose economies are far stronger than Britain's. Nevertheless, the economic importance of this newly evolving City within Britain is greater than in the past and its political influence is no less significant. Inexorably, it seems, even governments like Thatcher's, which began with a genuine commitment to encouraging industrial revival, soon fell into a pattern of decision-making which promoted the interests of the City, where gentlemanly capitalists still retain a strong presence. Yet the continuing economic and political importance of the City should come as no real surprise to those who are aware that it has been at the centre of the most dynamic region of the British economy for the last 150 years and that its leaders have had privileged access to the controllers of political power for twice as long. The empire has sunk leaving hardly a trace behind; the future of the gentleman in British life is uncertain; but the City adapts and survives.

CHAPTER TWELVE
Conclusion

Our decision to state our interpretation and to reveal its underpinnings at the outset of this study means that, at this point, we have neither a plot to unravel nor a surprise to spring. However, it is easy for authors to suppose that their presentation is as clear to others as it is to themselves. Our signposts to different centuries and continents may sometimes have suggested directions other than those we intended, and our argument may not always have been as visible as we would have wished, especially since it has been spread over two sizeable volumes. Consequently, these concluding remarks will try to set out our principal claims in a way that removes any residual uncertainties, makes some of the wider implications of the argument explicit, and ensures that we ourselves do not end, unintentionally, in 'the last dyke of prevarication'.[1]

BASES OF THE ANALYSIS

Our explanation of the causes of British imperialism is founded upon a reappraisal of the character of economic power and political authority in the metropolis itself: geopolitical considerations, like the 'peripheral thesis', have their place in the story, but only within the context of impulses emanating from the centre. Explanations which assign a leading role to historical developments in Britain do, of course, exist already; but, as we have suggested, the most influential of these are seriously weakened by the excessive emphasis they place on the Industrial Revolution and its consequences. This handicap is found

1. The phrase is Burke's, quoted in Volume I, p. 51.

most obviously in studies by Marxist writers, but it also pervades the work of the liberal historians who oppose them, even though it takes a less direct form. This perspective fails to incorporate much of the most interesting recent research on British economic and social history, and it tends to assume rather than to establish the existence of connections between the economy and the wider society, including the world inhabited by policy-makers. In this case, as in so much of the historiography of imperialism, the literature has been shaped either by assumptions about the political influence of a rising industrial bourgeoisie or by counter-claims which stress the distance of the 'official mind' from pressure groups representing manufacturers.

Our interpretation of this new evidence suggests that conventional approaches to modern British history need to be rethought. In particular, recognition needs to be given to the fact that economic development was not synonymous with the Industrial Revolution, and that non-industrial activities, especially those connected with finance and services, were far more important and independent than standard texts of economic history have allowed. Moreover, the upper reaches of these occupations, unlike those in manufacturing, were associated with high social status and gave access to political influence. Identifying these attributes establishes, in principle, the crucial connection between economic power and political authority, and hence offers a means of overcoming one of the central difficulties faced by current theories of imperialist expansion. By restating the main themes of British history during the past three centuries in these terms, it becomes possible to offer an alternative explanation of Britain's extraordinary and wide-ranging presence overseas.

We have addressed this task by tracing the growth and mutation of what we have called 'gentlemanly capitalism'. This concept is merely a convenient means of bringing coherence to a large body of evidence which does not fit into existing approaches to either British or imperial history. It has not been assigned special properties that allow it to rise above normal historical discourse, and the propositions derived from it are in principle falsifiable. We have used the term to represent a hitherto neglected theme in the historical transformation of British society, a process which we regard less as an exchange of 'tradition' for 'modernity' than as a selective amalgamation of elements inherited from the past with introductions from the continuously evolving present.[2] The particular transformation we have identified centred

---

2. The obvious analogy is with the findings of development studies following a generation of research on diverse parts of the 'Third World'.

upon the growth of the financial and service sector, an innovation which proved to be compatible with aristocratic power in the eighteenth century, supported a new gentlemanly order in the nineteenth century, and carried both into the twentieth century. It is perhaps worth repeating at this point that our concern has been to establish the historical significance of gentlemanly forms of capitalism: whether these are to be approved or disapproved on moral, economic or other grounds is a related but distinct issue which is sufficiently important and complex in itself to require separate treatment.

Gentlemen looked back to the mythical harmonies of Merrie England, to the knightly morals of the Arthurian legend, and beyond to Greece and Rome for their justificatory model of an elite dedicated to public service. The resulting ethos was a highly selective composite, but it was also singularly effective in drilling the guardians who presided over policy and in promoting a sense of national solidarity, focused on the monarchy, which blunted the edge of class divisions, diluted the appeal of subversive ideologies, and encouraged, as Bagehot observed, the deference of the parvenu to the privileges of the traditionally advantaged. A gentleman disdained those who were preoccupied with the mundane world of work and money, and accordingly distanced himself from manufacturing and from provincial urban life. But gentlemen looked forward as well as back. They invoked the past to fashion a morality for the present, not only to counter the encroachments of industry and democracy, but also to legitimise their own innovating activities. Moreover, property, privilege and order were defended by material wealth as well as by moral rearmament, even though a gentleman's means of support had ideally to be invisible as well as substantial. Gentlemen were directly involved in approved capitalist activities in relation to land, finance and associated businesses of high repute, or had a rentier interest in them. They may have been fascinated by armour, tournaments and castles, but they used history to protect new and sizeable forms of capitalist wealth which they themselves had created.[3]

The men who shaped Britain's imperial destinies were therefore neither representatives of the industrial bourgeoisie nor Olympian figures removed from material concerns. If their conception of the national interest rose above party and class, it was because they succeeded in projecting a view of the world which was sufficiently spacious to encompass other allegiances. But it was also a conception

3. Our argument is therefore clearly differentiated from that of Martin Wiener, *English Culture and the Decline of the Industrial Spirit, 1850–1980* (Cambridge, 1981).

that contained well-ordered, if usually unspoken, priorities. Income streams which fed gentlemanly interests were protected and promoted; industrial interests were given less weight in the formulation of policy. London was both the heartland of gentlemanly forms of business and the seat of government. It was there that the City, Whitehall and Parliament persuaded first themselves and then the wider constituency that the interests of finance and services were those of the nation, and that pressures issuing from Manchester, Birmingham or Glasgow were at best partial and at worst self-serving. Of course, no government could afford to ignore the wealth (and taxable incomes) created by Britain's manufactured exports, or the political threat posed by periodic unemployment in the staple industries. These considerations had their place on the agenda of domestic and international policy. But there was a difference between keeping industry content and allowing its claims to challenge the gentlemanly order; where a choice had to be made, as was increasingly the case after the mid-nineteenth century, gentlemanly interests invariably took precedence and did so, moreover, right down to the end of empire. As is now evident, this outcome was not the result of a conspiracy by a small, covert group who hijacked policy and made it serve their own ends, but the product of a gentlemanly elite whose position was openly acknowledged and widely accepted, even if its values and purposes have yet to be fully explored by historians of the 'official mind' of policy-making and imperialism.

THE HISTORICAL ARGUMENT

In the simplest terms, the argument we have advanced suggests that there is a broad unity of purpose underlying Britain's overseas expansion and her associated imperialist ventures during the three centuries spanning the rise and fall of the empire. This unity stems not from a stereotype of capitalist penetration or from an encompassing multicausal interpretation, but from a particular pattern of economic development, centred upon finance and commercial services, which was set in train at the close of the seventeenth century and survived to the end of empire and indeed beyond. However, since the continuities of history can easily be demonstrated by pitching generalisations at a sufficiently high level, we have also identified two principal chronological periods, before and after 1850, representing significant shifts of power within the gentlemanly order and related changes in the structure of Britain's activities overseas. Each period contains sub-divisions of its own which reflect alterations to the policies needed to sustain the gentlemanly order in question: in the first period, there was an important adjustment after 1815 which culminated in the point of transition in 1850; in the second, there was an adaptation after 1914 as Britain slowly came to terms with her inability to restore the pre-war international order. We recognise of course that chronological precision imposes a degree of unity which the past, being in constant transition, did not possess; but we accept, too, the counter-argument that historical analysis without dates is a contradiction in terms.

The first period, from 1688 to 1850, is defined by a system of political economy which a subsequent generation of reformers referred to as Old Corruption. This system was dominated by the landed interest, the aristocrats and country gentry whose power was confirmed by the Glorious Revolution, in association with a junior partner, the moneyed interest, which gained prominence after the financial revolution of the 1690s. Patronage and peculation were endemic to the system; but they were also consistent with the emergence of an effective military-fiscal state. The alliance between traditional authority and new sources of credit produced a strong and stable government, managed from London, which was capable of financing the defence of the realm and winning political loyalties without penalising wealth-holders or crushing the largely disenfranchised tax paying public. The mercantilist system attacked by Adam Smith was not inherited from a feudal past but was invented to raise the revenues needed to fund this structure of authority, which itself was the legacy of the Revolution Settlement. As mercantilism sheltered agriculture and manufactures, so it also promoted Britain's burgeoning shipping and commercial services, which forged ahead under a policy of aggressive protection and eventually captured most of the re-export trade in produce from the world beyond Europe.

What used to be known as the 'old colonial system' was the product of these domestic forces.[4] The American colonies were supposed to function as outer provinces of England, to reproduce a loyal gentry, and to render their appropriate contribution to the exchequer. India was to be assimilated to the military-fiscal order through the East India Company, which itself was an early manifestation of London's overseas influence and of gentlemanly capitalist interests. The growth

4. This term can still be used to refer to the period before the move to free trade in the mid-nineteenth century. However, we have avoided reference to the 'first' and 'second' British empires because these concepts are harder both to define and to date.

of the empire in the eighteenth century, we suggested, is better understood as an expression of these developments than through theories that search for a nascent industrial bourgeoisie or emphasise the role of atavistic social forces. When the crisis of empire came in the late eighteenth century, financial considerations were at its centre. The American Revolution, the first great act of decolonisation, linked taxation to representation. The French Revolution, and the wars that followed, brought the prospect of invasion, which endangered Britain's finance and credit as well as the political status quo, and threatened to close continental Europe to her re-export trade. These fears strengthened the body politic, despite the loss of the American colonies. As the national debt swelled to safeguard the realm, so too did national solidarity. The resurgent conservatism which caused gentlemen of wealth to rally to the defence of property postponed radical reform, encouraged a unifying religious revival, and authorised the suppression of dissidence. It also promoted firmer measures abroad, above all in India, where the extension of British power was part of an emerging global strategy for keeping the world safe from French imperialism and the attendant horrors, fostered by the United States too, of republicanism and democracy. Among Napoleon Bonaparte's various unintended legacies to Europe was the emergence in Britain of a sense of patriotism founded on the principles of godliness, social discipline and loyalty to the crown, which in turn prepared the way for the invention of the nineteenth-century gentleman.

Pressures contained during the emergency of war could no longer be controlled in conditions of peace. After 1815, reforms were set in train which reduced the national debt, abolished Old Corruption, enfranchised a larger cohort of property-owners and dismantled the machinery of protection. These measures were painful to vested interests and caused much anguish to die-hards. But by 1850, following the abolition of the Corn Laws and the Navigation Acts, the most important economic reforms were in place, and Britain had committed herself fully to a policy of free trade. The shift to free trade was a complex process, in which the growing need to import food and to find markets for manufactures were important considerations. But, as we have argued, the initiative was taken by governments which considered that Britain's comparative advantage lay in becoming the warehouse and banker of the world. After 1815, London replaced Amsterdam as Europe's leading financial centre, increased her control over the marketing of Britain's exports, and demonstrated her expanding value as a source of invisible income, which in turn was responsible for settling a sizeable and growing share of the import bill. Moreover, income from finance and services, being invisible, was socially acceptable and gave the playing classes, as Ruskin called them, material influence.[5] Even so, the transition was fraught with uncertainty: a leap had to be made from the familiar comforts of the national debt to the risky, if also unfolding, prospects of the wider world.

The transition from Old Corruption at home was thus complemented by expansionist policies abroad. These were entailed by the shift to free trade, which implied the integration of complementary trading partners into an international economy based on London's ability to finance and manage a multilateral payments system. As we have seen, however, these economic impulses were bound up with a wider mission, which can be summarised as the world's first comprehensive development programme. After 1815, Britain aimed to put in place a set of like-minded allies who would cooperate in keeping the world safe from what Canning called the 'youthful and stirring nations', such as the United States, which proclaimed the virtues of republican democracy, and from a 'league of worn-out governments' in Europe whose future lay too obviously in the past.[6] Britain offered an alternative vision of a liberal international order bound together by mutual interest in commercial progress and underpinned by a respect for property, credit, and responsible government, preferably of the kind found at home.

Expansionist tendencies expressed themselves most obviously in attempts to promote the growth of world trade after 1815 and in the increasing flow of capital to Europe and the United States. Manifestations of imperialism were found in the annexation of a chain of naval bases, from Aden to Singapore, which were taken to police the new international economic order, and in the more intensive efforts made to create cooperative satellites. In the colonies of white settlement, schemes were devised for filling empty spaces with emigrants who would reproduce, and hence safeguard, the institutions found in the mother country. In South America, an area of white settlement but not of colonies, Britain hoped to draw the new republics into her orbit by funding their nation-building activities and by tempting them with offers of free trade and liberal institutions. In India, where Britain was already a land power, it was possible to believe, for a time at least, that

5. John Ruskin, 'Work', in *The Works of John Ruskin*, 18 (1865), divided England into two classes: those who worked and those who played. For the playing classes, 'the first of all the English games is making money'.

6. Canning in 1825. Quoted in William W. Kaufmann, *British Policy and the Independence of Latin America, 1804–1828* (New Haven, Conn., 1951), p. 201.

a programme of social engineering would succeed in putting appropritate elites and institutions in place. In the Ottoman Empire, China and tropical Africa, policy rested on the less substantial hope that initial diplomatic and naval pressures would suffice to open up and integrate societies whose structures were very different, both from each other and from Britain's. These efforts were limited by technical constraints and considerations of cost, and the plan itself was hampered by a degree of naive optimism which assumed that other countries would see Britain's point of view as readily as she did herself.

Given the global sweep of these endeavours, it is hard to agree with Platt's contention that, before 1850, Britain's ambitions were contained within mercantilist targets of self-sufficiency which were met by the existing empire and by traditional trading partners in Europe and the United States.[7] In our view, this interpretation underestimates the importance of the house-breaking ventures needed to provide industry with new markets, of the transition to free trade, which required a more integrated world economy, and of the ideological commitment which associated economic progress with a vision of a new international order. But we do not accept, either, that the result of these intentions was an informal empire of influence which expressed Britain's competitive superiority in manufactured goods.[8] In the first place, Britain was already finding it difficult to hold, still more to expand, her place in the major markets of Europe and the United States; imperialist ventures, whether formal or informal, were partly a reflection of the need to keep industry satisfied – but also at arm's length. Secondly, as our case studies have shown, these efforts met with limited success. The colonies of white settlement grew, but far more slowly than had been hoped, while India disappointed the unrealistic expectations of a generation of eager reformers and improvers, and began to develop as a sizeable market only in the 1850s. Outside the confines of the constitutional empire, Britain was unable to create an alternative realm of informal sway in South America, the Ottoman Empire, China or tropical Africa, all of which demonstrated that there was a difference between knocking on the door and opening it.

After 1850, when our second period begins, the composition of the gentlemanly order experienced a change which reflected the growing influence of finance and associated service occupations, and the steady decline of the landed interest. The new gentlemen of the

7. Platt, 'The National Economy and British Imperial Expansion before 1914', *Jour. Imp. and Comm. Hist.*, 2 (1973–4).
8. J. Gallagher and R. Robinson, 'The Imperialism of Free Trade', *Econ. Hist. Rev.*, 2nd ser. VI (1953).

Victorian era eventually became the senior partners, though still in alliance with the landed interest, which responded to the erosion of agricultural wealth by marrying money and investing in it through the City and often overseas. After the middle of the century, service-sector occupations grew rapidly, especially in London and the aptly named Home Counties, and economic policy became permeated by assumptions about the centrality of the City. Given the rapid growth of overseas investment after 1850 and the increasingly vital role played by all forms of invisible earnings in the balance of payments, it is not surprising that the City succeeded in identifying its interests with those of the nation. Free trade and sound money became orthodoxies of such repute that they transcended policy and acquired the status of moral virtues which juxtaposed the gentlemanly ideals of liberty with discipline, and of progress with order. Attempts to dislodge economic orthodoxy merely confirmed its supremacy, as the campaigns favouring bimetallism and tariff reform demonstrated. Important manufacturing interests gained from free trade, and to this extent were accommodated within prevailing policy norms. The qualms of other manufacturers were rendered ineffective by disunity within their ranks and by their perception that a radical challenge to established policies might well bring down forms of property in which they themselves had a vested interest.

Between 1850 and 1914 Britain's overseas interests underwent a massive expansion. It was during this period that capital flows funded economic development and 'nation-building' across the world, and that effective integration based on complementarities between 'primary' and 'secondary' producers was finally achieved. The City stood at the centre of an increasingly complex network of multilateral payments, and Britain acquired the managerial obligation of ensuring that the system functioned smoothly. Britain's manufacturers gained from the opportunities opened up by finance, but, as we have seen, the gains were not unqualified and policy was not, in general, directed by industrial pressure groups. Indeed, the fact that Britain's industry was in relative decline from the late nineteenth century has often been cited as evidence that her arteries were hardening and that the initiative in international affairs was shifting to 'youthful and stirring nations', such as Germany, and to revitalised rivals, such as France.[9] From the perspective of the present study, however, the performance of Britain's industries is not the best index of her international priorities

9. See, for example, Ronald Robinson and John Gallagher, *Africa and the Victorians: The Official Mind of Imperialism* (1961; 2nd edn, 1981).

or power. Much more significant, we have suggested, were capital flows and invisible earnings, which continued to grow down to 1914. It was during this period that Britain moved from being an early lender to becoming a mature creditor.[10] In this stage, she financed, transported and insured an increasing proportion of the manufactured goods produced by other countries: the logic of free trade was precisely that debtors had to be given access to other markets so that they could acquire the foreign exchange needed to service their debts. If Britain's creditors had bought more British manufactures, they would have been less able to meet their obligations to the City of London. This irony, which has so far received little attention from historians of imperialism, provides a further reason for supposing that the ability of British manufacturers to shape international policy diminished rather than grew as the period advanced.

Our case studies have attempted to show that Britain was still a dynamic society, and that British imperialism during this period was far from being the weary response of a faltering power to the actions of fitter rivals. The Dominions became dependent on the supply of British capital even as they gained responsible government; if they used their new-found freedom to increase tariffs on British manufactured imports, this was to raise revenue to service their debts as well as to appease local industrial interests. India, which Marx thought would serve the needs of the industrial bourgeoisie, in fact became a vast arena for the pursuit of a whole gamut of gentlemanly activities – from the duties of administration to the pleasures of the chase. Manchester won markets but few privileges, and when a choice had to be made beween the interests of industry and the imperatives of finance, the gentlemen of the Indian Civil Service, like their counterparts in Whitehall, knew where their priorities lay. The argument that Britain was an ailing and defensive power fits even less well with the case most commonly cited to support it: the partition of Africa. The occupation of Egypt was a direct result of the khedive's external indebtedness, and was seen (in the end, even by Gladstone) as being a just penalty for 'oriental societies' which broke the rules of the game. The annexation of South Africa also sprang from a preoccupation with finance, though in this instance the aim was to realise the economic potential of the region by drawing British and Afrikaner settlers into a federation, based on Canadian precedents, which would create a viable unit and tie it more closely to London. Only in parts

10. For a succinct statement see Jeffrey A. Frieden, 'Capital Politics: Creditors and the International Political Economy', *Journal of Public Policy*, 8 (1989).

of tropical Africa did merchants representing manufacturing interests have a clear influence on policy, but this was mainly because the region was too poor to attract sizeable interest from the City, and could also be acquired at minimal cost.[11]

Evidence of the spread of Britain's informal influence outside the empire is equally telling. It was Britain, not her rivals, who promoted the surge of investment in South America in the second half of the nineteenth century, who extended her influence in the leading republics, and who set the terms that debtor governments had to meet if they were to continue to enjoy access to the London capital market. In the case of China, new research has made it possible to show that Britain's influence expanded rapidly after 1895, when Peking finally opened its doors to foreign loans. The British, led by the gentlemen of the Hongkong and Shanghai Bank, took the lion's share of this new business, and remained the dominant power in China down to the revolution of 1911. Finally, the fact that British investors were reluctant to finance the Ottoman Empire after 1875 was a sign of their strength and cannot be used as an example of Britain's decline and retreat, as some scholars have suggested. The Ottoman default was a serious one; the prospects for new investment were unattractive; and the City had better opportunities elsewhere. The City's attitude created problems for the Foreign Office, which was left to make bricks without straw, but British investors could not be directed against their will, and they would not move without gilt-edged guarantees. Even so, the City's authority was imprinted on the economic affairs of the Ottoman Empire through the organisation which administered the public debt, and its weight was felt right down to 1914. In all of these cases, the power exerted by Britain far exceeded that associated with normal business relations, and involved incursions into the sovereignty of independent states which can justly be classified as imperialist.

This analysis, we suggest, requires a restatement of the problem of imperialist expansion. The question is not why the long continuities of nineteenth-century expansion were interrupted; the answer, therefore, is not that Britain's informal empire was weakened by industrial decline, foreign rivals or proto-nationalists on the periphery. Britain was an expanding society in the nineteenth century, but expansion was not continuous. By dividing the period in 1850, we have tried to distinguish between a phase in which imperialist intentions had

---

11. We do not make this point to minimise an exception to our argument but rather to illustrate where London's priorities lay.

limited results in creating a fully integrated international economy, and a phase in which Britain's penetrative capacity was very greatly extended. Britain's invisible 'empire' had scarcely come into existence before 1850. Far from being in a state of advanced decay in the late nineteenth century, her informal influence was expanding vigorously at exactly that point. British imperialism, in both formal and informal guises, was the outgrowth of these successful expansionist impulses. Seen from another perspective, Britain's massive exports of capital not only encouraged economic growth but also gave rise to various types of development and managerial debt. Since a large proportion of Britain's foreign investments took the form of loans to foreign governments, the problem of sovereign debt inevitably touched the independence of the recipients. Britain may well have preferred to deal with these issues by informal means, though these still infringed the sovereignty of other countries; but the continuing dynamism of her expansion pushed her into situations where the range of choice was often limited. As the century advanced, an increasing number of patriotic officers and gentlemen were at hand to ensure that, at such moments, Britain did her duty.

World War I is conventionally regarded as marking the dividing line between the expansion and decline of empire, though, as we have seen, some historians prefer to date the transition from a point in the late nineteenth century. We have looked at the period from a different standpoint, one that carries forward the argument developed to explain imperialist expansion in the period after 1850. The power structure which arose from the debris of Old Corruption remained substantially intact after 1914, despite the ravages of two world wars and the hesitant emergence of 'corporatism'. The priorities of international policy were also unchanged, as Britain sought to maintain her role as banker to the world, first by returning to the gold standard in 1925, and then by nurturing the sterling bloc after 1931. These aims permeated Britain's wider diplomatic purposes: they entered Chamberlain's policy of appeasement in the 1930s, and they helped to mould the ambiguous 'special relationship' with the United States thereafter. Moreover, Britain's determination to retain her empire and her informal influence was undiminished, not only after 1914 but also after 1945. What changed after World War I was that Britain was no longer in a position to supply sufficient capital to fuel the international economy. Although successive governments struggled to create conditions which would encourage new overseas borrowing, they became increasingly preoccupied with the problem of securing repayments on existing loans. The gentlemanly order marched on;

but the adverse circumstances which affected the performance of overseas investment and other invisible earnings had a profound effect on the difficulties Britain faced and the means she adopted to meet her traditional priorities. It is for these reasons, and not because we accept standard assumptions contrasting 'expansion' with 'decline', that we have identified the years between World War I and decolonisation as being a sub-division of the longer period which began in the mid-nineteenth century.

Our approach suggests that British imperialism had a consistent and insistent theme which is imperfectly recognised, where it is recognised at all, in the majority of studies of the period, which tend to stress the continuing difficulties faced by Britain's manufactured exports, the gathering problems posed by the rise of colonial nationalism, and the failing will-power of the decision-making elite. The theme we have emphasised here was manifested most clearly in Britain's determination to use the empire to assist her return to the gold standard and subsequently to form the basis of the sterling bloc. As we have seen, the Dominions (with the exception of Canada) remained dependent on London for their external finance, and Britain used her authority to ensure that they continued to conform to the rules of the game. The Ottawa agreements, which are widely treated as a defeat for British policy, were in fact a success for British finance: the preferences granted to the empire were undoubtedly more generous than those given to Britain's manufacturers, but the imbalance was necessary to ensure that the Dominions had the means of servicing their debts. The same priorities made themselves felt in India: tariff autonomy fatally damaged Manchester's exports of cotton goods but helped to balance the budget and to service the external debt, while successive constitutional concessions left Delhi's subordination in financial and monetary affairs untouched. As for the tropical colonies, their subservience to the rigours of fiscal orthodoxy, their whole-hearted commitment to tax-gathering, and their much-needed contribution to Britain's faltering balance of payments was never more fully demonstrated than in the mother country's hour of need – which, in the event, extended from 1914 to the eve of decolonisation. The idea that there was a 'long retreat' from empire fits ill with evidence not only of the revitalisation of the colonial mission after the two world wars, but also of the firm grip which Britain retained in the areas of policy which mattered most.

Moreover, we argued that regions of informal influence also played their part in meeting Britain's priorities in the international economy, and did not simply disappear after 1914, as is generally thought. Their contribution could clearly be seen in the pressure exerted on the smaller European members of the sterling bloc in the 1930s and in the policies adopted towards the two great 'unclaimed' regions of the world, South America and China, where Britain worked hard and effectively to maintain her financial interests. Key decisions, such as the Roca–Runciman Pact with Argentina and the backing given to Chiang Kai-shek in China, were made with these priorities in mind, and in both cases it was Britain's staple manufactured exports that suffered. These examples, we suggested, also underlined the need to emphasise the continuing momentum of imperialist rivalries after 1914. The contest for supremacy in South America and China was not only hard-fought but also distinctive in deploying new weaponry devised by the service industries, especially radio, cinema and air-power. This struggle developed rapidly in the 1930s (when it also embraced schemes for redividing large parts of Africa), and was carried on by additional means during World War II. In the hierarchy of causes of the war, a prominent place has to be found, in our view, for the battle between the 'have' and the 'have not' powers arising out of the world slump and particularly out of the ensuing financial crisis – a crisis which signalled the final breakdown of the free-trade order which Britain had built by a combination of diplomacy and force from the middle of the nineteenth century.

THE WIDER CONTEXT

These general conclusions can themselves be set in an even wider context. Given the scope of the present study, the problem is not to think of possible connections but rather to limit their number so that they underline rather than overlay our principal theme. We shall confine ourselves here to three observations which should be of interest both to historians and to scholars who use the past principally as a guide to the present.

The first observation concerns the relationship between the rise and fall of empires. The question of the decline of 'hegemonic' powers has aroused a great deal of discussion in recent years, especially in the United States, where academic and political commentators have been much exercised by the belief that their country is less dominant today than it was in the years immediately after World War

II.[12] This perception has prompted considerable debate, and a good deal of heart-searching, about the causes of decline and its implications for the maintenance of world order. According to one influential interpretation, a hegemonic power is needed to guarantee international stability, and the conclusion drawn is that, if the influence of the United States is allowed to decline, disorder will follow. This cataclysmic view of the future will be familiar to historians of the British empire. Policy-makers were permanently fearful that they would be unable to maintain the legacy of eminence bequeathed by their predecessors, and they doubled their anxieties by assuming that what was good for London was also good for the rest of the world.[13] As commentators in the United States try to read the lessons of the British empire, so the British, in their time, looked to Greece and Rome for guidance – with a sideways glance at the fate of the Dutch.[14] In both cases, attempts to discern the laws of motion of large powers have often been variations, in modern dress, of the venerable organic metaphor of growth and decay, and the task of policy-oriented social scientists has been, in effect, to find the elixir of eternal life. Whatever their merits, the objectivity of these exercises in comparative history has often been compromised by their justificatory purpose, which stresses the weight of the burdens carried by the hegemonic power and the ingratitude of those who are presumed to benefit from its influence. Spokesmen of leading powers do not take readily to the idea that the end of their period of dominance is not necessarily the end of the world. Accordingly, they find it hard to envisage pluralistic alternatives to the rule of a single power, and harder still to accept the emergence of a more successful rival.

Since much of our argument is at variance with the historical interpretations of British imperialism usually drawn on by specialists in contemporary international relations, there is little point in examining the comparisons which have been made between the *Pax Britannica* and the *Pax Americana*. The question of imperial decline, however, requires comment because it bears particularly on our reconsideration of the period after 1914. The thrust of our argument, it will be recalled, emphasised Britain's continuing ambition and

12. For a critical introduction to what is now a vast literature see Isabelle Grunberg, 'Exploring the "Myth" of Hegemonic Stability', *International Organization*, 44 (1990), and the further references given there.
13. J.G. Darwin, 'The Fear of Falling: British Politics and Imperial Decline Since 1900', *Trans. Royal Hist. Soc.*, 36 (1986).
14. The comparisons are still made. See Gary B. Miles, 'Roman and Modern Imperialism: a Reassessment', *Comp. Stud. in Soc. and Hist.*, 32 (1990).

success as an imperialist power, and did so by identifying the priorities of policy-makers and tracing the ways in which they were implemented. But we also drew attention to the fact that Britain's ability to supply capital for overseas investment was more restricted after World War I, that her income from invisibles was less buoyant, and that she emerged from World War II as the world's largest debtor. Evidence of Britain's continuing stature as an international power might therefore seem to be at variance with evidence of her increasing weakness. However, this apparent paradox can be resolved by recalling that power is relative as well as absolute.[15] Objective measurements may show that Britain was weaker after 1914 than before, but her relative position with respect to her main rivals and satellites remained strong. Germany and France suffered severely as a result of World War I and the slump of the 1930s. The United States was only beginning to emerge as a world power before 1939, and some of the ground she had made up on Britain during the war and in the early 1920s was lost again during the depression. After 1945, with the onset of the Cold War, it was not in her interests to lean as heavily on Britain as she might have done. For their part, Britain's satellites were constrained by a lack of alternatives: even in adversity, they remained tied to sterling and to the London money market.

Viewed from this angle, Britain's decline as an imperial power became effective only when these relativities changed. The spreading influence of the United States during the period of 'competitive coexistence', combined with the recovery of continental Europe and Japan from the 1950s, created alternative centres of attraction which greatly reduced Britain's drawing power; and the irresistible rise of the dollar displaced sterling from its position as the chief currency of international trade. However, as we noted in Chapter 11, these developments also provided Britain with new opportunities: the growth of inter-industry trade directed capital and commerce towards the advanced economies and away from the more backward colonies and semi-colonies; and the appearance of novel financial instruments, notably the Eurodollar, gave the City a new lease of life.

These trends were associated with a historic shift in the structure

---

15. A dramatic illustration of this distinction has been provided by the collapse of the Soviet 'empire', an event which ought to prompt a review of the assumption that the power of the United States is withering away. Firm guidance on a slippery subject is provided by Joseph S. Nye, 'The Changing Nature of World Power', *Political Science Quarterly*, 105 (1990). For a remarkable piece of anticipation see Valerie Bunce, '"The Empire Strikes Back": the Transformation of the Eastern Bloc from a Soviet Asset to a Soviet Liability', *International Organization*, 39 (1985).

of the international economy which merits greater attention than it has received from students of 'late colonialism' and decolonisation. Our analysis has indicated that one of the most distinctive features of Britain's overseas expansion was that it integrated countries which lacked sizeable capital markets of their own by offering them sterling credits and the facilities of the City of London. Where the terms of the offer involved a loss of sovereignty, in ways described at the outset of this study, expansion became imperialism. The logic of this argument suggests that imperialism ends when these conditions cease or are greatly diminished. This is exactly what happened: the development of local capital markets and the indigenisation of the public foreign debt began in the Dominions before World War II; the growth of joint ventures started to alter the role of expatriate business in India, Argentina and China from the 1930s, and in the Dominions from an even earlier date; the recapture of public utilities by purchase, as in Argentina and Brazil, or by nationalisation, as in China and parts of the Middle East, occurred in the late 1940s and 1950s; the decline of sterling, and the failure of local Central Banks to 'play the game' according to traditional London rules, became apparent from the late 1950s onwards.

The purpose of these remarks is not to invent a new dialectic to explain the history of imperialism, but to call attention to an underestimated consequence of imperialist influences, which was to set in motion a series of structural changes that ultimately enabled the most important satellites to recover their independence. Neo-colonialism can undoubtedly be found in parts of the former empire, but so too can a new form of post-imperial capitalism based upon a cosmopolitan world order characterised by the unification of diverse capital markets through competing financial centres, the domestication of multinational corporations by hosts who have ceased to be hostages, and the separation of expatriate interests from the idea of a civilising mission.[16] The concept of decline therefore requires close definition, and even then it can easily mislead when applied to national aggregates. The decline of the British empire removed one of the props of the gentlemanly order, but it did not bring about the fall of

16. For these developments see David Fieldhouse, 'A New Imperial System? The Role of the Multinational Corporation Reconsidered', in Mommsen and Osterhammel, *Imperialism and After*; David G. Becker, Jeff Frieden, Sayre P. Schatz and Richard L. Sklar, *Post-Imperialism: International Capitalism and Development in the Late Twentieth Century* (1987); and Susan Strange, 'Finance, Information and Power', *Rev. Internat. Stud.*, 16 (1990). On current trends in global finance, see Susan Strange, *Casino Capitalism* (1986); and Jeffry A. Frieden, *Banking on the World: The Politics of International Finance* (1987).

the City, which may help to explain why the trauma of decolonisation was psychological rather than economic.

Our second observation concerns the implications of our analysis for the study of rival imperialist powers, especially those in Europe. We have focused on the domestic roots of imperialism because this approach seems to us to have greater explanatory power than one pitched at the level of international relations and removed from the interests which shape national policy.[17] We have brought international rivalries into the story at points where they exerted a particularly strong influence on British policy, but we are aware that more could have been said on this theme than space has allowed. However, the issue we wish to raise here is whether our approach is applicable to the cases which immediately suggest themselves: those of France and Germany.[18]

The answer to this question falls into two parts: one is easy; the other is difficult, and at present may not even be possible. The easy answer is to confirm our view that the analysis of metropolitan interests offers the most promising way of tracing imperialist impulses, and to support this judgement by citing the illuminating work of scholars such as Marseille, Wehler and Stern.[19] The hard part of the answer is to decide whether the particular configuration of interests we have identified was both present and of equal importance elsewhere, or whether it was specific to the British case. The reason for the difficulty is simply that the evidence currently available is insufficiently detailed to allow generalisations to be made with confidence.[20] Specialists who are familiar with the historical complexities of one country are still capable of adopting stereotypes of another. Analogies of this order can readily be made but they will also be flawed. Our caution on this question is, so we think, the product less of insularity than of an awareness that judgements about similarities and singularities need to be derived from a broadly comparable data

17. Here, as elsewhere, we are in agreement with Frieden, 'Capital Politics'.

18. This question has been one of the most frequently asked in seminars dealing with our general interpretation of British imperialism.

19. Jacques Marseille, *Empire colonial et capitalisme français: histoire d'un divorce* (Paris, 1984); Hans-Ulrich Wehler, *Bismarck und der Imperialismus* (Munich, 4th edn., 1976); Fritz Stern, *Gold and Iron: Bismarck, Bleichröder and the Building of the German Empire* (New York, 1977).

20. Notwithstanding the pioneering studies of Marseille, Wehler, Stern (see n.19) and others, and the high quality of the debates on, for example, the *parti colonial* in France and the nature of social imperialism in Germany. Dr Yussef Cassis of the University of Geneva is currently undertaking a study of bankers in London, Paris and Berlin, which, when finished, will be a considerable advance in comparative economic and social history, and will provide valuable information for students of imperialism.

base. On this subject, therefore, we have decided to confine ourselves to the hope that our work will join other studies in bringing nearer the prospect of a fully comparative approach to European imperialism.

Our final observation returns us to our starting point: the history of Britain and of the gentlemanly interests which have been our principal focus. We believe that the case we have presented has sufficient coherence and enough evidence to merit serious consideration, and we hope that it will carry forward the study of the subject in a constructive manner. At the same time, we are aware that our argument opens lines of inquiry rather than closes them: the relationship between the City and industry, the connection joining financial interests to political authority, the link between the domestic 'power elite' and imperialist expansion – all of these are large themes that invite further study. Whatever judgement is made of our particular interpretation, however, we hope that we have succeeded in making a case for reintegrating the analysis of British and imperial history in ways that unite economic, social and political branches of historical study and cross the boundaries of centuries divided by scholarly practice. These divisions are justified by the imperative of specialisation, and there is undoubtedly a price to be paid for stepping over them. Moreover, evidence of intention is no indication of the result of an enterprise, which must properly be left to the judgement of others. This being so, we should perhaps end this restatement of our wide-ranging claims by recalling Dr Johnson's salutory observation that he was confident of doing two things very well: one was the introduction to a literary work saying what it would contain and how it would be executed in the most perfect manner; the other was a conclusion revealing why the execution had fallen short of the promises made by the author to himself and to his readers.

Maps

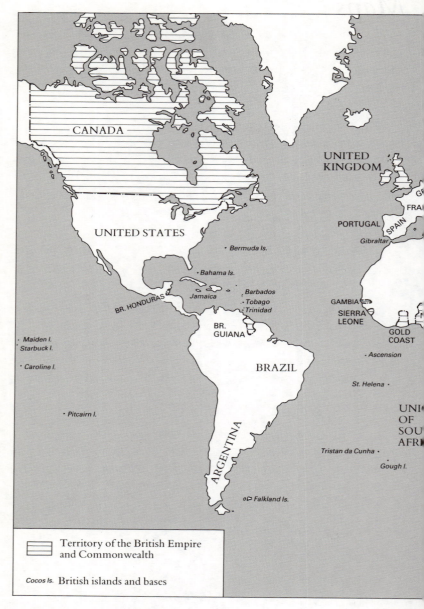

Map 1. The British empire in 1920
After: T.O. Lloyd, *The British Empire, 1558–1983* (Oxford, 1984)

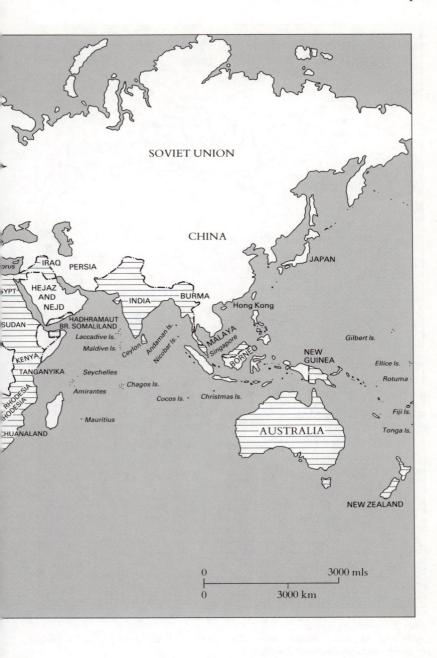

SOVIET UNION

CHINA

JAPAN

rus IRAQ PERSIA

EGYPT HEJAZ
AND
NEJD

SUDAN HADHRAMAUT
BR. SOMALILAND

INDIA BURMA

Hong Kong

Laccadive Is.

Maldive Is.

KENYA

TANGANYIKA

Ceylon

Andaman Is.

Nicobar Is.

MALAYA
Singapore

BORNEO

NEW
GUINEA

Gilbert Is.

Ellice Is.

Rotuma

Seychelles

RHODESIA
RHODESIA

Amirantes

Chagos Is.

Cocos Is.

Christmas Is.

Fiji Is.

CHUANALAND

Mauritius

AUSTRALIA

Tonga Is.

NEW ZEALAND

0		3000 mls
0		3000 km

Map 2. South America
After: D.C.M. Platt, *Business Imperialism, 1840–1930: An Inquiry Based on British Experience in Latin America* (Oxford, 1977)

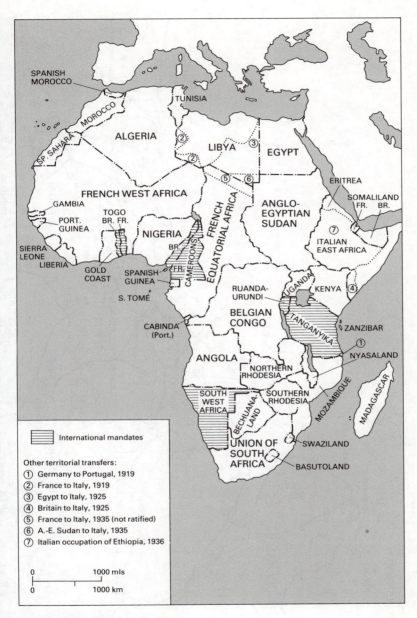

Map 3. Colonial Africa in 1939
After: A.D. Roberts, ed. *The Cambridge History of Africa, 1905–1940*, 7 (Cambridge, 1986)

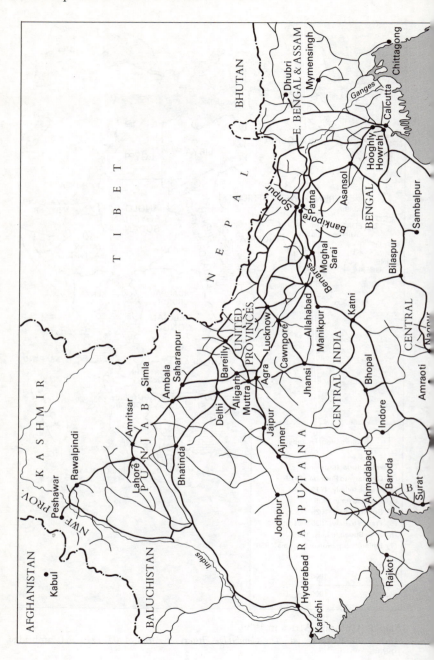

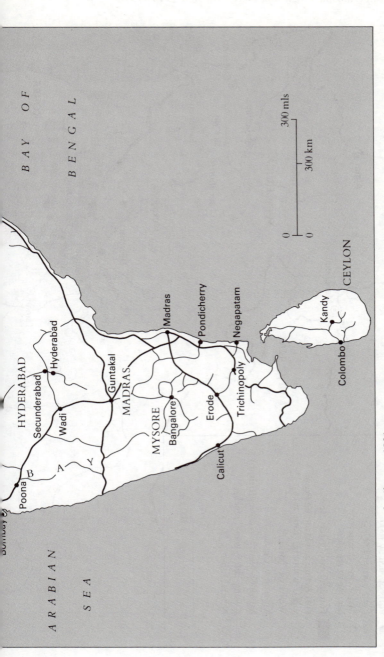

Map 4. India: provinces and railways, 1931

After: Dharma Kumar, ed. *The Cambridge Economic History of India, c. 1757–c. 1970,* 2 (Cambridge, 1983).

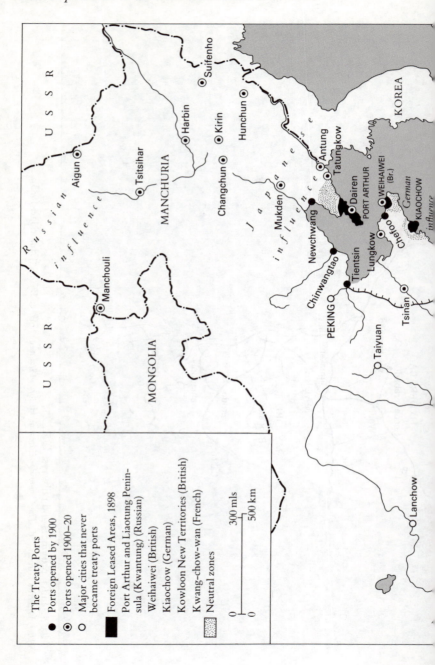

The Treaty Ports

Ports opened by 1900 ●
Ports opened 1900–20 ◉
Major cities that never ○
became treaty ports

Foreign Leased Areas, 1898 ■
Port Arthur and Liaotung Penin-
sula (Kwantung) (Russian)
Weihaiwei (British)
Kiaochow (German)
Kowloon New Territories (British)
Kwang-chow-wan (French)
Neutral zones

300 mls
500 km

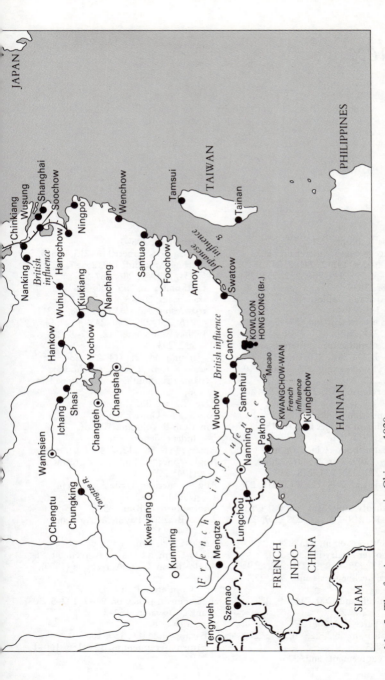

Map 5. The foreign presence in China, c. 1920
After: John K. Fairbank, ed. *The Cambridge History of China,* 12 (Cambridge, 1983)

Index